BICENTENNIAL
1807
WILEY
2007
BICENTENNIAL

THE WILEY BICENTENNIAL—KNOWLEDGE FOR GENERATIONS

*E*ach generation has its unique needs and aspirations. When Charles Wiley first opened his small printing shop in lower Manhattan in 1807, it was a generation of boundless potential searching for an identity. And we were there, helping to define a new American literary tradition. Over half a century later, in the midst of the Second Industrial Revolution, it was a generation focused on building the future. Once again, we were there, supplying the critical scientific, technical, and engineering knowledge that helped frame the world. Throughout the 20th Century, and into the new millennium, nations began to reach out beyond their own borders and a new international community was born. Wiley was there, expanding its operations around the world to enable a global exchange of ideas, opinions, and know-how.

For 200 years, Wiley has been an integral part of each generation's journey, enabling the flow of information and understanding necessary to meet their needs and fulfill their aspirations. Today, bold new technologies are changing the way we live and learn. Wiley will be there, providing you the must-have knowledge you need to imagine new worlds, new possibilities, and new opportunities.

Generations come and go, but you can always count on Wiley to provide you the knowledge you need, when and where you need it!

WILLIAM J. PESCE
PRESIDENT AND CHIEF EXECUTIVE OFFICER

PETER BOOTH WILEY
CHAIRMAN OF THE BOARD

Microsoft Certified Application Specialist (MCAS)

Approved Courseware

▪ What does this logo mean?

It means this courseware has been approved by the Microsoft® Certified Application Specialist program to be among the finest available for learning Microsoft® Office Word 2007, Microsoft® Office Excel 2007, Microsoft® Office PowerPoint 2007, Microsoft® Office Access 2007, or Microsoft® Office Outlook 2007. It also means that upon completion of this courseware, you may be prepared to take an exam for Microsoft Certified Application Specialist qualification.

▪ What is a Microsoft Certified Application Specialist?

A Microsoft Certified Application Specialist is an individual who has passed exams for certifying his or her skills in one or more of the Microsoft Office desktop applications such as Microsoft Word, Microsoft Excel, Microsoft PowerPoint, Microsoft Outlook, or Microsoft Access. The Microsoft Certified Application Specialist program is the only program approved by Microsoft for testing proficiency in Microsoft Office desktop applications. This testing program can be a valuable asset in any job search or career development.

▪ More Information

To learn more about becoming a Microsoft Certified Application Specialist and exam availability, visit www.microsoft.com/learning/msbc.

Microsoft, the Microsoft Office Logo, PowerPoint, and Outlook are trademarks or registered trademarks of Microsoft Corporation in the United States and/or other countries, and the Microsoft Certified Application Specialist logo is used under license from the owner.

Microsoft® Official Academic Course

Microsoft® Office PowerPoint® 2007

BICENTENNIAL
BICENTENNIAL
1807
WILEY
2007
BICENTENNIAL
BICENTENNIAL

Credits

EXECUTIVE EDITOR	John Kane
SENIOR EDITOR	Gary Schwartz
DIRECTOR OF MARKETING AND SALES	Mitchell Beaton
EDITORIAL ASSISTANT	Jennifer Lartz
PRODUCTION MANAGER	Kelly Tavares
DEVELOPMENT AND PRODUCTION	Custom Editorial Productions, Inc
CREATIVE DIRECTOR	Harry Nolan
TEXT DESIGN	Brian Salisbury
TECHNOLOGY AND MEDIA	Phyllis Bregman
COVER PHOTO	Corbis

Wiley 200th Anniversary logo designed by: Richard J. Pacifico

This book was set in Garamond by Aptara, Inc. and printed and bound by Bind Rite Graphics. The cover was printed by Phoenix color.

Microsoft, ActiveX, Excel, InfoPath, Microsoft Press, MSDN, OneNote, Outlook, PivotChart, PivotTable, PowerPoint, SharePoint, Visio, Windows, Windows Mobile, and Windows Vista are either registered trademarks or trademarks of Microsoft Corporation in the United States and/or other countries. Other product and company names mentioned herein may be the trademarks of their respective owners.

The example companies, organizations, products, domain names, e-mail addresses, logos, people, places, and events depicted herein are fictitious. No association with any real company, organization, product, domain name, e-mail address, logo, person, place, or event is intended or should be inferred.

The book expresses the author's views and opinions. The information contained in this book is provided without any express, statutory, or implied warranties. Neither the authors, John Wiley & Sons, Inc., Microsoft Corporation, nor their resellers or distributors will be held liable for any damages caused or alleged to be caused either directly or indirectly by this book.

ISBN-13 978-0-47006951-6 (U.S.)
ISBN-13 978-0-47016383-2 (International)
Printed in the United States of America

10 9 8 7 6 5 4

www.wiley.com/college/microsoft *or* call the MOAC Toll-Free Number: 1+(888) 764-7001

Foreword from the Publisher

Wiley's publishing vision for the Microsoft Official Academic Course series is to provide students and instructors with the skills and knowledge they need to use Microsoft technology effectively in all aspects of their personal and professional lives. Quality instruction is required to help both educators and students get the most from Microsoft's software tools and to become more productive. Thus our mission is to make our instructional programs trusted educational companions for life.

To accomplish this mission, Wiley and Microsoft have partnered to develop the highest quality educational programs for Information Workers, IT Professionals, and Developers. Materials created by this partnership carry the brand name "Microsoft Official Academic Course," assuring instructors and students alike that the content of these textbooks is fully endorsed by Microsoft, and that they provide the highest quality information and instruction on Microsoft products. The Microsoft Official Academic Course textbooks are "Official" in still one more way—they are the officially sanctioned courseware for Microsoft IT Academy members.

The Microsoft Official Academic Course series focuses on *workforce development*. These programs are aimed at those students seeking to enter the workforce, change jobs, or embark on new careers as information workers, IT professionals, and developers. Microsoft Official Academic Course programs address their needs by emphasizing authentic workplace scenarios with an abundance of projects, exercises, cases, and assessments.

The Microsoft Official Academic Courses are mapped to Microsoft's extensive research and job-task analysis, the same research and analysis used to create the Microsoft Certified Application Specialist (MCAS) and Microsoft Certified Application Professional (MCAP) exams. The textbooks focus on real skills for real jobs. As students work through the projects and exercises in the textbooks they enhance their level of knowledge and their ability to apply the latest Microsoft technology to everyday tasks. These students also gain resume-building credentials that can assist them in finding a job, keeping their current job, or in furthering their education.

The concept of life-long learning is today an utmost necessity. Job roles, and even whole job categories, are changing so quickly that none of us can stay competitive and productive without continuously updating our skills and capabilities. The Microsoft Official Academic Course offerings, and their focus on Microsoft certification exam preparation, provide a means for people to acquire and effectively update their skills and knowledge. Wiley supports students in this endeavor through the development and distribution of these courses as Microsoft's official academic publisher.

Today educational publishing requires attention to providing quality print and robust electronic content. By integrating Microsoft Official Academic Course products, *WileyPLUS*, and Microsoft certifications, we are better able to deliver efficient learning solutions for students and teachers alike.

Bonnie Lieberman
General Manager and Senior Vice President

Welcome to the Microsoft Official Academic Course (MOAC) program for the 2007 Microsoft Office system. MOAC represents the collaboration between Microsoft Learning and John Wiley & Sons, Inc. publishing company. Microsoft and Wiley teamed up to produce a series of textbooks that deliver compelling and innovative teaching solutions to instructors and superior learning experiences for students. Infused and informed by in-depth knowledge from the creators of Microsoft Office and Windows Vista™, and crafted by a publisher known worldwide for the pedagogical quality of its products, these textbooks maximize skills transfer in minimum time. With MOAC, students are hands on right away—there are no superfluous text passages to get in the way of learning and using the software. Students are challenged to reach their potential by using their new technical skills as highly productive members of the workforce.

Because this knowledgebase comes directly from Microsoft, architect of the 2007 Office system and creator of the Microsoft Certified Application Specialist (MCAS) exams, you are sure to receive the topical coverage that is most relevant to students' personal and professional success. Microsoft's direct participation not only assures you that MOAC textbook content is accurate and current; it also means that students will receive the best instruction possible to enable their success on certification exams and in the workplace.

■ The Microsoft Official Academic Course Program

The *Microsoft Official Academic Course* series is a complete program for instructors and institutions to prepare and deliver great courses on Microsoft software technologies. With MOAC, we recognize that, because of the rapid pace of change in the technology and curriculum developed by Microsoft, there is an ongoing set of needs beyond classroom instruction tools for an instructor to be ready to teach the course. The MOAC program endeavors to provide solutions for all these needs in a systematic manner in order to ensure a successful and rewarding course experience for both instructor and student—technical and curriculum training for instructor readiness with new software releases; the software itself for student use at home for building hands-on skills, assessment, and validation of skill development; and a great set of tools for delivering instruction in the classroom and lab. All are important to the smooth delivery of an interesting course on Microsoft software, and all are provided with the MOAC program. We think about the model below as a gauge for ensuring that we completely support you in your goal of teaching a great course. As you evaluate your instructional materials options, you may wish to use the model for comparison purposes with available products.

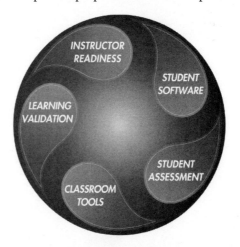

▪ Organization

MOAC for 2007 Microsoft Office system is designed to cover all the learning objectives in the MCAS exams, referred to as "objective domains." The Microsoft Certified Application Specialist (MCAS) exam objectives are highlighted throughout the textbooks. Unique features of our task-based approach include a Lesson Skills Matrix that correlates skills taught in each lesson to the MCAS objectives; Certification, Workplace, and Internet Ready exercises; and three levels of increasingly rigorous lesson-ending activities: Competency, Proficiency, and Mastery Assessment.

Following is a list of key features in each lesson designed to prepare your students for success on these exams and in the workplace:

- Each lesson begins with a **Lesson Skill Matrix.** More than a standard list of learning objectives, the Skill Matrix correlates each software skill covered in the lesson to the specific MCAS "objective domain."

- Every lesson features a real-world **Business Case** scenario that places the software skills and knowledge to be acquired in a real-world setting.

- Every lesson opens with a **Software Orientation.** This feature provides an overview of the software features students will be working with in the lesson. The orientation includes a large, labeled screen image.

- Engaging point-of-use **Reading Aids** provide students with hints, introduce alternative methods for producing results, alert them to pitfalls, provide learning cross-references, and tell them the names of files found on the Student CD.

- **Certification Ready?** features throughout the text signal students where a specific certification objective is covered. It provides students with a chance to check their understanding of that particular MCAS objective and, if necessary, review the section of the lesson where it is covered. MOAC offers complete preparation for MCAS certification.

- Concise and frequent **Step-by-Step** instructions teach students new features and provide an opportunity for hands-on practice.

- **Circling Back.** These integrated projects provide students with an opportunity to review and practice skills learned in previous lessons.

- **Competency, Proficiency, and Mastery Assessment** provide three progressively more challenging lesson-ending activities.

- **Internet Ready.** Projects combine the knowledge students acquire in a lesson with a Web-based research task.

- **Workplace Ready.** These features preview how 2007 Microsoft Office system applications are used in real-world situations.

■ Pedagogical Features

Many pedagogical features have been developed specifically for *Microsoft Official Academic Course* programs. Presenting the extensive procedural information and technical concepts woven throughout the textbook raises challenges for the student and instructor alike. The Illustrated Book Tour that follows provides a guide to the rich features contributing to *Microsoft Official Academic Course* program's pedagogical plan.

Each book within the *Microsoft Official Academic Course* series features:

- **Lesson Skill Matrix:** The skill matrix lists the instructional goals for the lesson so that you know what skills you will be asked to master. The Matrix previews the lesson structure, helping you grasp key concepts and prepares you for learning software skills. These skills are also linked directly to the Microsoft Certified Application Specialist (MCAS) certification skill, when appropriate.

- **Key Terms:** Important technical vocabulary is listed at the beginning of the lesson. When these terms are used later in the lesson, they appear in bold italic type and are defined. The Glossary contains all of the key terms and their definitions.

- **Software Orientation:** This feature provides an overview of the software you will be using in the lesson. The orientation will detail the general properties of the software or specific features, such as a ribbon or dialog box.

- **The Bottom Line:** Each main topic within the lesson has a summary of why this topic is relevant.

- **Hands-on practice:** Numbered steps give detailed, step-by-step instructions to help you learn software skills. The steps also show results and screen images to match what you should see on your computer screen.

- **Student CD:** The companion CD contains the data files needed for each lesson. These files are indicated by the CD icon in the margin of the textbook.

- **Informational text for each topic:** Easy-to-read, technique-focused information can be found following each exercise.

- **Illustrations:** Screen images provide visual feedback as you work through the exercises. The images reinforce key concepts, provide visual clues about the steps, and allow you to check your progress.

- **Reader aids:** Helpful hints, such as *Take Note,* and alternate ways to accomplish tasks (*Another Way*) are located throughout the lessons. Reader aids provide additional relevant or background information that adds value to the lesson. Reader aids, such as *Troubleshooting,* also point out things to watch out for or things to avoid.

- **Button images:** When the text instructs you to click a particular toolbar button, an image of the button is shown in the margin.

- **Certification Ready?:** This feature signals the point in the text where a specific certification objective is covered. It provides you with a chance to check your understanding of that particular MCAS objective and, if necessary, review the section of the lesson where it is covered.

- **New Feature:** The New Feature icon appears in the margin next to any software feature that is new to Office 2007.

- **Workplace Ready:** These special features provide a glimpse of how the software application can be put into practice in a real-world situation.
- **Circling Back:** This feature provides you with an opportunity to review and practice skills learned in previous lessons.
- **Knowledge Assessment:** True/false, multiple choice, matching, or fill-in-the-blank questions test or reinforce your understanding of key lesson topics.
- **Competency Assessment:** These projects are similar to the exercises you completed within the lesson. Specific steps for completion are provided so that you can practice what you have learned.
- **Proficiency Assessment:** These projects give you additional opportunity to practice skills that you learned in the lesson. Not all the steps for completion are provided. Completing these exercises helps you verify whether you understand the lesson and reinforces your learning.
- **Mastery Assessment:** These projects require you to work independently—as you would in the workplace. Steps needed to complete the problems are not supplied. You must apply the knowledge you have acquired in the lesson to complete the problems successfully.
- **Internet Ready:** These projects combine what you have learned with research on the Internet.
- **Glossary:** Technical vocabulary is defined in the Glossary. Terms in the Glossary also appear in boldface italic type and are defined within the lessons.
- **Index:** All Glossary terms and application features appear in the Index.

■ Lesson Features

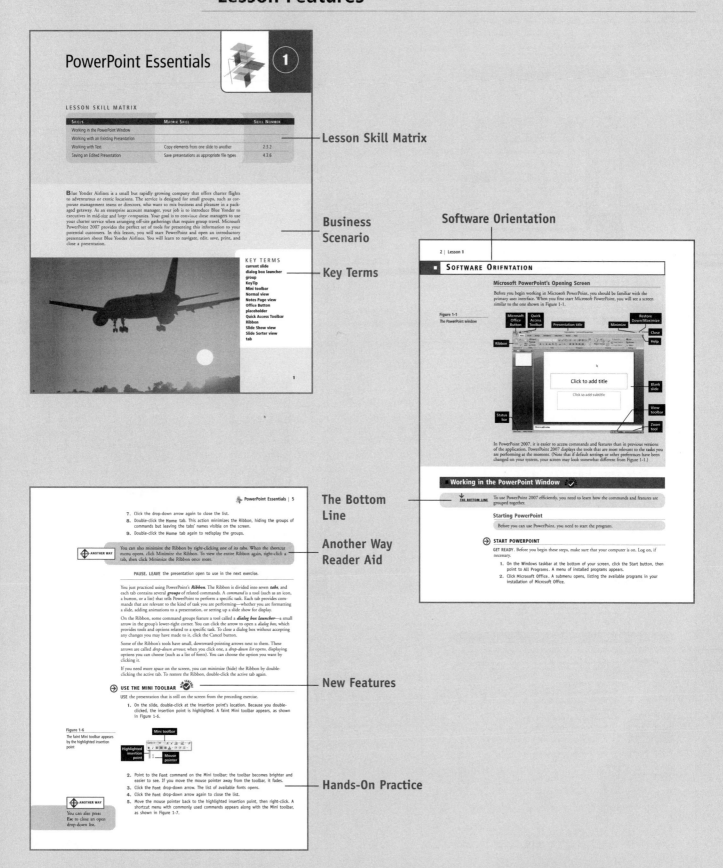

Lesson Skill Matrix

Business Scenario

Key Terms

Software Orientation

The Bottom Line

Another Way Reader Aid

New Features

Hands-On Practice

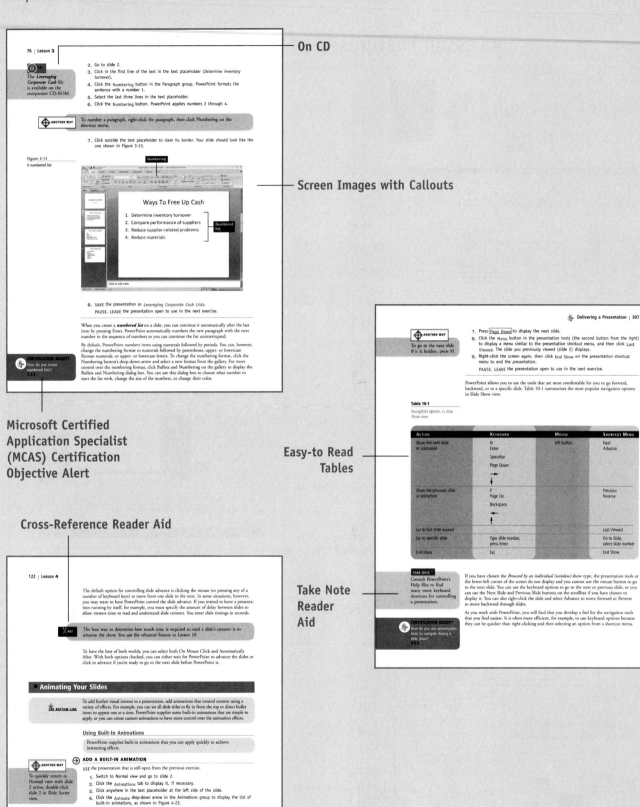

On CD

Screen Images with Callouts

Microsoft Certified
Application Specialist
(MCAS) Certification
Objective Alert

Cross-Reference Reader Aid

Easy-to Read
Tables

Take Note
Reader
Aid

Working with Text | 97

SUMMARY SKILL MATRIX

In This Lesson You Learned	Matrix Skill	Skill Number
To format characters		
To choose fonts and font sizes	Format font attributes	2.2.3
To apply font styles and effects	Format font attributes	2.2.3
To copy character formats using the Format Painter	Use the Format Painter to format text	2.2.4
To format paragraphs	Format paragraphs	2.2.6
To create and format bulleted and numbered lists	Create and format bulleted and numbered lists	2.2.5
To insert and format WordArt	Insert and modify WordArt	2.2.7
To add a text box to a slide	Insert and remove text boxes	2.1.1
To resize text boxes	Size text boxes	2.1.2
To set formatting options for a text box	Format text boxes	2.1.3
To format text with Quick Styles	Apply Quick Styles from the Style Gallery	2.2.2
To orient text in a text box	Select text orientation and alignment	2.1.4
To set up margins in a text box	Set margins	2.1.5
To set up columns in a text box	Create columns in text boxes	2.1.6
To delete a text box	Insert and remove text boxes	2.1.1

— Summary Skill Matrix

Knowledge Assessment

Fill in the Blank

Fill in each blank with the term or phrase that best completes the statement.

1. A(n) _____ is a container for text or a picture on a slide.
2. A font _____ is an attribute such as boldface or italic.
3. The small white boxes on the borders of a text box are called _____.
4. You can paint the background of a text box with a(n) _____ color.
5. The border of a WordArt character is called a(n) _____.
6. A(n) _____ is sometimes also called a typeface.
7. _____ text is aligned to both the left and right margins of a text box.
8. A(n) _____ object is text in the form of a graphic.
9. You should use a(n) _____ list to show items in a specific order.
10. A(n) _____ is a small character, such as a dot or a square, that appears before an item in a list.

— Knowledge Assessment Questions

Proficiency Assessment Projects

100 | Lesson 3

10. Go to slide 2, then drag the Format Painter pointer over the text on the right side of the slide.
11. SAVE the presentation as *Graphic Designs Final* and CLOSE the file.
LEAVE PowerPoint open for the next project.

Proficiency Assessment

Project 3-3: Destinations

As the owner and operator of Margie's Travel, you are involved with many aspects of sales, marketing, customer service, and new products and services. Today you want to format the text in a slide presentation that includes new European destinations.

The *New Destinations* file is available on the companion CD-ROM.

1. OPEN the *New Destinations* presentation.
2. Go to slide 2 and select the slide's title text. Click the Bold button to make the title boldface.
3. Select all the text in the bulleted list. Click the Align Text Left button to align the list along the left side of the text placeholder.
4. With the list still selected, open the Bullets and Numbering dialog box. Change the bullets' color to Orange, Accent 2, then resize the bullets so they are 90% of the text's size.
5. Click the Font Color drop-down arrow, then change the list's font color to Dark Green, Background 2, Lighter 80%.
6. Click Text Box on the Insert tab, then click below the picture on the slide to create a nonwrapping text box.
7. In the text box, key Companion Files Free until Jan. 1!
8. Click the Quick Styles button and apply the Colored Outline – Accent 1 Quick Style to the text box.
9. SAVE the presentation as *New Destinations Final* and CLOSE the file.
LEAVE PowerPoint open for the next project.

Project 3-4: Business To Business Imports

You are the lone marketing research person in your company, World Wide Importers. You often find exciting and potentially highly profitable new products that go overlooked by some of the senior staff. You need to draw attention to these products, and PowerPoint can help. Create a short presentation that uses WordArt to jazz up your presentation. This presentation will focus on precision equipment your company can start importing.

The *World Wide Importers* file is available on the companion CD-ROM.

1. OPEN the *World Wide Importers* presentation.
2. With slide 1 on the screen, open the WordArt gallery and select Gradient Fill – Accent 1, Outline – White, Glow – Accent 2.
3. In the WordArt text box that appears, key World Wide Importers. Reposition the text box so it is just above the subtitle and centered between the left and right edges of the slide.
4. In the WordArt Styles group, open the Text Fill color palette and click Aqua, Accent 1, Darker 25%.
5. Open the Text Effects menu and select the Cool Slant bevel effect.
6. Go to slide 2 and select all the text in the bulleted list.
7. Change the font size to 24, then change the line spacing to 1.5.

Competency Assessment Projects

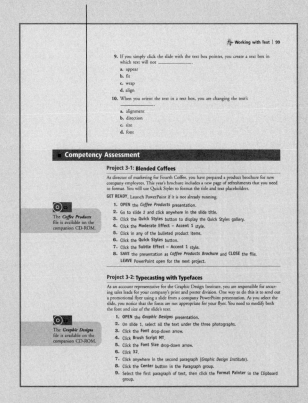

Working with Text | 99

9. If you simply click the slide with the text box pointer, you create a text box in which text will not _____.
  a. appear
  b. fit
  c. wrap
  d. align
10. When you orient the text in a text box, you are changing the text's _____.
  a. alignment
  b. direction
  c. size
  d. font

Competency Assessment

Project 3-1: Blended Coffees

As director of marketing for Fourth Coffee, you have prepared a product brochure for new company employees. This year's brochure includes a new page of refreshments that you need to format. You will use Quick Styles to format the title and text placeholders.

GET READY. Launch PowerPoint if it is not already running.

The *Coffee Products* file is available on the companion CD-ROM.

1. OPEN the *Coffee Products* presentation.
2. Go to slide 2 and click anywhere in the slide title.
3. Click the Quick Styles button to display the Quick Styles gallery.
4. Click the Moderate Effect – Accent 1 style.
5. Click in any of the bulleted product items.
6. Click the Quick Styles button.
7. Click the Subtle Effect – Accent 1 style.
8. SAVE the presentation as *Coffee Products Brochure* and CLOSE the file.
LEAVE PowerPoint open for the next project.

Project 3-2: Typecasting with Typefaces

As an account representative for the Graphic Design Institute, you are responsible for securing sales leads for your company's print and poster division. One way to do this is to send out a promotional flyer using a slide from a company PowerPoint presentation. As you select the slide, you notice that the fonts are not appropriate for your flyer. You need to modify both the font and size of the slide's text.

The *Graphic Designs* file is available on the companion CD-ROM.

1. OPEN the *Graphic Designs* presentation.
2. On slide 1, select all the text under the three photographs.
3. Click the Font drop-down arrow.
4. Click Brush Script MT.
5. Click the Font Size drop-down arrow.
6. Click 32.
7. Click anywhere in the second paragraph (Graphic Design Institute).
8. Click the Center button in the Paragraph group.
9. Select the first paragraph of text, then click the Format Painter in the Clipboard group.

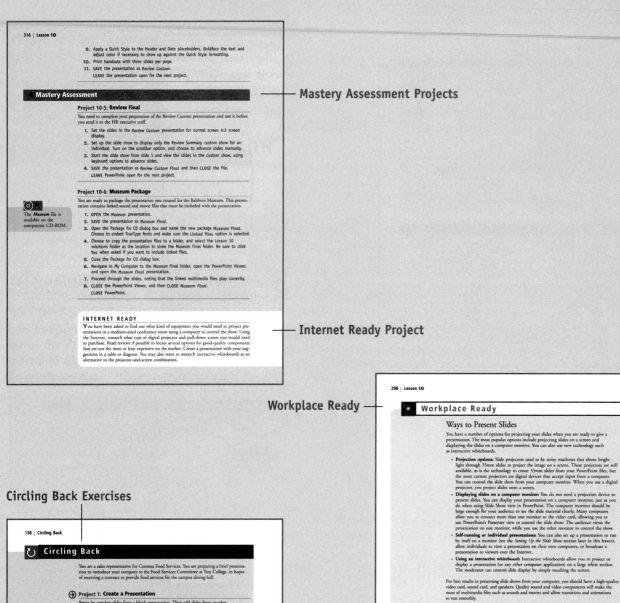

Mastery Assessment Projects

Internet Ready Project

Workplace Ready

Circling Back Exercises

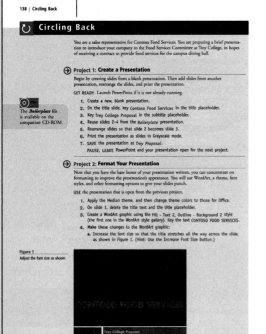

Conventions and Features Used in This Book

This book uses particular fonts, symbols, and heading conventions to highlight important information or to call your attention to special steps. For more information about the features in each lesson, refer to the Illustrated Book Tour section.

CONVENTION	MEANING
NEW FEATURE	This icon indicates a new or greatly improved Office 2007 feature in this version of the software.
↓ **THE BOTTOM LINE**	This feature provides a brief summary of the material to be covered in the section that follows.
CLOSE	Words in all capital letters and in a different font color than the rest of the text indicate instructions for opening, saving, or closing files or programs. They also point out items you should check or actions you should take.
CERTIFICATION READY?	This feature signals the point in the text where a specific certification objective is covered. It provides you with a chance to check your understanding of that particular MCAS objective and, if necessary, review the section of the lesson where it is covered.
◎ **CD**	This indicates a file that is available on the student CD.
TAKE NOTE *	Reader aids appear in shaded boxes found in your text. *Take Note* provides helpful hints related to particular tasks or topics.
⬦ **ANOTHER WAY**	*Another Way* provides an alternative procedure for accomplishing a particular task.
TROUBLESHOOTING	*Troubleshooting* covers common problems and pitfalls.
X REF	These notes provide pointers to information discussed elsewhere in the textbook or describe interesting features of Office 2007 that are not directly addressed in the current topic or exercise.
SAVE 🔲	When a toolbar button is referenced in an exercise, the button's picture is shown in the margin.
Alt + Tab	A plus sign (+) between two key names means that you must press both keys at the same time. Keys that you are instructed to press in an exercise will appear in the font shown here.
A *cell* is the area where data is entered.	Key terms appear in bold italic.
Key **My Name is.**	Any text you are asked to key appears in color.
Click **OK.**	Any button on the screen you are supposed to click on or select will also appear in color.
OPEN *FitnessClasses*.	The names of data files will appear in bold, italic, and color for easy identification.

www.wiley.com/college/microsoft *or* call the MOAC Toll-Free Number: 1+(888) 764-7001

Instructor Support Program

The *Microsoft Official Academic Course* programs are accompanied by a rich array of resources that incorporate the extensive textbook visuals to form a pedagogically cohesive package. These resources provide all the materials instructors need to deploy and deliver their courses. Resources available online for download include:

- **6-Month Office 2007 Trial Edition.** Students receive 6-months' access to Microsoft Office Professional 2007 when you adopt a MOAC 2007 Microsoft Office system textbook. The textbook includes the trial CD and a product key that allows students to activate the CD for a 6-month period.

- The **Instructor's Guide** contains Solutions to all the textbook exercises, Syllabi for various term lengths, Data Files for all the documents students need to work the exercises. The Instructor's Guide also includes chapter summaries and lecture notes. The Instructor's Guide is available from the Book Companion site (http://www.wiley.com/college/microsoft) and from WileyPLUS.

- The **Test Bank** contains hundreds of multiple-choice, true-false, and short answer questions and is available to download from the Instructor's Book Companion site (http://www.wiley.com/college/microsoft) and from WileyPLUS. A complete answer key is provided.

- **PowerPoint Presentations and Images.** A complete set of PowerPoint presentations is available on the Instructor's Book Companion site (http://www.wiley.com/college/microsoft) and in WileyPLUS to enhance classroom presentations. Approximately 50 PowerPoint slides are provided for each lesson. Tailored to the text's topical coverage and Skills Matrix, these presentations are designed to convey key Office 2007 concepts addressed in the text.

  All figures from the text are on the Instructor's Book Companion site (http://www.wiley.com/college/microsoft) and in WileyPLUS. You can incorporate them into your PowerPoint presentations, or create your own overhead transparencies and handouts.

  By using these visuals in class discussions, you can help focus students' attention on key elements of Office 2007 and help them understand how to use it effectively in the workplace.

- **Microsoft Business Certification Pre-Test and Exams**. With each MOAC textbook, students receive information allowing them to access a Pre-Test, Score Report, and Learning Plan, either directly from Certiport, one of Microsoft's exam delivery partners, or through links from WileyPLUS Premium. They also receive a code and information for taking the certification exams.

- The **MSDN Academic Alliance** is designed to provide the easiest and most inexpensive way for university departments to make the latest Microsoft software available to faculty and students in labs, classrooms, and on student PCs. A free 1-year membership is available to qualified MOAC adopters.

- **The Wiley Faculty Network** lets you tap into a large community of your peers effortlessly. Wiley Faculty Network mentors are faculty like you, from educational institutions around the country, who are passionate about enhancing instructional efficiency and effectiveness through best practices. Faculty Network activities include technology training and tutorials, virtual seminars, peer-to-peer exchanges of experience and ideas, personal consulting, and sharing of resources. To register for a seminar, go to www.wherefacultyconnect.com or phone 1-866-4FACULTY.

WileyPLUS

Broad developments in education over the past decade have influenced the instructional approach taken in the Microsoft Official Academic Course programs. The way that students learn, especially about new technologies, has changed dramatically in the Internet era. Electronic learning materials and Internet-based instruction is now as much a part of classroom instruction as printed textbooks. *WileyPLUS* provides the technology to create an environment where students reach their full potential and experience academic success that will last them a lifetime!

WileyPLUS is a powerful and highly-integrated suite of teaching and learning resources designed to bridge the gap between what happens in the classroom and what happens at home and on the job. *WileyPLUS* provides Instructors with the resources to teach their students new technologies and guide them to reach their goals of getting ahead in the job market by having the skills to become certified and advance in the workforce. For students, WileyPLUS provides the tools for study and practice that are available to them 24/7, wherever and whenever they want to study. *WileyPLUS* includes a complete online version of the student textbook; PowerPoint presentations; homework and practice assignments and quizzes; links to Microsoft's Pre-Test, Learning Plan, and a code for taking the certification exam (in WileyPLUS Premium); image galleries; test-bank questions; gradebook; and all the instructor resources in one easy-to-use website.

Organized around the everyday activities you and your students perform in the class, *WileyPLUS* helps you:

- **Prepare & Present** outstanding class presentations using relevant PowerPoint slides and other *WileyPLUS* materials—and you can easily upload and add your own.
- **Create Assignments** by choosing from questions organized by lesson, level of difficulty, and source—and add your own questions. Students' homework and quizzes are automatically graded, and the results are recorded in your gradebook.
- **Offer context-sensitive help to students, 24/7.** When you assign homework or quizzes, you decide if and when students get access to hints, solutions, or answers where appropriate—or they can be linked to relevant sections of their complete, online text for additional help whenever—and wherever they need it most.
- **Track Student Progress:** Analyze students' results and assess their level of understanding on an individual and class level using the *WileyPLUS* gradebook, or export data to your own personal gradebook.
- **Administer Your Course:** Wiley PLUS can easily be integrated with another course management system, gradebook, or other resources you are using in your class, providing you with the flexibility to build your course, your way.
- **Seamlessly integrate all of the rich WileyPLUS content and resources with WebCT and Blackboard**—with a single sign-on.

Please view our online demo at **www.wiley.com/college/wileyplus.** Here you will find additional information about the features and benefits of Wiley PLUS, how to request a "test drive" of Wiley PLUS for this title, and how to adopt it for class use.

MICROSOFT BUSINESS CERTIFICATION PRE-TEST AND EXAMS AVAILABLE THROUGH WILEY*PLUS* PREMIUM

Enhance your students' knowledge and skills and increase their performance on Microsoft Business Certification exams with adoption of the Microsoft Official Academic Course program for Office 2007.

With the majority of the workforce classified as *information workers*, certification on the 2007 Microsoft Office system is a critical tool in terms of validating the desktop computing knowledge and skills required to be more productive in the workplace. Certification is the primary tool companies use to validate the proficiency of desktop computing skills among employees. It gives organizations the ability to help assess employees' actual computer skills and select job candidates based on verifiable skills applying the latest productivity tools and technology.

Microsoft Pre-tests, delivered by Certiport, provide a simple, low-cost way for individuals to identify their desktop computing skill level. Pre-Tests are taken online, making the first step towards certification easy and convenient. Through the Pre-Tests, individuals can receive a custom learning path with recommended training.

To help students to study for and pass the Microsoft Certified Application Specialist, or MCAS exam, each MOAC textbook includes information allowing students to access a Pre-Test, Score Report, and Learning Plan, either directly from Certiport or through links from the Wiley*PLUS* Premium course. Students also receive a code and information for taking the certification exams. Students who do not have access to Wiley*PLUS* Premium can find information on how to purchase access to the Pre-Test and a code for taking the certification exams by clicking on their textbook at:

http://www.wiley.com/college/microsoft.

The Pre-Test can only be taken once. It provides a simple, low-cost way for students to evaluate and identify their skill level. Through the Pre-Test, students receive a recommended study plan that they can print out to help them prepare for the live certification exams. The Pre-Test is comprised of a variety of selected response questions, including matching, sequencing exercises, "hot spots" where students must identify an item or function, and traditional multiple-choice questions. After students have mastered all the certification objectives, they can use their code to take the actual Microsoft Certified Application Specialist (MCAS) exams for Office 2007.

Wiley*PLUS* Premium includes a complete online version of the student textbook, PowerPoint® presentations, homework and practice assignments and quizzes, links to Microsoft's Pre-Test, Learning Plan and a certification voucher, image galleries, test bank questions, gradebook, and all the instructor resources in one, easy-to-use website. Together, with Wiley*PLUS* and the MCAS Pre-Test and exams delivered by Certiport, we are creating the best of both worlds in academic learning and performance based validation in preparation for a great career and a globally recognized Microsoft certification—the higher education learning management system that accesses the industry-leading certification pre-test.

Contact your Wiley rep today about this special offer.

MSDN ACADEMIC ALLIANCE—FREE 1-YEAR MEMBERSHIP AVAILABLE TO QUALIFIED ADOPTERS!

MSDN Academic Alliance (MSDN AA) is designed to provide the easiest and most inexpensive way for universities to make the latest Microsoft software available in labs, classrooms, and on student PCs. MSDN AA is an annual membership program for departments teaching Science, Technology, Engineering, and Mathematics (STEM) courses. The membership provides a complete solution to keep academic labs, faculty, and students on the leading edge of technology.

As a bonus to this free offer, faculty will be introduced to Microsoft's Faculty Connection and Academic Resource Center. It takes time and preparation to keep students engaged while giving them a fundamental understanding of theory, and the Microsoft Faculty Connection is designed to help STEM professors with this preparation by providing articles, curriculum, and tools that professors can use to engage and inspire today's technology students.

Software provided in the MSDN AA program carries a high retail value but is being provided here through the Wiley and Microsoft publishing partnership and is made available to your department free of charge with the adoption of any Wiley qualified textbook.*

* Contact your Wiley rep for details.

For more information about the MSDN Academic Alliance program, go to:

http://msdn.microsoft.com/academic/

Adoption Options

To provide you and your students with the right choices for learning, studying, and passing the MCAS certification exams, we have put together various options for your adoption requirements.

All selections include the student CD. Please contact your Wiley rep for more information:
- Textbook with 6-month Microsoft Office Trial
- Textbook, 6-month Microsoft Office Trial, WileyPLUS
- Textbook, 6-month Microsoft Office Trial, WileyPLUS Premium (includes access to Certiport)
- WileyPLUS (includes full e-book)
- WileyPLUS Premium (includes full e-book and access to Certiport)

Important Web Addresses and Phone Numbers

To locate the Wiley Higher Education Rep in your area, go to the following Web address and click on the "*Who's My Rep?*" link at the top of the page.

http://www.wiley.com/college

Or Call the MOAC Toll Free Number: 1 + (888) 764-7001

To learn more about becoming a Microsoft Certified Application Specialist and exam availability, visit www.microsoft.com/learning/msbc.

http://www.wiley.com/college/microsoft *or* call the MOAC Toll-Free Number: 1+(888) 764-7001

Book Companion Website (www.wiley.com/college/microsoft)

The book companion site for the MOAC series includes the Instructor Resources and Web links to important information for students and instructors.

WileyPLUS

WileyPLUS is a powerful and highly-integrated suite of teaching and learning resources designed to bridge the gap between what happens in the classroom and what happens at home and on the job. For students, WileyPLUS provides the tools for study and practice that are available 24/7, wherever and whenever they want to study. WileyPLUS includes a complete online version of the student textbook; PowerPoint presentations; homework and practice assignments and quizzes; links to Microsoft's Pre-Test, Learning Plan, and a code for taking the certification exam (in WileyPLUS Premium); image galleries; test bank questions; gradebook; and all the instructor resources in one easy-to-use website.

WileyPLUS provides immediate feedback on student assignments and a wealth of support materials. This powerful study tool will help your students develop their conceptual understanding of the class material and increase their ability to answer questions.

- A **Study and Practice** area links directly to text content, allowing students to review the text while they study and answer. Access to Microsoft's Pre-Test, Learning Plan, and a code for taking the MCAS certification exam is available in Study and Practice. Additional Practice Questions tied to the MCAS certification that can be re-taken as many times as necessary, are also available.

- An **Assignment** area keeps all the work you want your students to complete in one location, making it easy for them to stay on task. Students have access to a variety of interactive self-assessment tools, as well as other resources for building their confidence and understanding. In addition, all of the assignments and quizzes contain a link to the relevant section of the multimedia book, providing students with context-sensitive help that allows them to conquer obstacles as they arise.

- A **Personal Gradebook** for each student allows students to view their results from past assignments at any time.

Please view our online demo at www.wiley.com/college/wileyplus. Here you will find additional information about the features and benefits of WileyPLUS, how to request a "test drive" of WileyPLUS for this title, and how to adopt it for class use.

6-MONTH MICROSOFT OFFICE 2007 TRIAL EDITION

MOAC textbooks provide an unparalleled value to students in today's performance-based courses. All MOAC 2007 Microsoft Office system textbooks are packaged with a 6-month trial CD of Microsoft Office Professional 2007. The textbook includes the CD and a product key that allows students to activate Microsoft Office Professional 2007 for the 6-month trial period. After purchasing the textbook containing the Microsoft Office Professional 2007 Trial CD, students must install the CD onto their computer and, when prompted, enter the Office Trial product key that allows them to activate the software.

Installing the Microsoft Office Professional 2007 Trial CD provides students with the state-of-the-art 2007 Microsoft Office system software, allowing them to use the practice files on the Student CD and in WileyPLUS to learn and study by doing, which is the best and most effective way to acquire and remember new computing skills.

TAKE NOTE

For the best performance, the default selection during Setup is to uninstall previous versions of Office. There is also an option to remove previous versions of Office. With all trial software, Microsoft recommends that you have your original CDs available to reinstall if necessary. If you want to return to your previous version of Office, you need to uninstall the trial software. This should be done through the Add or Remove Programs icon in Microsoft Windows Control Panel (or Uninstall a program in the Control Panel of Windows Vista).

Installation of Microsoft Office Professional 2007 6-Month Trial software will remove your existing version of Microsoft Outlook. However, your contacts, calendar, and other personal information will not be deleted. At the end of the trial, if you choose to upgrade or to reinstall your previous version of Outlook, your personal settings and information will be retained.

Installing the 2007 Microsoft Office System 6-Month Trial

1. Insert the trial software CD-ROM into the CD drive on your computer. The CD will be detected, and the Setup.exe file should automatically begin to run on your computer.
2. When prompted for the Office Product Key, enter the Product Key provided with the software, and then click **Next.**
3. Enter your name and organization user name, and then click **Next.**
4. Read the End-User License Agreement, select the *I Accept the Terms in the License Agreement* check box, and then click **Next.**
5. Select the install option, verify the installation location or click **Browse** to change the installation location, and then click **Next.**
6. Verify the program installation preferences, and then click **Next.**
7. Click **Finish** to complete the setup.

Upgrading Microsoft Office Professional 2007 6-Month Trial Software to the Full Product

You can convert the software into full use without removing or reinstalling software on your computer. When you complete your trial, you can purchase a product license from any Microsoft reseller and enter a valid Product Key when prompted during Setup.

Uninstalling the Trial Software and Returning to Your Previous Office Version

If you want to return to your previous version of Office, you need to uninstall the trial software. This should be done through the Add or Remove Programs icon in Control Panel (or Uninstall a program in the Control Panel of Windows Vista).

Uninstall Trial Software

1. Quit any programs that are running.
2. In Control Panel, click **Add or Remove Programs** (or **Uninstall a program** in Windows Vista).
3. Click **Microsoft Office Professional 2007,** and then click **Remove** (or **Uninstall** in Windows Vista).

TAKE NOTE

If you selected the option to remove a previous version of Office during installation of the trial software, you need to reinstall your previous version of Office. If you did not remove your previous version of Office, you can start each of your Office programs either through the Start menu or by opening files for each program. In some cases, you may have to recreate some of your shortcuts and default settings.

Student CD

The CD-ROM included with this book contains the practice files that you will use as you perform the exercises in the book. By using the practice files, you will not waste time creating the samples used in the lessons, and you can concentrate on learning how to use Microsoft Office 2007. With the files and the step-by-step instructions in the lessons, you will learn by doing, which is an easy and effective way to acquire and remember new skills.

IMPORTANT

This course assumes that the 2007 Microsoft Office system has already been installed on the PC you are using. Note that Microsoft Product Support does not support this trial version.

Copying the Practice Files

Your instructor might already have copied the practice files before you arrive in class. However, your instructor might ask you to copy the practice files on your own at the start of class. Also, if you want to work through any of the exercises in this book on your own at home or at your place of business after class, you may want to copy the practice files. Note that you can also open the files directly from the CD-ROM, but you should be cautious about carrying the CD-ROM around with you as it could become damaged.

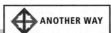

If you only want to copy the files for one lesson, you can open the Data folder and right-click the desired Lesson folder within the Data folder.

1. Insert the CD-ROM in the CD-ROM drive of your computer.
2. Start Windows Explorer.
3. In the left pane of Explorer, locate the icon for your CD-ROM and click on this icon. The folders and files contained on the CD will appear listed on the right.
4. Locate and select the **PowerPoint Data** folder. This is the folder that contains all of the practice files, separated by Lesson folders.
5. Right-click on the **PowerPoint Data** folder and choose **Copy** from the menu.
6. In the left pane of Windows Explorer, locate the location to which you would like to copy the practice files. This can be a drive on your local PC or an external drive.
7. Right-click on the drive/location to which you want to copy the practice files and choose **Paste.** This will copy the entire Data folder to your chosen location.
8. Close Windows Explorer.

Deleting the Practice Files

Use the following steps when you want to delete the practice files from your hard disk or other drive. Your instructor might ask you to perform these steps at the end of class. Also, you should perform these steps if you have worked through the exercises at home or at your place of business and want to work through the exercises again. Deleting the practice files and then reinstalling them ensures that all files and folders are in their original condition if you decide to work through the exercises again.

1. Start Windows Explorer.
2. Browse through the drives and folders to locate the practice files.
3. Select the **PowerPoint Data** folder.
4. Right-click on the **PowerPoint Data** folder and choose **Delete** from the menu.
5. Close Windows Explorer.

Locating and Opening Practice Files

ANOTHER WAY

If you only want to delete only the files for one lesson, you can open the Data folder and right-click the desired Lesson folder within the Data folder.

After you (or your instructor) have copied the practice files, all the files you need for this course will be stored in a folder named Data located on the disk you choose.

1. Click the **Office Button** in the top left corner of your application.
2. Choose **Open** from the menu.
3. In the Open dialog box, browse through the Folders panel to locate the drive and folder where you copied the files.
4. Double-click on the **PowerPoint Data** folder.
5. Double-click on the **Lesson** folder for the lesson in which you are working.
6. Select the file that you want and click **Open** or double-click on the file that you want.

Wiley Desktop Editions

ANOTHER WAY

You can use the Search function in the Open dialog box to quickly find the specific file for which you are looking.

Wiley MOAC Desktop Editions are innovative, electronic versions of printed textbooks. Students buy the desktop version for 60% off the price of the printed text, and get the added value of permanence and portability. Wiley Desktop Editions provide students with numerous additional benefits that are not available with other e-text solutions:

Wiley Desktop Editions are NOT subscriptions; students download the Wiley Desktop Edition to their computer desktops. Students own the content they buy to keep for as long as they want. Once a Wiley Desktop Edition is downloaded to the computer desktop, students have instant access to all of the content without being online. Students can also print out the sections they prefer to read in hard copy. Students also have access to fully integrated resources within their Wiley Desktop Edition. From highlighting their e-text to taking and sharing notes, students can easily personalize their Wiley Desktop Edition as they are reading or following along in class.

Microsoft® Office Online

Please visit Microsoft Office Online for help using Office 2007, Clip Art, Templates, and other valuable information:
http://office.microsoft.com/

Preparing to Take the Microsoft Certified Application Specialist (MCAS) Exam

The Microsoft Certified Application Specialist program is part of the new and enhanced Microsoft Business Certifications. It is easily attainable through a series of verifications that provide a simple and convenient framework for skills assessment and validation.

For organizations, the new certification program provides better skills verification tools that help with assessing not only in-demand skills on the 2007 Microsoft Office system, but also the ability to quickly complete on-the-job tasks. Individuals will find it easier to identify and work towards the certification credential that meets their personal and professional goals.

To learn more about becoming a Microsoft Certified Application Specialist and exam availability, visit www.microsoft.com/learning/msbc.

Microsoft Certified Application Specialist (MCAS) Program

The core Microsoft Office Specialist credential has been upgraded to validate skills with the 2007 Microsoft Office system as well as the new Windows Vista operating system. The Application Specialist certifications target information workers and cover the most popular business applications such as Word 2007, PowerPoint 2007, Excel 2007, Access 2007, and Outlook 2007.

By becoming certified, you demonstrate to employers that you have achieved a predictable level of skill in the use of a particular Office application. Employers often require certification either as a condition of employment or as a condition of advancement within the company or other organization. The certification examinations are sponsored by Microsoft but administered through exam delivery partners like Certiport.

Preparing to Take an Exam

Unless you are a very experienced user, you will need to use a test preparation course to prepare to complete the test correctly and within the time allowed. The *Microsoft Official Academic Course* series is designed to prepare you with a strong knowledge of all exam topics, and with some additional review and practice on your own. You should feel confident in your ability to pass the appropriate exam.

After you decide which exam to take, review the list of objectives for the exam. This list can be found in the MCAS Objectives Appendix at the back of this book. You can also easily identify tasks that are included in the objective list by locating the Lesson Skill Matrix at the start of each lesson and the Certification Ready sidebars in the margin of the lessons in this book.

To take the MCAS test, visit *www.microsoft.com/learning/msbc* to locate your nearest testing center. Then call the testing center directly to schedule your test. The amount of advance notice you should provide will vary for different testing centers, and it typically depends on the number of computers available at the testing center, the number of other testers who have already been scheduled for the day on which you want to take the test, and the number of times per week that the testing center offers MCAS testing. In general, you should call to schedule your test at least two weeks prior to the date on which you want to take the test.

When you arrive at the testing center, you might be asked for proof of identity. A driver's license or passport is an acceptable form of identification. If you do not have either of these items of documentation, call your testing center and ask what alternative forms of identification will be accepted. If you are retaking a test, bring your MCAS identification number, which will have been given to you when you previously took the test. If you have not prepaid or if your organization has not already arranged to make payment for you, you will need to pay the test-taking fee when you arrive.

Test Format

All MCAS certification tests are live, performance-based tests. There are no true/false, or short-answer questions. Instructions are general: you are told the basic tasks to perform on the computer, but you aren't given any help in figuring out how to perform them. You are not permitted to use reference material or the application's Help system.

As you complete the tasks stated in a particular test question, the testing software monitors your actions. An example question might be:

Open the file named *Wiley Guests* and select the word *Welcome* in the first paragraph. Change the font to 12 point, and apply bold formatting. Select the words *at your convenience* in the second paragraph, move them to the end of the first paragraph using drag and drop, and then center the first paragraph.

When the test administrator seats you at a computer, you will see an online form that you use to enter information about yourself (name, address, and other information required to process your exam results). While you complete the form, the software will generate the test from a master test bank and then prompt you to continue. The first test question will appear in a window. Read the question carefully, and then perform all the tasks stated in the test question. When you have finished completing all tasks for a question, click the Next Question button.

You have 45 to 50 minutes to complete all questions, depending on the test that you are taking. The testing software assesses your results as soon as you complete the test, and the test administrator can print the results of the test so that you will have a record of any tasks that you performed incorrectly. If you pass, you will receive a certificate in the mail within two to four weeks. If you do not pass, you can study and practice the skills that you missed and then schedule to retake the test at a later date.

Tips for Successfully Completing the Test

The following tips and suggestions are the result of feedback received from many individuals who have taken one or more MCAS tests:

- Make sure that you are thoroughly prepared. If you have extensively used the application for which you are being tested, you might feel confident that you are prepared for the test. However, the test might include questions that involve tasks that you rarely or never perform when you use the application at your place of business, at school, or at home. You must be knowledgeable in all the MCAS objectives for the test that you will take.

- Read each exam question carefully. An exam question might include several tasks that you are to perform. A partially correct response to a test question is counted as an incorrect response. In the example question on the previous page, you might apply bold formatting and move the words *at your convenience* to the correct location, but forget to center the first paragraph. This would count as an incorrect response and would result in a lower test score.

- Keep track of your time. The test does display the amount of time that you have left, so keep track of the time. The test program displays the number of items that you have completed along with the total number of test items (for example, "35 of 40 items have been completed"). Use this information to gauge your pace.

If You Do Not Pass the Test

If you do not pass, you can use the assessment printout as a guide to practice the items that you missed. There is no limit to the number of times that you can retake a test; however, you must pay the fee each time that you take the test. When you retake the test, expect to see some of the same test items on the subsequent test; the test software randomly generates the test items from a master test bank before you begin the test. Also expect to see several questions that did not appear on the previous test.

MOAC Instructor Advisory Board

We would like thank to our Instructor Advisory Board, an elite group of educators who has assisted us every step of the way in building these products. Advisory Board members have acted as our sounding board on key pedagogical and design decisions leading to the development of these compelling and innovative textbooks for future Information Workers. Their dedication to technology education is truly appreciated.

Catherine Binder, Strayer University & Katharine Gibbs School–Philadelphia

Catherine currently works at both Katharine Gibbs School in Norristown, PA and Strayer University in King of Prussia, PA. Catherine has been at Katharine Gibbs School for 4 years. Catherine is currently the Department Chair/Lead instructor for PC Networking at Gibbs and the founder/advisor of the TEK Masters Society. Since joining Strayer University a year and a half ago she has risen in the ranks from adjunct to DIT/Assistant Campus Dean.

Catherine has brought her 10+ year's industry experience as Network Administrator, Network Supervisor, Professor, Bench Tech, Manager and CTO from such places as Foster Wheeler Corp, KidsPeace Inc., Victoria Vogue, TESST College, AMC Theatres, Blue Mountain Publishing and many more to her teaching venue.

Catherine began as an adjunct in the PC Networking department and quickly became a full-time instructor. At both schools she is in charge of scheduling, curricula and departmental duties. She happily advises about 80+ students and is committed to Gibbs/Strayer life, her students, and continuing technology education every day.

Penny Gudgeon, CDI College

Penny is the Program Manager for IT curriculum at Corinthian Colleges, Inc. Until January 2006, Penny was responsible for all Canadian programming and web curriculum for five years. During that time, Corinthian Colleges, Inc. acquired CDI College of Business and Technology in 2004. Before 2000 she spent four years as IT instructor at one of the campuses. Penny joined CDI College in 1997 after her working for 10 years first in programming and later in software productivity education. Penny previously has worked in the fields of advertising, sales, engineering technology and programming. When not working from her home office or indulging her passion for life long learning, and the possibilities of what might be, Penny likes to read mysteries, garden and relax at home in Hamilton, Ontario, with her Shih-Tzu, Gracie, and husband, Al.

Jana Hambruch, School District of Lee County

Ms. Hambruch currently serves as Director for the Information Technology Magnet Programs at The School District of Lee County in Ft Myers, Florida. She is responsible for the implementation and direction of three schools that fall under this grant program. This program has been recognized as one of the top 15 most innovative technology programs in the nation. She is also co-author of the grant proposal for the IT Magnet Grant prior to taking on the role of Director.

Ms. Hambruch has over ten years experience directing the technical certification training programs at many Colleges and Universities, including Barry University, the University of

South Florida, Broward Community College, and at Florida Gulf Coast University, where she served as the Director for the Center for Technology Education. She excels at developing alternative training models that focus on the tie between the education provider and the community in which it serves.

Ms. Hambruch is a past board member and treasurer of the Human Resources Management Association of SW Florida, graduate of Leadership Lee County Class of 2002, Steering Committee Member for Leadership Lee County Class of 2004 and a former board member of the Career Coalition of Southwest Florida. She has frequently lectured for organizations such as Microsoft, American Society of Training and Development, Florida Gulf Coast University, Florida State University, University of Nevada at Las Vegas, University of Wisconsin at Milwaukee, Canada's McGill University, and Florida's State Workforce Summit.

Dee Hobson, Richland College

Dee Hobson is currently a faculty member of the Business Office Systems and Support Division at Richland College. Richland is one of seven colleges in the Dallas County Community College District and has the distinction of being the first community college to receive the Malcolm Baldrige National Quality Award in 2005. Richland also received the Texas Award for Performance Excellence in 2005.

The Business Office Systems and Support Division at Richland is also a Certiport Authorized Microsoft Office testing center. All students enrolling in one of Microsoft's application software courses (Word, Excel, PowerPoint, and Access) are required to take the respective Microsoft certification exam at the end of the semester.

Dee has taught computer and business courses in K-12 public schools and at a proprietary career college in Dallas. She has also been involved with several corporate training companies and with adult education programs in the Dallas area. She began her computer career as an employee of IBM Corporation in St. Louis, Missouri. During her ten-year IBM employment, she moved to Memphis, Tennessee, to accept a managerial position and to Dallas, Texas, to work in a national sales and marketing technical support center.

Keith Hoell, Katharine Gibbs School–New York

Keith has worked in both non-profit and proprietary education for over 10 years, initially at St. John's University in New York, and then as full-time faculty, Chairperson and currently Dean of Information Systems at the Katharine Gibbs School in New York City. He also worked for General Electric in the late 80's and early 90's as the Sysop of a popular bulletin board dedicated to ASCII-Art on GE's pioneering GEnie on-line service before the advent of the World Wide Web. He has taught courses and workshops dealing with many mainstream IT issues and varied technology, especially those related to computer hardware and operating system software, networking, software applications, IT project management and ethics, and relational database technology. An avid runner and a member of The New York Road Runners, he won the Footlocker Five Borough Challenge representing Queens at the 2005 ING New York City Marathon while competing against the 4 other borough reps. He currently resides in Queens, New York.

Michael Taylor, Seattle Central Community College

Michael worked in education and training for the last 20 years in both the public and private sector. He currently teaches and coordinates the applications support program at Seattle Central Community College and also administers the Microsoft IT Academy. His experience outside the educational world is in Travel and Tourism with wholesale tour operations and cruise lines.

Interests outside of work include greyhound rescue. (He adopted 3 x-racers who bring him great joy.) He also enjoys the arts and is fortunate to live in downtown Seattle where there is much to see and do.

MOAC Office 2007 Reviewers

We also thank the many reviewers who pored over the manuscript providing invaluable feedback in the service of quality instructional materials.

Access

Susan Fry, Boise State University
Leslie Jernberg, Eastern Idaho Technical College
Dr. Deborah Jones, South Georgia Technical College
Suzanne Marks, Bellevue Community College
Harvey Munroe, Compu College Atlantic
Kim Styles, Tri-County Technical College & Anderson School District 5

Excel

Christie Hovey, Lincoln Land Community College
Barbara Lave, Portland Community College
Donna Madsen, Kirkwood Community College
James M. Veneziano, Davenport University—Caro
Dorothy Weiner, Manchester Community College

PowerPoint

Barbara Gillespie, Cuyamaca College
Tatyana Pashnyak, Bainbridge College
Michelle Poertner, Northwestern Michigan College
Janet Sebesy, Cuyahoga Community College

Outlook

Julie Boyles, Portland Community College
Joe LaMontagne, Davenport University—Grand Rapids
Randy Nordell, American River College
Echo Rantanen, Spokane Community College

Project

Janis DeHaven, Central Community College
Dr. Susan Jennings, Stephen F. Austin State University
Diane D. Mickey, Northern Virginia Community College
Linda Nutter, Peninsula College
Marika Reinke, Bellevue Community College

Word

Diana Anderson, Big Sandy Community & Technical College
Donna Hendricks, South Arkansas Community College
Dr. Donna McGill-Cameron, Yuba Community College—Woodland Campus
Patricia McMahon, South Suburban College
Nancy Noe, Linn-Benton Community College
Teresa Roberts, Wilson Technical Community College

Focus Group and Survey Participants

Finally we thank the hundreds of instructors who participated in our focus groups and surveys to ensure that the Microsoft Official Academic Courses best met the needs of our customers.

Jean Aguilar, Mt. Hood Community College
Konrad Akens, Zane State College
Michael Albers, University of Memphis
Diana Anderson, Big Sandy Community & Technical College
Phyllis Anderson, Delaware County Community College

Judith Andrews, Feather River College
Damon Antos, American River College
Bridget Archer, Oakton Community College
Linda Arnold, Harrisburg Area Community College–
    Lebanon Campus

Neha Arya, Fullerton College

Mohammad Bajwa, Katharine Gibbs School–New York

Virginia Baker, University of Alaska Fairbanks

Carla Bannick, Pima Community College

Rita Barkley, Northeast Alabama Community College

Elsa Barr, Central Community College – Hastings

Ronald W. Barry, Ventura County Community College District

Elizabeth Bastedo, Central Carolina Technical College

Karen Baston, Waubonsee Community College

Karen Bean, Blinn College

Scott Beckstrand, Community College of Southern Nevada

Paulette Bell, Santa Rosa Junior College

Liz Bennett, Southeast Technical Institute

Nancy Bermea, Olympic College

Lucy Betz, Milwaukee Area Technical College

Meral Binbasioglu, Hofstra University

Catherine Binder, Strayer University & Katharine Gibbs School–Philadelphia

Terrel Blair, El Centro College

Ruth Blalock, Alamance Community College

Beverly Bohner, Reading Area Community College

Henry Bojack, Farmingdale State University

Matthew Bowie, Luna Community College

Julie Boyles, Portland Community College

Karen Brandt, College of the Albemarle

Stephen Brown, College of San Mateo

Jared Bruckner, Southern Adventist University

Pam Brune, Chattanooga State Technical Community College

Sue Buchholz, Georgia Perimeter College

Roberta Buczyna, Edison College

Angela Butler, Mississippi Gulf Coast Community College

Rebecca Byrd, Augusta Technical College

Kristen Callahan, Mercer County Community College

Judy Cameron, Spokane Community College

Dianne Campbell, Athens Technical College

Gena Casas, Florida Community College at Jacksonville

Jesus Castrejon, Latin Technologies

Gail Chambers, Southwest Tennessee Community College

Jacques Chansavang, Indiana University–Purdue University Fort Wayne

Nancy Chapko, Milwaukee Area Technical College

Rebecca Chavez, Yavapai College

Sanjiv Chopra, Thomas Nelson Community College

Greg Clements, Midland Lutheran College

Dayna Coker, Southwestern Oklahoma State University–Sayre Campus

Tamra Collins, Otero Junior College

Janet Conrey, Gavilan Community College

Carol Cornforth, West Virginia Northern Community College

Gary Cotton, American River College

Edie Cox, Chattahoochee Technical College

Rollie Cox, Madison Area Technical College

David Crawford, Northwestern Michigan College

J.K. Crowley, Victor Valley College

Rosalyn Culver, Washtenaw Community College

Sharon Custer, Huntington University

Sandra Daniels, New River Community College

Anila Das, Cedar Valley College

Brad Davis, Santa Rosa Junior College

Susan Davis, Green River Community College

Mark Dawdy, Lincoln Land Community College

Jennifer Day, Sinclair Community College

Carol Deane, Eastern Idaho Technical College

Julie DeBuhr, Lewis-Clark State College

Janis DeHaven, Central Community College

Drew Dekreon, University of Alaska–Anchorage

Joy DePover, Central Lakes College

Salli DiBartolo, Brevard Community College

Melissa Diegnau, Riverland Community College

Al Dillard, Lansdale School of Business

Marjorie Duffy, Cosumnes River College

Sarah Dunn, Southwest Tennessee Community College

Shahla Durany, Tarrant County College–South Campus

Kay Durden, University of Tennessee at Martin

Dineen Ebert, St. Louis Community College–Meramec

Donna Ehrhart, State University of New York–Brockport

Larry Elias, Montgomery County Community College

Glenda Elser, New Mexico State University at Alamogordo

Angela Evangelinos, Monroe County Community College

Angie Evans, Ivy Tech Community College of Indiana

Linda Farrington, Indian Hills Community College

Dana Fladhammer, Phoenix College

Richard Flores, Citrus College

Connie Fox, Community and Technical College at Institute of Technology West Virginia University

Wanda Freeman, Okefenokee Technical College

Brenda Freeman, Augusta Technical College

Susan Fry, Boise State University

Roger Fulk, Wright State University–Lake Campus

Sue Furnas, Collin County Community College District

Sandy Gabel, Vernon College

Laura Galvan, Fayetteville Technical Community College

Candace Garrod, Red Rocks Community College

Sherrie Geitgey, Northwest State Community College

Chris Gerig, Chattahoochee Technical College

Barb Gillespie, Cuyamaca College

Jessica Gilmore, Highline Community College

Pamela Gilmore, Reedley College

Debbie Glinert, Queensborough Community College

Steven Goldman, Polk Community College

Bettie Goodman, C.S. Mott Community College

Mike Grabill, Katharine Gibbs School–Philadelphia

Francis Green, Penn State University

Walter Griffin, Blinn College

Fillmore Guinn, Odessa College

Helen Haasch, Milwaukee Area Technical College

John Habal, Ventura College

Joy Haerens, Chaffey College

Norman Hahn, Thomas Nelson Community College

Kathy Hall, Alamance Community College

Teri Harbacheck, Boise State University

Linda Harper, Richland Community College

Maureen Harper, Indian Hills Community College

Steve Harris, Katharine Gibbs School–New York

Robyn Hart, Fresno City College

Darien Hartman, Boise State University

Gina Hatcher, Tacoma Community College

Winona T. Hatcher, Aiken Technical College

BJ Hathaway, Northeast Wisconsin Tech College

Cynthia Hauki, West Hills College – Coalinga

Mary L. Haynes, Wayne County Community College

Marcie Hawkins, Zane State College

Steve Hebrock, Ohio State University Agricultural
  Technical Institute

Sue Heistand, Iowa Central Community College

Heith Hennel, Valencia Community College

Donna Hendricks, South Arkansas Community College

Judy Hendrix, Dyersburg State Community College

Gloria Hensel, Matanuska-Susitna College University
  of Alaska Anchorage

Gwendolyn Hester, Richland College

Tammarra Holmes, Laramie County Community College

Dee Hobson, Richland College

Keith Hoell, Katharine Gibbs School–New York

Pashia Hogan, Northeast State Technical
  Community College

Susan Hoggard, Tulsa Community College

Kathleen Holliman, Wallace Community College Selma

Chastity Honchul, Brown Mackie College/Wright
  State University

Christie Hovey, Lincoln Land Community College

Peggy Hughes, Allegany College of Maryland

Sandra Hume, Chippewa Valley Technical College

John Hutson, Aims Community College

Celia Ing, Sacramento City College

Joan Ivey, Lanier Technical College

Barbara Jaffari, College of the Redwoods

Penny Jakes, University of Montana College of Technology

Eduardo Jaramillo, Peninsula College

Barbara Jauken, Southeast Community College

Susan Jennings, Stephen F. Austin State University

Leslie Jernberg, Eastern Idaho Technical College

Linda Johns, Georgia Perimeter College

Brent Johnson, Okefenokee Technical College

Mary Johnson, Mt. San Antonio College

Shirley Johnson, Trinidad State Junior College–
  Valley Campus

Sandra M. Jolley, Tarrant County College

Teresa Jolly, South Georgia Technical College

Dr. Deborah Jones, South Georgia Technical College

Margie Jones, Central Virginia Community College

Randall Jones, Marshall Community and Technical College

Diane Karlsbraaten, Lake Region State College

Teresa Keller, Ivy Tech Community College of Indiana

Charles Kemnitz, Pennsylvania College of Technology

Sandra Kinghorn, Ventura College

Bill Klein, Katharine Gibbs School–Philadelphia

Bea Knaapen, Fresno City College

Kit Kofoed, Western Wyoming Community College

Maria Kolatis, County College of Morris

Barry Kolb, Ocean County College

Karen Kuralt, University of Arkansas at Little Rock

Belva-Carole Lamb, Rogue Community College

Betty Lambert, Des Moines Area Community College

Anita Lande, Cabrillo College

Junnae Landry, Pratt Community College

Karen Lankisch, UC Clermont

David Lanzilla, Central Florida Community College

Nora Laredo, Cerritos Community College

Jennifer Larrabee, Chippewa Valley Technical College

Debra Larson, Idaho State University

Barb Lave, Portland Community College

Audrey Lawrence, Tidewater Community College

Deborah Layton, Eastern Oklahoma State College

Larry LeBlanc, Owen Graduate School–
  Vanderbilt University

Philip Lee, Nashville State Community College

Michael Lehrfeld, Brevard Community College

Vasant Limaye, Southwest Collegiate Institute for the
  Deaf – Howard College

Anne C. Lewis, Edgecombe Community College

Stephen Linkin, Houston Community College

Peggy Linston, Athens Technical College

Hugh Lofton, Moultrie Technical College

Donna Lohn, Lakeland Community College

Jackie Lou, Lake Tahoe Community College

Donna Love, Gaston College

Curt Lynch, Ozarks Technical Community College

Sheilah Lynn, Florida Community College–Jacksonville

Pat R. Lyon, Tomball College

Bill Madden, Bergen Community College

Heather Madden, Delaware Technical &
  Community College

Donna Madsen, Kirkwood Community College

Jane Maringer-Cantu, Gavilan College

Suzanne Marks, Bellevue Community College

Carol Martin, Louisiana State University–Alexandria

Cheryl Martucci, Diablo Valley College

Roberta Marvel, Eastern Wyoming College

Tom Mason, Brookdale Community College

Mindy Mass, Santa Barbara City College

Dixie Massaro, Irvine Valley College

Rebekah May, Ashland Community & Technical College

Emma Mays-Reynolds, Dyersburg State
  Community College

Timothy Mayes, Metropolitan State College of Denver

Reggie McCarthy, Central Lakes College

Matt McCaskill, Brevard Community College
Kevin McFarlane, Front Range Community College
Donna McGill, Yuba Community College
Terri McKeever, Ozarks Technical Community College
Patricia McMahon, South Suburban College
Sally McMillin, Katharine Gibbs School–Philadelphia
Charles McNerney, Bergen Community College
Lisa Mears, Palm Beach Community College
Imran Mehmood, ITT Technical Institute–King of Prussia Campus
Virginia Melvin, Southwest Tennessee Community College
Jeanne Mercer, Texas State Technical College
Denise Merrell, Jefferson Community & Technical College
Catherine Merrikin, Pearl River Community College
Diane D. Mickey, Northern Virginia Community College
Darrelyn Miller, Grays Harbor College
Sue Mitchell, Calhoun Community College
Jacquie Moldenhauer, Front Range Community College
Linda Motonaga, Los Angeles City College
Sam Mryyan, Allen County Community College
Cindy Murphy, Southeastern Community College
Ryan Murphy, Sinclair Community College
Sharon E. Nastav, Johnson County Community College
Christine Naylor, Kent State University Ashtabula
Haji Nazarian, Seattle Central Community College
Nancy Noe, Linn-Benton Community College
Jennie Noriega, San Joaquin Delta College
Linda Nutter, Peninsula College
Thomas Omerza, Middle Bucks Institute of Technology
Edith Orozco, St. Philip's College
Dona Orr, Boise State University
Joanne Osgood, Chaffey College
Janice Owens, Kishwaukee College
Tatyana Pashnyak, Bainbridge College
John Partacz, College of DuPage
Tim Paul, Montana State University–Great Falls
Joseph Perez, South Texas College
Mike Peterson, Chemeketa Community College
Dr. Karen R. Petitto, West Virginia Wesleyan College
Terry Pierce, Onandaga Community College
Ashlee Pieris, Raritan Valley Community College
Jamie Pinchot, Thiel College
Michelle Poertner, Northwestern Michigan College
Betty Posta, University of Toledo
Deborah Powell, West Central Technical College
Mark Pranger, Rogers State University
Carolyn Rainey, Southeast Missouri State University
Linda Raskovich, Hibbing Community College
Leslie Ratliff, Griffin Technical College
Mar-Sue Ratzke, Rio Hondo Community College
Roxy Reissen, Southeastern Community College
Silvio Reyes, Technical Career Institutes
Patricia Rishavy, Anoka Technical College
Jean Robbins, Southeast Technical Institute

Carol Roberts, Eastern Maine Community College and University of Maine
Teresa Roberts, Wilson Technical Community College
Vicki Robertson, Southwest Tennessee Community College
Betty Rogge, Ohio State Agricultural Technical Institute
Lynne Rusley, Missouri Southern State University
Claude Russo, Brevard Community College
Ginger Sabine, Northwestern Technical College
Steven Sachs, Los Angeles Valley College
Joanne Salas, Olympic College
Lloyd Sandmann, Pima Community College–Desert Vista Campus
Beverly Santillo, Georgia Perimeter College
Theresa Savarese, San Diego City College
Sharolyn Sayers, Milwaukee Area Technical College
Judith Scheeren, Westmoreland County Community College
Adolph Scheiwe, Joliet Junior College
Marilyn Schmid, Asheville-Buncombe Technical Community College
Janet Sebesy, Cuyahoga Community College
Phyllis T. Shafer, Brookdale Community College
Ralph Shafer, Truckee Meadows Community College
Anne Marie Shanley, County College of Morris
Shelia Shelton, Surry Community College
Merilyn Shepherd, Danville Area Community College
Susan Sinele, Aims Community College
Beth Sindt, Hawkeye Community College
Andrew Smith, Marian College
Brenda Smith, Southwest Tennessee Community College
Lynne Smith, State University of New York–Delhi
Rob Smith, Katharine Gibbs School–Philadelphia
Tonya Smith, Arkansas State University–Mountain Home
Del Spencer – Trinity Valley Community College
Jeri Spinner, Idaho State University
Eric Stadnik, Santa Rosa Junior College
Karen Stanton, Los Medanos College
Meg Stoner, Santa Rosa Junior College
Beverly Stowers, Ivy Tech Community College of Indiana
Marcia Stranix, Yuba College
Kim Styles, Tri-County Technical College
Sylvia Summers, Tacoma Community College
Beverly Swann, Delaware Technical & Community College
Ann Taff, Tulsa Community College
Mike Theiss, University of Wisconsin–Marathon Campus
Romy Thiele, Cañada College
Sharron Thompson, Portland Community College
Ingrid Thompson-Sellers, Georgia Perimeter College
Barbara Tietsort, University of Cincinnati–Raymond Walters College
Janine Tiffany, Reading Area Community College
Denise Tillery, University of Nevada Las Vegas
Susan Trebelhorn, Normandale Community College
Noel Trout, Santiago Canyon College

Cheryl Turgeon, Asnuntuck Community College
Steve Turner, Ventura College
Sylvia Unwin, Bellevue Community College
Lilly Vigil, Colorado Mountain College
Sabrina Vincent, College of the Mainland
Mary Vitrano, Palm Beach Community College
Brad Vogt, Northeast Community College
Cozell Wagner, Southeastern Community College
Carolyn Walker, Tri-County Technical College
Sherry Walker, Tulsa Community College
Qi Wang, Tacoma Community College
Betty Wanielista, Valencia Community College
Marge Warber, Lanier Technical College–Forsyth Campus
Marjorie Webster, Bergen Community College
Linda Wenn, Central Community College
Mark Westlund, Olympic College
Carolyn Whited, Roane State Community College
Winona Whited, Richland College
Jerry Wilkerson, Scott Community College
Joel Willenbring, Fullerton College

Barbara Williams, WITC Superior
Charlotte Williams, Jones County Junior College
Bonnie Willy, Ivy Tech Community College of Indiana
Diane Wilson, J. Sargeant Reynolds Community College
James Wolfe, Metropolitan Community College
Marjory Wooten, Lanier Technical College
Mark Yanko, Hocking College
Alexis Yusov, Pace University
Naeem Zaman, San Joaquin Delta College
Kathleen Zimmerman, Des Moines Area
    Community College

We would also like to thank Lutz Ziob, Sanjay Advani, Jim DiIanni, Merrick Van Dongen, Jim LeValley, Bruce Curling, Joe Wilson, and Naman Kahn at Microsoft for their encouragement and support in making the Microsoft Official Academic Course programs the finest instructional materials for mastering the newest Microsoft technologies for both students and instructors.

Brief Contents

Contents

Lesson 4: Designing a Presentation   103

Lesson 5: Adding Tables to Slides   141

FOR INSTRUCTORS

WileyPLUS is built around the activities you perform in your class each day. With WileyPLUS you can:

Prepare & Present
Create outstanding class presentations using a wealth of resources such as PowerPoint™ slides, image galleries, interactive simulations, and more. You can even add materials you have created yourself.

Create Assignments
Automate the assigning and grading of homework or quizzes by using the provided question banks, or by writing your own.

Track Student Progress
Keep track of your students' progress and analyze individual and overall class results.

Now Available with WebCT and Blackboard!

"It has been a great help, and I believe it has helped me to achieve a better grade."

Michael Morris,
Columbia Basin College

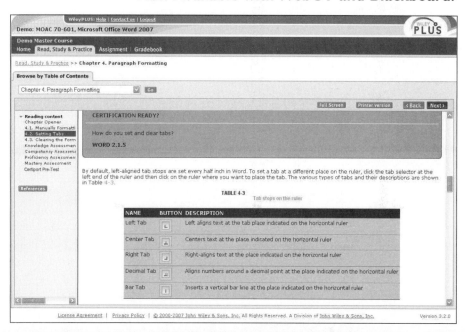

FOR STUDENTS

You have the potential to make a difference!

WileyPLUS is a powerful online system packed with features to help you make the most of your potential and get the best grade you can!

With WileyPLUS you get:

A complete online version of your text and other study resources.

•

Problem-solving help, instant grading, and feedback on your homework and quizzes.

•

The ability to track your progress and grades throughout the term.

•

Access to Microsoft's Assessment, Learning Plan, and MCAS examination voucher.

For more information on what *WileyPLUS* can do to help you and your students reach their potential, please visit www.wiley.com/college/*wileyplus*.

76% of students surveyed said it made them better prepared for tests.*

*Based on a survey of 972 student users of *WileyPLUS*

www.wiley.com/college/microsoft *or* **call the MOAC Toll-Free Number: 1+(888) 764-7001**

PowerPoint Essentials

LESSON SKILL MATRIX

SKILLS	MATRIX SKILL	SKILL NUMBER
Working in the PowerPoint Window		
Working with an Existing Presentation		
Working with Text	Copy elements from one slide to another	2.3.2
Saving an Edited Presentation	Save presentations as appropriate file types	4.3.6

Blue Yonder Airlines is a small but rapidly growing company that offers charter flights to adventurous or exotic locations. The service is designed for small groups, such as corporate management teams or directors, who want to mix business and pleasure in a packaged getaway. As an enterprise account manager, your job is to introduce Blue Yonder to executives in mid-size and large companies. Your goal is to convince these managers to use your charter service when arranging off-site gatherings that require group travel. Microsoft PowerPoint 2007 provides the perfect set of tools for presenting this information to your potential customers. In this lesson, you will start PowerPoint and open an introductory presentation about Blue Yonder Airlines. You will learn to navigate, edit, save, print, and close a presentation.

KEY TERMS
current slide
dialog box launcher
group
KeyTip
Mini toolbar
Normal view
Notes Page view
Office Button
placeholder
Quick Access Toolbar
Ribbon
Slide Show view
Slide Sorter view
tab

■ Software Orientation

Microsoft PowerPoint's Opening Screen

Before you begin working in Microsoft PowerPoint, you should be familiar with the primary user interface. When you first start Microsoft PowerPoint, you will see a screen similar to the one shown in Figure 1-1.

Figure 1-1

The PowerPoint window

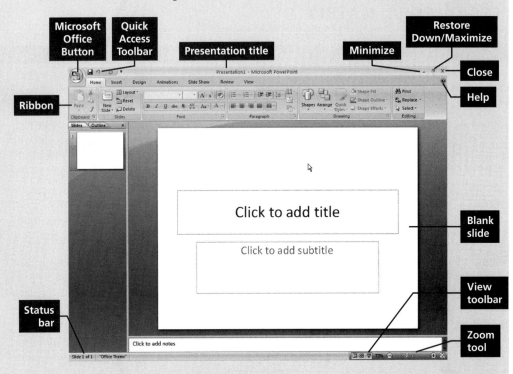

In PowerPoint 2007, it is easier to access commands and features than in previous versions of the application. PowerPoint 2007 displays the tools that are most relevant to the tasks you are performing at the moment. (Note that if default settings or other preferences have been changed on your system, your screen may look somewhat different from Figure 1-1.)

■ Working in the PowerPoint Window

 THE BOTTOM LINE To use PowerPoint 2007 efficiently, you need to learn how the commands and features are grouped together.

Starting PowerPoint

Before you can use PowerPoint, you need to start the program.

➔ START POWERPOINT

GET READY. Before you begin these steps, make sure that your computer is on. Log on, if necessary.

1. On the Windows taskbar at the bottom of your screen, click the Start button, then point to **All Programs**. A menu of installed programs appears.
2. Click **Microsoft Office**. A submenu opens, listing the available programs in your installation of Microsoft Office.

3. Click **Microsoft Office PowerPoint 2007**, as shown in Figure 1-2. PowerPoint starts and a new, blank presentation appears in the PowerPoint window.

 **ANOTHER WAY**

When Office was installed on your computer, a PowerPoint shortcut icon may have been added to your desktop. You can double-click the desktop icon to start PowerPoint without first opening the Start menu.

Figure 1-2

Starting PowerPoint

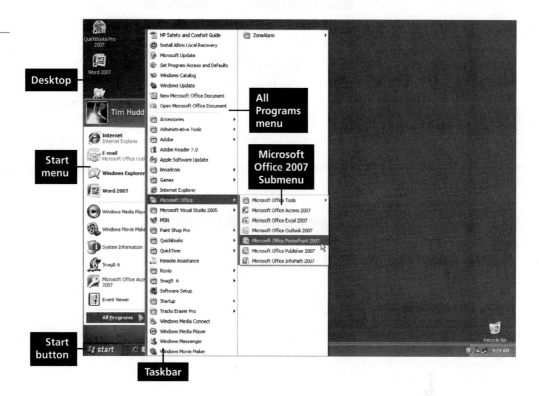

PAUSE. LEAVE the blank presentation open to use in the next exercise.

To launch PowerPoint, you can click the Start button to open the Start menu, which gives you access to all the programs, documents, and other resources (such as disks or a printer) on your computer. On the Start menu, point to All Programs, click Microsoft Office, then click Microsoft Office PowerPoint 2007.

Using the Onscreen Tools

PowerPoint's tools are grouped by common function. For example, if you want to format a slide, you will find all the formatting tools grouped together. This arrangement lets you work quickly, without searching for the tools you need. The following exercises introduce you to some of PowerPoint's most prominent (and essential) features, including the Ribbon, the Mini toolbar, the Quick Access Toolbar, and PowerPoint's KeyTips. These features can help you easily create and manage presentations.

 USE THE RIBBON   NEW FEATURE

USE the new, blank presentation that is still open from the previous exercise.

1. Look at the Ribbon, which appears in Figure 1-3. The Ribbon is divided into seven tabs. Each tab displays several groups of related commands. By default, the Home tab is active.

Figure 1-3

The Ribbon

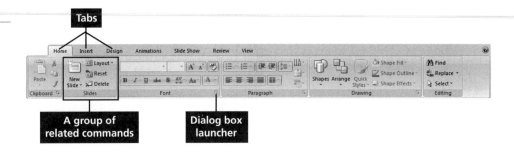

2. Click the **Design** tab to make it active. The groups of commands change.

3. Click the **Home** tab.

4. On the slide, click anywhere in the text **Click to add title**. The text disappears and a blinking insertion point appears.

5. In the lower-right corner of the Font group, click the dialog box launcher (the small box with a diagonal, downward-pointing arrow, as shown in Figure 1-3). Clicking this button opens PowerPoint's Font dialog box, as shown in Figure 1-4. Click **Cancel** to close the dialog box.

REF

You will learn about adding and editing text later in this lesson.

Figure 1-4

The Font dialog box

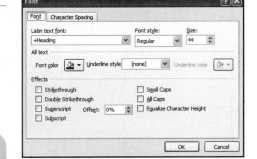

ANOTHER WAY

You can also open the Font dialog box by pressing **Ctrl+Shift+F**.

6. In the Font group, click the drop-down arrow next to the **Font** list. A drop-down list appears, as shown in Figure 1-5. This list shows all the fonts that are currently available for use.

Figure 1-5

The Font list

7. Click the drop-down arrow again to close the list.
8. Double-click the **Home** tab. This action minimizes the Ribbon, hiding the groups of commands but leaving the tabs' names visible on the screen.
9. Double-click the **Home** tab again to redisplay the groups.

ANOTHER WAY

You can also minimize the Ribbon by right-clicking one of its tabs. When the shortcut menu opens, click Minimize the Ribbon. To view the entire Ribbon again, right-click a tab, then click Minimize the Ribbon once more.

PAUSE. LEAVE the presentation open to use in the next exercise.

You just practiced using PowerPoint's **Ribbon**. The Ribbon is divided into seven **tabs**, and each tab contains several **groups** of related commands. A *command* is a tool (such as an icon, a button, or a list) that tells PowerPoint to perform a specific task. Each tab provides commands that are relevant to the kind of task you are performing—whether you are formatting a slide, adding animations to a presentation, or setting up a slide show for display.

On the Ribbon, some command groups feature a tool called a **dialog box launcher**—a small arrow in the group's lower-right corner. You can click the arrow to open a *dialog box*, which provides tools and options related to a specific task. To close a dialog box without accepting any changes you may have made to it, click the Cancel button.

Some of the Ribbon's tools have small, downward-pointing arrows next to them. These arrows are called *drop-down arrows*; when you click one, a *drop-down list* opens, displaying options you can choose (such as a list of fonts). You can choose the option you want by clicking it.

If you need more space on the screen, you can minimize (hide) the Ribbon by double-clicking the active tab. To restore the Ribbon, double-click the active tab again.

USE THE MINI TOOLBAR

USE the presentation that is still on the screen from the preceding exercise.

1. On the slide, double-click at the insertion point's location. Because you double-clicked, the insertion point is highlighted. A faint Mini toolbar appears, as shown in Figure 1-6.

Figure 1-6

The faint Mini toolbar appears by the highlighted insertion point

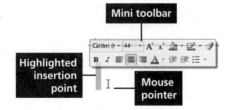

2. Point to the **Font** command on the Mini toolbar; the toolbar becomes brighter and easier to see. If you move the mouse pointer away from the toolbar, it fades.
3. Click the **Font** drop-down arrow. The list of available fonts opens.
4. Click the **Font** drop-down arrow again to close the list.
5. Move the mouse pointer back to the highlighted insertion point, then right-click. A shortcut menu with commonly used commands appears along with the Mini toolbar, as shown in Figure 1-7.

ANOTHER WAY

You can also press **Esc** to close an open drop-down list.

Figure 1-7

The shortcut menu and Mini toolbar

6. Move the mouse pointer to a blank area of the slide (such as the upper-left corner), then click twice. The first click removes the Mini toolbar and shortcut menu from the screen; the second click restores the slide to its original state.

   PAUSE. LEAVE the presentation open to use in the next exercise.

You just practiced working with the *Mini toolbar*, a small toolbar that appears when you point to text that has been *selected* (highlighted). The Mini toolbar displays tools for formatting text appearance and alignment. The Mini toolbar is faint and transparent until you point to it; then it becomes bright and opaque, indicating that the toolbar is active.

If you right-click selected text, PowerPoint displays both the Mini toolbar and a *shortcut menu*, which displays additional commands.

 USE THE QUICK ACCESS TOOLBAR

USE the presentation that is still open from the previous exercise.

1. Look for the Quick Access Toolbar in the upper-left corner of the PowerPoint window. The Quick Access Toolbar appears in Figure 1-8, with its tools labeled.

Figure 1-8

The Quick Access Toolbar

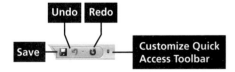

You can also press **Esc** to close a dialog box.

2. Click the **Save** button on the Quick Access Toolbar. The Save As dialog box appears.
3. Click **Cancel** to close the dialog box.
4. Click the **Customize Quick Access Toolbar** button. A menu appears, as shown in Figure 1-9. This menu lets you choose the tools you want to appear on the Quick Access Toolbar.

Figure 1-9

This menu lets you customize the Quick Access Toolbar

5. Click **Show Below the Ribbon**. The toolbar moves down and appears directly beneath the Ribbon.
6. Click the **Customize Quick Access Toolbar** button again. Click **Show Above the Ribbon**. The toolbar moves back to its original location.
   PAUSE. LEAVE the presentation open to use in the next exercise.

The *Quick Access Toolbar* displays commands that you use frequently. By default, the Save, Undo, and Redo commands appear on the toolbar. The Save command quickly saves an existing presentation while you are working on it or when you are done with it. If you have not yet given the presentation a file name, PowerPoint will prompt you for a name by launching the Save As dialog box, as happened in the preceding exercise.

TAKE NOTE * When you click the Customize Quick Access Toolbar button, the menu lets you add or remove commands from the toolbar. To add or remove a tool, click its name on the menu. If a tool's name has a checkmark, it is already on the toolbar.

The Undo command lets you reverse ("undo") the action of your last command. The Redo button lets you reverse an undo action. If either the Undo or Redo command is gray, then you cannot undo or redo.

 USE KEYTIPS NEW FEATURE

USE the presentation that is still open from the previous exercise.

1. Press **Alt**. Letters and numbers appear on the Ribbon and the Quick Access Toolbar, as shown in Figure 1-10. These characters show you which keyboard keys you can press to access the tabs or the items on the Quick Access Toolbar.

Figure 1-10

KeyTips

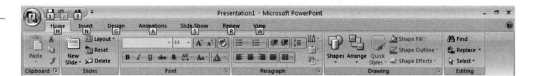

ANOTHER WAY

If you accidentally press **Alt**, you can clear KeyTips from the screen by pressing **Esc**.

2. Press **N** to activate the Insert tab. When the Insert tab opens, notice that a new set of letters appears. These characters show you which keys to use to insert different kinds of objects in the current slide.
3. Press **P** to open the Insert Picture dialog box.
4. Click **Cancel** to close the dialog box.

PAUSE. LEAVE the presentation open to use in the next exercise.

When you press the Alt key, small letters and numbers—called *KeyTips*—appear on the Ribbon. To issue a command by using its KeyTip, press the Alt key, then press the key or keys that correspond to the command you want to use. Every command on the Ribbon has a KeyTip.

In earlier versions of PowerPoint, key combinations that let you issue commands were called *shortcut keys* or *keyboard shortcuts*. Some shortcut keys worked with the Alt key; those shortcut combinations are now KeyTips in PowerPoint 2007. Other shortcut keys worked with the Ctrl key, and those shortcuts still work the same in PowerPoint 2007. For example, you can press Ctrl+S to save a presentation or Ctrl+P to print a presentation.

KeyTips and shortcut keys let you issue commands without using the mouse. This method is handy for experienced typists who prefer to keep their hands on the keyboard as much as possible. In fact, if you master KeyTips and shortcut keys, you may find that you use the mouse less often over time.

TAKE NOTE You must press **Alt** each time you want to see a tab's KeyTips. If you issue one command by keyboard shortcut, you have to press **Alt** again to redisplay the tab's KeyTips before you can issue another one.

Using the Office Button

The Office Button opens a menu of commands that help you manage the presentations on your computer or network. These commands are not used for creating or formatting a slide show. Instead, they let you save a presentation as a file, open an existing set of slides, print your slides, distribute a presentation through e-mail, and perform other tasks with the files you create in PowerPoint.

⊕ **USE THE OFFICE BUTTON**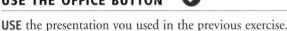

USE the presentation you used in the previous exercise.

1. Click the **Office Button**. A menu appears, as shown in Figure 1-11.

Figure 1-11

The Office Button and menu

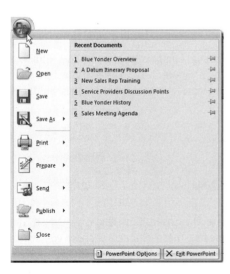

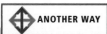
ANOTHER WAY

To open the Office Button's menu by using KeyTips, press **Alt**, then press **F**.

2. Point to the Save As command to view its options.

3. Point to other commands to see their options. (A command has options if there is a right-pointing arrow next to it.)

4. Click the Office Button to close the menu.

   PAUSE. LEAVE the presentation open to use in the next exercise.

You can find the *Office Button* in the upper-left corner of the PowerPoint window. When you click the button, PowerPoint displays a menu of commands for opening, saving, and printing files. The menu offers several other options as well, some of which are more advanced than others:

- **New:** Lets you create a new presentation.
- **Open:** Opens an existing presentation stored on a disk, either on your computer's disk or a network drive.
- **Save:** Saves the current presentation using PowerPoint's default file format.
- **Save as:** Lets you save a presentation in PowerPoint's default format or in several other file formats.
- **Print:** Provides three options for printing a presentation; you can open the Print dialog box and set print options, send the slides directly to the printer without setting options, or use the Print Preview option to see how your slides will look on paper before you actually print them.
- **Prepare:** Offers a variety of options that let you prepare your slide show for distribution. You can edit the presentation's properties, check it for sensitive information, restrict other users' access to the file, add a digital signature, mark the slides as final so they cannot be changed, or make sure the presentation is compatible with other versions of PowerPoint.
- **Send:** Allows you to send the file to someone else, either as an e-mail attachment or as a fax delivered over the Internet.
- **Publish:** Enables you to store the presentation and all media links on a CD, save the slides in a library, create handouts of a presentation in Microsoft Word, save the slide show to a document management server for sharing, or create a new document workspace.
- **Close:** Closes the currently open presentation.

When you click the Office Button, the menu lists the presentations you have most recently opened. You can quickly reopen one of those presentations by choosing from this list.

The PowerPoint Options button lets you customize PowerPoint so it best suits your needs.

To close the PowerPoint application and all open presentations, you can click the Exit PowerPoint button.

Working with PowerPoint's Help System

PowerPoint's Help system is rich in information, illustrations, and tips that can help you complete any task as you create a presentation. When PowerPoint was installed on your computer, hundreds of help topics were installed along with it. PowerPoint can also access thousands of other help topics that are available online. Finding the right information is easy: You can pick a topic from the Help system's table of contents, browse a directory of help topics, or perform keyword searches by entering terms that best describe the task you want to complete.

→ USE THE HELP SYSTEM

If you aren't sure what an onscreen tool does, just point to it. When the mouse pointer rests on a tool, a box called a ScreenTip appears. A basic ScreenTip displays the tool's name and shortcut key (if a shortcut exists for that tool). Some of the Ribbon's tools have enhanced ScreenTips, which also provide a brief description of the tool.

USE the presentation that is open from the previous exercise.

1. Click the **Microsoft Office PowerPoint Help** button at the right end of the Ribbon. (The Help button is a blue circle with a question mark on it.) The PowerPoint Help window appears, as shown in Figure 1-12.

   In the lower-right corner of the Help window, you should see the Connection Status button, which indicates whether PowerPoint is connected to Office Online. If your system is configured not to use online help, your screen will look different. **NEW FEATURE** ✓

Figure 1-12

The PowerPoint Help window

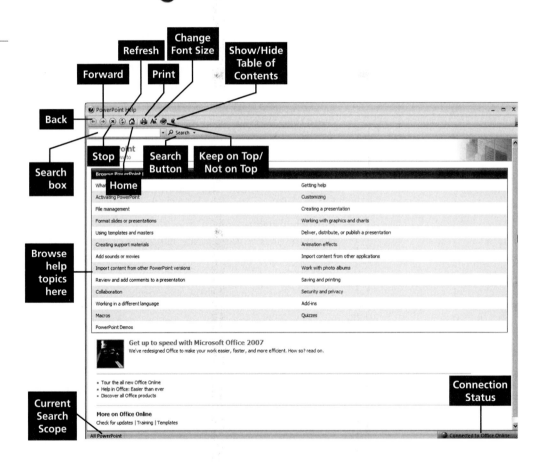

ANOTHER WAY

You can also open the Help window by pressing **F1**.

2. Click the **Connection Status** button. The Connection Status menu appears, as shown in Figure 1-13.

Figure 1-13

The Connection Status menu

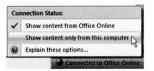

3. Click **Show content only from this computer**. Notice that the Connection Status button now displays the message Offline. From this point forward, PowerPoint (and all the other Office applications) will use only the offline help system.

> **TAKE NOTE**
>
> Even if Office is set to work offline, you can still search for help online. Instead of clicking the Search button, click the drop-down arrow button next to it. When the menu opens, click Content from Office Online. The choice will affect only the current search.

4. Click the **Search** box, key **ribbon**, then click the **Search** button. A list of help topics appears, as shown in Figure 1-14.

Figure 1-14

Searching for Help about the Ribbon

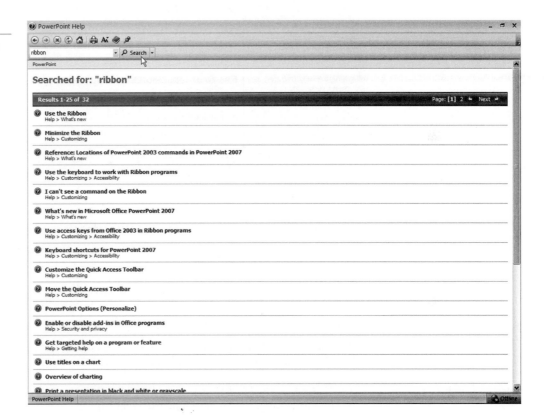

5. Click the **Use the Ribbon** link. The help topic appears.
6. Click the **Show Table of Contents** button. The Table of Contents opens in a pane on the left side of the Help window.
7. Click the **Getting help** link in the Table of Contents.
8. Click **Work with the Help window**. The help topic appears in the window, as shown in Figure 1-15.

Figure 1-15

The Table of Contents pane

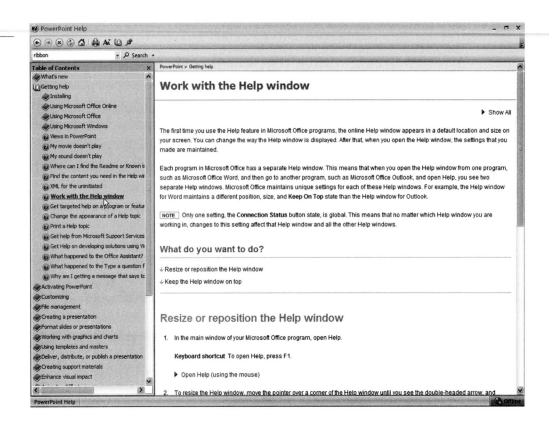

9. Click the **Home** button.
10. Click the **Close** button to close the Help window.

PAUSE. LEAVE the presentation open to use in the next exercise.

PowerPoint's Help window gives you access to many different help topics. A help topic is a window of information about a specific PowerPoint feature. Help topics can assist you with virtually any task or problem you encounter while working with PowerPoint.

The Help window is set up like a browser window and features some of the same tools you will find in your Web browser, including:

- **Back:** Jumps to the previously opened Help topic.
- **Forward:** Jumps to the next opened Help topic.
- **Stop:** Stops any action in progress.
- **Refresh:** Reloads the current Help topic.
- **Home:** Returns to the initial Help window.
- **Print:** Prints the currently open Help topic.

TAKE NOTE Many PowerPoint dialog boxes contain a Help button. When you click it, a Help window opens with information about the dialog box.

You can find help in several ways. For example, you can open the Table of Contents and scan the list for help on a specific topic. You can also key a word or phrase into the Search box, then click the Search button. A list of related help topics appears in the Help window.

The Search button gives you more options when looking for help. If you click the drop-down arrow next to the Search button, you can search for help online or offline, look for PowerPoint templates, find information for developers, and more.

The Connection Status menu lets you use help topics that are available online, or just those topics that are installed on your computer (called "offline help"). If your computer has an "always on" connection to the Internet—such as a cable modem or a LAN connection—you may want to set the Connection Status to *Show content from Office Online,* which is a Web-based help system that Microsoft provides for Office 2007 users. Office Online complements Office's built-in help system. If your computer has a dial-up connection, or if you simply do not want to download help topics every time you click the Help button, you can choose *Show content only from this computer* to work with offline help topics.

Closing a Presentation

When you close a presentation, PowerPoint removes it from the screen. PowerPoint continues running so you can work with other files. You should always save and close any open presentations before you exit PowerPoint or shut down your computer. In this exercise, you will practice closing an open presentation.

⊕ CLOSE A PRESENTATION

USE the presentation that is open from the previous exercise.

1. Click the **Office Button**.
2. When the menu opens, click **Close.** PowerPoint clears the presentation from the screen.

   PAUSE. LEAVE PowerPoint open to use in the next exercise.

The Close command removes the current presentation from the PowerPoint window. If another presentation is open, it will appear. When multiple presentations are open, you can close them by clicking the Close button in the upper-right corner of the PowerPoint window. If only one presentation is open, clicking the Close button will clear the presentation and exit PowerPoint.

■ Working with an Existing Presentation

THE BOTTOM LINE

If you want to work with an existing presentation, you need to open it. When you open a presentation, your slides appear on the screen exactly as they did when the presentation was last saved to disk, but you can easily change your view of the presentation to make it easier to perform certain tasks. You can also use PowerPoint's zoom tools to make slides look larger or smaller on the screen. The following exercises show you how to view your slides in different ways, and how to add, edit, and delete text on your slides. You will then learn how to print a presentation and to save it to a disk.

Opening an Existing Presentation

PowerPoint makes it easy to work on a presentation over time. If you can't finish a slide show today, you can reopen it later and resume working on it. This exercise shows you how to open an existing presentation—one that has already been created and saved as a file on a disk.

⊕ OPEN AN EXISTING PRESENTATION

1. Click the **Office Button**.
2. Click **Open.** The Open dialog box appears, as shown in Figure 1-16.

Figure 1-16

The Open dialog box

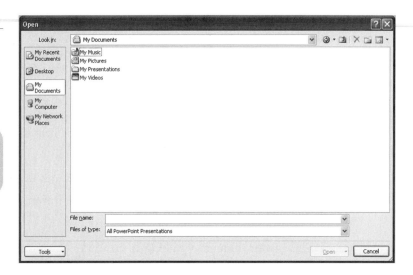

ANOTHER WAY

You can also open the Open dialog box by pressing **Ctrl+O**.

3. Locate and open *Blue Yonder Overview*. The presentation appears on your screen, as shown in Figure 1-17.

Figure 1-17

The Blue Yonder Overview presentation

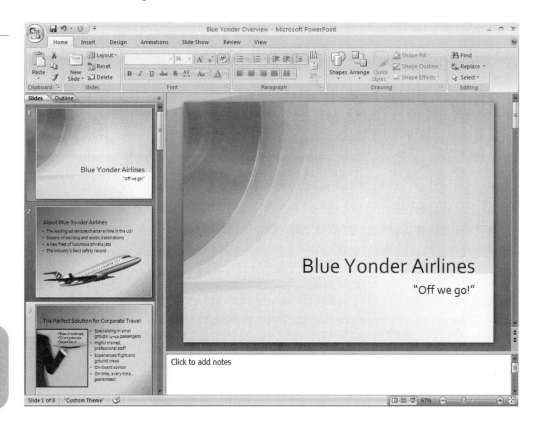

CD

The *Blue Yonder Overview* file is available on the companion CD-ROM.

ANOTHER WAY

Instead of clicking the file's name and then clicking the Open button, you can double-click the file's name to open the presentation.

PAUSE. LEAVE the presentation open to use in the next exercise.

Use the Office Button to access the Open dialog box, which lets you open a presentation that has already been saved on a disk. Presentations can be stored on any disk or removable media (such as a CD) on your PC or network. You can use the Look in box to navigate to the file's location, then click the file to select it. Use the Open button to open the presentation on your screen.

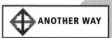 **ANOTHER WAY** If a presentation has been opened recently, its name should appear on the Recent Documents list. Just click the presentation's name to open it.

Viewing a Presentation in Different Ways

PowerPoint lets you see your presentation in a variety of ways. For example, you can work with just one slide at a time, which is helpful when you are adding text or graphics to a slide. Or, you can view all the slides in a presentation at the same time, which makes it easy to rearrange the slides. The following exercises show you how to change PowerPoint's views and how to change the magnification level of your slides for easier viewing.

⊕ CHANGE POWERPOINT'S VIEWS

USE the presentation that you opened during the previous exercise.

1. Click the **View** tab, as shown in Figure 1-18. Notice that the Normal button is highlighted; this is the default view.

Figure 1-18

Normal view, with the View tab selected

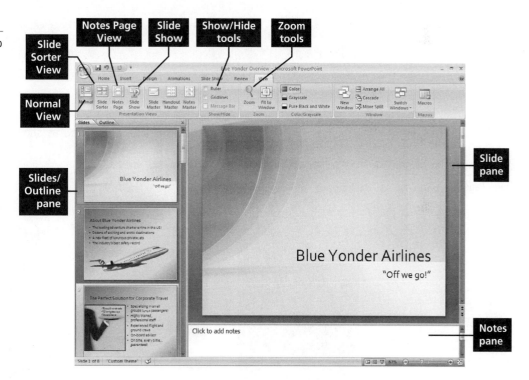

2. In the Presentation Views group, click the **Slide Sorter View** button to change to Slide Sorter view, as shown in Figure 1-19.

TAKE NOTE If formatted slides are hard to read in Slide Sorter view, press **Alt** and click a slide to see its heading clearly.

Figure 1-19

Slide Sorter view

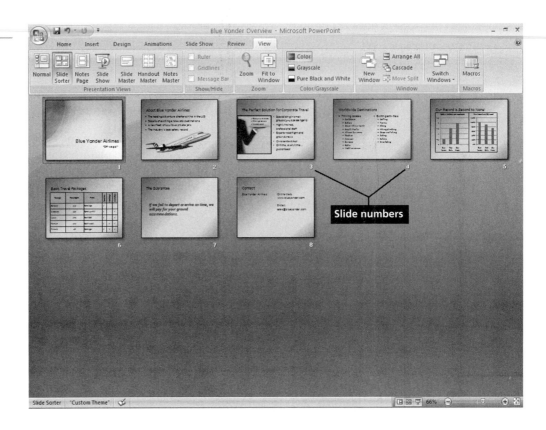

3. Click slide 2, then click the **Notes Page View** button in the Presentation Views group. PowerPoint switches to Notes Page view, as shown in Figure 1-20.

Figure 1-20

Notes Page view

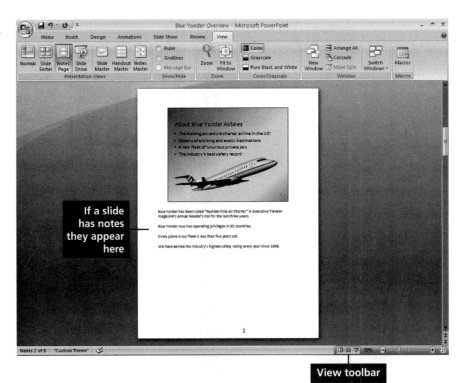

ANOTHER WAY

Instead of using the Ribbon to change views, you can use the View toolbar in the lower-right corner of the PowerPoint window.

4. In the Presentation Views group, click **Slide Show**. The first slide of the presentation fills the screen, as shown in Figure 1-21.

Figure 1-21

Slide Show view

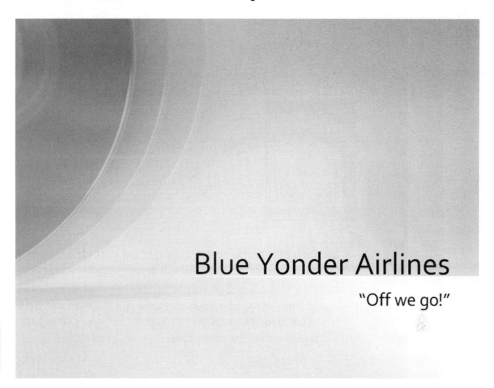

Blue Yonder Airlines

"Off we go!"

**ANOTHER WAY**

You can switch to Slide Show view by pressing **F5**.

5. Press (Esc) to exit Slide Show view and return to Notes Page view.

6. Click the **Normal View** button in the Presentation Views group. PowerPoint switches back to Normal view.

PAUSE. LEAVE the presentation open to use in the next exercise.

PowerPoint has four main views:

- *Normal view* is the default view that lets you focus on an individual slide. The slide you are currently editing is called the *current slide*. The current slide appears in the Slide pane, which is the largest of the view's three panes. Below the Slide pane is the Notes pane, where you can add and edit notes you want to associate with the current slide. In the left pane—called the Slides/Outline pane—you can use the Slides tab to jump from one slide to another, as you will see later in this lesson. On the Outline tab, you can add text to a slide or copy or move text from one slide to another.

- *Slide Sorter view* displays all the slides in a presentation on a single screen. (If there are more slides than can fit in one screen, you can use scroll bars to move slides in and out of view.) In Slide Show view, you can reorganize a slide show by dragging slides to different positions. You can also duplicate and delete slides in this view.

- *Notes Page view* shows one slide at a time, along with any notes that are associated with the slide. This view lets you create and edit notes. You may find it easier to work with notes in this view than in Normal view. You can also print out notes pages for your presentation; they are printed as they appear in Notes Page view.

- *Slide Show view* lets you preview your presentation on the screen, so you can see it the way your audience will see it.

X REF

You will work with PowerPoint's printing options and practice previewing a presentation in Lesson 2.

ANOTHER WAY

You can drag the Zoom control's slider bar to the right or left to change the zoom level.

USE ZOOM

USE the presentation that is open from the previous exercise.

1. Make sure that the View tab is active on the Ribbon.
2. On the View tab, click the **Zoom** button. The Zoom dialog box appears, as shown in Figure 1-22.

Figure 1-22

The Zoom dialog box

ANOTHER WAY

You can click the Zoom level indicator at the far left of the Zoom control to display the Zoom dialog box.

3. Click the **200%** option button, then click **OK**. In the Slide pane, the slide is magnified by 200%. Notice that you can no longer see the entire slide.
4. Click the **Zoom Out** button at the left end of the Zoom control, at the lower-right of the screen, as shown in Figure 1-23. Continue clicking the button until the zoom level drops to 100%. Notice that, even at 100% magnification, the slide is too large for the Slide pane.

Figure 1-23

Using the Zoom control

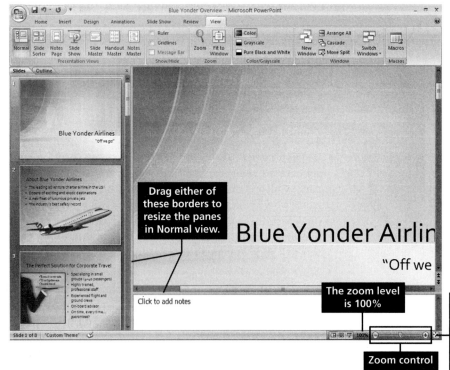

TAKE NOTE

You can resize the Slide pane by dragging its bottom border up or down, or by dragging its left-hand border to the right or left. The Slides/Outline pane and Notes pane also change size when you drag the borders.

5. Click the Fit slide to current window button at the far right end of the Zoom control. PowerPoint zooms out to fit the entire slide in the Slide pane.

PAUSE. LEAVE the presentation open to use in the next exercise.

PowerPoint's zoom tools let you change the magnification of slides on the screen. By zooming out, you can see an entire slide; by zooming in, you can inspect one area of the slide. Both views have advantages: Higher magnifications make it easier to position objects on the slide, and lower magnifications enable you to see how all the parts of a slide look as a whole.

You can use either the Zoom dialog box or the Zoom control to change magnification levels. In the Zoom dialog box, you can zoom in or out by choosing one of seven pre-set magnification levels, or you can use the Percent spin control to set the zoom level precisely. If you click the *Fit slide to current window* button on the Zoom control (there is also one on the View tab), PowerPoint changes the magnification level so the entire slide fits in the Slide pane.

All zoom options are available in Normal view. In Slide Sorter view, some zoom options are available, but the *Fit slide to current window* tool is not.

Navigating a Presentation

PowerPoint provides a number of tools that let you move around in—or navigate—a presentation. You can use onscreen tools such as scroll bars to view your slides in order, moving either forward or backward. There are also ways to jump from one slide to another in any order. Like all the Microsoft Office applications, PowerPoint also lets you use the keyboard to navigate a presentation. In the following exercise, you will practice using all these navigation tools.

⊕ SCROLL WITH THE MOUSE

USE the presentation that is open from the previous exercise.

1. Click the scroll down button on the right side of the Slide pane, as shown in Figure 1-24. Because the zoom level is set at *Fit slide to current window*, slide 2 appears on the screen.

Figure 1-24

Scroll tools

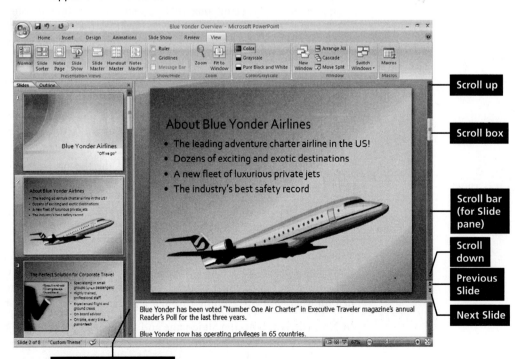

2. Change the zoom level to 100%, then click the **scroll down** button twice. Because the slide is now larger than the Slide pane, the scroll button scrolls the slide down in small increments instead of jumping to the next slide.

3. Click the **Fit to Window** button on the Ribbon.

4. At the bottom of the scroll bar, click the **Next Slide** button twice. Slide 3 appears, then slide 4 appears.

5. In the Slides tab of the Slides/Outline pane, click slide 5. The selected slide appears in the Slide pane, as shown in Figure 1-25.

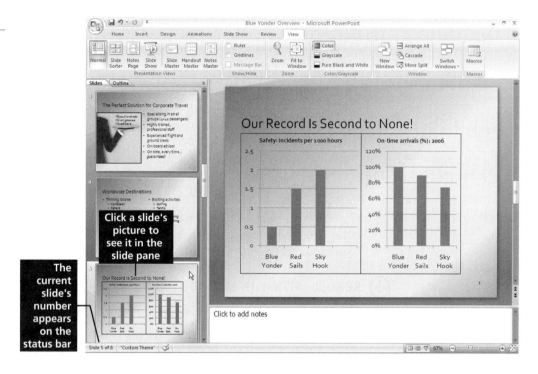

TAKE NOTE

The current slide's number always appears in the lower-left corner of the status bar.

Figure 1-25

You can click a slide's picture on the Slides tab to jump to that slide

6. Point to the **scroll box** that appears to the right of the Slides/Outline pane, then drag the scroll box all the way down to the bottom of the scroll bar. The last slide (slide 8) appears on the Slides tab, but slide 5 remains visible in the Slide pane.

7. Click the **Previous Slide** button (at the bottom right of the Slide pane, as shown earlier in Figure 1-24). Slide 4 appears in the Slide pane; notice that the slide also appears highlighted on the Slides tab.

8. Point to the **scroll box** that appears to the right of the Slide pane, then drag the scroll box all the way up to the top of the scroll bar. You return to the beginning of the presentation.

   PAUSE. LEAVE the presentation open for the next exercise.

PowerPoint's scroll bars let you move up and down through your presentation. Click the scroll buttons to move up or down one line at a time or one slide at a time, depending on the current zoom level. Click and hold a scroll button to move more quickly. You can also drag a scroll box to move even more quickly. When you drag the scroll box in the Slide pane, PowerPoint displays a ScreenTip with the slide number and slide title to show you which slide will appear on screen when you release the mouse button. The scroll box's ScreenTip is helpful when you are scrolling through a presentation with a lot of slides.

In Normal view, both the Slide pane and the Slides/Outline pane have scroll bars, buttons, and boxes. If there is text in the Notes pane, scroll tools will appear there to let you move up and down through the text, if necessary. In Slide Sorter view and Notes Page view, scroll tools will appear on the right side of the window if they are needed.

In Normal view, you can click the Previous Slide button to move up to the previous slide and click the Next Slide button to move to the following slide.

→ NAVIGATE A PRESENTATION FROM THE KEYBOARD

USE the presentation that is open from the previous exercise.

1. With slide 1 visible in the Slide pane, press ↓ on your keyboard. Slide 2 appears.
2. Press Page Down to jump to slide 3.
3. Press —→ to jump to slide 4.
4. Press Page Up to go back to slide 3.
5. Press ←— to move up to slide 2.
6. Press ↑ to view slide 1.
7. Press End to jump to slide 8, the last slide in the presentation.
8. Press Home to return to slide 1.

   PAUSE. LEAVE the presentation open to use in the next exercise.

Your keyboard's cursor control keys let you jump from one slide to another, as long as no text or object is selected on a slide. If text is selected, the arrow keys move the insertion point within the text; however, the Page Up, Page Down, Home, and End keys will still let you move from slide to slide.

Working with Text

It is easy to add text to a slide. In most slides, text is contained in boxes called placeholders. You can work with text directly in a placeholder, or you can use the Outline tab. PowerPoint offers many of the same editing and formatting tools found in Microsoft Word. In the following exercises, you will practice adding text to a placeholder; adding text to the Outline tab; selecting, replacing, and deleting text on a slide; and copying and moving text from one slide to another.

→ ADD TEXT TO A TEXT PLACEHOLDER

USE the presentation that is open from the previous exercise.

1. Click the **Home** tab. On slide 1, click at the beginning of the slide's title (*Blue Yonder Airlines*). The borders of the title's placeholder appear, as shown in Figure 1-26, and a blinking insertion point appears before the word *Blue*.

Figure 1-26

The title placeholder and insertion point

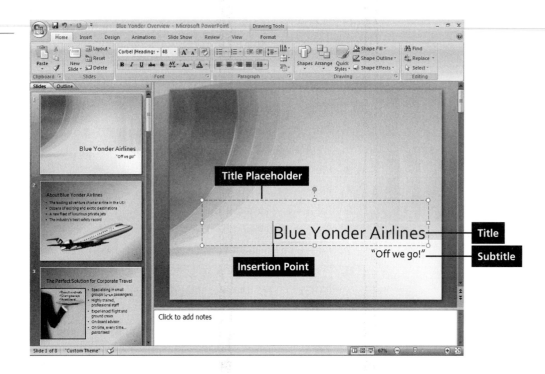

2. Click the slide's subtitle, which is the second line of text. The subtitle's placeholder appears, as does the insertion point.
3. Go to slide 4.
4. Click after the word *Snorkeling* in the second column. The insertion point appears.
5. Press Enter to start a new line, and key **Scuba**.
6. Press Enter, then key **Sightseeing**. Your slide should look like the one shown in Figure 1-27.

Figure 1-27

Slide 4 with added text

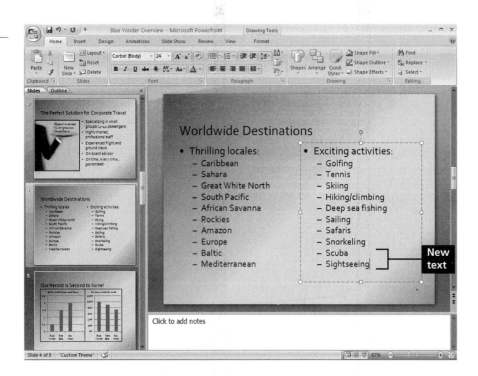

PAUSE. LEAVE the presentation open for the next exercise.

In this exercise, you practiced entering text in a *placeholder*, which is a special box that holds text on a slide. (As you will see in upcoming lessons, placeholders can also hold objects such as pictures, tables, or charts.) Several types of slides, such as title slides, have text placeholders built into them. In the Blue Yonder presentation, slide 1 is an example of a title slide. A title slide almost always includes a title and a subtitle. Placeholders make it easy to add text—just click in the placeholder, then key the text.

ADD TEXT ON THE OUTLINE TAB

USE the presentation that is open from the previous exercise.

1. Go to slide 8. This slide is supposed to contain contact information, but the mailing address and telephone number are missing.
2. In the Slides/Outline pane, click the **Outline** tab. Because slide 8 is the current slide, its text is highlighted on the tab.
3. On the Outline tab, click after the word *Airlines* to place the insertion point there.
4. Press **Enter** to start a new line.
5. On the new line, key **12 Ferris St.**, then press **Enter**. As you key the new text on the Outline tab, notice that it appears on the slide.
6. Key **Diehard, TN 34567**, then press **Enter**.
7. Key **(707) 555-AWAY.** Your slide should look like the one shown in Figure 1-28.

Figure 1-28

Text added to the Outline tab appears on the slide

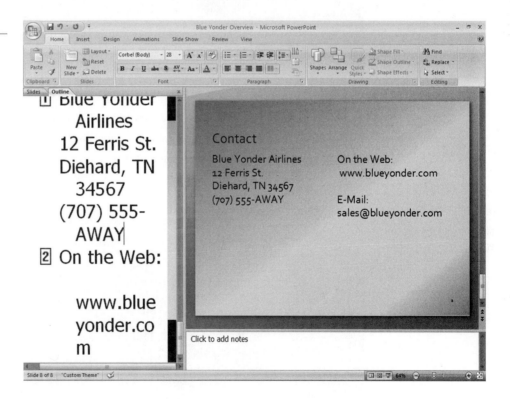

8. In the Slides/Outline pane, click the **Slides** tab.
   PAUSE. LEAVE the presentation open for the next exercise.

Working on the Outline tab is like working in a word processor. PowerPoint displays the text from each slide on the Outline tab, without any backgrounds, placeholders, or anything else that might distract you from your writing. You can navigate a presentation on the Outline tab the same way you use the Slides tab—scroll to the desired slide's outline, then click it.

⊕ SELECT, REPLACE, AND DELETE TEXT

USE the presentation that is open from the previous exercise.

1. Go to slide 3 and look at the right-hand column of text.
2. In the fourth item of the bulleted list, double-click the word *advisor* to select it, as shown in Figure 1-29.

Figure 1-29

Selected text

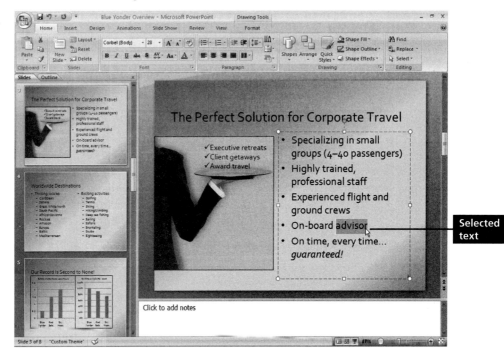

3. While the text is selected, key **concierge**. The new text replaces the selected text.
4. Go to slide 7. This slide contains an unneeded word.
5. Select the word *ground* by dragging the mouse pointer over it. (The mouse pointer changes from an arrow to an I-beam whenever it is in a text placeholder, as shown in Figure 1-30.)

Figure 1-30

Selecting text and the I-beam pointer

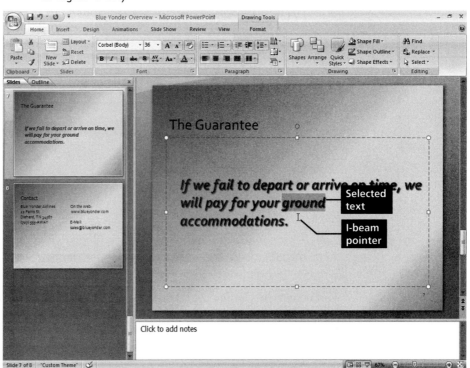

6. Press Delete to delete the word from the slide.

PAUSE. LEAVE the presentation open for the next exercise.

As mentioned previously, working with text in PowerPoint is a lot like using a word processor. You can edit, replace, and delete text directly on a slide. First, you must select the text, to let PowerPoint know you want to edit it. You can select any amount of text by dragging the mouse pointer across it. When you move the mouse pointer over text, it changes to an *I-beam pointer*, a vertically oriented pointer that resembles the letter *I*. This pointer makes it easy to select text precisely. Whenever you select text in PowerPoint—whether it is a single character or all the text on a slide—it is highlighted with a colored background. Once the text is selected, you can type new text in its place or delete it.

COPY AND MOVE TEXT FROM ONE SLIDE TO ANOTHER

USE the presentation that is open from the previous exercise.

1. Go to slide 2.

2. In the slide's title placeholder, select B*lue Yonder Airline*s by dragging the mouse pointer across the text. You will make a copy of the selected text, then paste the copy into another slide.

3. On the Home tab, click the **Copy** button, as shown in Figure 1-31.

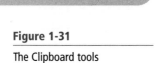
ANOTHER WAY

You can issue the Copy command by pressing **Ctrl+C**.

Figure 1-31

The Clipboard tools

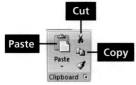

4. Go to slide 7.

5. Click between the two words of the title to place the insertion point before the word *Guarantee*.

ANOTHER WAY

You can issue the Paste command by pressing **Ctrl+V**.

6. On the Home tab, click the **Paste** button. PowerPoint inserts the copied text at the insertion point's position, as shown in Figure 1-32. Press Spacebar if necessary to insert a space before the word *Guarantee*.

Figure 1-32

The selected text has been copied to slide 7

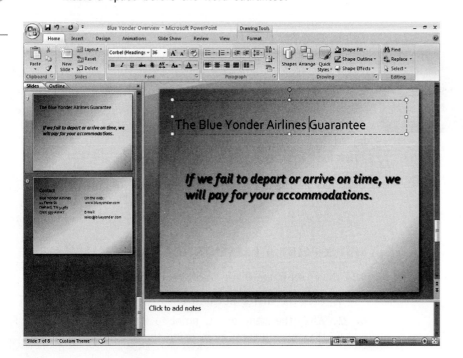

7. Go to slide 3.

8. Select the last item of the bulleted list, on the right side of the slide.

9. On the Home tab, click the **Cut** button. The selected item is removed from the list.

10. Go to slide 2.

11. Click below the last item of the bulleted list, just above the airplane's tail.

12. On the Home tab, click the **Paste** button. The item appears at the bottom of the list.

13. Click anywhere in the blank area around the slide to clear the placeholder's border from the screen. Your slide should look like the one shown in Figure 1-33.

ANOTHER WAY

You can issue the Cut command by pressing **Ctrl+X**.

Figure 1-33

The selected text has been moved to slide 2

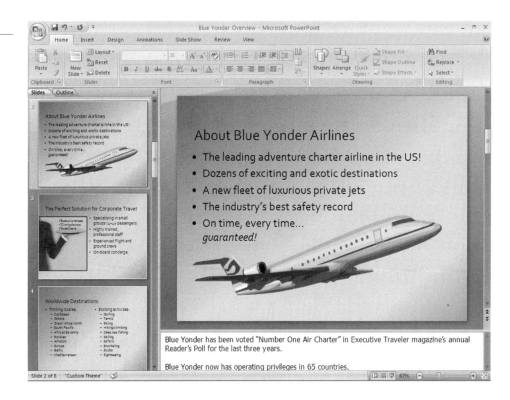

PAUSE. LEAVE the presentation open for the next exercise.

In this exercise, you practiced copying and moving text from one slide to another, using the Copy, Cut, and Paste commands. Don't be surprised if these commands become your most frequently used tools, because they can save you a great deal of typing.

You can use these commands on many kinds of objects in PowerPoint, including pictures, charts, and placeholders. The Cut, Copy, and Paste commands are used throughout the remaining lessons of this book.

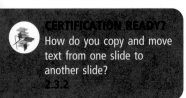
CERTIFICATION READY?

How do you copy and move text from one slide to another slide?

2.3.2

Quick-Printing a Presentation

PowerPoint's Quick Print command sends the currently open presentation to the printer. When you use the Quick Print feature, PowerPoint prints the presentation one slide per page, with the slide taking up most of the page in landscape orientation.

⊕ QUICK-PRINT A PRESENTATION

USE the presentation that is open from the previous exercise.

1. Click the **Office Button**.

2. When the menu opens, point to **Print**, then click **Quick Print**. PowerPoint prints the entire presentation, using the default print settings.

If the Quick Print button is available on the Quick Access Toolbar, click it instead of using the Office Button. If the Quick Print button is not visible on the Quick Access Toolbar, you can add it to the toolbar by clicking the Customize Quick Access Toolbar drop-down arrow, then clicking Quick Print.

PAUSE. LEAVE the document open to use in the next exercise.

X REF

Other printing options are discussed in Lesson 2.

Sometimes you need to change printer settings before printing a presentation. For example, you may want to use a different printer or print only selected slides. Use the Quick Print command when you want to print an entire presentation without changing any settings.

Saving an Edited Presentation

Whenever you work on a presentation, you should save it to a disk—especially if you have made changes that you want to keep. You can save a presentation in different ways. In this exercise, you will practice saving a presentation with a different file name.

⊘ SAVE AN EDITED PRESENTATION

USE the presentation that is open from the previous exercise.

1. Click the **Office Button**.
2. When the menu opens, click **Save As**. The Save As dialog box appears, as shown in Figure 1-34.

Figure 1-34

The Save As dialog box

3. Select the location where you want to save your files, then key **Blue Yonder Introduction** in the File name box.
4. Click **Save**.
5. Close the presentation.

PAUSE. LEAVE PowerPoint open to use in the next exercise.

X REF

You will learn other ways to save files in Lesson 2.

When you need to save an existing presentation in a new location or with a different file name, use the Save As command. In the Save As dialog box, you can specify a different disk drive and folder to store the file; you can also give the file a different name in the File name box. After the presentation is saved in the new location and with its new file name, you can click the Save button on the Quick Access Toolbar when you need to resave the file.

CERTIFICATION READY?

How do you save a presentation with a different file name?

4.3.6

By default, PowerPoint saves files in extensible markup language (XML) format. This format makes PowerPoint 2007 presentations incompatible with presentations created in previous versions of PowerPoint. However, PowerPoint 2007 can open and convert presentations from earlier versions.

Exiting PowerPoint

When you exit PowerPoint, the program closes and is removed from your computer's memory. In this exercise, you will practice exiting PowerPoint.

⊕ EXIT POWERPOINT

1. Click the **Office Button**.
2. When the menu opens, click **Exit PowerPoint**. PowerPoint disappears from the screen.

SUMMARY SKILL MATRIX

IN THIS LESSON YOU LEARNED	MATRIX SKILL	SKILL NUMBER
To work with tools in the PowerPoint window		
To work with an existing presentation		
To copy and move text from one slide to another	Copy elements from one slide to another	2.3.2
To save an edited presentation	Save presentations as appropriate file types	4.3.6

■ Knowledge Assessment

Matching

Match the term in Column 1 to its description in Column 2.

Column 1		Column 2
1. tab	a.	includes the Slide, Notes, and Slide/Outline panes
2. Ribbon	b.	a small toolbar that appears when you point to selected text
3. Normal view	c.	shows the keyboard key that will issue a command
4. current slide	d.	to highlight text for editing
5. Office Button	e.	a set of related tools on the Ribbon
6. Mini toolbar	f.	displays commands for managing files
7. placeholder	g.	the slide you are editing
8. KeyTip	h.	a Ribbon tool that opens a dialog box
9. dialog box launcher	i.	a large toolbar that presents tools in related groups
10. select	j.	a box, built into many slides, that holds text or an object

True / False

Circle T if the statement is true or F if the statement is false.

T F **1.** If you need more room on the screen, you can hide the Ribbon.

T F **2.** When you start PowerPoint, the last presentation you worked on appears on the screen.

T F **3.** The Ribbon is divided into sections, called tabs.

T F **4.** The Quick Access Toolbar appears faint, but turns brighter as the mouse pointer gets closer.

T F **5.** To close a dialog box without accepting any changes you may have made to it, click the Cancel button.

T F **6.** You can use the Undo command to reverse the last action you took.

T F **7.** KeyTips allow you to select commands from the keyboard.

T F **8.** The Office Button gives you access to all of PowerPoint's design tools.

T F **9.** You can use the Cut and Paste commands to move text from one slide to another slide.

T F **10.** In Normal view, PowerPoint displays five different panes for viewing different aspects of your slides.

■ Competency Assessment

Project 1-1: The Central City Job Fair

As personnel manager for Woodgrove Bank, you have accepted an invitation to give a presentation at a local job fair. Your goal is to recruit applicants for positions as bank tellers. You have created the presentation but need to finish it.

GET READY. Launch PowerPoint if it is not already running.

The *Job Fair* file is available on the companion CD-ROM.

1. Click the **Office Button** and open the presentation named *Job Fair* from the data files for this lesson.

2. On slide 1, click in the subtitle box to place the insertion point there, then key **Central City Job Fair.** Go to slide 2.

3. In the title of slide 2, select the words *Woodgrove Bank* by dragging the mouse pointer over them, then replace the selected text by keying **Us**.

4. In the bulleted list, click after the word *assets* to place the insertion point there.

5. Press **Enter** to move the insertion point down to a new, blank line.

6. Key **Voted "Best Local Bank" by City Magazine, 2005.** The new text will wrap to fit in the box.

7. Click the **Next Slide** button to go to slide 3. In the slide's outline, select the words *Help Wanted* (do not select the colon), then press **Delete** to delete the text.

8. Key **Now Hiring.**

9. Click at the end of the first item in the bulleted list, then press **Enter** to create a new line in the list.

10. Key **Responsible for cash drawer and station bookkeeping.**

11. Click the **Slides** tab, then press **Page Down** to go to slide 4.

12. Select the last item in the bulleted list by dragging the mouse pointer across it.

13. On the Ribbon, click the **Home** tab, if necessary, then click the **Cut** button. On the Slides tab, click slide 5.

14. Click at the end of the last item in the bulleted list to place the insertion point there, then press [Enter].

15. On the Ribbon, click the **Paste** button. The item you cut from slide 4 is pasted into slide 5.

16. **SAVE** the presentation as *Central City Job Fair* and **CLOSE** the file.

    LEAVE PowerPoint open for the next project.

Project 1-2: Messenger Service

Consolidated Messenger is a new company offering in-town courier service to corporate and private customers. As the company's owner, you want to tell as many people as possible about your new service, and a presentation can help you do it. You need to review your presentation, make some minor changes, and print it.

GET READY. Launch PowerPoint if it is not already running.

1. Click the **Office Button** and open the presentation named *Pitch* from the data files for this lesson.

2. Read slide 1. On the Slides tab, click slide 2 and read it.

3. Click the **scroll down** box to go to slide 3, then read it.

4. Click the **Next Slide** button to go to slide 4, then read it.

5. Press [Page Down] to go to slide 5, then read it.

6. Press ↓ to go to slide 6, then read it.

7. Press [Home] to return to the beginning of the presentation.

8. On slide 1, select the words *and Delivery* by dragging the mouse pointer over them.

9. Press [Delete] to delete the selected text from the subtitle. Go to slide 2.

10. On slide 2, select the word *delayed* and key **scheduled** in its place.

11. Select the third item in the bulleted list (*24-hour emergency service*) by dragging the mouse pointer over it.

12. On the Home tab of the Ribbon, click the **Copy** button. Go to slide 5.

13. On slide 5, click at the end of the last item in the bulleted list to place the insertion point there.

14. Press [Enter] to move the insertion point down to a new, blank line. On the Ribbon, click the **Paste** button.

15. Click at the end of the newly pasted line to move the insertion point there, then key : $250. Go to slide 6.

16. On slide 6, click at the end of the last line of text in the left-hand column, then press [Enter].

17. Key 555-1087 (daytime), then press [Enter].

18. Key 555-1088 (emergency), then press [Enter].

19. Key 555-1089 (fax).

20. Go to slide 1. Click the **Office Button**.

21. When the menu opens, point to **Print**, then click **Quick Print** to print the presentation.

22. **SAVE** the presentation as *Messenger Pitch* and **CLOSE** the file.

    LEAVE PowerPoint open for the next project.

The *Pitch* file is available on the companion CD-ROM.

■ Proficiency Assessment

Project 1-3: The Big Meeting

You are the director of documentation at Litware, Inc., which develops software for use in elementary schools. You have scheduled a conference with the writing staff and are working on an agenda for the meeting. Because the agenda is a single PowerPoint slide, you can display it on a projection screen for reference during the meeting.

1. **OPEN** the *Agenda* file from the data files for this lesson.
2. Copy the second line of the bulleted list. Paste the copied item below the currently selected item.
3. In the newly pasted line, replace the word *Upcoming* with **Revised**.
4. On the Outline tab, add a new line to the end of the agenda. On the new line, key **Adjourn**.
5. Quick-print the presentation.
6. **SAVE** the presentation as *Final Agenda* and then **CLOSE** the file.

   LEAVE PowerPoint open for the next project.

The *Agenda* file is available on the companion CD-ROM.

Project 1-4: Job Fair, Part 2

You have decided to make some last-minute changes to your presentation before going to the job fair.

1. **OPEN** *Central City Job Fair* from the data files for this lesson.
2. Copy the word *Woodgrove* on slide 1. In the title of slide 2, delete the word *Us* and paste the copied word in its place.
3. On slide 2, change the word *owned* to **managed**.
4. On slide 4, add the line **References a must** to the bottom of the bulleted list.
5. Quick-print the presentation.
6. **SAVE** the presentation as *Final Job Fair* and then **CLOSE** the file.

   LEAVE PowerPoint open for the next project.

The *Central City Job Fair* file is available on the companion CD-ROM.

■ Mastery Assessment

Project 1-5: Price-Fixing

You are the general manager of the restaurant at Coho Winery. It's time to update the staff on the restaurant's new wine selections and prices, and a slide show is a good way to give everyone the details. An easy way to handle this job is to open last season's presentation and update it with new wines and prices.

1. **OPEN** *Wine List* from the data files for this lesson.
2. Move *Coho Premium Chardonnay - $29.99* from slide 2 to the bottom of slide 4.
3. On slide 3, increase the price of every wine by one dollar.
4. Quick-print the presentation.
5. **SAVE** the presentation as *New Wine List* and then **CLOSE** the file.

   LEAVE PowerPoint open for the next project.

The *Wine List* file is available on the companion CD-ROM.

Project 1-6: A Trip to Toyland

As a product manager for Tailspin Toys, you introduce new products to many other people in the company, such as the marketing and sales staff. You need to finalize a presentation about several new toys.

1. **OPEN** *Toys* from the data files for this lesson.
2. Copy *List Price: $14.99* on slide 2 and paste it at the bottom of the bulleted lists on slides 3 and 4.
3. Change the teddy bear's name from *Rory* to **George**.
4. Change the top's speed from *800* to **1,200**.
5. Quick-print the presentation.
6. **SAVE** the presentation as *New Toys* and then **CLOSE** the file.
   CLOSE PowerPoint.

The *Toys* file is available on the companion CD-ROM.

INTERNET READY

Use PowerPoint Help to access online information about *What's New in PowerPoint 2007*. *Up to Speed with PowerPoint 2007* provides a short online course or demo explaining the new features. Browse these or other topics in PowerPoint's Help online.

Presentation Basics

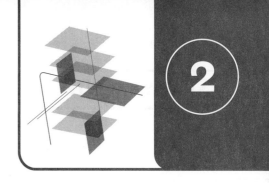

2

LESSON SKILL MATRIX

Skills	Matrix Skill	Skill Number
Creating a New Blank Presentation	Create presentations from blank presentations	1.1.1
Saving a Presentation for the First Time	Save presentations as appropriate file types	4.3.6
Creating a Presentation from a Template	Create presentations from templates	1.1.2
Reusing a Slide from Another Presentation	Reuse slides from an existing presentation	2.3.1
Creating a New Presentation from an Existing One	Create presentations from existing presentations	1.1.3
Starting a Presentation from a Microsoft Word Outline	Create presentations from Microsoft Office Word outlines	1.1.4
Organizing Your Slides		
Rearranging the Slides in a Presentation	Arrange slides	1.5
Adding Notes to Your Slides		
Printing a Presentation		
Printing a Presentation in Grayscale Mode	Print a presentation in various formats	4.4.2
Previewing a Presentation on the Screen		

Northwind Traders is a retailer of high-quality outdoor apparel and accessories for men, women, and children. The company has six stores in the Minneapolis–St. Paul area and a thriving online presence. As an assistant general manager, you help oversee the company's daily operations, hire and train new employees, and develop strategic plans. You also perform day-to-day functions assigned by the general manager. Your job frequently requires you to present information to an audience—for example, when training new workers on company policies or when providing executives with information about revenue or expenses. These duties often require you to create presentations from scratch, and PowerPoint 2007 lets you do that in several ways. In this lesson, you will learn different methods for creating presentations. You will also learn how to organize the slides in a presentation, add notes to your slides, select printing options, preview a slide show, and save a presentation for the first time.

KEY TERMS
handout
indent level
layout
note
Presenter view
template
theme
thumbnails

SOFTWARE ORIENTATION

Microsoft PowerPoint's New Presentation Dialog Box

PowerPoint's New Presentation window gives you many choices for creating a new presentation. Figure 2-1 shows the New Presentation window.

Figure 2-1

The New Presentation window

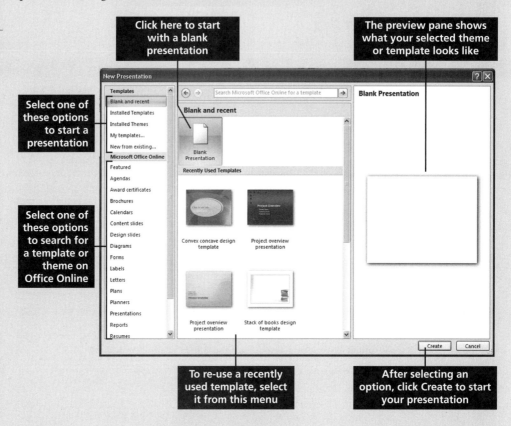

This window enables you to create a new, blank presentation; work from a template or theme stored on your computer; search for templates online; or create a new presentation from an existing one. (Note that if your copy of PowerPoint already has been used to create presentations, your screen may look somewhat different from Figure 2-1.)

Creating A New Blank Presentation

THE BOTTOM LINE
The fastest and simplest way to create a new presentation is to start with a blank presentation. You can add text to the presentation, then format the slides later.

Opening a Blank Presentation

In the following exercises, you will create a short slide show from a blank presentation.

⊖ OPEN A BLANK PRESENTATION

GET READY. Before you begin these steps, make sure that your computer is on. Log on, if necessary.

1. Start PowerPoint, if the program is not already running.
2. Click the **Office Button**.

3. Click **New**. The New Presentation window opens, as shown previously in Figure 2-1.

When you start PowerPoint, a new, blank slide appears. You can use that slide to create a new presentation. You need to use the New Presentation window only when another presentation is open or when no presentation is open.

4. Click the **Blank Presentation** icon, then click **Create**. A new, blank presentation appears in Normal view, as shown in Figure 2-2.

Figure 2-2

A blank presentation begins with a title slide

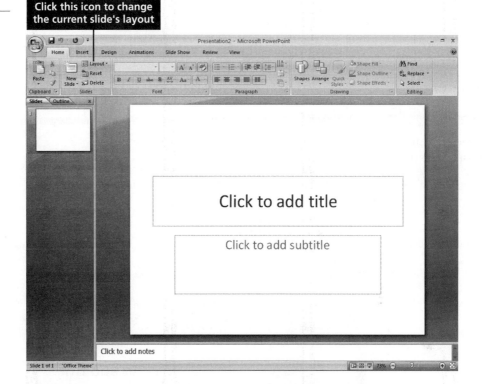

Press **Ctrl+N** to open a new, blank presentation without using the New Presentation window. If another presentation is on the screen, the blank presentation opens on top of it.

PAUSE. LEAVE the blank presentation open to use in the next exercise.

There are two advantages to using a blank presentation to start a slide show. First, PowerPoint displays a blank presentation every time the program starts, so you always have immediate access to the first slide of a new presentation. Second, because the presentation is not formatted (meaning there are no backgrounds, colors, or pictures), you can focus on writing your text. Many experienced PowerPoint users prefer to start with a blank presentation because they know they can format their slides after the text is finished.

Changing a Slide's Layout

You can change a slide's layout at any time to arrange text or objects on the slide exactly the way you want. The following exercise shows you how to apply a different layout to the current slide.

→ CHOOSE A DIFFERENT LAYOUT

USE the new, blank presentation that is still open from the previous exercise.

1. Click the **Home** tab to make it active, if necessary, then click **Layout**. A drop-down menu (called a *gallery*) appears, displaying PowerPoint's default layouts, as shown in Figure 2-3.

Figure 2-3

Choosing a new layout

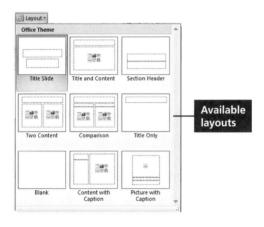

Available layouts

ANOTHER WAY

To change a slide's layout, right-click a blank area of the slide outside a placeholder. When the shortcut menu opens, click Layout, then click a layout.

2. Click **Title and Content**. The gallery closes and PowerPoint applies the chosen layout to the current slide, as shown in Figure 2-4.

Figure 2-4

The new layout applied to the current slide

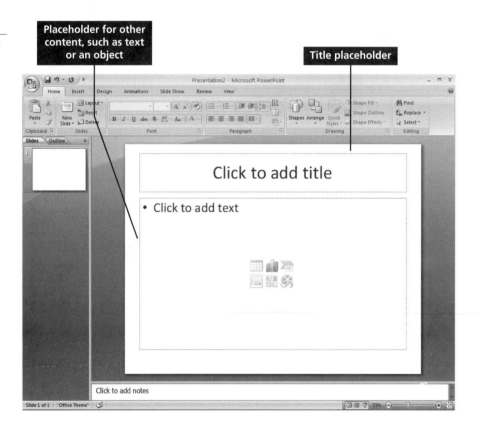

Placeholder for other content, such as text or an object

Title placeholder

PAUSE. LEAVE the presentation open to use in the next exercise.

X REF

You will work with other slide layouts in Lesson 4.

Most slides have a *layout*—a predefined arrangement of placeholders for text or objects (such as charts or pictures). PowerPoint has a variety of built-in layouts that you can use any time. Layouts are shown in the Layout gallery as *thumbnails*—small pictures showing each available layout. Choose the layout that is best suited to display the text or objects you want to place on the slide. In this exercise, you chose the Title and Content layout, which contains a placeholder for the slide's title and a second placeholder that can display text, a picture, a table, or some other kind of object.

You can change a slide's layout whether the slide is blank or contains text. If the slide already has text, PowerPoint will fit the text into the new layout's placeholders.

Adding Text to a Blank Slide

If a blank slide has one or more text placeholders, you can easily add text to the slide. In the following exercise, you will enter text into a blank slide's placeholders to create a set of discussion points for a meeting of store managers.

⊕ ADD TEXT TO A BLANK SLIDE

USE the slide that is still on the screen from the preceding exercise.

1. Click the title placeholder at the top of the slide. The text *Click to add title* disappears and a blinking insertion point appears in the placeholder.

2. Key **Discussion Points**.

3. Click the text at the top of the lower placeholder. The words *Click to add text* disappear and the insertion point appears.

4. Key **Customer surveys**, then press [Enter] to move the insertion point down to a new line.

5. Key **Inventory tracking** and press [Enter].

6. Key **Absenteeism policy** and press [Enter].

7. Key **Break** and press [Enter].

8. Key **Store security** and press [Enter].

9. Key **Store closing procedures** and press [Enter].

10. Key **Cash drawer management**, then click anywhere in the blank area outside the placeholder to clear its borders from the screen. Your slide should look like the one shown in Figure 2-5.

TAKE NOTE

If you click any of the icons in the lower placeholder, PowerPoint will display tools for adding non-text content, such as a table or chart. These types of content are covered in later lessons.

Figure 2-5

The completed slide

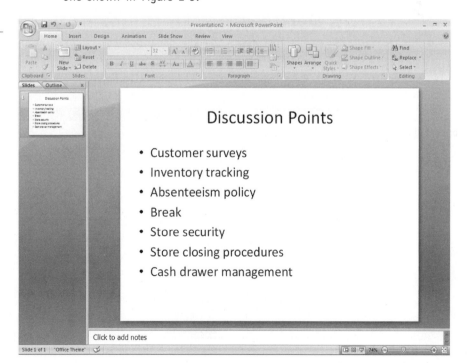

PAUSE. LEAVE the presentation open to use in the next exercise.

CERTIFICATION READY?
How do you create a presentation from a blank presentation?
1.1.1

In this exercise, you practiced adding text to a blank slide, creating a one-slide presentation that can be left on the screen for reference during a meeting. Even when a multiple-slide presentation is not needed at a meeting, displaying an agenda, a list of discussion points, or a list of breakout rooms can be helpful for the group.

PowerPoint makes it easy to add text to a slide with built-in text placeholders. In this exercise, the slide has a title placeholder and a content placeholder that can hold text and other types of content. To enter text, just click the sample text in the placeholder, then type your text.

■ Saving a Presentation for the First Time

↓
THE BOTTOM LINE

If you want to keep a presentation, you must save it on a disk. The following exercises show you how to save a new presentation to a disk and how to save the presentation in a different file format.

Saving a New Presentation

In this exercise, you will name and save the presentation you created earlier.

⊕ SAVE A NEW PRESENTATION

USE the presentation that is still on the screen from the preceding exercise.

1. On the Quick Access Toolbar, click **Save**. The Save As dialog box appears.

⊕ **ANOTHER WAY**

When saving a presentation for the first time, you can open the Save As dialog box by pressing **Ctrl+S**.

2. Navigate to the folder where you want to save your files.

3. Select the text in the File name box by dragging the mouse pointer over it, then press **Delete** to delete it.

4. Key **Managers Meeting**, as shown in Figure 2-6.

Figure 2-6

Naming the presentation

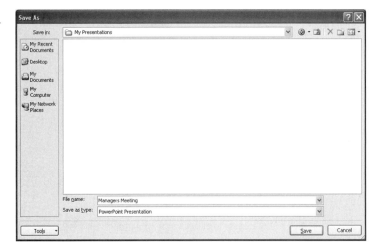

5. Click **Save**. PowerPoint saves the presentation in the folder you chose, under the name you have given it.

PAUSE. LEAVE the presentation open to use in the next exercise.

When you create a new presentation, it exists only in your computer's memory. If you want to keep the presentation, you must save it on a disk. After you save a file, you can close it, then re-open it again later and resume working on it. When you save a presentation for the first time, PowerPoint displays the Save As dialog box so you can give the presentation a name before saving it.

When you save a presentation (or any type of document), be sure to give it a name that describes its contents. This will help you identify your presentations more easily when you are trying to find the right one.

Choosing a Different File Format

PowerPoint can save presentations in several different file formats. In this exercise, you will save your presentation in a format that is compatible with earlier versions of PowerPoint.

 **CHOOSE A DIFFERENT FILE FORMAT**

USE the presentation that is still open from the previous exercise.

1. Click the **Office Button**, then point to the **Save As** command. A submenu of options appears.
2. On the submenu, click **PowerPoint 97-2003 Presentation**, as shown in Figure 2-7. The Save As box opens.

Figure 2-7

PowerPoint's Save As options

3. Navigate to the folder where you want to save your files. (This step is not necessary if you want to save the file in the same folder you used in the previous exercise.)
4. Select the file's name in the File name box, delete the name, then key **Old Format Discussion Points**.
5. Look at the Save as type box. Notice that the PowerPoint 97-2003 file format is already selected. Click the drop-down arrow at the right end of the box to view other available file formats, as shown in Figure 2-8.

CERTIFICATION READY?
How do you name and save a new presentation?
4.3.6

TAKE NOTE

Because you are saving the presentation in a different file format, it is not necessary to give it a new name. Files of different formats can have the same file name.

Figure 2-8

Viewing formats for saving presentations

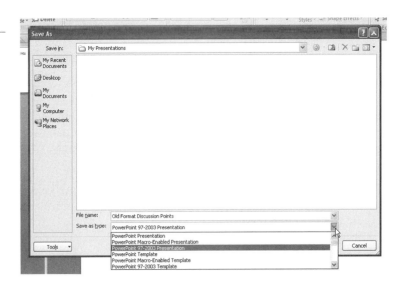

6. Because the desired format is already selected, click in the blank area to the right of the Save as type box to close the drop-down list.

7. Click **Save**, then **CLOSE** the presentation.

PAUSE. LEAVE PowerPoint open to use in the next exercise.

By default, PowerPoint 2007 saves presentations in XML format, which is not compatible with earlier versions of PowerPoint. If you want to be able to use a presentation with an older version of PowerPoint, you can save it by using the PowerPoint 97-2003 Presentation file format.

CERTIFICATION READY?
How do you save a presentation in a different file format?
4.3.6

You can save a presentation in other formats, as well. For example, if you select the PowerPoint Show format, the presentation will always open in Slide Show view, rather than in Normal view. You can also save a presentation as a template or save it so that special built-in commands called macros are enabled.

■ Creating a Presentation from a Template

↓ THE BOTTOM LINE

PowerPoint's templates give you a jump start to creating complete presentations. A template is a pre-designed presentation that includes backgrounds, fonts, and other design elements. You can insert your own text and objects (such as charts or pictures) and build a finished presentation very quickly.

Using a Template as the Basis for a Presentation

PowerPoint has several built-in templates, and you can create your own templates or download new ones from Microsoft Office Online. In this exercise, you will use a built-in template to start a presentation that, when finished, will help you show pictures and descriptions of new products to a group of store managers.

⊕ CREATE A PRESENTATION FROM A TEMPLATE

1. Click the **Office Button**.

2. Click **New** to open the New Presentation window.

3. Under Templates, click **Installed Templates**. A menu of PowerPoint's built-in templates appears in the center of the New Presentation window, as shown in Figure 2-9.

Figure 2-9

Selecting an installed template

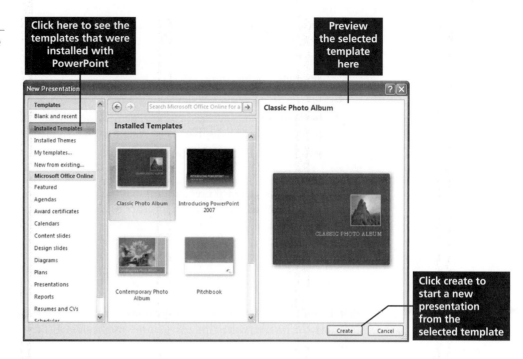

Click here to see the templates that were installed with PowerPoint

Preview the selected template here

Click create to start a new presentation from the selected template

4. Click **Classic Photo Album**, then click **Create**. PowerPoint opens a new presentation based on the selected template.

TAKE NOTE

If none of the installed templates suits your needs, download one from Office Online. In the New Presentation window, click one of the categories under Microsoft Office Online. Select a template in the center of the window to preview it. If you like it, click Download. The template appears in the PowerPoint window, ready to edit.

5. On the Zoom control, click the **Fit slide to current window** button. Your screen should look like the one shown in Figure 2-10.

Figure 2-10

A new presentation based on the Classic Photo Album template

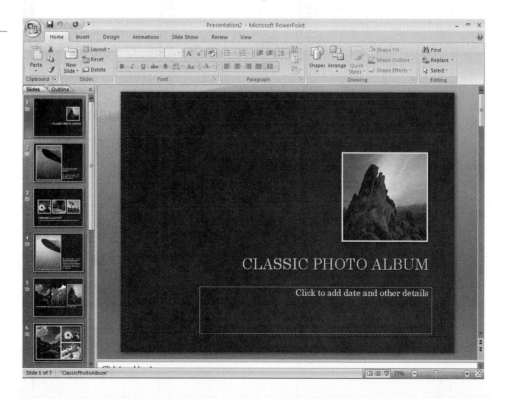

6. On slide 1, select the type *CLASSIC PHOTO ALBUM* and replace it with **NORTHWIND TRADERS**.

7. Click the text in the subtitle placeholder to place the insertion point there, then key **New Product Preview**.

8. On the Quick Access Toolbar, click **Save**. The Save As dialog box appears.

9. Navigate to the folder where you want to save your files, then save the presentation with the file name *New Product Preview*.

   PAUSE. LEAVE the presentation open to use in the next exercise.

A ***template*** is a predesigned presentation that includes a background, layouts, coordinating fonts, and other elements that work together to create an attractive finished slide show. Most templates also have a ***theme***, which is a color scheme with complementing colors for the backgrounds, bullets, text, borders, and other parts of the presentation.

PowerPoint's templates, however, are more than just formatting. They can help you decide what kinds of information to add to your presentations. Some templates contain just one slide—for example, to display a meeting agenda. But most templates include multiple slides that are set up to hold specific combinations of content. For example, one slide may be ready to display pictures and descriptions, another might hold a chart and a bulleted list, and another might contain a table. Such templates often display instructions that tell you what kind of information to place in each slide.

You can choose from many different templates. A few templates are included with PowerPoint, but you can find many more on Office Online.

It is important to choose a template that is appropriate for your audience and your message. If you need to deliver business information to a group of managers, for example, choose a template that looks professional and does not have elements that will distract the audience from getting your message. Conversely, a whimsical template might work better for a group of young people.

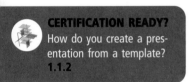

CERTIFICATION READY?
How do you create a presentation from a template?
1.1.2

Adding a New Slide to a Presentation

You can add as many new slides as you want to a presentation. The following exercise shows you how to insert a new slide into the current presentation.

⊕ ADD A NEW SLIDE

USE the presentation that is still open from the previous exercise.

1. With slide 1 still selected, make sure that the Home tab is active.

2. Click the drop-down arrow under the **New Slide** button. A gallery opens, showing thumbnail images of the slide layouts that are available for this template, as shown in Figure 2-11.

Figure 2-11

The New Slide gallery

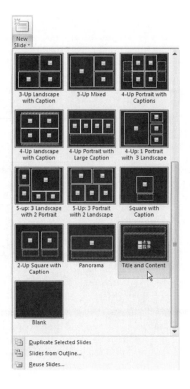

3. Scroll down to the bottom of the gallery, then click **Title and Content**.

To view the New Slide gallery, you must click the New Slide button's drop-down arrow. If you click the New Slide button, PowerPoint will insert the default new slide for the current template.

4. On the new slide, click the title placeholder and key **THIS YEAR'S NEW PRODUCTS**.

5. Click the sample text at the top of the second placeholder, then key the following items, placing each item on its own line:

Women's jackets

Men's jackets

Boots

Backpacks

Flannel shirts

Fleece

Turtlenecks

Underwear

Socks

6. Click in the area surrounding the slide to clear the placeholder's border. When you are done, your slide should look like the one shown in Figure 2-12.

Figure 2-12

The inserted slide

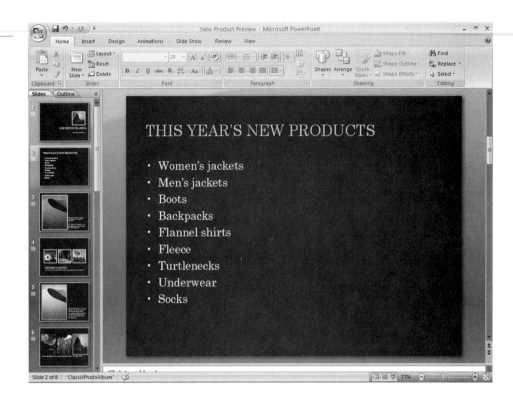

PAUSE. LEAVE the presentation open to use in the next exercise.

Reusing a Slide from Another Presentation

It is easy to reuse a slide from one presentation in another. This technique frees you from creating the same slide from scratch more than once. The following exercise shows you how to locate a slide from a different presentation and insert it into the current presentation.

⊕ REUSE A SLIDE FROM A DIFFERENT PRESENTATION

USE the presentation that is still open from the previous exercise.

1. Click the drop-down arrow under the **New Slide** button. At the bottom of the gallery, click **Reuse Slides**. The Reuse Slides task pane opens on the right side of the PowerPoint window, as shown in Figure 2-13.

Figure 2-13

The Reuse Slides task pane

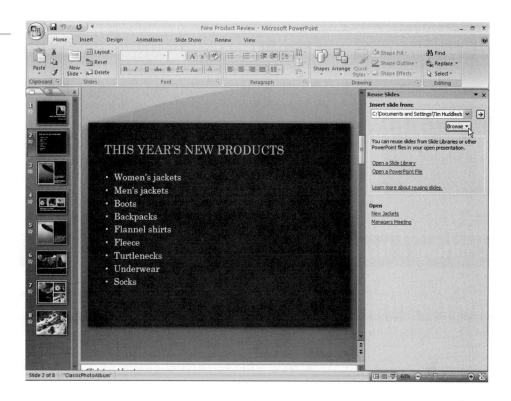

The *New Jackets* file
is available on the
companion CD-ROM.

2. In the task pane, click the **Browse** button. A drop-down list opens. Click **Browse File**. The Browse dialog box opens.

3. Locate and open *New Jackets*. The presentation's slides appear in the task pane, as shown in Figure 2-14.

Figure 2-14

Selecting a slide to reuse in the New Product Preview presentation

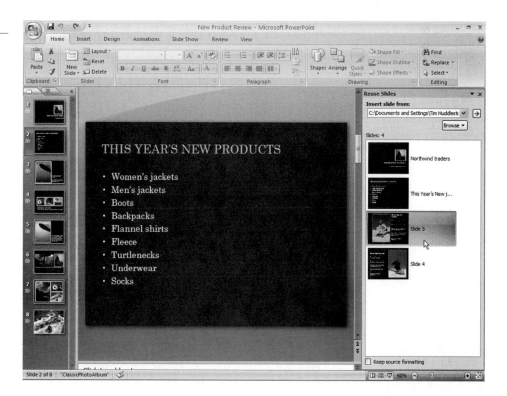

4. In the task pane, click slide 3. The slide is inserted into the *New Product Preview* presentation.

5. Click the **Close** button in the upper-right corner of the task pane.

6. **SAVE** and **CLOSE** the *New Product Preview* presentation.

PAUSE. LEAVE PowerPoint open to use in the next exercise.

CERTIFICATION READY?
How do you reuse a slide from one presentation in another presentation?
2.3.1

Over time, you will probably create many presentations, and some of them may share common information. The Reuse Slide command lets you copy slides from one presentation to another. By copying finished slides in this manner, you can avoid re-creating similar slides over and over again.

■ Creating a New Presentation from an Existing One

↓ **THE BOTTOM LINE**

You don't need to start a new presentation from scratch if you have already created another one that is similar. Instead, you can use the existing presentation as the basis for the new one.

➔ **CREATE A NEW PRESENTATION FROM AN EXISTING ONE**

1. Click the **Office Button**.

2. Click **New** to open the New Presentation window.

3. Under Templates, click **New from existing**. The New from Existing Presentation dialog box opens, as shown in Figure 2-15.

Figure 2-15

The New from Existing Presentation dialog box

CD

The *Cashier Training* file is available on the companion CD-ROM.

4. Locate and open *Cashier Training*.

5. Look at PowerPoint's title bar, at the top of the screen. Notice that the presentation's name does not appear there. You can now save this presentation as though you just created it from scratch.

6. On the Quick Access Toolbar, click **Save**. The Save As dialog box appears.

CERTIFICATION READY?
How do you create a new presentation from an existing one?
1.1.3

7. **SAVE** the presentation as *Phone Sales Training*. You can now edit the slides as needed to suit a different audience or message.

8. **CLOSE** the file without making any changes to it.

PAUSE. LEAVE PowerPoint open to use in the next exercise.

■ Starting a Presentation from a Microsoft Word Outline

THE BOTTOM LINE

You can use text created in another application (such as Microsoft Word) as the basis for a new presentation. In the following exercises, you create a new presentation, then add content from a Microsoft Word outline. You also learn how to change the indent levels of items in a list.

➔ START A PRESENTATION FROM A WORD OUTLINE

1. Click the **Office Button**.
2. Click **New** to open the New Presentation window.
3. Click **Create**. A new, blank title slide appears in the PowerPoint window.
4. Click in the slide's title placeholder, then key **Computer Use Policy**.
5. Click in the subtitle placeholder, then key **Northwind Traders**.

TAKE NOTE

Don't worry if a wavy red line appears under some words, such as *Northwind*. This is PowerPoint's spelling checker telling you that the word may be misspelled. To clear the underlining, right-click the word, then click Ignore All. PowerPoint will ignore the word from now on.

6. Click outside the text placeholder to clear its border.
7. On the Ribbon's Home tab, click the **New Slide** drop-down arrow. At the bottom of the gallery of slide layouts, click **Slides from Outline**. The Insert Outline dialog box appears, as shown in Figure 2-16.

Figure 2-16

The Insert Outline dialog box

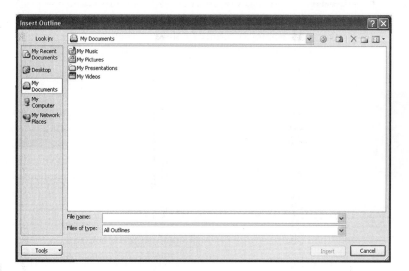

The *Computer Use Policy* file is available on the companion CD-ROM.

8. Locate and select the Microsoft Word document named *Computer Use Policy*. Click **Insert**. PowerPoint imports the text from the outline and uses it to create five new slides, as shown in Figure 2-17.

Figure 2-17

New slides created from a Word outline

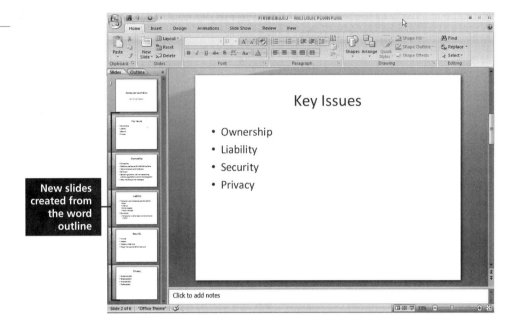

New slides created from the word outline

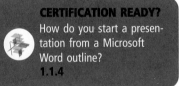 **ANOTHER WAY**

You can also create a presentation from an outline by opening a properly formatted Word outline in PowerPoint. Click the Office Button, then click Open. In the Open dialog box, click the Files of type drop-down arrow, then click All Files. Select the outline, then click Open.

9. Press **Home** to return to slide 1, then navigate through the slides to see them all. When you have seen all the slides, go to slide 3.

PAUSE. LEAVE the presentation open to use in the next exercise.

If you create an outline in Microsoft Word, you can import it into PowerPoint and generate slides from it. Before you can create slides from a Word outline, the outline must be formatted correctly. Paragraphs formatted with Word's Heading 1 style become slide titles. Paragraphs formatted with subheading styles (such as Heading 2 or Heading 3) are converted into bulleted lists in the slides' subtitle placeholders.

⊕ CHANGE INDENT LEVELS IN A LIST

USE the presentation that is still open from the previous exercise.

1. With slide 3 still selected, click the second line of the bulleted list (*Desktops, laptops and handheld systems*).

2. On the Ribbon, click the **Increase List Level** button. In the list, the line's indent increases, making it subordinate to the preceding line (*Computers:*), as shown in Figure 2-18.

Figure 2-18

Increasing the indent of an item in a list

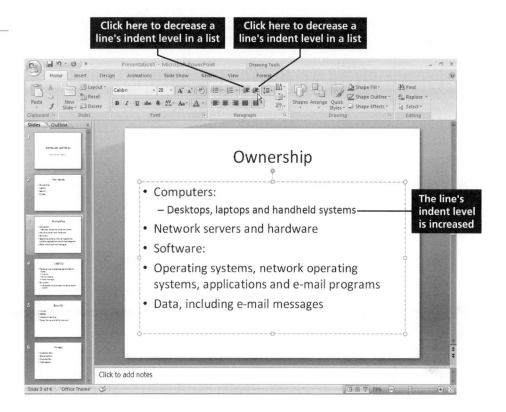

3. Click the next line in the list (*Network servers and hardware*), then click the **Increase List Level** button.

 **ANOTHER WAY**   You can click the Repeat button on the Quick Access Toolbar to repeat the last action you took.

4. In the Slides/Outline pane, click the **Outline** tab. On the Outline tab, notice that all the text from slide 3 is highlighted.

5. Click just outside the highlighting to clear it from the text, then select the last two bulleted items by dragging the mouse pointer across them.

6. Click the **Increase List Level** button to increase the indent level of the two selected items.

7. In the Slides/Outline pane, click the **Slides** tab.

8. On the Quick Access Toolbar, click **Save**. The Save As dialog box appears.

9. **SAVE** the presentation as *Computer Use Policy*, then **CLOSE** the file.

PAUSE. LEAVE PowerPoint open to use in the next exercise.

Just like the headings in a book's outline, some of the items in a list are superior while others are subordinate. In a PowerPoint slide, the relationship between items in a list is shown by indent level. An item's ***indent level*** is the distance it is indented from the placeholder's left border. Superior items are indented less than subordinate ones. You can change the indent level of an item in a list by using the Decrease List Level and Increase List Level buttons on the Home tab of the Ribbon.

Another way to increase a paragraph's indent level is to press Tab at the beginning of a line. To reduce a paragraph's indent level (called *outdenting*), press Shift+Tab. This method is especially helpful when you are keying text, because you don't have to remove your fingers from the keyboard to click a button to change indent levels.

■ Organizing Your Slides

THE BOTTOM LINE

As you work on a presentation, you may decide that some of the slides need to be in different places. PowerPoint makes it easy to view multiple slides and move them to different positions. The following exercises show you how to rearrange the slides in a presentation and how to remove a slide from a presentation.

Rearranging the Slides in a Presentation

You can reorganize your slides in either Normal view or Slide Sorter view. Moving a slide is a simple procedure, as you will learn in the following exercise.

⊕ REARRANGE THE SLIDES IN A PRESENTATION

CD

The *Management Values* file is available on the companion CD-ROM.

1. Locate and open the *Management Values* presentation.
2. Switch to Slide Sorter view. The presentation's slides appear together in a single window, as shown in Figure 2-19.

Figure 2-19

Viewing the presentation in Slide Sorter view

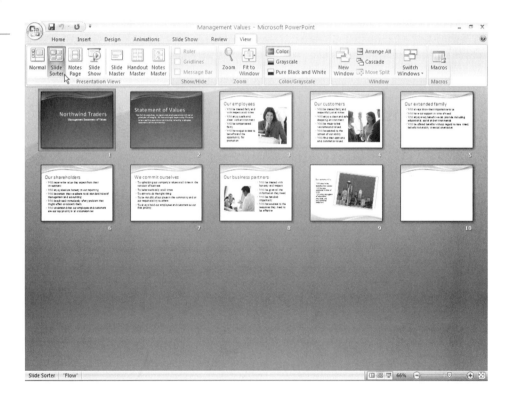

3. Click slide 5 and drag it to the left. When a vertical line appears between slides 3 and 4 (as shown in Figure 2-20), release the mouse button. The moved slide is now slide 4.

Figure 2-20

Moving a slide in Slide Sorter
view

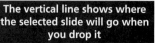

The vertical line shows where
the selected slide will go when
you drop it

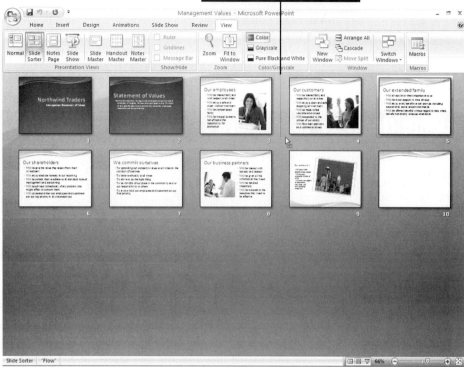

4. Click slide 7 and drag it to the right. When a vertical line appears between slides 9 and 10, release the mouse button. The moved slide is now slide 9.

 **ANOTHER WAY**

You can also drag slides to new positions in the Slides tab (Normal view). Click a slide and drag it up or down in the tab, then drop it where you want it.

PAUSE. LEAVE the presentation open to use in the next exercise.

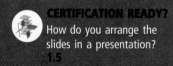 **CERTIFICATION READY?**
How do you arrange the slides in a presentation?
1.5

It is important to organize your slides so they best support your message. In PowerPoint, reorganizing slides is a simple drag-and-drop procedure. In Slide Sorter view (or on the Slides tab in Normal view), you can click a slide and drag it to a new location in the presentation. A line shows you where the slide will be placed when you drop it.

Deleting a Slide

When you don't want to keep a slide in a presentation, you can delete it. The following exercise shows you how.

⊕ DELETE A SLIDE

USE the presentation that is still open from the previous exercise.

1. In Slide Sorter view, click slide 10.
2. On the Ribbon, click the **Home** tab to activate it, if necessary.
3. In the Slides group, click the **Delete** button. The selected slide is removed from the presentation.
4. **SAVE** the presentation as *New Management Values*.

PAUSE. LEAVE the presentation open to use in the next exercise.

 **ANOTHER WAY**

You can also delete a selected slide by pressing **Delete**.

PowerPoint does not ask whether you are sure if you want to delete a slide, so it's important to be careful before deleting. If you accidentally delete a slide, click the Undo button right away to bring the slide back.

To select more than one slide at a time for deletion, hold down the Ctrl key and click each slide you want to delete. (If you change your mind, you can deselect the selected slides by clicking in a blank area of the PowerPoint window.) Then delete all the selected slides at the same time.

■ Adding Notes to Your Slides

↓ THE BOTTOM LINE A note is a piece of additional information you associate with a slide. Notes do not appear on the screen when you show your presentation to an audience, but you can view notes in a couple of ways. The following exercises show you how to add notes to your slides.

→ ADD NOTES IN THE NOTES PANE

USE the presentation that is still open from the previous exercise.

ANOTHER WAY

You can move from one pane to another in Normal view by pressing **F6**.

1. Switch to Normal view, then go to slide 2.
2. Click in the Notes pane (below the Slide pane) to place the insertion point there.
3. In the Notes pane, key **All Northwind employees are required to sign a statement of values, which binds them to ethical behavior on the job.** Your screen should look like the one shown in Figure 2-21.

Figure 2-21

Adding a note in the Notes pane

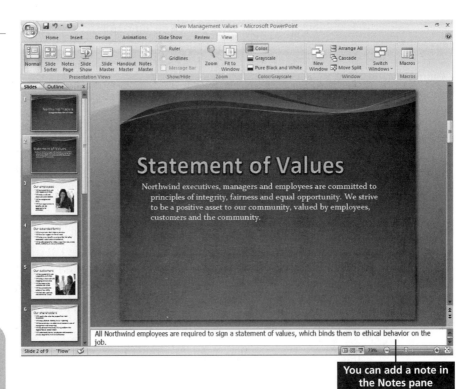

You can add a note in the Notes pane

TAKE NOTE

You can edit and delete text in the Notes pane just as you can in the Slide pane or on the Outline tab. Select text with the mouse pointer; use the **Delete** and **Backspace** keys to delete text.

4. **SAVE** the presentation.

PAUSE. LEAVE the presentation open to use in the next exercise.

Notes are extra information that might not fit on a slide, but which the presenter wants to tell the audience as they view the slide. Suppose, for example, you are using a chart to show financial data to the audience but do not have room on the slide for a lot of details. You can add those details as notes, and they will remind you to share the details with your audience during your presentation.

Notes do not appear on the screen in Slide Show view, so the audience does not see them. You can see your notes by printing them or by using PowerPoint's *Presenter view*. Presenter view lets you use two monitors when delivering your presentation to an audience. One monitor displays your slides in Slide Show view. You can use the second monitor to view your notes, among other things.

REF

You will learn more about preparing your presentation for delivery in Lesson 10.

⊕ ADD NOTES IN NOTES PAGE VIEW

USE the presentation that is still open from the previous exercise.

1. Switch to Notes Page view. On the scroll bar, click **Next Slide** to go to slide 3. Your screen should look like the one shown in Figure 2-22.

Figure 2-22

Viewing a slide and its notes in Notes Page view

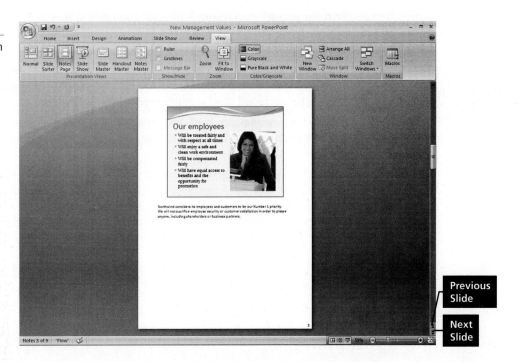

2. Go to slide 5. Click in the notes placeholder (below the slide) to place the insertion point there.
3. In the notes placeholder, key **All Northwind employees receive special training in customer relations.**
4. **SAVE** the presentation.

   PAUSE. LEAVE the presentation open to use in the next exercise.

TAKE NOTE

If your slides' content is too small to read in Notes Page view, use the Zoom control to enlarge the view.

Notes Page view is a special view that displays each slide along with its associated notes. Each slide and its notes appear on a white background; the content is sized as it would appear when printed on a standard sheet of paper. You can view and edit notes directly in the note placeholder, which is located below the slide.

✳ Workplace Ready

Presenting with a Purpose

Many professionals have experienced "death by PowerPoint." They can tell you what it's like to sit through a presentation that is boring or too long and will usually tell you that the presenter did not understand how to use slides effectively. But an ineffective presentation can be worse than dull; it can actually prevent your audience from getting your message.

The following guidelines will help you (and your audience) get the most from a slide show:

- **Be brief:** Make only one major point per slide, using only a few bullets to support that point. A presentation should include only enough slides to support its major points.
- **Write concisely:** Keep your text short; sentence fragments work well on slides.
- **Focus on content:** Formatting is nice, but too much formatting can overwhelm the text and obscure your message.
- **Keep graphics relevant:** A nice picture can enhance a slide's meaning; a chart or table may support your point better than words alone. But use graphics only where they are needed.
- **Be consistent:** Use the same fonts, background, and colors throughout the presentation. If you use different design elements on each slide, your audience will become distracted (and maybe irritated).
- **Make sure slides are readable:** Ask someone else to review your slides before you show them to your audience. Make sure the reviewer can read all the text and see the graphics clearly.
- **Practice, practice, practice:** Never deliver a presentation "cold." Practice running the slide show and delivering your comments along with it. Practice your spoken parts out loud. Be sure to work on your timing, so you know just how long to keep each slide on the screen before going to the next one. Ask someone to watch you practice and offer feedback.

■ Printing a Presentation

THE BOTTOM LINE PowerPoint gives you many options for printing your slides. In the following exercises, you learn how to preview a presentation before printing it, how to choose a printer, how to set print options, and how to print a presentation in both color and grayscale mode.

Using Print Preview

PowerPoint's Print Preview feature shows you how your slides will look on paper before you print them. This exercise shows you how to use Print Preview.

➔ USE PRINT PREVIEW

USE the presentation that is still open from the previous exercise.

1. Go to slide 1. Click the Office Button. When the menu appears, point to Print, then click Print Preview. The presentation's first slide appears in the Print Preview window, as shown in Figure 2-23.

Figure 2-23

Viewing a presentation in Print Preview

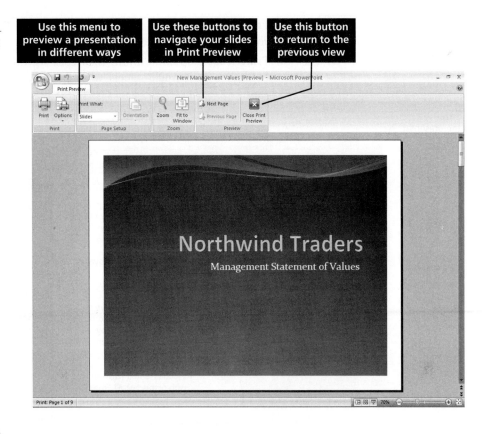

Use this menu to preview a presentation in different ways

Use these buttons to navigate your slides in Print Preview

Use this button to return to the previous view

TAKE NOTE

If you are using a black-and-white printer, Print Preview will display your slides in grayscale.

2. On the Print Preview tab, click the **Next Page** button eight times to view each slide in the presentation. Then press the Home key to return to slide 1.

3. Click the **Print What** drop-down arrow, then click **Handouts (2 Slides Per Page)**. PowerPoint shows you how a printed handout would appear with two slides printed on each page, as shown in Figure 2-24.

Figure 2-24

Previewing a handout with two slides per page

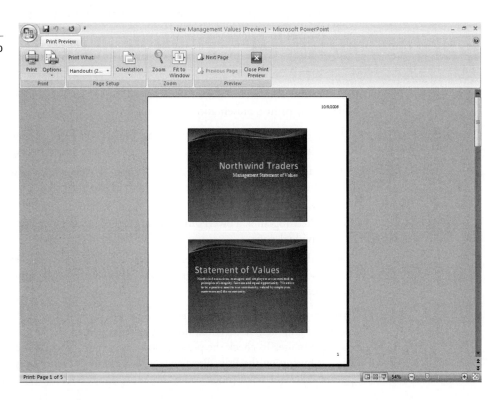

4. Click the **Print What** drop-down arrow, then click **Notes Pages**. PowerPoint shows you how your notes pages will appear when printed.

5. Click the **Print What** drop-down arrow, then click **Outline View**. PowerPoint displays the outline as it would appear when printed, as shown in Figure 2-25.

Figure 2-25

Previewing the presentation's outline

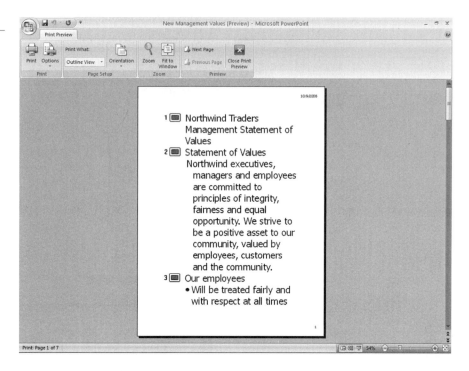

TAKE NOTE

If the preview does not fit in the window, use the Zoom button or the Fit slide to current window button on the Print Preview tab to change the magnification. These tools function in Print Preview just as they do in Normal view.

6. Click the **Close Print Preview** button to return to Notes Page view.

7. Switch to Normal view.

PAUSE. LEAVE the presentation open to use in the next exercise.

Print Preview allows you to see how your slides will appear before you print them. You can preview and print a presentation in several different formats:

- **Slides:** When you select this option, PowerPoint shows you how the slides will look when printed one per page, using your current print settings.
- **Handouts:** A *handout* is a printed copy of your slides, which you can give to the audience. You can print handouts with up to nine slides on each sheet.
- **Notes Pages:** This view shows you how your slides and notes will appear when printed together. PowerPoint prints each slide and its associated notes on an individual page.
- **Outline View:** PowerPoint allows you to print only the text (the outline) of your presentation, without any graphics. This view shows you how the outline will appear when printed.

If you are using a color printer, Print Preview will display your slides in color mode, showing all colors and graphics. To save ink, however, you may want to print your slides in grayscale or black and white. To check the presentation's appearance in a different color mode, click the Options button on the Print Preview tab, then point to Color/Grayscale; a submenu of options appears. Click the color mode you want, and Print Preview will display the slides in that mode.

Setting Print Options

PowerPoint lets you set a number of attributes before printing a presentation. The following exercise shows you how to set some of these printing options.

⊕ SET PRINT OPTIONS

USE the presentation that is still open from the previous exercise.

1. Click the **Office Button**. When the menu appears, point to Print, then click Print. The Print dialog box appears, as shown in Figure 2-26.

Figure 2-26

The Print dialog box

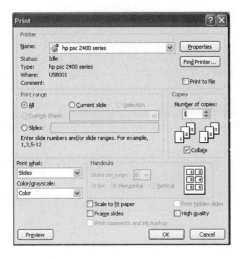

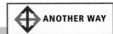

Press **Ctrl+P** to open the Print dialog box.

2. To select a different printer, click the **Name** drop-down arrow, then click the name of the printer you want to use.

3. In the Print range group, click the **All** option button if it is not already selected.

4. Click the **Print what** drop-down arrow, then click **Handouts**. Notice that the Handouts group becomes available.

5. In the Handouts group, click the **Slides per page** drop-down arrow, then click **2**.

6. Click the **Color/grayscale** drop-down arrow and click **Color**, if it is not already selected.

7. If the **Frame slides** check box is selected, click it to deselect it.

8. Click **OK**. PowerPoint prints your presentation, using the options you just selected.

PAUSE. LEAVE the presentation open to use in the next exercise.

The Print dialog box provides an array of options that help you print your presentations exactly the way you want. You can select a printer by choosing one from the Name drop-down list or choose properties that are specific to your chosen printer by clicking the Properties button. The Find Printer button helps you locate a printer that is attached to your computer or network but which does not appear in the Name list.

The Print range group lets you determine how many of the slides to print:

- **All:** Prints all the slides in the presentation.
- **Current slide:** Prints only the slide that is currently active on the screen.
- **Slides:** Prints only the slides you specify. For example, if you want to print only the first four slides of your presentation, click the Slides option button, then key 1-4 in the text box. If you want to print only the first and third slides, key 1,3 in the box.

TAKE NOTE

When you set printing options and then save your presentation, the options are saved as well.

The Copies group lets you determine how many copies of the presentation (or selected slides) to print. Click the Number of copies spinner control to set the number of copies. By default, PowerPoint collates multiple copies when printing. If you do not want the copies to be collated, clear the Collate check box.

Use the Print what drop-down list to determine how to print your presentation. You can print a presentation as slides only, handouts with multiple slides per page, notes pages, or outline.

The Color/grayscale drop-down list lets you set the color mode for printing. The following exercise shows you how to use this tool.

The Print dialog box offers the following options as well:

X REF

Comments are covered in Lesson 9.

- **Scale to fit paper:** If your printer uses odd size sheets, this option tells PowerPoint to scale the slides to fit on the paper.
- **Frame slides:** This option prints a fine black border around each slide.
- **Print comments and ink markup:** This option lets you print out any comments and handwritten notes that have been added to the presentation. The option is not available if the presentation does not include comments or markups.
- **Print hidden slides:** Click this option if you want to include hidden slides in the printout.
- **High quality:** If your slides are formatted with shadows under text or graphics, choose this option to print the shadows.
- **Preview:** This button switches PowerPoint to Print Preview mode.

Printing a Presentation in Grayscale Mode

Grayscale mode lets you print a presentation without color. This setting can save time and reduce your use of colored ink or toner.

⊙ PRINT A PRESENTATION IN GRAYSCALE MODE

USE the presentation that is still open from the previous exercise.

1. Click the **Office Button**. When the menu appears, point to **Print**, then click **Print**. The Print dialog box appears.
2. Click the **Color/grayscale** drop-down arrow, then click **Grayscale**.
3. Click **OK**. PowerPoint prints your presentation in grayscale mode.
4. **SAVE** the presentation.

   PAUSE. LEAVE the presentation open to use in the next exercise.

Even if you have a color printer and your presentation uses a colored background or fonts, you can still print the slides in grayscale mode. In this mode, PowerPoint converts the colors to shades of gray for printing. (The colors in the presentation itself are not changed.) Grayscale mode offers a couple of advantages over color printing. First, it saves time because color printers generally print faster in grayscale or black-and-white mode. Second, by omitting the colors from your printout, you reduce your use of colored ink or toner.

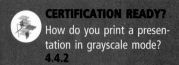

CERTIFICATION READY?

How do you print a presentation in grayscale mode?
4.4.2

PowerPoint can also print slides in pure black and white. To choose this option, click the Color/grayscale drop-down arrow, then click Pure Black and White. In this mode, slides are printed in black and white only, without any gray. This is the fastest way to print, but only the darkest parts of your presentation will print recognizably. Use black-and-white mode only for presentations that have no color or shading in them.

■ Previewing a Presentation on the Screen

THE BOTTOM LINE

Before you show your presentation to an audience, you should preview it in Slide Show view. This exercise shows you how to use PowerPoint's tools for running a slide show on your own computer's screen.

⊕ PREVIEW A PRESENTATION

USE the presentation that is still open from the previous exercise.

TAKE NOTE

You can also switch to Slide Show view by pressing **F5**.

1. Go to slide 1, if necessary.
2. On the Ribbon, click the View tab, if necessary.
3. Click **Slide Show**. PowerPoint changes to Slide Show view and the first slide appears in full-screen mode, as shown in Figure 2-27.

Figure 2-27

Previewing a presentation in Slide Show view

TAKE NOTE

You can exit from Slide Show view at any time by pressing **Esc**.

4. Click the left mouse button nine times to view the slides in order. When you click the mouse on the last slide, PowerPoint displays a black screen.
5. Click the left mouse button once more to return to Normal view.
6. **SAVE** and **CLOSE** the presentation.

   CLOSE PowerPoint.

TAKE NOTE

You will learn more about using Slide Show view in Lesson 10.

In Slide Show view, PowerPoint displays every slide in the presentation, in order from beginning to end. To advance to the next slide, you can click the left mouse button.

SUMMARY SKILL MATRIX

IN THIS LESSON YOU LEARNED	MATRIX SKILL	SKILL NUMBER
To create a new blank presentation	Create presentations from blank presentations	1.1.1
To save a presentation for the first time	Save presentations as appropriate file types	4.3.6
To create a new presentation from a PowerPoint template	Create presentations from templates	1.1.2
To copy a slide from one presentation and use it in another presentation	Reuse slides from an existing presentation	2.3.1
To create a new presentation from an existing one	Create presentations from existing presentations	1.1.3
To create a new presentation from a Microsoft Word outline	Create presentations from Microsoft Office Word outlines	1.1.4
To organize and rearrange slides	Arrange slides	1.5
To add notes to slides		
To print a presentation		
To print a presentation in grayscale mode	Print a presentation in various formats	4.4.2
To preview a presentation		

■ Knowledge Assessment

Matching

Match the term in Column 1 to its description in Column 2.

Column 1	Column 2
1. note	a. shows how a presentation will appear on paper
2. template	b. a printing mode that saves colored ink or toner
3. handout	c. additional information associated with a slide
4. Print Preview	d. a predefined arrangement of placeholders
5. Presenter view	e. a scheme of complementing colors
6. theme	f. a small picture of a slide
7. layout	g. the distance from a placeholder's left border
8. thumbnail	h. a predesigned presentation
9. grayscale	i. a printed copy of a presentation
10. indent level	j. lets you see notes on one screen while the audience sees slides on another

True / False

Circle T if the statement is true or F if the statement is false.

T | F **1.** A new, blank presentation appears on your screen when you launch PowerPoint.

T | F **2.** Once a layout has been applied to a slide, it cannot be changed.

T | F **3.** When you save a presentation for the first time, the Save As dialog box appears.

T | F **4.** If you want to be able to use a presentation with an older version of PowerPoint, you can save it by using the PowerPoint 97-2003 Presentation file format.

T | F **5.** Many PowerPoint templates feature a set of complementing colors, called a layout.

T | F **6.** If you click the New Slide button, PowerPoint displays the New Slide gallery.

T | F **7.** To copy a slide, right-click its thumbnail, then click Copy.

T | F **8.** Notes appear on the screen with the slides in Slide Show view.

T | F **9.** PowerPoint can print just the text of your slide, without printing any graphics.

T | F **10.** If you use a black-and-white printer, your slides will appear in grayscale when viewed in Print Preview.

■ Competency Assessment

Project 2-1: Tonight's Guest Speaker

As director of the Citywide Business Alliance, one of your jobs is to introduce the guest speaker at the organization's monthly meeting. To do this, you will create a new presentation from a template, then reuse a slide with information about the speaker from a different presentation.

GET READY. Launch PowerPoint if it is not already running.

1. Click the **Office Button**, then click **New** to open the New Presentation window.

2. Click **Installed Templates**. Click **Introducing PowerPoint 2007** then click **Create**.

3. Switch to Slide Sorter view, then delete slides 2 through 18.

4. Switch to Normal view.

5. On slide 1, select the title by dragging the mouse pointer over it. Press (Delete), then key **Citywide Business Alliance**.

6. Select the subtitle by dragging the mouse pointer over it. Press (Delete), then key **Tonight's Guest Speaker**. Click outside the subtitle's placeholder to deselect it.

7. On the Ribbon, click the **New Slide** button. At the bottom of the gallery, click **Reuse Slides**.

8. In the Reuse Slides task pane, click the **Browse** button, then click **Browse File**.

9. When the Browse dialog box appears, locate and open the presentation named *Bourne*.

The *Bourne* file is available on the companion CD-ROM.

10. In the Reuse Slides task pane, click slide 1. The slide is added to your new presentation. Close the task pane.

11. Click the **Office Button**, point to **Print**, then click **Print**. The Print dialog box opens.

12. In the Print dialog box, click the **Color/grayscale** drop-down arrow, then click **Grayscale**. Click **OK** to print the presentation in grayscale mode.

13. Click the **Office Button**, point to **Save As**, then click **PowerPoint 97-2003 Presentation**. The Save As dialog box opens.

14. Navigate to the folder where you want to save the presentation.

15. Select the text in the File name box, press [Delete], then key **Speaker**.

16. Click **Save**. If the Compatibility Checker task pane appears, click **Continue**. **CLOSE** the file.

LEAVE PowerPoint open for the next project.

Project 2-2: Advertise with Us

As an account manager for The Phone Company, you are always trying to convince potential customers of the benefits of advertising in the local phone directory. A PowerPoint presentation can help you make your case. You need to create a presentation from a Word document that lists some reasons why businesses should purchase ad space in your directory.

1. **OPEN** the New Presentation window and click **Create**. A new, blank title slide appears in the PowerPoint window.

2. Click in the slide's title placeholder, then key **Why Advertise with Us?**

3. Click in the subtitle placeholder, then key **The Phone Company**.

4. Click outside the text placeholder to clear its border.

5. On the Ribbon's Home tab, click the **New Slide** drop-down arrow. At the bottom of the gallery of slide layouts, click **Slides from Outline**.

6. In the Insert Outline dialog box, locate and select the Microsoft Word document named **Ad Benefits**. Click **Insert**. PowerPoint inserts five new slides using content from the outline.

7. Switch to Slide Sorter view. Click slide 5 and drag it to the left, then drop it after slide 1.

8. Click slide 6, then press [Delete] to remove the slide from the presentation.

9. Switch to Notes Page view, then go to slide 1.

10. Click in the text box below the slide, then key **Give the client a copy of the directory**.

11. Switch to Normal view.

12. On the Quick Access Toolbar, click **Save**. The Save As dialog box opens.

13. Navigate to the folder where you want to save the presentation.

14. Select the text in the File name box, then key **Benefits**.

15. Click **Save**. **CLOSE** the file.

LEAVE PowerPoint open for the next project.

The *Ad Benefits* file is available on the companion CD-ROM.

■ Proficiency Assessment

Project 2-3: Send People to Their Room

You are an assistant marketing manager at Contoso, Ltd., which develops process control software for use in manufacturing. You are coordinating a set of panel discussions at the company's annual sales and marketing meeting. At the start of the afternoon session, you must tell the groups which conference rooms to use for their discussions. To help deliver your message, you need to create a single-slide presentation that lists the panels' room assignments. You can display the slide on a projection screen for reference while you announce the room assignments.

1. **CREATE** a new, blank presentation.

2. Change the blank slide's layout to Title and Content. In the slide's title placeholder, key **Panel Discussions**.

3. In the second placeholder, key the following items, placing each item on its own line:

Aligning with Partners, Room 104
Building Incentives, Room 101
Creating New Value, Room 102
Managing Expenses, Room 108
Opening New Markets, Room 112
Recapturing Lost Accounts, Room 107
Strengthening Client Relationships, Room 110

4. In the Notes pane, key **Refreshments will be delivered to each room during the 3:00 PM break.**

5. Print the presentation in grayscale mode.

6. SAVE the presentation as *Room Assignments*, then CLOSE the file.

LEAVE PowerPoint open for the next project.

Project 2-4: Editorial Services

You are the editorial director for Lucerne Publishing, a small publishing house that provides editorial services to other businesses. Your sales manager has asked you to prepare a simple presentation that lists the services offered by your editorial staff. You can create this presentation from an outline that was created earlier.

1. CREATE a new, blank presentation.

2. Key **Lucerne Publishing** in the title placeholder.

3. Key **Editorial Services** in the subtitle placeholder, then click outside the placeholder.

4. Use the **Slides from Outline** command to locate the Microsoft Word document named *Editorial Services*, then click **Insert**.

5. In the Slides/Outline pane, click slide 6.

6. Use the Reuse Slides command to locate and open the *About Lucerne* presentation, then add slide 3 from that presentation to the end of your new presentation.

7. Print the presentation in grayscale mode.

8. SAVE the presentation as *Lucerne Editorial Services*, then CLOSE the file.

LEAVE PowerPoint open for the next project.

The *Editorial Services* file is available on the companion CD-ROM.

The *About Lucerne* file is available on the companion CD-ROM.

■ Mastery Assessment

Project 2-5: The Final Gallery Crawl

As director of the Graphic Design Institute, you have volunteered to coordinate your city's last-ever gallery crawl—an annual charity event that enables the public to visit several art galleries for one price. Fortunately, this year's event is almost identical to last year's crawl, so when you create a presentation for the local arts council, you can use last year's presentation as the basis for a new one.

1. OPEN the New Presentation window, then click **New from existing**. Locate and open *Gallery Crawl*.

2. In Slide Sorter view, switch slides 6 and 7.

3. In Normal view, reword the subtitle of slide 1 to read **Our last ever!**

4. View the presentation in Print Preview.

5. Print the presentation in grayscale mode.

The *Gallery Crawl* file is available on the companion CD-ROM.

6. Preview the presentation from beginning to end in Slide Show view.

7. SAVE the presentation as *Final Gallery Crawl*, then CLOSE the file.

   LEAVE PowerPoint open for the next project.

Project 2-6: The Final, Final Gallery Crawl

The *Final Gallery Crawl* file is available on the companion CD-ROM.

Having just finished your presentation for the last-ever gallery crawl, you realize that one of the museum curators uses an older version of PowerPoint. You need to save a copy of the presentation so he can use it on his computer.

1. OPEN *Final Gallery Crawl* from the data files for this lesson.

2. SAVE the presentation with the file name *Compatible Gallery Crawl* in PowerPoint 97-2003 format. CLOSE the file without making any other changes.

   CLOSE PowerPoint.

INTERNET READY

Use PowerPoint Help to access online information about presentation templates. Learn how to download new templates from Office Online, then download at least one new template to your computer.

Working with Text

3

LESSON SKILL MATRIX

SKILLS	MATRIX SKILL	SKILL NUMBER
Formatting Characters		
Choosing Fonts and Font Sizes	Format font attributes	2.2.3
Applying Font Styles and Effects	Format font attributes	2.2.3
Copying Character Formats Using the Format Painter	Use the Format Painter to format text	2.2.4
Formatting Paragraphs	Format paragraphs	2.2.6
Working with Lists	Create and format bulleted and numbered lists	2.2.5
Inserting and Formatting WordArt	Insert and format WordArt	2.2.7
Creating and Formatting Text Boxes		
Adding a Text Box to a Slide	Insert and remove text boxes	2.1.1
Resizing a Text Box	Size text boxes	2.1.2
Setting Formatting Options for a Text Box	Format text boxes	2.1.3
Applying a Quick Style to a Text Box	Apply Quick Styles from the Style Gallery	2.2.2
Aligning Text in a Text Box	Select text orientation and alignment	2.1.4
Orienting Text in a Text Box	Select text orientation and alignment	2.1.4
Setting the Margins in a Text box	Set margins	2.1.5
Setting Up Columns in a Text Box	Create columns in text boxes	2.1.6
Deleting a Text Box	Insert and remove text boxes	2.1.1

Fourth Coffee is a "boutique" company devoted to producing and distributing fine coffees and teas. As the sales manager for Fourth Coffee, you often produce and deliver presentations to your staff and managers on topics such as realizing the full profit potential of your delivery systems. Whenever you create a presentation, consider how the information appears to your viewers. If the text in your slides is difficult to read or haphazardly formatted, or if

KEY TERMS
bulleted list
fonts
Format Painter
formatting
line spacing
numbered list
Quick Style
text box
WordArt

you cram too much text into your slides, then your presentations will not be professional-looking. In this lesson, you learn some basics of text formatting, including formatting characters and paragraphs, creating and formatting lists, using WordArt to "jazz up" your text, and creating and modifying text boxes.

■ SOFTWARE ORIENTATION

Microsoft PowerPoint's Basic Text Formatting Tools

Most of PowerPoint's basic text formatting tools are found on the Home tab of the Ribbon, as shown in Figure 3-1. These are the tools you will use most often when working with text.

Figure 3-1

Basic text formatting tools

There are two groups of text formatting tools on the Ribbon: the Font group and the Paragraph group. They allow you to fine-tune the text on your slides, right down to an individual character. These groups also provide access to the Font and Paragraph dialog boxes, which give you even more control over your text's appearance.

■ Formatting Characters

THE BOTTOM LINE

All PowerPoint presentations are formatted with specific fonts, font sizes, and font attributes such as style and color. You can change the way characters look on a slide by using commands in the Font group on the Home tab or the Mini toolbar. The Format Painter can save you time by allowing you to copy formats from selected text to other text items.

Choosing Fonts and Font Sizes

You can change the font and font size at any time on your slides. The following exercise shows you how.

⊕ CHOOSE FONTS AND FONT SIZES

GET READY. Before you begin these steps, make sure that your computer is on. Log on, if necessary.

1. Start PowerPoint, if the program is not already running.
2. Locate and open *Sales Pipeline*.
3. Go to slide 2. In the first row of the table, double-click Timing. The Mini toolbar appears above the selected text.
4. Move the mouse pointer up to the Mini toolbar so you can see it better.
5. Click the Font drop-down arrow. A list of fonts appears, as shown in Figure 3-2.

CD

The *Sales Pipeline* file is available on the companion CD-ROM.

TAKE NOTE*

When you select text to change its font or font size, the Mini toolbar that appears is at first transparent.

Figure 3-2

Choosing a new font

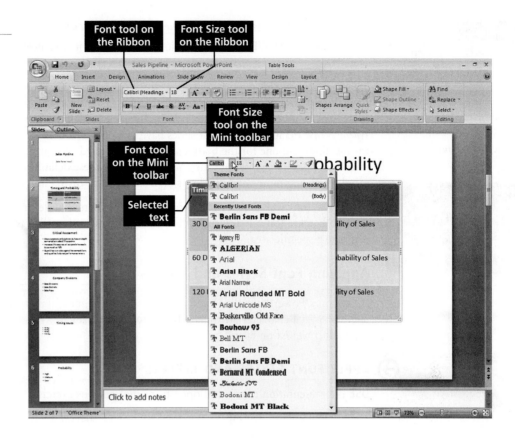

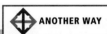 **ANOTHER WAY**

You can also select a font and font size from the Font group on the Ribbon's Home tab.

6. Click **Berlin Sans FB Demi**. PowerPoint applies the chosen font to the selected text.

7. Click the **Font Size** drop-down arrow. A list of font sizes appears.

8. Click **32**. PowerPoint applies the chosen font size to the selected text.

9. Double-click **Probability** in the top right cell of the table.

10. Select the **Berlin Sans FB Demi** font and size **32** from the Mini toolbar.

11. Click anywhere in the blank area outside the table to clear the Mini toolbar from your screen. Your slide should look like the one shown in Figure 3-3.

Figure 3-3

The new font and font size applied to the current slide

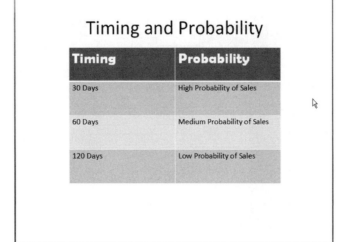

X REF

You will work with tables in Lesson 5.

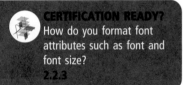

CERTIFICATION READY?
How do you format font attributes such as font and font size?
2.2.3

12. **SAVE** the presentation as *Sales Pipeline Formats*.

PAUSE. LEAVE the presentation open to use in the next exercise.

The term *formatting* refers to the appearance of text or objects on a slide. Most of PowerPoint's tools are devoted to formatting the various parts of your slides. *Fonts* are sets of characters, numbers, and symbols in a specific style or design. (Fonts are sometimes also called *typefaces*.) By default, PowerPoint slides have one or two fonts per presentation: one font for the headings and one for the body text, such as bulleted or numbered items. Each PowerPoint theme supplies its own set of fonts. You can change these default fonts as you like, but keep in mind that using more than two fonts on a slide can be distracting to the viewer.

Like fonts, font sizes are controlled by the current theme. Slide titles have a larger font size than body text. You can adjust the font size of any text on a slide to emphasize it or fit the text into a specific area.

Applying Font Styles and Effects

Text on a PowerPoint slide can be boldfaced, underlined, italicized, or formatted with other special character attributes. In the following exercise, you will apply a font style and an effect to text on a slide.

➔ APPLY FONT STYLES AND EFFECTS

USE the presentation that is still open from the previous exercise.

1. Double-click **Timing** in the top left cell of the table. The Mini toolbar appears above the selected text.
2. Point to the Mini toolbar so you can see it better.
3. Click the **Italic** button on the Mini toolbar. PowerPoint formats the selected text in italic, as shown in Figure 3-4.

Figure 3-4

Text formatted in italics

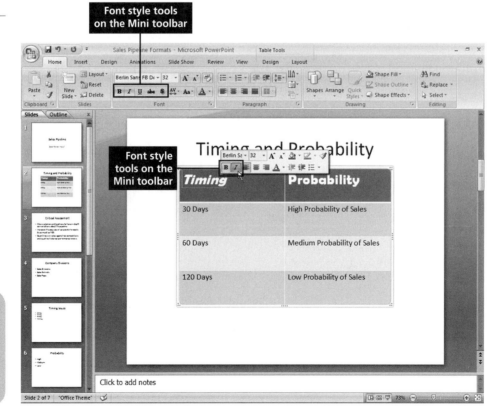

4. Double-click **Probability** in the top right cell of the table.

5. Click the **Italic** button on the Mini toolbar. PowerPoint formats the selected text in italic.

6. Double-click **Timing** in the top left cell of the table, then click the Font dialog box launcher.

7. In the Font dialog box, click the **Character Spacing** tab, as shown in Figure 3-5.

Figure 3-5

Setting the character spacing for the selected text

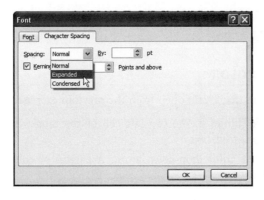

8. Click the **Spacing** drop-down arrow, click **Expanded**, then click **OK**. PowerPoint places 1 point of spacing between the letters.

9. Double-click **Probability** in the top right cell of the table, then click the **Repeat** button on the Quick Access Toolbar. PowerPoint repeats the last command you issued, applying the new character spacing to the selected text. Your slide should look like the one shown in Figure 3-6.

ANOTHER WAY

To repeat the last command you issued, press **Ctrl+Y**.

Figure 3-6

The slide with new character spacing in the table's column headings

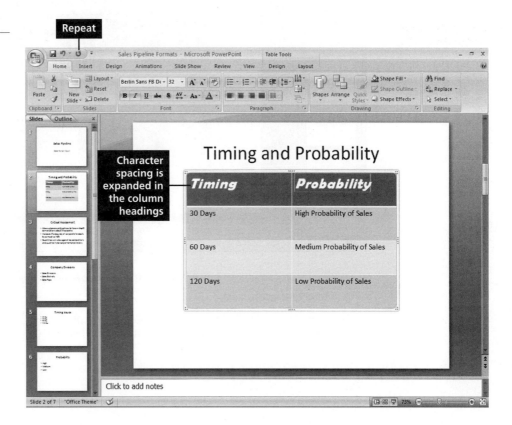

PAUSE. LEAVE the presentation open to use in the next exercise.

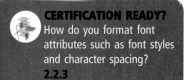

Use font styles and effects to emphasize text on a slide. Besides the standard font styles—bold, italic, and underline—PowerPoint provides strikethrough and shadow styles. You can also adjust character spacing and case to give your text a special look. To access more font effects, click the Font group's dialog box launcher to open the Font dialog box. The Font dialog box allows you to apply effects such as superscripts and subscripts, all caps, and small caps.

Changing Font Color

An easy way to change text appearance is to modify its color. Use the Font Color button in the Font group to access a palette of colors you can apply to selected text.

→ CHANGE FONT COLOR

USE the presentation that is still open from the previous exercise.

1. Double-click **Timing** in the top left cell of the table. The Mini toolbar appears above the selected text.
2. Click the **Font Color** drop-down arrow. A palette of colors appears, as shown in Figure 3-7.

Figure 3-7

Changing a font's color

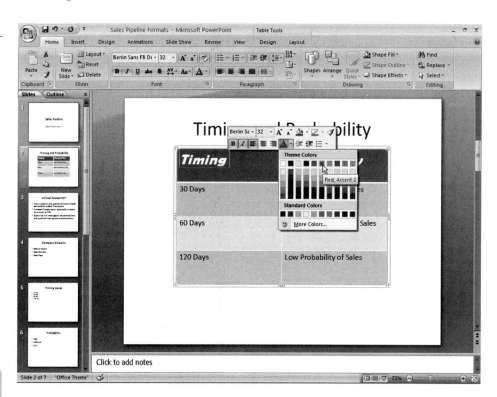

When you hold the mouse pointer over a color box, the color's name appears in a ScreenTip.

3. In the first row of theme colors, click **Red, Accent 2**. PowerPoint applies the color to the selected text.
4. Double-click **Probability** in the top right cell of the table, then apply the color **Red, Accent 2** to it. Your slide should resemble the one shown in Figure 3-8.

Figure 3-8

The slide with the new color applied

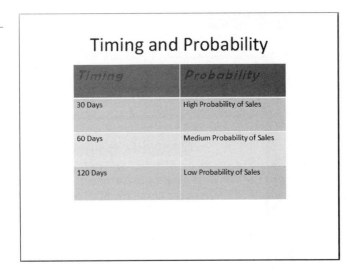

PAUSE. **LEAVE** the presentation open to use in the next exercise.

PowerPoint provides an almost limitless selection of colors that can be applied to fonts. You can select any color for your text, but it is usually best to use one of the colors provided by the presentation's theme. Each PowerPoint theme includes a set of coordinating colors, which appear in the color palette when you click the Font Color button. By selecting one of the theme's colors, you can be sure that all the font colors in your slides will look good together on the screen, making them easier to read.

If you want to use a color that is not included in the theme, select one of the Standard Colors at the bottom of the color palette or click More Colors to open the Colors dialog box. In the Colors dialog box, you can choose from dozens of standard colors or create a custom color.

Copying Character Formats with the Format Painter

As you format text in your presentations, you will want to keep similar types of text formatted the same way. Use the Format Painter to copy formatting from one character, word, phrase, or paragraph to another character, word, phrase, or paragraph.

➔ COPY CHARACTER FORMATS WITH THE FORMAT PAINTER

USE the presentation that is still open from the previous exercise.

1. Go to slide 2, if necessary.
2. Select the text in the title placeholder.
3. Change the font color to **Blue, Accent 1, Darker 25%**.
4. Click the **Bold** button in the Ribbon's Font group to apply the bold font style.
5. Click the **Shadow** button in the Font group to apply the shadow font style.
6. With the text still selected, click the **Format Painter** button in the Clipboard group.
7. Go to slide 3. Click just to the left of the first word in the title so that the placeholder border displays, hold down the mouse button, and then drag the Format Painter pointer over the title text. The title displays the same character formats you applied on slide 2, as shown in Figure 3-9.

Figure 3-9

Formatting copied to the
title of slide 3

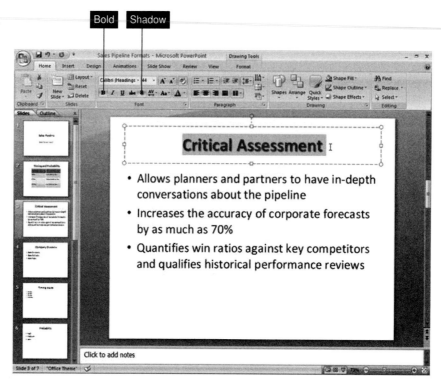

8. With the title text on slide 3 still selected, double-click the Format Painter button in the Clipboard group.

9. Go to each remaining slide and drag the Format Painter pointer over the title text.

10. Click the Format Painter in the Clipboard group to deselect it.

PAUSE. LEAVE the presentation open to use in the next exercise.

Consistency is the name of the game in a presentation. PowerPoint provides a number of tools to help you format text consistently on every slide. The **Format Painter** is one of those tools. Use it to copy formats from one text item to another on the same slide or on another slide. If you want to copy a format only once, simply click the button. To copy a format multiple times, double-click the button. Not only does this tool reduce your workload, it also ensures consistency throughout a presentation.

The Format Painter copies not only character formats but paragraph formats such as alignments and line spacing. You learn about paragraph formats in the next section.

CERTIFICATION READY?
How do you copy character formatting with the Format Painter?
2.2.4

■ Formatting Paragraphs

↓
THE BOTTOM LINE

You can change the look of paragraph text by modifying alignment or line spacing. When you apply formatting to a paragraph, all the text within that paragraph receives the same formatting.

Aligning Paragraphs

In this exercise, you change the default alignment of items in a bulleted list to customize a slide's appearance.

⊕ ALIGN PARAGRAPHS

USE the presentation that is still open from the previous exercise.

1. Go to slide 4.
2. Click in the second bulleted item (*Sales Districts*).
3. Click the **Center** button in the Ribbon's Paragraph group. PowerPoint aligns the paragraph in the center of the text box.
4. Click in the third bulleted item (*Sales Reps*).
5. Click the **Align Text Right** button in the Paragraph group. PowerPoint aligns the paragraph to the right side of the text placeholder. Your slide should look like the one shown in Figure 3-10.

Figure 3-10

Aligning paragraphs to the left, center, and right

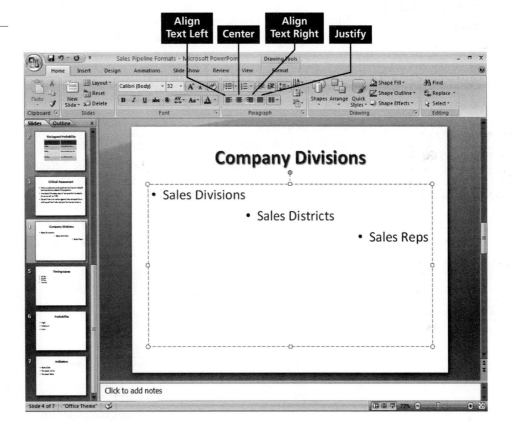

 The paragraph alignment tools also appear on the Mini toolbar when you right-click within a paragraph of text.

PAUSE. LEAVE the presentation open to use in the next exercise.

When you apply paragraph formats such as alignment, you do not have to select the entire paragraph of text. Just click anywhere in the paragraph and apply the format. The formatting applies to the entire paragraph, even if the paragraph is several lines or sentences long.

When you begin a new paragraph by pressing Enter after an existing paragraph, the new paragraph keeps the same alignment and formatting as the paragraph above it. For example, if you start a new paragraph after a paragraph aligned to the right, the new paragraph aligns to the right as well.

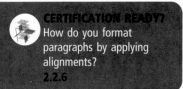

ANOTHER WAY

To left-align text, press **Ctrl+L**. To center text, press **Ctrl+E**. To right-align text, press **Ctrl+R**.

CERTIFICATION READY?
How do you format paragraphs by applying alignments?
2.2.6

PowerPoint provides four paragraph-alignment options:

- Align Text Left aligns the paragraph at the left edge of the object in which the text resides, whether the object containing the text is a placeholder, a table cell, or a text box.
- Center aligns the paragraph in the center of the object.
- Align Text Right aligns the paragraph at the right edge of the object.
- Justify distributes the paragraph of text evenly across the width of the object, if possible. PowerPoint justifies text by adding spaces between words and characters.

Setting Paragraph Line Spacing

Adjust paragraph *line spacing* to allow more or less room between lines of a paragraph. Line spacing changes can help you display text more attractively or fit more text on a slide.

SET PARAGRAPH LINE SPACING

USE the presentation that is still open from the previous exercise.

1. Go to slide 3.
2. Click in the first bulleted item (*Allows planners and partners . . .*).
3. Click the **Line Spacing** drop-down arrow in the Paragraph group. A list of line spacing options appears, as shown in Figure 3-11.

Figure 3-11

PowerPoint's Line Spacing options

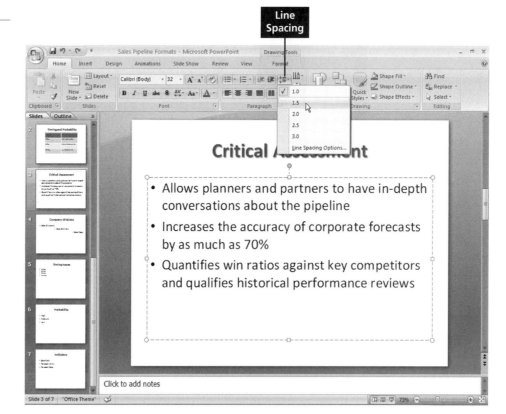

4. Select **1.5**. PowerPoint formats the paragraph's lines so they are separated by 1.5 lines of blank space.
5. Drag the mouse pointer over the first bulleted item to select the text.

TAKE NOTE★ PowerPoint enables you to specify spacing before and after paragraphs. Click the Line Spacing button's drop-down arrow and click Line Spacing Options. Set the Before and After options to the settings you desire.

6. Click the **Format Painter** button once to copy the paragraph format.

7. Drag the Format Painter pointer over the remaining two bulleted items to apply the 1.5 line spacing. Your slide should look like the one shown in Figure 3-12.

Figure 3-12

The text with different line spacing

Critical Assessment

- Allows planners and partners to have in-depth conversations about the pipeline

- Increases the accuracy of corporate forecasts by as much as 70%

- Quantifies win ratios against key competitors and qualifies historical performance reviews

8. **SAVE** the presentation and **CLOSE** it.

PAUSE. LEAVE PowerPoint open to use in the next exercise.

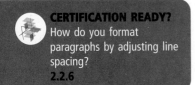

CERTIFICATION READY?
How do you format paragraphs by adjusting line spacing?
2.2.6

By default, PowerPoint formats your paragraphs so that one line of blank space lies between each paragraph and between the lines within a paragraph. Use the Line Spacing button to adjust the spacing to 1.0, 1.5, 2.0, 2.5, or 3.0. You also can use the Line Spacing Options command to display the Paragraph dialog box. With this dialog box, you can finely tune the spacing between each paragraph.

■ Working with Lists

THE BOTTOM LINE

Lists make the information on slides easy to read and remember. PowerPoint provides for several levels of bulleted lists that you can modify for a special effect. You can also create numbered lists when your slide text implies a specific order.

Creating Numbered Lists

PowerPoint enables you to create numbered lists to place your information in numeric order. Numbered lists are used for procedural steps, action items, and other information where order is required. In the following exercise, you create a numbered list from a list of items on a slide.

⊙ CREATE NUMBERED LISTS

1. **OPEN** the *Leveraging Corporate Cash* presentation.

CD

The *Leveraging Corporate Cash* file is available on the companion CD-ROM.

2. Go to slide 2.

3. Click in the first line of the text in the text placeholder (*Determine inventory turnover*).

4. Click the Numbering button in the Paragraph group. PowerPoint formats the sentence with a number 1.

5. Select the last three lines in the text placeholder.

6. Click the Numbering button. PowerPoint applies numbers 2 through 4.

 ANOTHER WAY

To number a paragraph, right-click the paragraph, then click Numbering on the shortcut menu.

7. Click outside the text placeholder to clear its border. Your slide should look like the one shown in Figure 3-13.

Figure 3-13

A numbered list

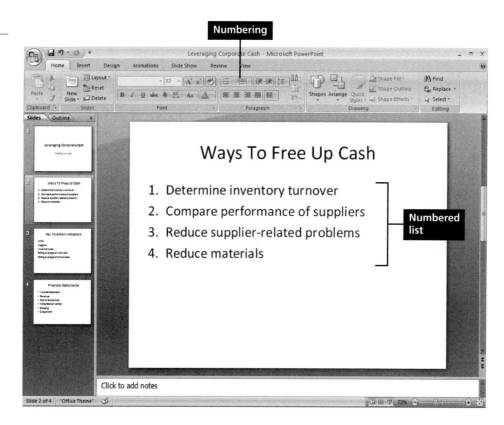

8. SAVE the presentation as *Leveraging Corporate Cash Lists*.

PAUSE. LEAVE the presentation open to use in the next exercise.

When you create a ***numbered list*** on a slide, you can continue it automatically after the last item by pressing Enter. PowerPoint automatically numbers the new paragraph with the next number in the sequence of numbers so you can continue the list uninterrupted.

By default, PowerPoint numbers items using numerals followed by periods. You can, however, change the numbering format to numerals followed by parentheses, upper- or lowercase Roman numerals, or upper- or lowercase letters. To change the numbering format, click the Numbering button's drop-down arrow and select a new format from the gallery. For more control over the numbering format, click Bullets and Numbering on the gallery to display the Bullets and Numbering dialog box. You can use this dialog box to choose what number to start the list with, change the size of the numbers, or change their color.

CERTIFICATION READY?
How do you create numbered lists?
2.2.5

Working with Bulleted Lists

Bulleted lists are the most popular way to present items on PowerPoint presentations. In fact, most of PowerPoint's text placeholders automatically format text as a bulleted list. In the following exercise, you will change the formats of a bulleted list.

→ WORK WITH BULLETED LISTS

USE the presentation that is still open from the previous exercise.

1. Go to slide 3. In this slide, the text is already set up as a bulleted list.
2. Select all of the text in the text placeholder by dragging the mouse pointer over it.
3. Click the **Bullets** drop-down arrow in the Paragraph group. PowerPoint displays a gallery of bullet styles, as shown in Figure 3-14.

Figure 3-14

Gallery of bullet styles

TAKE NOTE   If a series of paragraphs does not have bullets, you can add them by selecting the paragraphs, then clicking the Bullets button in the Paragraph group.

4. Click **Hollow Square Bullets**. PowerPoint applies the bullet style to the selected paragraphs.
5. With the text still selected, click the **Bullets** drop-down arrow again, then click **Bullets and Numbering**. The Bullets and Numbering dialog box appears, as shown in Figure 3-15.

Figure 3-15

The Bullets and Numbering dialog box

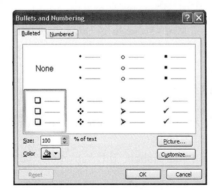

6. Select the value in the Size spin control by dragging the mouse pointer over it, then key **80**. This reduces the bullets' size to 80% of the text's size.
7. Click the **Color** drop-down arrow, then click **Blue, Accent 1**. This changes the color of the bullets.

8. Click **OK**. Your slide should look like the one shown in Figure 3-16.

Figure 3-16

The bullets with different formatting

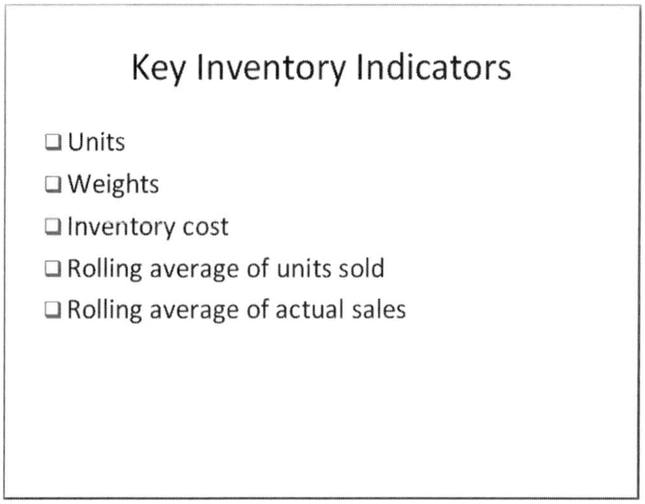

Key Inventory Indicators

❑ Units
❑ Weights
❑ Inventory cost
❑ Rolling average of units sold
❑ Rolling average of actual sales

9. **SAVE** the presentation and **CLOSE** it.

PAUSE. LEAVE PowerPoint open to use in the next exercise.

CERTIFICATION READY?
How do you create and format bulleted lists?
2.2.5

Bullets are small dots, arrows, circles, diamonds, or other graphics that appear before a short phrase or word. Each PowerPoint theme supplies bullet characters for up to nine levels of bullets, and these characters differ according to theme. When you create a ***bulleted list*** on your slide, you can continue it automatically after the last item by pressing Enter. PowerPoint automatically adds the new paragraph with a bullet.

■ Inserting and Formatting WordArt

↓
THE BOTTOM LINE

PowerPoint's WordArt feature can change standard text into flashy, eye-catching graphics. Use WordArt's formatting options to change the WordArt fill or outline color or apply special effects. You can also apply WordArt styles to any slide text to give it special emphasis.

Inserting a WordArt Graphic

In this exercise, you choose a WordArt style and then key your own text to create the graphic.

⊕ INSERT A WORDART GRAPHIC

CD

The ***Full Profit Potential*** file is available on the companion CD-ROM.

1. **OPEN** the *Full Profit Potential* presentation. Notice that the first slide has a subtitle, but no title placeholder.

2. Click the **Insert** tab on the Ribbon. This tab allows you to insert a number of different objects.

3. Click the **WordArt** button to display a gallery of WordArt styles, as shown in Figure 3-17.

Figure 3-17

Gallery of WordArt styles

4. Click the **Gradient Fill – Accent 1** WordArt style. PowerPoint displays the WordArt graphic with the sample text *Your Text Here*.
5. Key **Full Profit** to replace the sample text. Your slide should resemble Figure 3-18.

Figure 3-18

A new WordArt graphic on a slide

6. **SAVE** the presentation as *Full Profit*.

PAUSE. LEAVE the presentation open to use in the next exercise.

The ***WordArt*** feature allows you to use text to create a graphic object. WordArt graphics can add special "pizzazz" on a slide. For the best appearance, limit the number of words in the graphic.

TAKE NOTE

When you create WordArt, the information appears as text, but PowerPoint treats the object as a graphics object—a picture. However, you can search for text formatted as WordArt when using the Find tool.

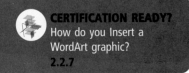

CERTIFICATION READY?
How do you Insert a WordArt graphic?
2.2.7

After you have inserted the WordArt graphic, you can format it in a number of ways. You can change the style from the WordArt gallery, you can modify the fill or the outline, or you can apply any of a number of interesting special effects. You can also modify the text of the graphic at any time. Click the graphic to open the placeholder, just as when editing a slide's title or body text, and then edit the text as desired.

Formatting a WordArt Graphic

To format a WordArt graphic, you use the tools on one of PowerPoint's contextual tabs, the Drawing Tools Format tab. In the next several exercises, you will use these tools to modify the WordArt's fill and outline and apply an effect.

→ CHANGING THE WORDART FILL COLOR

The WordArt fill color is the color you see inside the WordArt characters. You can change the fill color by using the color palette for the current theme or any other available color.

→ CHANGE THE WORDART FILL COLOR

USE the presentation that is still open from the previous exercise.

1. Select the WordArt graphic on slide 1. Note that the Drawing Tools Format tab becomes active on the Ribbon.
2. Click the **Drawing Tools Format** tab and locate the WordArt Styles group.
3. Click the **Text Fill** drop-down arrow. PowerPoint displays the Theme Colors palette as shown in Figure 3-19.

Figure 3-19

Selecting a new WordArt fill color

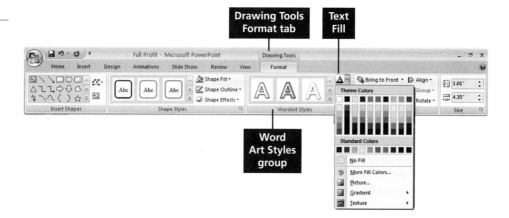

4. Click the **Blue, Accent 2, Darker 25%** theme color as the fill color. PowerPoint changes the fill of the graphic.

 **ANOTHER WAY**   You can right-click a WordArt object, select Format Text Effects, and then click Text Fill in the Format Text Effects dialog box. Click the Color button's drop-down arrow and select a fill color.

5. Click outside the graphic to clear its border. Your slide should look like the one in Figure 3-20.

Figure 3-20

The WordArt object with a new fill color

PAUSE. **LEAVE** the presentation open to use in the next exercise.

One way to fine-tune the graphic you have inserted is to change the fill color of the WordArt object. You can use any of the colors on the Theme Colors palette to make sure the object coordinates with other items in the presentation.

You can also choose from the Standard Colors palette or select another color from the Colors dialog box. To access these colors, click More Fill Colors on the Theme Colors palette to open the Colors dialog box. You can "mix" your own colors on the Custom tab or click the Standard tab to choose from a palette of premixed colors.

The Theme Colors palette gives you additional fill options. You can search for a picture that will fill the graphic characters, apply a gradient (a gradient is a gradation of several colors), or apply one of PowerPoint's default textures.

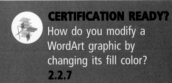

CERTIFICATION READY?
How do you modify a WordArt graphic by changing its fill color?
2.2.7

CHANGING THE WORDART OUTLINE COLOR

Most WordArt styles include a colored outline around the edges of the WordArt characters. You can change the outline color to fine-tune the graphic.

CHANGE THE WORDART OUTLINE COLOR

USE the presentation that is still open from the previous exercise.

1. Select the WordArt graphic on slide 1 if necessary.
2. Click the **Text Outline** drop-down arrow. PowerPoint displays the Theme Colors palette.
3. Click **Blue, Accent 2, Darker 50%**.

You can right-click a WordArt object, select Format Text Effects, and then click Text Outline in the Format Text Effects dialog box. Click the Color button's drop-down arrow and select an outline color.

4. Click outside the graphic to clear its border. Your slide should look like the one in Figure 3-21.

Figure 3 21

The WordArt object with a
new outline color

PAUSE. LEAVE the presentation open to use in the next exercise.

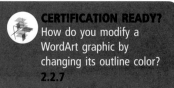

CERTIFICATION READY?
How do you modify a
WordArt graphic by
changing its outline color?
2.2.7

Just as with a WordArt object's fill color, you can fine-tune the outline color of the object.
You have the same color options as for changing a fill color. The Text Outline Theme Colors
palette also allows you to remove the outline, change its weight, or apply a dash style to the
outline.

→ APPLYING SPECIAL EFFECTS TO WORDART

You can apply special effects to your WordArt objects, such as shadows, reflections,
glows, transformations, and more.

→ APPLY SPECIAL EFFECTS TO WORDART

USE the presentation that is still open from the previous exercise.

1. Select the WordArt graphic on slide 1, if necessary.
2. Click the **Text Effects** drop-down arrow. PowerPoint displays the Text Effects menu.
3. Click **Reflection**. PowerPoint displays the reflection special effects, as shown in
   Figure 3-22.

Figure 3-22

WordArt special effects

4. Click **Tight Reflection, touching**. PowerPoint adds the reflection special effect to
   the WordArt object.
5. Click outside the graphic to clear its border.
6. Move the WordArt graphic close to the subtitle, approximately where the slide title
   would be, as shown in Figure 3-23.

Figure 3-23

A reflection special effect added to the WordArt object

PAUSE. LEAVE the presentation open to use in the next exercise.

WordArt special effects provide a way to spice up an ordinary slide. Although you should not use WordArt special effects on all your slides, you may want to look for spots in your presentations where a little artistic punch will liven up your slide show. Always consider your audience and your topic when adding special effects. For example, a presentation discussing plant closings and layoffs would not be an appropriate place for a cheerful-looking WordArt graphic.

Formatting Text with WordArt Styles

You do not have to insert a WordArt graphic to use the WordArt styles. You can apply WordArt styles to any text in a slide.

➔ FORMAT TEXT WITH WORDART STYLES

USE the presentation that is still open from the previous exercise.

1. Go to slide 2.
2. Select the slide title, *On-Time Delivery*.
3. Click the **Drawing Tools Format** tab.
4. Click the **More** button for the WordArt styles gallery to display all available styles.
5. Click the **Fill – Accent 2, Warm Matte Bevel** WordArt style.
6. Click outside the text placeholder to clear its border. Your slide should look like the one shown in Figure 3-24.

CERTIFICATION READY?
How do you modify a WordArt graphic by applying special effects?
3.3.7

Figure 3-24

Formatting text with a WordArt style

7. **SAVE** and **CLOSE** the presentation.

PAUSE. LEAVE PowerPoint open to use in the next exercise.

Applying WordArt styles to regular text in a presentation is an additional way to format the text to customize the presentation. You can use the same features you used to format the WordArt graphic to format a title or bulleted text: Text Fill, Text Outline, and Text Effects.

■ Creating and Formatting Text Boxes

THE BOTTOM LINE   You can use text boxes as containers for text or graphics. Text boxes make it easy to position content anywhere on a slide.

Adding a Text Box to a Slide

Text boxes can be used to place text on a slide anyplace you want it. In this exercise, you add a text box to a slide and then insert text into the text box.

→ ADD A TEXT BOX TO A SLIDE

The *Profit Analysis* file is available on the companion CD-ROM.

1. **OPEN** the *Profit Analysis* presentation.

2. Go to slide 1, if necessary.

3. Click the **Insert** tab on the Ribbon.

4. Click **Text Box** in the Text group. The cursor changes to a text insertion pointer.

5. Move the pointer to the right side of the slide about two-thirds of the way up.

6. Click and hold down the mouse button. Drag the mouse down and to the right to create a rectangle.

7. Release the mouse button. The rectangle changes to a text box, as shown in Figure 3-25.

Figure 3-25

Inserting a text box

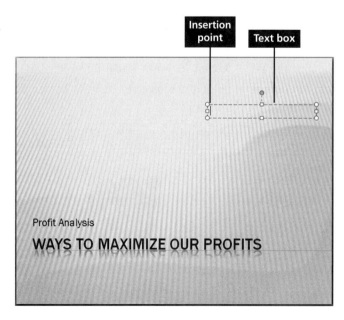

TAKE NOTE When you release the mouse button after creating a text box, the Ribbon automatically displays the Home tab once more.

8. Key **Fourth Coffee** in the text box.
9. Click outside the text box to clear its border. Your slide should look like the one shown in Figure 3-26.

Figure 3-26

A text box with text inserted

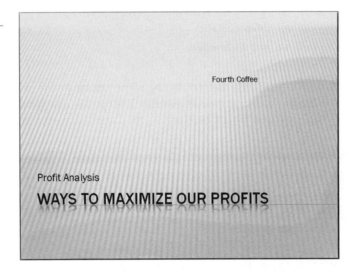

Fourth Coffee

Profit Analysis

WAYS TO MAXIMIZE OUR PROFITS

10. **SAVE** the presentation as *Profit Analysis Boxes*.

PAUSE. LEAVE the presentation open to use in the next exercise.

Although PowerPoint layouts are very flexible and provide a number of ways to insert text, you may occasionally need to insert text in a location for which there is no default placeholder. *Text boxes* are the answer in this circumstance. You can use a text box to hold a few words, an entire paragraph of text, or even several paragraphs of text.

You have two options when creating a text box. If you simply click the slide with the text box pointer, you create a text box in which text will not wrap. As you enter text, the text box expands horizontally to accommodate the text. If you want to create a text box that will contain the text in a specific area, with text wrapping from line to line, you draw a desired width with the text box pointer. When text reaches that border, it wraps to the next line.

Resizing a Text Box

Text boxes can be resized so other text boxes or objects can be added to a slide without interfering with the text box or to rearrange a text box's contents.

CERTIFICATION READY?
How do you insert a text box?
2.1.1

→ **RESIZE A TEXT BOX**

USE the presentation that is still open from the previous exercise.

1. Go to slide 2.
2. Click the **Insert** tab on the Ribbon.
3. Click **Text Box** in the Text group.
4. Drag to draw a text box under the *Divisional Breakdown* title.

5. Key the following items into the text box, placing each item on its own line:

Sales

Marketing

Purchasing

Production

Distribution

Customer Service

Human Resources

Product Development

Information Technology

Administration

6. Move the mouse pointer to the white square in the middle of the text box's right border. This is a resizing handle. The pointer changes to a double-headed arrow, as shown in Figure 3-27.

Figure 3-27

A text box with resizing handle selected

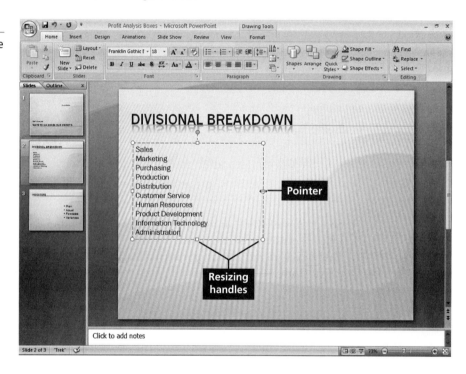

7. Click and hold down the mouse button.

> **TAKE NOTE** A text box has eight resizing handles: one in each corner and one in the middle of each side.

8. Move the mouse pointer to the left until the text box's right border is close to the text (all entries should still be on a single line).

9. Release the mouse button. The text box resizes to a smaller size. Your slide should look like the one in Figure 3-28.

Figure 3-28

The resized text box

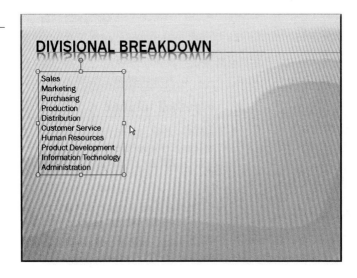

10. Click outside the text box to clear its border.

   PAUSE. LEAVE the presentation open to use in the next exercise.

If the only object you have on your slide is a text box, you do not have to resize it. However, if you plan to add other objects, such as additional text boxes, WordArt, charts, pictures, and other items, you may want to resize text boxes so they do not consume too much space on your slides.

Setting Formatting Options for a Text Box

When you add a text box to a slide, you can see it because it has a resizing border around it. However, once you deselect the text box, you cannot see the text box itself, only its contents. You can use formatting options such as a Quick Style, a fill, or a border to make the text box more visible on the slide.

 APPLYING A QUICK STYLE TO A TEXT BOX

PowerPoint's Quick Styles allow you to quickly format any text box or placeholder with a combination of fill, border, and effect formats to make the object stand out on the slide.

 APPLY A QUICK STYLE TO A TEXT BOX

USE the presentation that is still open from the previous exercise.

1. Go to slide 1.
2. Click the *Fourth Coffee* text box to select it.
3. Click the **Quick Styles** button on the Home tab to display a gallery of Quick Styles.
4. Select the **Intense Effect – Accent 6** Quick Style, the last thumbnail in the last row. Click outside the text box to clear its border. The Quick Style formatting is applied to the text box, as shown in Figure 3-29.

Figure 3-29

A Quick Style applied to a
text box

PAUSE. LEAVE the presentation open to use in the next exercise.

There are several advantages to using **Quick Styles** to format an object. Each Quick Style provides a number of formatting options that would take more time to apply separately. Quick Styles also give a professional appearance to slides. Using Quick Styles can also make it easy to format consistently throughout a presentation.

CERTIFICATION READY?
How do you apply Quick
Styles to a slide?
2.2.2

In this exercise, you applied a Quick Style to a text box, but you will find that PowerPoint also provides Quick Styles for other features such as tables, SmartArt graphics, charts, and pictures.

APPLYING FILL AND BORDER FORMATTING TO A TEXT BOX

If you want more control over formatting applied to a text box, you can use the Shape Fill and Shape Outline tools.

APPLY FILL AND BORDER FORMATTING TO A TEXT BOX

USE the presentation that is still open from the previous exercise.

1. Go to slide 2.
2. Click any item in the text box list. PowerPoint displays the text box border and sizing handles.
3. Click the **Shape Fill** drop-down arrow in the Drawing group. The Theme Colors palette for the text box fill color appears, as shown in Figure 3-30.

Figure 3-30

Choosing a color for a
text box fill

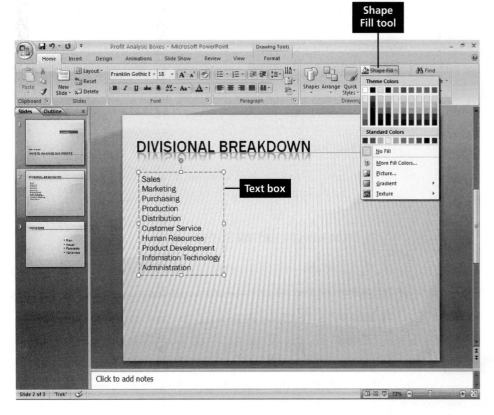

4. Click the **Light Yellow, Background 2, Darker 25%** theme color. PowerPoint formats the text box fill with this color.

5. Click the **Shape Outline** drop-down arrow. The Theme Colors palette for the text box border color appears.

6. Click the **Orange, Accent 1, Darker 25%** theme color. PowerPoint formats the text box border with this color.

7. Click the **Shape Outline** drop-down arrow again.

8. Click **Weight**. A menu with line weights appears.

9. Click **3 pt**. PowerPoint resizes the text box border to a 3-point border size.

10. Click outside the text box to clear its border. Your slide should look like the one in Figure 3-31.

Figure 3-31

The formatted text box

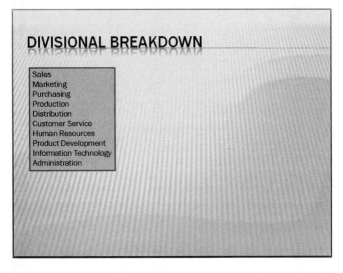

PAUSE. LEAVE the presentation open to use in the next exercise.

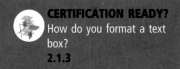

CERTIFICATION READY?
How do you format a text box?
2.1.3

Applying a fill color that contrasts with the text inside the box and with the slide background makes the text in a text box easy to read. If you choose not to use a fill in the text box (text boxes are not filled by default), consider boldfacing the text and enlarging it so that it shows up clearly against the slide background.

To make a text box stand out even more, you can apply special effects such as reflections or shadows. Use the Shape Effects button to access the different effects. You can also right-click the text box, select Format Shape, and choose options such as 3-D Format or 3-D Rotation.

Working with Text in a Text Box

You can format the text within a text box in a number of ways: adjust alignment, change text orientation, set text margins, and even set the text in columns.

⊕ ALIGNING TEXT IN A TEXT BOX

Text that appears in a text box can be aligned left, center, or right. In the following exercise, you align text to the center of the text box.

⊕ ALIGN TEXT IN A TEXT BOX

USE the presentation that is still open from the previous exercise.

1. On slide 2, click anywhere in the first line in the text box.
2. Click the **Center** button. PowerPoint aligns the text so that it is centered between the left and right border of the text box.
3. Select the rest of the text in the text box.
4. Click the **Center** button.
5. Click outside the text box to clear its border. Your slide should look like the one in Figure 3-32.

TAKE NOTE*

If you resize a text box that has centered text, the text re-centers automatically based on the final size of the text box.

Figure 3-32

Text aligned in a text box

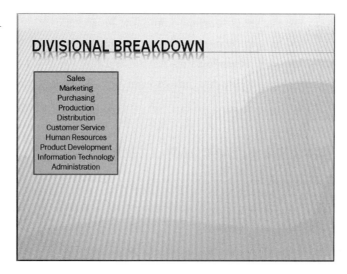

PAUSE. LEAVE the presentation open to use in the next exercise.

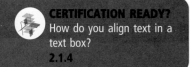

CERTIFICATION READY?
How do you align text in a text box?
2.1.4

You use the same alignment options in a text box that are available for a text placeholder: left, center, right, and justify. By default, PowerPoint aligns text in new text boxes to the left. If you align text to a different position, such as right, and then add a new paragraph by pressing Enter from that text, the new paragraph keeps the right-aligned formatting.

The Justify alignment option keeps long passages of text even on the left and right margins of a text box, similar to the way newspapers and many books align text. PowerPoint adds extra space between words if necessary to stretch a line to meet the right margin. This can result in a very "gappy" look that you can improve by adjusting font size and/or the width of the text box.

⊕ ORIENTING TEXT IN A TEXT BOX

You can change the text direction in a text box so that text runs from bottom to top or stacks one letter atop the other. This can make text in the text box more visually interesting. You can also change orientation by rotating the text box itself.

⊕ ORIENT TEXT IN A TEXT BOX

USE the presentation that is still open from the previous exercise.

1. Go to slide 1.
2. Select the *Fourth Coffee* text box.
3. Click the **Text Direction** drop-down arrow in the Paragraph group. A menu of text direction choices displays.
4. Click **Rotate all text 270°**. PowerPoint changes the orientation of the text in the text box to run from the bottom of the text box to the top, as shown in Figure 3-33.

Figure 3-33

The text in a different orientation

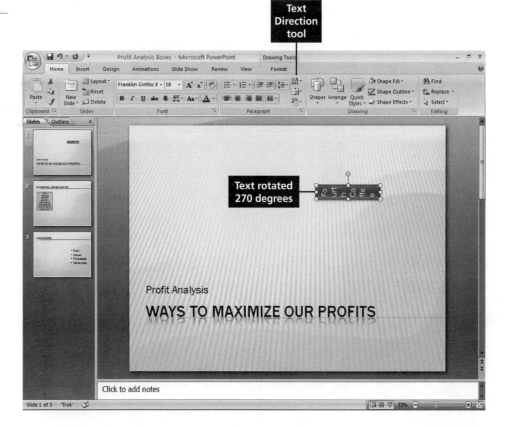

5. Resize the text box so the text appears in a single vertical column.

6. Increase the text size to 32 points. Resize the text box again if necessary so the text is on a single line.

7. Move the text box to the left side of the slide, above the subtitle.

8. Click outside the text box to clear its border. Your slide should look like the one in Figure 3-34.

Figure 3-34

The repositioned text box

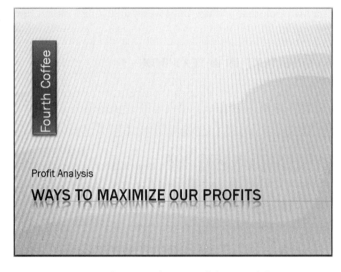

9. Draw another text box on slide 1 and key **Sales Dept.** in the text box.

10. Move the mouse to the round, green rotation handle at the top center of the text box. The mouse pointer changes to an open-ended circle with an arrow point.

11. Click and hold down the mouse button.

12. Move the mouse to the right so that the outline of the text box starts to rotate around its center, as shown in Figure 3-35.

Figure 3-35

Rotating a text box

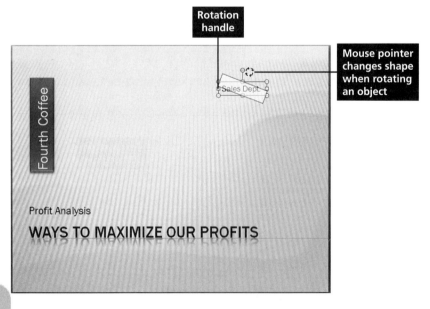

TAKE NOTE

When you drag an object's rotation handle, the mouse pointer turns into a small circle made of arrows.

13. Rotate the text box to about a 45-degree angle, then release the mouse button.

14. Move the rotated text box into the upper-right corner of the slide.

15. Click outside the text box to clear its sizing handles. Your slide should look like the one in Figure 3-36.

Figure 3-36

The rotated and repositioned text box

PAUSE. LEAVE the presentation open to use in the next exercise.

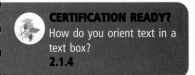

CERTIFICATION READY?
How do you orient text in a text box?
2.1.4

Orienting text boxes can be a design enhancement for your slides. For example, you might create a text box that includes your company name in it. Instead of drawing the text box horizontally on the slide, draw it so it is taller than wide and then choose one of the Text Direction button options to change text orientation. You can also rotate a text box or any placeholder for a special effect.

SETTING THE MARGINS IN A TEXT BOX

PowerPoint enables you to set the margins in a text box. Margins control the distance between the text and the outer border of the text box.

SET THE MARGINS IN A TEXT BOX

USE the presentation that is still open from the previous exercise.

1. Go to slide 3.
2. Select the text box on the right side of the slide.
3. Right-click inside the text box and click **Format Shape** on the shortcut menu. The Format Shape dialog box opens.
4. Click **Text Box** in the left pane of the Format Shape dialog box. Text box layout options appear, as shown in Figure 3-37.

Figure 3-37

Text box layout options

5. Click the ↑ in the Left spin control to set the left margin at **0.5″**.

6. Click the ↑ in the Right spin control to set the right margin at **0.5″**.

7. Click **Close**. PowerPoint applies the margin changes to the text box.

8. Select the top border of the text box and move the text box up so all of the text in the text box appears on the slide.

9. Grab the resizing handle on the left side of the text box.

10. Resize the text box so all the text appears readable on the slide. Your slide should look like the one shown in Figure 3-38.

Figure 3-38

Text box with new margins

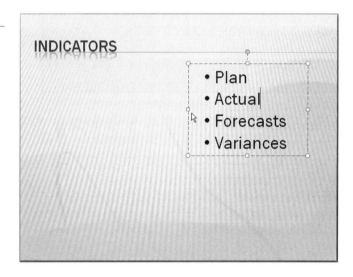

PAUSE. LEAVE the presentation open to use in the next exercise.

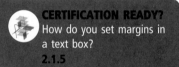

CERTIFICATION READY?
How do you set margins in a text box?
2.1.5

Resizing text box margins enables you to fine-tune text placement within a text box. For example, if you want text to appear 1 inch away from the left side of the text box, change the Left box to 1.0. You might want to do this if your slide design needs to have text align with other items placed on the slide. If you have chosen to format a text box or placeholder with a fill, increasing margins can also prevent the text from appearing to crowd the edges of the text box.

⊙ **SETTING UP COLUMNS IN A TEXT BOX**

Another way to format text in a text box is to format the text in columns. Columns can make text more readable.

⊙ **SET UP COLUMNS IN A TEXT BOX**

USE the presentation that is still open from the previous exercise.

1. Go to slide 2 and click inside the text box you formatted earlier.

2. Click the **Columns** drop-down arrow in the Paragraph group. A menu appears, as shown in Figure 3-39.

Figure 3-39

Setting up columns in a text box

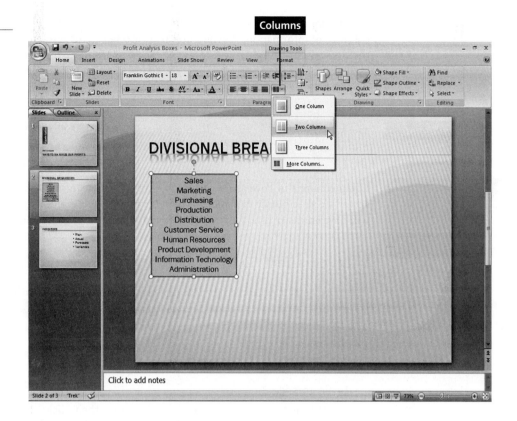

3. Click **Two Columns**. PowerPoint formats the list of items into two columns.

ANOTHER WAY   If you need two lists on a slide but do not want to use columns, create two text boxes and position them side by side.

4. Drag the right sizing handle to the right so the text box contents are readable.
5. Drag the bottom resizing handle upward until an equal number of items appear in each column. You may need to resize the right side of the text box again. Each column should contain five lines of text, as shown in Figure 3-40.

Figure 3-40

The text box with two columns

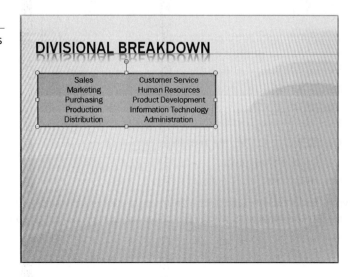

PAUSE. LEAVE the presentation open to use in the next exercise.

PowerPoint enables you to create columns in text boxes to help you format your text into columns of information. As you enter text or other items into a column, PowerPoint fills up the first column and then wraps text to the next column. You can create columns in any text box, placeholder, or shape.

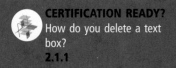

TAKE NOTE If the column choices in the Column drop-down menu do not meet your needs, click the More Columns option to display the Columns dialog box. Here you can set any number of columns and adjust the spacing between columns.

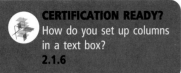

CERTIFICATION READY?
How do you set up columns in a text box?
2.1.6

Using columns in PowerPoint is a good way to present information you want to set up in lists across the slide but do not want to place in PowerPoint tables. Viewers of your presentation will have an easier time reading and remembering lists formatted into multiple columns.

Deleting a Text Box

Text boxes you no longer need on a slide can be deleted very easily in PowerPoint. In the following exercise, you delete a text box.

⊖ DELETE A TEXT BOX

USE the presentation that is still open from the previous exercise.

1. Go to slide 3.
2. Click in the text box under the slide title, then click the text box's border to select the text box, as shown in Figure 3-41. The text box's border is a solid line when selected.

Figure 3-41

Selecting a text box to delete

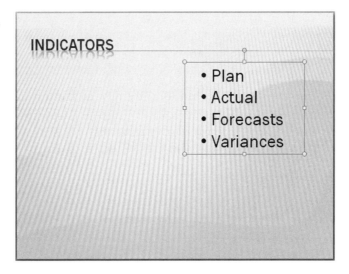

3. Press Delete. PowerPoint deletes the text box.
4. **SAVE** and **CLOSE** the presentation.
   CLOSE PowerPoint.

CERTIFICATION READY?
How do you delete a text box?
2.1.1

If you decide after you delete a text box that you want to undo your deletion, click the Undo button on the Quick Access Toolbar. You also can press Ctrl+Z to undo the deletion.

SUMMARY SKILL MATRIX

IN THIS LESSON YOU LEARNED	MATRIX SKILL	SKILL NUMBER
To format characters		
To choose fonts and font sizes	Format font attributes	2.2.3
To apply font styles and effects	Format font attributes	2.2.3
To copy character formats using the Format Painter	Use the Format Painter to format text	2.2.4
To format paragraphs	Format paragraphs	2.2.6
To create and format bulleted and numbered lists	Create and format bulleted and numbered lists	2.2.5
To insert and format WordArt	Insert and modify WordArt	2.2.7
To add a text box to a slide	Insert and remove text boxes	2.1.1
To resize text boxes	Size text boxes	2.1.2
To set formatting options for a text box	Format text boxes	2.1.3
To format text with Quick Styles	Apply Quick Styles from the Style Gallery	2.2.2
To orient text in a text box	Select text orientation and alignment	2.1.4
To set up margins in a text box	Set margins	2.1.5
To set up columns in a text box	Create columns in text boxes	2.1.6
To delete a text box	Insert and remove text boxes	2.1.1

■ Knowledge Assessment

Fill in the Blank

Fill in each blank with the term or phrase that best completes the statement.

1. A(n) _____ is a container for text or a picture on a slide.

2. A font _____ is an attribute such as boldface or italic.

3. The small white boxes on the borders of a text box are called _____.

4. You can paint the background of a text box with a(n) _____ color.

5. The border of a WordArt character is called a(n) _____.

6. A(n) _____ is sometimes also called a typeface.

7. _____ text is aligned to both the left and right margins of a text box.

8. A(n) _____ object is text in the form of a graphic.

9. You should use a(n) _____ list to show items in a specific order.

10. A(n) _____ is a small character, such as a dot or a square, that appears before an item in a list.

Multiple Choice

Circle the correct answer.

1. This PowerPoint feature lets you perform sophisticated formatting to text very quickly.
   a. Quick Styles
   b. Paragraph group
   c. Insert tab
   d. Line Spacing

2. You can select fonts and font sizes from the Ribbon or the _____.
   a. Quick Access Toolbar
   b. Format Painter
   c. Mini toolbar
   d. Shape Outline gallery

3. Which of the following is not a standard paragraph-alignment option?
   a. Left
   b. Center
   c. Right
   d. Under

4. Text attributes such as superscript and all caps are called _____.
   a. fonts
   b. effects
   c. bullets
   d. points

5. Most of PowerPoint's text placeholders automatically format text as a(n) _____ list.
   a. numbered
   b. bulleted
   c. sorted
   d. itemized

6. Each PowerPoint theme supplies bullet characters for up to _____ levels of bullets.
   a. 3
   b. 5
   c. 7
   d. 9

7. The characters in a WordArt graphic include _____.
   a. an outline and a fill
   b. a bullet
   c. a shape and a shadow
   d. boldface and underlining

8. To apply a WordArt style to existing text on a slide, you must first _____.
   a. format the text with a Quick Style
   b. insert a text box
   c. select the text
   d. change the text's alignment

9. If you simply click the slide with the text box pointer, you create a text box in which text will not _____.

   a. appear
   b. fit
   c. wrap
   d. align

10. When you orient the text in a text box, you are changing the text's _____.

   a. alignment
   b. direction
   c. size
   d. font

■ Competency Assessment

Project 3-1: Blended Coffees

As director of marketing for Fourth Coffee, you have prepared a product brochure for new company employees. This year's brochure includes a new page of refreshments that you need to format. You will use Quick Styles to format the title and text placeholders.

GET READY. Launch PowerPoint if it is not already running.

The **Coffee Products** file is available on the companion CD-ROM.

1. OPEN the *Coffee Products* presentation.
2. Go to slide 2 and click anywhere in the slide title.
3. Click the **Quick Styles** button to display the Quick Styles gallery.
4. Click the **Moderate Effect – Accent 1** style.
5. Click in any of the bulleted product items.
6. Click the **Quick Styles** button.
7. Click the **Subtle Effect – Accent 1** style.
8. SAVE the presentation as *Coffee Products Brochure* and CLOSE the file.
   LEAVE PowerPoint open for the next project.

Project 3-2: Typecasting with Typefaces

As an account representative for the Graphic Design Institute, you are responsible for securing sales leads for your company's print and poster division. One way to do this is to send out a promotional flyer using a slide from a company PowerPoint presentation. As you select the slide, you notice that the fonts are not appropriate for your flyer. You need to modify both the font and size of the slide's text.

The **Graphic Designs** file is available on the companion CD-ROM.

1. OPEN the *Graphic Designs* presentation.
2. On slide 1, select all the text under the three photographs.
3. Click the **Font** drop-down arrow.
4. Click **Brush Script MT**.
5. Click the **Font Size** drop-down arrow.
6. Click **32**.
7. Click anywhere in the second paragraph (*Graphic Design Institute*).
8. Click the **Center** button in the Paragraph group.
9. Select the first paragraph of text, then click the **Format Painter** in the Clipboard group.

10. Go to slide 2, then drag the Format Painter pointer over the text on the right side of the slide.

11. **SAVE** the presentation as *Graphic Designs Final* and **CLOSE** the file.

    LEAVE PowerPoint open for the next project.

■ Proficiency Assessment

Project 3-3: Destinations

As the owner and operator of Margie's Travel, you are involved with many aspects of sales, marketing, customer service, and new products and services. Today you want to format the text in a slide presentation that includes new European destinations.

The *New Destinations* file is available on the companion CD-ROM.

1. **OPEN** the *New Destinations* presentation.

2. Go to slide 2 and select the slide's title text. Click the **Bold** button to make the title boldface.

3. Select all the text in the bulleted list. Click the **Align Text Left** button to align the list along the left side of the text placeholder.

4. With the list still selected, open the Bullets and Numbering dialog box. Change the bullets' color to **Orange, Accent 2**, then resize the bullets so they are 90% of the text's size.

5. Click the **Font Color** drop-down arrow, then change the list's font color to **Dark Green, Background 2, Lighter 80%**.

6. Click **Text Box** on the Insert tab, then click below the picture on the slide to create a nonwrapping text box.

7. In the text box, key **Companion Flies Free until Jan. 1!**

8. Click the **Quick Styles** button and apply the **Colored Outline – Accent 1** Quick Style to the text box.

9. **SAVE** the presentation as *New Destinations Final* and **CLOSE** the file.

    LEAVE PowerPoint open for the next project.

Project 3-4: Business To Business Imports

You are the lone marketing research person in your company, World Wide Importers. You often find exciting and potentially highly profitable new products that go overlooked by some of the senior staff. You need to draw attention to these products, and PowerPoint can help. Create a short presentation that uses WordArt to jazz up your presentation. This presentation will focus on precision equipment your company can start importing.

The *World Wide Importers* file is available on the companion CD-ROM.

1. **OPEN** the *World Wide Importers* presentation.

2. With slide 1 on the screen, open the WordArt gallery and select **Gradient Fill - Accent 1, Outline - White, Glow – Accent 2**.

3. In the WordArt text box that appears, key **World Wide Importers**. Reposition the text box so it is just above the subtitle and centered between the left and right edges of the slide.

4. In the WordArt Styles group, open the Text Fill color palette and click **Aqua, Accent 1, Darker 25%**.

5. Open the Text Effects menu and select the **Cool Slant** bevel effect.

6. Go to slide 2 and select all the text in the bulleted list.

7. Change the font size to **24**, then change the line spacing to **1.5**.

8. Click the **Numbering** button to convert the list into a numbered list.

9. Go to slide 3. Insert a text box under the slide's title. Key the following items into the text box, putting each item on its own line:

   Digital controls

   Heat sensors

   Laser guides

   Light sensors

   Motion detectors

   Pressure monitors

   Regulators

   Timing systems

10. Select all the text in the text box and change the font size to 24.

11. Open the Quick Styles gallery and click **Colored Fill – Accent 4**.

12. Click the **Columns** button, then click **Two Columns**.

13. Resize the text box by dragging its sizing handles, as needed, so that four items appear in each column within the text box.

14. **SAVE** the presentation as *World Wide Importers Final* and **CLOSE** the file.

    LEAVE PowerPoint open for the next project.

■ Mastery Assessment

Project 3-5: Pop Quiz

As an instructor at the School of Fine Art, you decide to use a slide show to give beginning students the first pop quiz on art history. You need to finish the presentation by formatting the text and removing some unneeded text boxes.

The *Art History* file is available on the companion CD-ROM.

1. **OPEN** the *Art History* presentation.

2. On slides 2, 3, and 4, do each of the following:

   a. Format the slide's title with the **Intense Effect – Dark 1 Quick Style**.

   b. Convert the bulleted list of answers into a numbered list.

   c. Delete the text box (containing the correct answer) at the bottom of the slide.

3. **SAVE** the presentation as *Art History Final* and **CLOSE** the file.

   LEAVE PowerPoint open for the next project.

Project 3-6: Graphic Design Drafts

As the manager of the account representative that prepared the Graphic Designs slide, you want to put a few finishing touches on the slide before it is published. To protect against someone inadvertently printing the slide, you need to add a text box across the entire slide that announces the slide as a "Draft."

The *Graphic Designs Final* file is available on the companion CD-ROM.

1. **OPEN** the *Graphic Designs Final* presentation you completed in Project 3-2.

2. **SAVE** the presentation as *Graphic Designs Draft*.

3. Add a text box to the slide.

4. Key the word **DRAFT** into the text box.

5. Rotate the text box at a 45 degree angle across the center photo on the slide.

6. Enlarge the text to **88** points. Resize the text box as needed by dragging its sizing handles so the text fits properly inside the box.

7. **SAVE** and **CLOSE** the presentation.

   CLOSE PowerPoint.

INTERNET READY

Launch your browser and visit the Microsoft Web site at http://www.microsoft.com. On the Microsoft home page, click in the Search box, key the word *fonts*, then click the Search button. Look for pages on the Microsoft site that offer information about fonts; read the information to learn about how fonts are created and to find tips for using fonts wisely in your documents and presentations.

Designing a Presentation

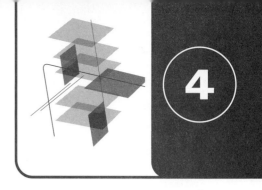

4

LESSON SKILL MATRIX

SKILLS	MATRIX SKILL	SKILL NUMBER
Formatting Presentations with Themes		
Changing Slide Backgrounds		
Changing a Slide Layout		
Inserting a Date, Footer, and Slide Numbers		
Linking to Web Pages and Other Programs		
Adding a Hyperlink to a Slide	Insert hyperlinks	2.3.3
Setting Up Slide Transitions		
Applying a Transition	Add, change, and remove transitions between slides	1.4.2
Modifying a Transition	Add, change, and remove transitions between slides	1.4.2
Animating Your Slides		
Using Built-In Animations	Apply built-in animations	2.4.1
Modifying an Animation	Modify animations	2.4.2
Creating a Customized Animation	Create custom animations	2.4.3
Customizing Slide Masters		
Applying a Theme to a Slide Master	Apply themes to slide masters	1.2.1
Changing a Slide Master's Background	Format slide master backgrounds	1.2.2
Adding New Elements to a Slide Master	Add elements to slide masters	1.3

KEY TERMS
action
animation
footer
header
slide master
slide transition
target

Southridge Video is a small company that offers video services to the community, such as videography for special events, video editing services, and duplication and conversion services. As a sales representative for Southridge Video, you often present information on the company to those who are considering the use of professional-level video services. In this lesson, you will add design elements to a simple presentation to polish and improve its appearance. Themes, animations, and transitions provide visual interest that will convince new clients of your company's commitment to quality. You will also learn how to customize slide masters to make global changes to a presentation.

SOFTWARE ORIENTATION

Microsoft PowerPoint's Themes Gallery

PowerPoint's Themes gallery offers 20 unique designs you can apply to presentations to format the slides with colors, fonts, effects, and backgrounds. Figure 4-1 shows the Themes gallery.

Figure 4-1

The Themes gallery

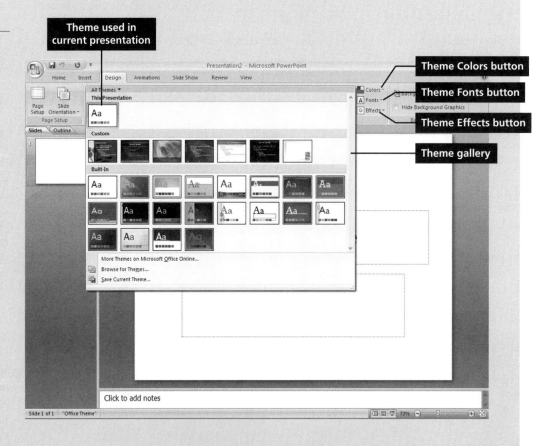

Use PowerPoint's built-in themes to give your presentation a polished, professional look without a lot of trial and error. Like Quick Styles, themes are designed to provide an immediate visual impact to a presentation.

■ Formatting Presentations with Themes

Themes are new in PowerPoint 2007. Use a theme to quickly apply a unified set of colors, fonts, and effects to one or more slides in a presentation. You can modify a theme as desired to customize it for a particular presentation.

Applying a Theme to a Presentation

Select a theme from the Themes gallery to change the default "blank" formatting into a more visually striking slide show.

⊕ **APPLY A THEME TO A PRESENTATION**

GET READY. Before you begin these steps, make sure that your computer is on. Log on, if necessary.

1. Start PowerPoint, if the program is not already running.
2. Locate and open the *Special Events* presentation.
3. Click the **Design** tab and then click the **More** button in the Themes group. PowerPoint's available themes display in the Themes gallery, as shown in Figure 4-2.

The *Special Events* file is available on the companion CD-ROM.

Figure 4-2

The Themes gallery

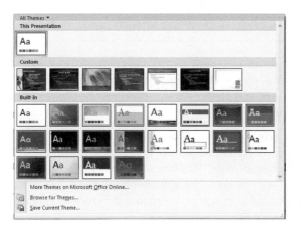

TAKE NOTE

The theme names are in alphabetical order in the gallery.

4. Point to any of the themes in the gallery. Notice that a ScreenTip displays the theme's name and the theme formats are instantly applied to the slide behind the gallery.
5. Point to the **Origin** theme to see its formats applied to the active slide, and then click the theme to apply it.
6. Scroll through the slides to see how the theme has supplied new colors, fonts, bullet symbols, and layouts. Slide 1 should resemble Figure 4-3.

Figure 4-3

Origin theme applied to slides

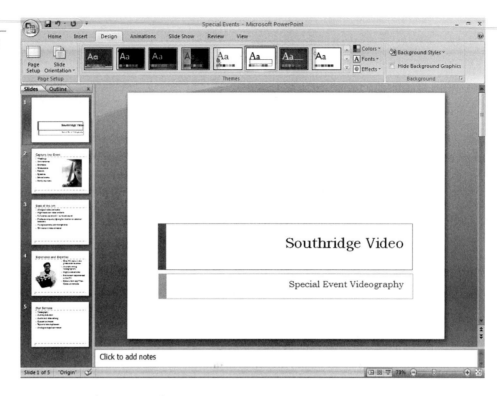

7. **SAVE** the presentation as *Special Events Final*.

PAUSE. LEAVE the presentation open to use in the next exercise.

A PowerPoint theme includes a set of colors designed to work well together, a set of fonts (one for headings and one for body text), special effects that can be applied to objects such as pictures or shapes, and often a graphic background. The theme also controls the layout of placeholders on each slide.

PowerPoint makes it easy to see how a theme will look on your slides by offering a *live preview*. As you move the mouse pointer over each theme in the gallery, that theme's formats display on the current slide. This formatting feature takes a great deal of guesswork out of the design process—if you don't like a theme's appearance, just move the pointer to a different theme or click outside the gallery to restore the previous appearance.

Clicking a theme applies it to all slides in a presentation. You can also apply a theme to a single slide or a selection of slides by making the selection, right-clicking the theme, and choosing Apply to Selected Slides. You can save any presentation you have customized as a new theme. Your custom themes display in the Custom area of the Themes gallery.

TAKE NOTE

The name of the current theme displays on the status bar to the right of the slide number information.

Changing Theme Colors

You can change theme colors by applying the colors of another theme or by creating a new theme color scheme.

⊕ **CHANGE THEME COLORS**

USE the presentation that is still open from the previous exercise.

1. Click the **Theme Colors** button in the Themes group. A gallery displays showing color palettes for all available themes.

2. Move the pointer over some of the color palettes to see the live preview of those colors on the current slide.

3. Click the **Aspect** theme color palette. The new colors are applied to the presentation, as shown in Figure 4-4.

Figure 4-4

The Aspect theme colors applied to all slides

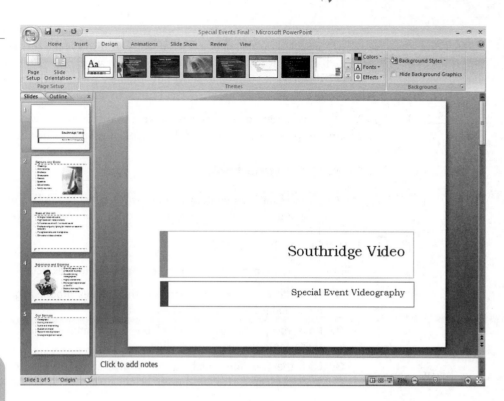

TAKE NOTE

Color palettes and font combinations are identified by theme name to make it easy to select them.

Figure 4-5

The Create New Theme Colors dialog box

4. Click the **Theme Colors** button again, then click **Create New Theme Colors** at the bottom of the gallery. The dialog box shown in Figure 4-5 opens to allow you to replace colors in the current color palette.

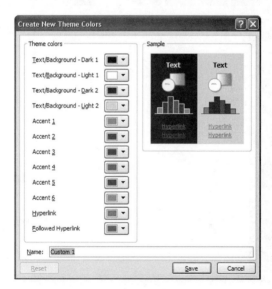

5. Click the drop-down arrow next to the light green color designated for Hyperlinks.
6. Click **Background 2, Lighter 25%** on the Theme Colors palette to change the color for hyperlinks to a medium gray.
7. Select the text in the **Name** box and key **Southridge** in its place. Click **Save** to save the new color palette.

   PAUSE. LEAVE the presentation open to use in the next exercise.

Although PowerPoint supplies specific colors for a theme, you do not have to use those colors if you prefer the colors of another theme. When you apply the colors from another theme, your current theme layout remains the same—only the colors of text and other elements change.

To create a unique appearance, you can choose new colors for theme elements in the Create New Theme Colors dialog box. This dialog box displays the theme's color palette and shows you what element each color applies to. A preview area shows the colors in use; as you change colors, the preview changes to show how the new colors work together. If you don't like the choices you have made, use the Reset button to restore the default colors.

You can save a new color scheme to make it available for use with any theme. Saved color schemes display at the top of the Theme Colors gallery in the Custom section.

Changing Theme Fonts

Each theme supplies a combination of two fonts to be applied to headings and text. You can select another set of theme fonts or create your own new combination.

⊕ CHANGE THEME FONTS

USE the presentation that is still open from the previous exercise.

1. Click the **Theme Fonts** button in the Themes group. A gallery displays showing font combinations for all available themes.

2. Move the pointer over some of the font combinations to see the live preview of those fonts on the current slide.

3. Click the **Trek** font combination to give a crisper look to the slide text. The new fonts are applied to the presentation, as shown in Figure 4-6.

Figure 4-6

New fonts change the slides' appearance

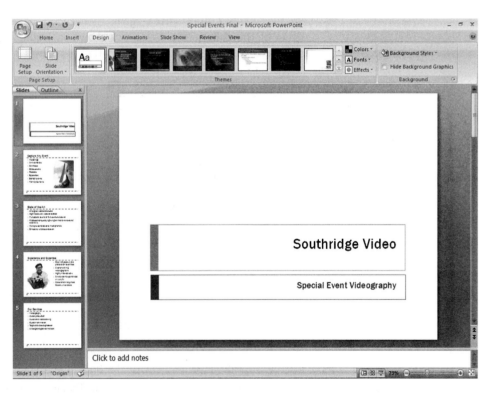

PAUSE. Leave the presentation open to use in the next exercise.

PowerPoint supplies a wide variety of font combinations to allow you to choose among traditional serif fonts and contemporary sans serif fonts. The choice you make depends a great deal on the subject of your presentation and the impression you are trying to convey with your slides.

As with theme colors, you can select your own theme fonts and save them to be available to apply to any theme. Click Create New Theme Fonts at the bottom of the Theme Fonts gallery, select a heading font and body font, and then save the combination with a new name.

■ Changing Slide Backgrounds

THE BOTTOM LINE Themes provide a default background for all slides formatted with that theme. To customize a theme or draw attention to one or more slides, apply a different background.

Selecting a Theme Background

Use the Background Styles gallery to quickly apply a different background based on theme colors. You can apply a background to one or more selected slides or to all slides in the presentation.

⊕ SELECT A THEME BACKGROUND

USE the presentation that is still open from the previous exercise.

1. Go to slide 1, if necessary.
2. Click the **Background Styles** button in the Background group. A gallery displays as shown in Figure 4-7, showing 12 background styles created using the theme's designated background colors.

Figure 4-7

Background Styles gallery

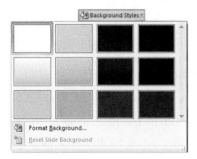

TAKE NOTE Rest the pointer on a background style to see its name and preview it on the current slide.

3. Right-click **Style 6**, then click **Apply to Selected Slides**. The background style is applied to slide 1 only.

    PAUSE. LEAVE the presentation open to use in the next exercise.

The Background Styles gallery allows you to choose from plain light or dark backgrounds and gradient backgrounds that gradually change from light to dark. Background colors are determined by the theme. Some background styles include graphic effects such as fine lines or textures over the entire background.

The area of the slide that is considered to be background can change depending on the theme. For example, the Aspect theme displays a shadowed graphic text box on top of the background, so the background displays as only a narrow border around some slide layouts.

Applying a Textured Background

Theme backgrounds are usually simple colors or color gradients. You can add more visual interest to a slide by changing the background to show a texture or even a picture.

⊙ APPLY A TEXTURED BACKGROUND

USE the presentation that is still open from the previous exercise.

1. With slide 1 still active, click the **Background Styles** button, then click **Format Background** at the bottom of the gallery. The Format Background dialog box opens, as shown in Figure 4-8.

Figure 4-8

The Format Background dialog box

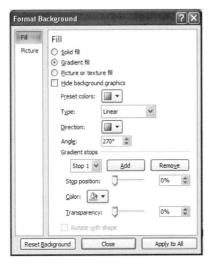

 **ANOTHER WAY**

Display the Format Background dialog box by right-clicking any blank area of the slide background and then clicking Format Background from the shortcut menu. Or, click the Background group's dialog box launcher.

2. Click **Picture or texture fill** in the right pane of the dialog box.
3. Click the **Texture** drop-down arrow to display a gallery of textures, as shown in Figure 4-9.

Figure 4-9

Texture gallery

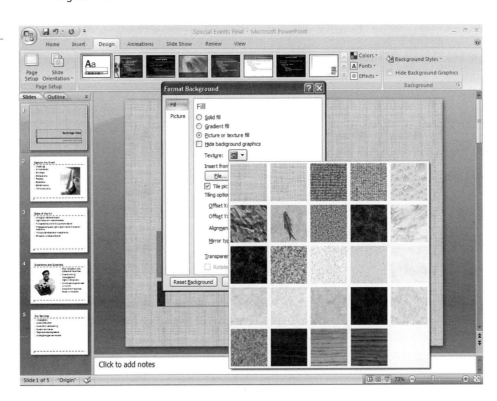

4. Click the **Stationery** texture, the fourth thumbnail in the first column, then click **Close**. The new texture gives slide 1 a brighter, warmer look.

PAUSE. LEAVE the presentation open to use in the next exercise.

Use the Format Background dialog box to create and modify any background, even a default theme background. You can apply a solid color or gradient fill, or select a picture or texture for the background. Options for each of these fill types allow you to modify the fill to suit your needs.

For any background choice, you can increase transparency to "wash out" the background so it doesn't overwhelm your text. For a gradient fill background, you can adjust the gradient by adding or removing colors. For a picture fill background, you can choose where to position a picture on the slide. For a texture, you can choose whether or not to tile the texture—position multiple copies of the texture over the slide background—or stretch the texture file over the whole slide.

By default, a new slide background created in this dialog box applies only to the current slide. Click the Apply to All button to apply the background to the entire presentation.

■ Working with Different Layouts

THE BOTTOM LINE

Slide layouts control the position of text and objects on a slide. Select a layout according to the content you need to add to it. If your current layout does not present information as you want it, you can change the layout.

⊕ WORK WITH A DIFFERENT SLIDE LAYOUT

USE the presentation that is still open from the previous exercise.

1. Click the **Home** tab on the Ribbon.

2. Go to slide 5 and click **New Slide** in the Slides group. PowerPoint adds a new slide with the same layout as slide 5, Title and Content.

3. Key the title **Contact Information**.

4. Key the following information in the text placeholder:

Address

457 Gray Road

North Hills, OH 45678

Phone

(513) 555-6543

Fax

(513) 555-5432

5. Turn off bullet formatting for the subordinate bullet items (the street address, phone number, and fax number). Your slide should look like Figure 4-10.

Figure 4-10

Add contact information
to the slide

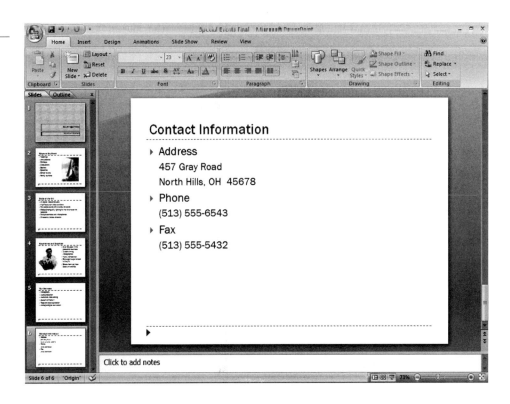

6. To make it easy to add an e-mail and Web site address in a separate placeholder, change the slide layout: Click the **Layout** button to display the slide layout gallery shown in Figure 4-11.

Figure 4-11

Slide layout gallery

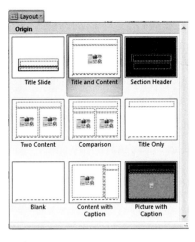

7. Click **Two Content** to change the layout to two side-by-side content placeholders.
8. In the second placeholder, key the following information:

   E-mail

   sales@southridgevideo.com

TAKE NOTE If you press the spacebar after keying an e-mail or Web address, PowerPoint automatically formats the text as a hyperlink.

9. Below the e-mail address, key the following information:

Web site

www.southridgevideo.com

When you press **Enter** at the end of the Web address, PowerPoint formats the address as a hyperlink (formatting the address as gray, underlined text). Click the Undo button immediately to undo the formatting. You will learn how to insert an actual hyperlink into a slide later in this lesson.

10. Turn off the bullets for the subordinate e-mail address and Web address. Your slide should look similar to Figure 4-12.

Figure 4-12

E-mail and Web addresses added to the slide

PAUSE. LEAVE the presentation open to use in the next exercise.

If you have applied a theme, the slide layout gallery shows available layouts with theme formats. Generally, several of the available layouts show the darker slide background supplied by the theme, which can add variety to a presentation while still coordinating with colors shown on other slides. If you have applied more than one theme to a presentation, the slide layout gallery shows available layouts from all themes so you can pick and choose among a greater variety of layout options.

All of PowerPoint's built-in themes offer a choice of nine layouts. PowerPoint's special purpose templates, however, may offer additional layouts required by the template's subject.

■ Inserting a Date, Footer, and Slide Numbers

THE BOTTOM LINE

Adding a date, footer, and slide numbers to a presentation can help you identify and organize slides. In this exercise, you learn how to apply these useful elements to one or more slides.

⊕ INSERT A DATE, FOOTER, AND SLIDE NUMBERS

USE the presentation that is still open from the previous exercise.

1. Click the **Insert** tab, and then click the **Header & Footer** button. The Header and Footer dialog box opens, as shown in Figure 4-13.

Figure 4 13

Header and Footer dialog box

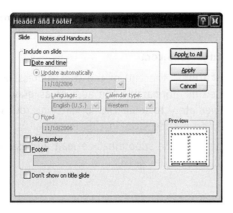

ANOTHER WAY

You can also open the Header and Footer dialog box by clicking the Date & Time button or the Slide Number button.

2. Click the **Date and time** check box, and then click **Update automatically** if necessary.

3. Click the **Slide number** check box.

4. Click the **Footer** check box and then key **Special Events** in the text box below the check box.

5. Click the **Don't show on title slide** check box.

6. Click **Apply to All** to apply the date, footer, and slide number to all slides except the title slide. Your slide 6 should look similar to Figure 4-14.

Figure 4-14

Slide number, footer, and date on a slide

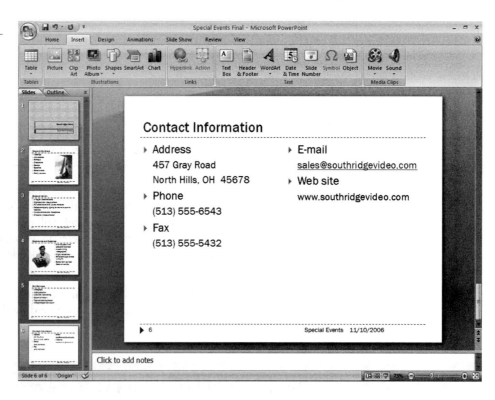

PAUSE. LEAVE the presentation open to use in the next exercise.

A *footer* is text that repeats at the bottom of each slide in a presentation. Use a footer to record the slide title, company name, or other important information that you want the audience to keep in mind as they view the slides.

You have two choices when inserting a date: A date that automatically updates changes to the current date each time the presentation is opened. A fixed date stays the same until you decide to change it. If it is important to indicate when slides were created or presented, use a fixed date.

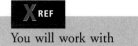

You will work with handouts in Lesson 10.

You may have noticed that the Header and Footer dialog box has another tab, the Header tab. When you create notes pages and handouts, you can specify a *header* to appear at the top of every page. You can also create footers for notes pages and handouts.

■ Linking to Web Pages and Other Programs

THE BOTTOM LINE

You can set up links on slides that allow you to jump from one slide to another or from a slide to a Web page. Action buttons allow you to quickly move from slide to slide, play sounds, or even run other programs. Links and action buttons contribute an element of interactivity to a presentation.

Adding a Hyperlink to a Slide

Use the Insert Hyperlink dialog box to set up links between slides or from slides to other targets.

 ADD A HYPERLINK TO A SLIDE

USE the presentation that is still open from the previous exercise.

1. Go to slide 6, if necessary, and select the Web site address (*www.southridgevideo.com*).
2. Click the **Hyperlink** button on the Insert tab. The Insert Hyperlink dialog box opens, as shown in Figure 4-15.

Figure 4-15

Insert Hyperlink dialog box

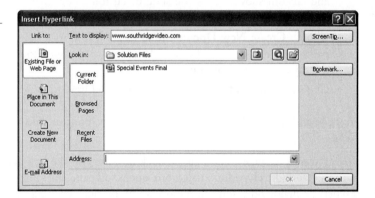

TAKE NOTE

If www.southridgevideo.com was already underlined when you selected it, the Edit Hyperlink dialog box will open instead.

3. Click in the **Address** box and key **http://www.southridgevideo.com** as the target of the link text.
4. Click **OK**. The Web site address is formatted with the theme's hyperlink color and an underline, as shown in Figure 4-16.

Figure 4-16

Text formatted as a hyperlink

PAUSE. LEAVE the presentation open to use in the next exercise.

You can create links to a number of different types of **targets** using the Insert Hyperlink dialog box. The target is the page, file, or slide that opens when you click a link.

- Choose **Existing File or Web Page** to link to any Web page or any file on your system or network. Use the Look in box, the Browse the Web button, or the Browse File button to locate the desired page or file, or type the URL or path in the Address box.
- Choose **Place in This Document** to display a list of the current presentation's slides and custom shows. Click the slide or custom show that you want to display when the link is clicked.
- Choose **Create New Document** to create a link to a new document. You supply the path and the name for the new document and then choose whether to add content to the document now or later.
- Choose **E-mail Address** to key an e-mail address to which you want to link.

You can add hyperlinks to a slide in Normal view, but the links will work only in Slide Show view.

If you need to change a link's target, click anywhere in the link and then click the Hyperlink button. The Edit Hyperlink dialog box opens, offering the same functionality as the Insert Hyperlink dialog box. You can remove a link by right-clicking the link and selecting Remove Hyperlink from the shortcut menu.

CERTIFICATION READY?
How do you insert a hyperlink?
2.3.3

Adding an Action to a Slide

Use **actions** to perform tasks such as jumping to a new slide or starting a different program. Actions can be applied to text or shapes such as buttons.

⊕ ADD AN ACTION TO A SLIDE

USE the presentation that is still open from the previous exercise.

1. Go to slide 5.
2. Click the **Shapes** button on the Insert tab to display a gallery of drawing shapes.
3. Click the **Action Button: Information** shape in the middle of the last row of shapes, as shown in Figure 4-17.

ANOTHER WAY

The Shapes button is also available on the Home tab.

Figure 4-17

Select the Information action button shape

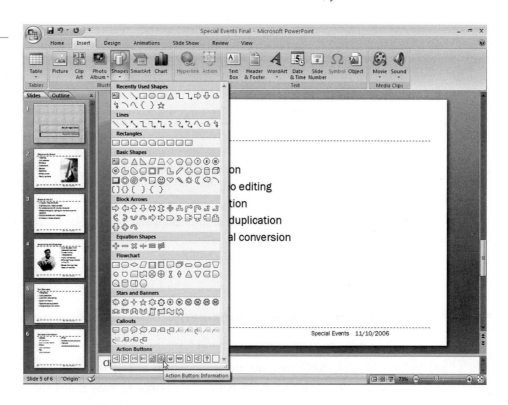

The *Service Fees* file is available on the companion CD-ROM.

4. The pointer changes to a crosshair. Use the crosshair to draw a button shape near the bottom of the slide. As soon as you release the mouse button, the Action Settings dialog box opens.

5. Click **Hyperlink to** and then click the drop-down arrow of the box that displays *Next Slide*.

6. Scroll to the bottom of the list of possible link targets and click **Other File**. The Hyperlink to Other File dialog box opens.

7. Navigate to the data files for this lesson, click the *Service Fees* file, and then click **OK**.

8. Click **OK** again to close the Action Settings dialog box. Your slide should look similar to Figure 4-18.

Figure 4-18

Action button on slide 5

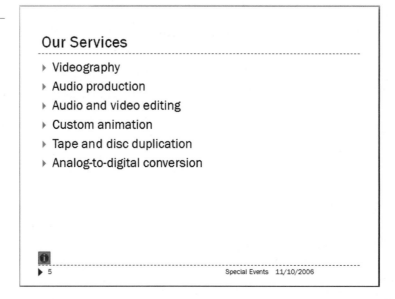

PAUSE. **LEAVE** the presentation open to use in the next exercise.

The Action Settings dialog box has two tabs that contain identical options. The default tab, Mouse Click, offers actions that will occur when you click the mouse pointer on the action item, such as the action button you drew in this exercise. The Mouse Over tab offers actions that will occur when you move the mouse pointer over the action item. It is therefore possible to attach two different actions to the same item. For example, you can specify that an action button will play a sound if you rest the mouse pointer on it and display a new slide if you click it.

Besides allowing you to set up links to specific slides or files, you can use action settings to run a particular program, run a macro, or perform an action with an object such as an embedded Excel worksheet. You can also play a sound from a list of default sounds or any sound file on your system.

As with hyperlink text, an action item works only in Slide Show view.

Testing Links in a Slide Show

Run a slide show to test the link and action you added in the previous exercises.

⊕ TEST LINKS IN A SLIDE SHOW

USE the presentation that is still open from the previous exercise.

1. **SAVE** the presentation and then press F5 to start the slide show from slide 1.
2. Click the mouse button to advance to slide 5 and then click the action button. An Excel worksheet opens, containing sample service fees, as shown in Figure 4-19.

Figure 4-19

The action button opens an Excel file

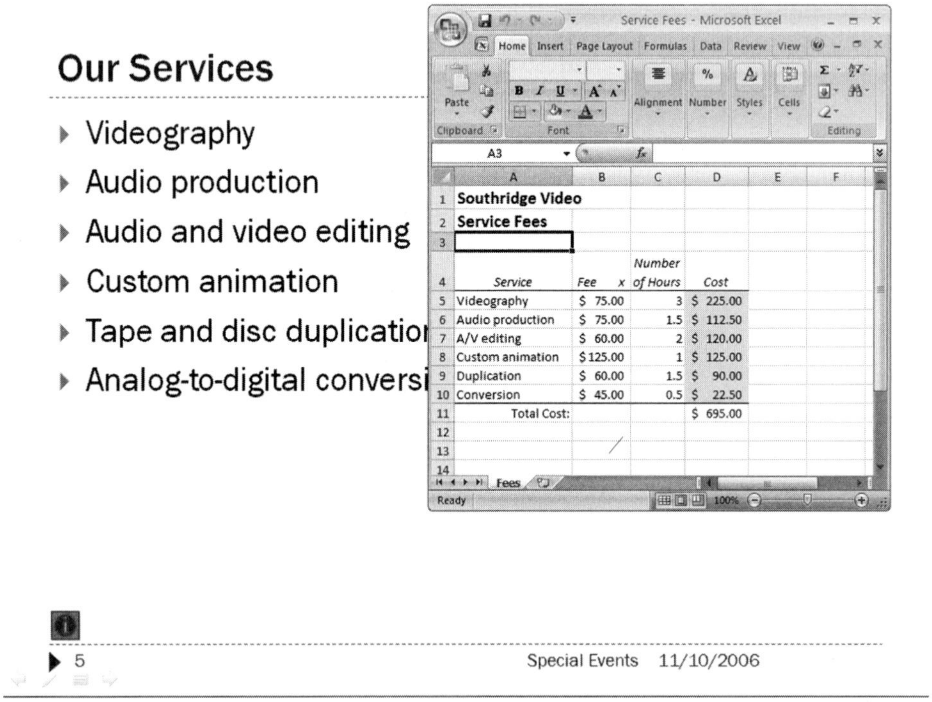

TROUBLESHOOTING

If you are prompted to enable PowerPoint to run an external program, click Enable and then continue with the exercise.

TAKE NOTE

The Web site address you entered is a dummy address supported by Microsoft to allow you to practice creating links.

3. Close the Excel worksheet to return to Slide Show view.
4. Advance to slide 6 and click the Web site address, **www.southridgevideo.com**. Your Web browser opens and displays a Microsoft Web page.

5. Close the Web browser and end the slide show.

PAUSE. LEAVE the presentation open to use in the next exercise.

When you activate links or actions during a slide show, the target of the link or action displays in the full screen, like the slides in the slide show. If you open a Web browser using a link, you can use the Web browser's Back button to return to your slide.

■ Setting up Slide Transitions

↓
THE BOTTOM LINE

Slide transitions supply another form of visual interest to slides and as such help to hold audience attention. PowerPoint offers over 50 different transitions that can be customized to create just the effect you want.

Applying a Transition

Transitions display in the Transition gallery on the Animations tab. Applying a transition is as simple as clicking one of the thumbnails in the gallery.

➔ APPLY A TRANSITION

USE the presentation that is still open from the previous exercise.

1. Go to slide 1.
2. Click the **Animations** tab, and then click the **More** button for the Transition gallery. The gallery displays with the transition effects divided into categories, as shown in Figure 4-20.

Figure 4-20

The Transition gallery

3. Point to several of the transitions in the gallery to see the live preview of the effect on slide 1.
4. Click **Fade Smoothly**, the first transition effect in the Fades and Dissolves section of the gallery. The star transition symbol displays under the slide number in the Slides tab.

PAUSE. LEAVE the presentation open to use in the next exercise.

TAKE NOTE*

You can click the star transition symbol or the Preview button on the Animations tab to preview the animation.

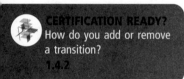

TAKE NOTE*

You can apply transition effects in either Normal view or Slide Sorter view.

CERTIFICATION READY?
How do you add or remove a transition?
1.4.2

A *slide transition* is a special effect that occurs when one slide is being replaced by another during a slide show. Effects such as fades, dissolves, wipes, and covers hold audience attention until the next slide displays. You may want to choose transitions according to content, so that all section title slides, for example, have the same transition, or you can apply the Random transition to format each slide with a different transition.

By default, a transition is applied only to the current slide. You can also select several slides to apply the same transition or use the Apply To All button to apply the same transition effects to all slides in the presentation.

If you decide you don't want a transition, select the No Transition thumbnail in the Transition gallery. This option removes all transition formatting you have applied to the current slide.

Modifying a Transition

You have options for modifying a transition you have already applied: You can add a sound effect to the transition or change the transition speed.

⊕ MODIFY A TRANSITION

USE the presentation that is still open from the previous exercise.

1. With slide 1 displayed, click the **Transition Sound** drop-down arrow. A menu of transition sounds displays, as shown in Figure 4-21.

Figure 4-21

Sound effects that can be applied to transitions

2. Preview several of the transition sounds by resting the mouse pointer on the sound name in the menu.
3. Click the **Applause** sound effect, an appropriate one for special events.
4. Click the **Transition Speed** drop-down arrow to display the speed options.
5. Click **Medium**. The transition previews on the slide at a slower speed.
   PAUSE. LEAVE the presentation open to use in the next exercise.

PowerPoint supplies a list of short, distinctive sound effects you can add to transitions, but you can also choose any sound file on your system by selecting Other Sound on the Transition Sound menu and then navigating to the sound file you want to use. When choosing a sound of your own, make sure the sound duration is short to avoid holding up the slides while the sound plays.

Take care when adding sound effects. Repeating a sound over and over can become irritating, as can playing many different sounds during the presentation. For best results, use sound sparingly to introduce significant content.

CERTIFICATION READY?
How do you change a slide
transition?
1.4.2

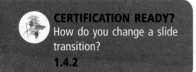

By default, transitions are set to display at the Fast speed. If your projector system or computer has a fast processor speed, transitions can go by very quickly indeed. Changing transition speed allows the audience to enjoy the effects and gives you more time between slides to conclude remarks or prepare for the next topic.

Determining How Slides Will Advance

You can choose to control slide advance by clicking the mouse button to display the next slide, or you can have PowerPoint display slides automatically based on a specific time delay that you set. Automatic slide timings allow a presentation to run by itself in venues such as trade shows or kiosks.

⊖ DETERMINE HOW SLIDES WILL ADVANCE

USE the presentation that is still open from the previous exercise.

1. Click the **Automatically After** check box and then click the up spin control arrow ten times to set a slide timing of 00:10.
2. Click the **Apply To All** button to apply all transition effects to all slides.
3. Switch to Slide Sorter view. Notice that the slide timing displays under each slide, along with the star transition symbol, as shown in Figure 4-22.

Figure 4-22

Transition and timing symbols display in Slide Sorter view

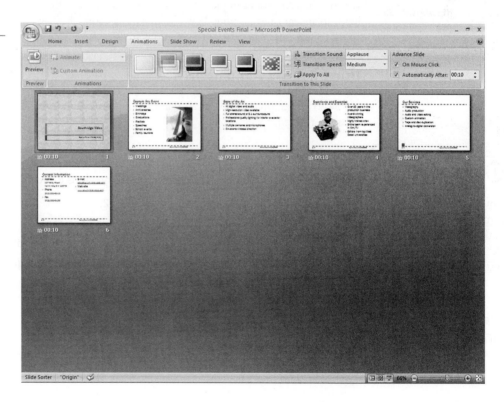

4. Click slide 2, hold down **Shift**, and then click slide 6 to select a group of slides. Click the **Transition Sound** drop-down arrow, and then click **[No Sound]** to remove the sound effect from transitions on these slides.
5. Press **F5** to start the slide show. Allow PowerPoint to control the slide advance. When you reach the end of the show, click the mouse button to return to Slide Sorter view.
6. Select all slides and click the **Automatically After** check box to remove the checkmark. You have turned off automatic slide timings.
7. **SAVE** your changes.

   PAUSE. LEAVE the presentation open to use in the next exercise.

The default option for controlling slide advance is clicking the mouse (or pressing any of a number of keyboard keys) to move from one slide to the next. In some situations, however, you may want to have PowerPoint control the slide advance. If you intend to leave a presentation running by itself, for example, you must specify the amount of delay between slides to allow viewers time to read and understand slide content. You enter slide timings in seconds.

 The best way to determine how much time is required to read a slide's content is to rehearse the show. You use the rehearsal feature in Lesson 10.

To have the best of both worlds, you can select both On Mouse Click and Automatically After. With both options checked, you can either wait for PowerPoint to advance the slides or click to advance if you're ready to go to the next slide before PowerPoint is.

■ Animating Your Slides

 To add further visual interest to a presentation, add animations that control content using a variety of effects. For example, you can set all slide titles to fly in from the top or direct bullet items to appear one at a time. PowerPoint supplies some built-in animations that are simple to apply, or you can create custom animations to have more control over the animation effects.

Using Built-In Animations

PowerPoint supplies built-in animations that you can apply quickly to achieve interesting effects.

ADD A BUILT-IN ANIMATION

To quickly return to Normal view with slide 2 active, double-click slide 2 in Slide Sorter view.

USE the presentation that is still open from the previous exercise.

1. Switch to Normal view and go to slide 2.
2. Click the **Animations** tab to display it, if necessary.
3. Click anywhere in the text placeholder at the left side of the slide.
4. Click the **Animate** drop-down arrow in the Animations group to display the list of built-in animations, as shown in Figure 4-23.

Figure 4-23

Menu of built-in animations

5. Click **By 1st Level Paragraphs** in the Fade section of the menu. The animation effect previews on the slide, displaying bullet items one by one.
6. Press **F5** to start the slide show and advance to slide 2. Click to display the first bulleted item, and continue to click until you move to slide 3.

7. Press [Esc] to end the slide show to return to Normal view.

PAUSE. LEAVE the presentation open to use in the next exercise.

Animations are effects you apply to placeholders or other content to move the content in unique ways on the slide. Animations supply visual interest, but they also allow the presenter to control when content displays on the slide. Displaying content in a controlled fashion allows the audience to concentrate more completely on each bullet point or chart element.

PowerPoint's built-in animations can supply interesting effects with a minimum of fuss. You have a limited selection of animation options that are easy to apply, so it is possible to animate an entire presentation with only a few button clicks. Use the All At Once option to display all content of a placeholder or other object at one time. The By 1st Level Paragraphs option displays bullet items or other paragraphs one at a time.

By default, built-in animations are set up to display when you click the mouse button. You can modify a built-in effect to have PowerPoint control the display of content, as well as adjust other options such as speed of the effect.

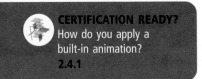

CERTIFICATION READY?
How do you apply a built-in animation?
2.4.1

Modifying an Animation

While built-in animations provide quick effects, you may find that you need to modify those effects for your presentation. You use the Custom Animation task pane to modify built-in animations.

⊕ **MODIFY AN ANIMATION**

USE the presentation that is still open from the previous exercise.

1. Go to slide 2 and click the **Custom Animation** button in the Animations group. The Custom Animation task pane opens, as shown in Figure 4-24. The built-in animation effect you applied in the last exercise displays in the effects list area of the task pane.

Figure 4-24

The Custom Animation task pane

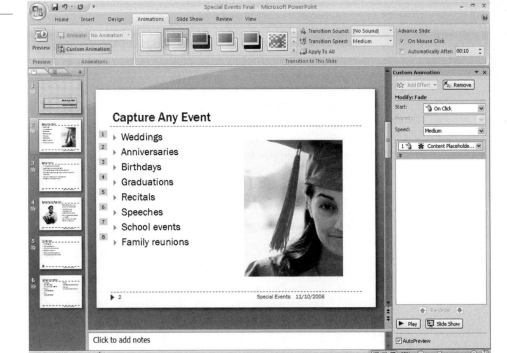

2. Click the **Content Placeholder 2** animation effect in the list area to select it.

3. Click the **Start** drop-down arrow near the top of the task pane and then click **After Previous**.

4. Click the Speed drop-down arrow and then click **Fast**. The modified effect previews on the slide.

5. Press F5 to start the slide show. Advance to slide 2 and notice that PowerPoint starts displaying the bullet items immediately after the transition has ended and controls their entry so you don't have to click the mouse.

6. Press Esc to end the show to return to Normal view. Leave the Custom Animation task pane open.

   PAUSE. LEAVE the presentation open to use in the next exercise.

Use the Custom Animation task pane to modify built-in animations or create new custom animations. The Custom Animation task pane displays buttons at the top of the pane for adding, changing, or removing an animation effect. Below the buttons are Start, Property, and Speed options that allow you to change how an object starts, how it plays, and how fast it occurs.

PowerPoint offers three options for starting an effect:

- **On Mouse Click** starts the effect when you click the mouse button. This gives you the most control over animations but can be tedious when you have to click repeatedly to display a bulleted list or the bars of a chart.

- **With Previous** starts the effect at the same time as the previous effect. Using this option can prevent delays from occurring between animations. You might use it, for example, for a text placeholder if you have also animated the title placeholder.

- **After Previous** starts the effect after the previous effect (either an animation or transition) has ended.

The Property option varies according to the effect; it may give you a choice of directions, for example, for objects that are flying in. You have five speed options, from Very Fast to Very Slow. The speed choice will depend on what you are animating. Your audience may find Very Fast to be disorienting for a text animation.

Use the Play button at the bottom of the task pane to preview animations. Use the Slide Show button at the bottom of the task pane to run the slide show from the current slide to check animations.

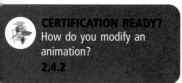

CERTIFICATION READY?
How do you modify an animation?
2.4.2

Creating a Customized Animation

For the most control over animations, select the effects and modify their settings yourself in the Custom Animation task pane. The Effect Options dialog box for an effect gives you further options for controlling the animation.

⊙ CREATE A CUSTOMIZED ANIMATION

USE the presentation that is still open from the previous exercise.

1. Go to slide 6 and select the left-hand text placeholder (click the outside border so it appears as a solid line).

2. In the Custom Animations task pane, click the **Add Effect** button, point to **Entrance**, and then click **More Effects**. The Add Entrance Effect dialog box opens, as shown in Figure 4-25.

Figure 4-25

Choose a new entrance effect from the Add Entrance Effect dialog box

3. Click **Wipe** in the Basic area of the dialog box, and then click **OK**.

4. Click the **Start** drop-down arrow, then click **After Previous**.

5. Click the **Direction** drop-down arrow, then click **From Left**.

6. Click the **Speed** drop-down arrow, then click **Fast**.

7. Click the drop-down arrow at the right side of the content placeholder animation effect in the effects list. A shortcut menu displays.

8. Click **Effect Options** to open the Wipe dialog box, as shown in Figure 4-26.

Figure 4-26

The Wipe dialog box

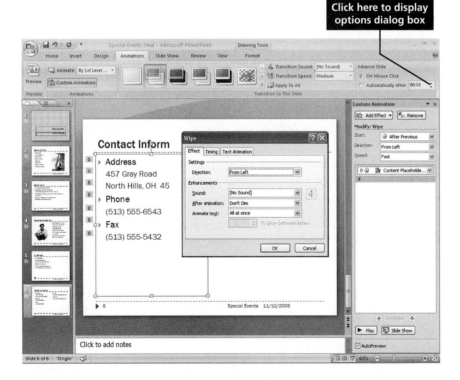

9. Click the **Text Animation** tab.

10. Click the **Group text** drop-down arrow, and then click **By 2nd Level Paragraphs**.

11. Click **OK**.

12. Click in **E-mail** in the right-hand placeholder. Add the **Wipe** entrance effect, start it **With Previous**, set the direction to **From Left**, and change the speed to **Fast**.

13. Open the Wipe effect options dialog box, click the **Text Animation** tab, and choose to group **By 2nd level paragraphs**. Click **OK**.

14. Click the double downward-pointing arrows in the blue bar below the Content Placeholder 3 effect to expand the effect so you can see the effects applied to all items in the placeholder, as shown in Figure 4-27.

Figure 4-27

Expand the effect

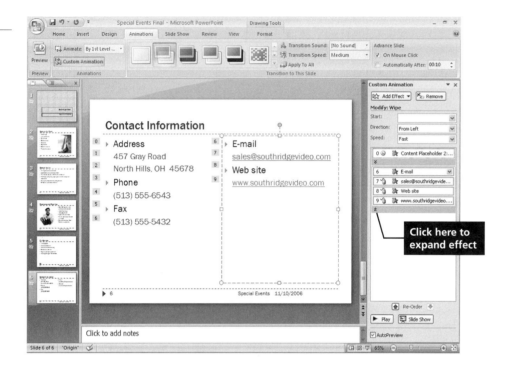

15. Notice that the last three items have the mouse symbol indicating that they are controlled by mouse click. Click each of these three lines, then click **After Previous**.

16. Click the Slide Show button at the bottom of the task pane to check the animation. Notice that the first item in the right-hand placeholder starts with the last item in the left-hand placeholder.

17. End the slide show to return to Normal view, then close the Custom Animation task pane.

18. SAVE and CLOSE the presentation.

PAUSE. LEAVE PowerPoint open to use in the next exercise.

The Custom Animation task pane provides options for creating very sophisticated animation effects. By default, all built-in animations are entrance effects—they occur as content appears on a slide. When you choose to create a new custom animation, you can select from the following options:

- **Entrance** effects control how the object appears on the slide. Use these effects to add information to a slide.
- **Emphasis** effects control objects that already display on the slide. Use these effects to draw attention to existing slide content.
- **Exit** effects control how an object disappears from a slide. Use these effects to remove content from a slide.
- **Motion Path** effects cause an object such as a picture or placeholder to follow a path on the slide.

You can insert more than one animation on a slide. You can, for example, animate the slide title; text; pictures; and objects such as tables, SmartArt graphics, and charts. Animations are listed in the task pane as you apply them. You can reorder the list to control the order in which the animations occur. Numbers on the slide in the Slide pane show the order in which content is animated. If content is set to animate using With Previous or After Previous, these numbers are 0s to indicate that the content is automatically controlled.

If a placeholder contains more than one line of text, you can expand the effect in the effects list to apply separate settings to each item.

The amount of time available for animations depends on slide advance options. If you have not set an automatic advance time, animations proceed according to the speed you have set. If an automatic slide timing has been set, the animations take place within that time. If you decide to set slide timings, make sure you allow time for all animations to play at a reasonable speed.

You can set further options for any animation in the effect's Options dialog box. The tabs in this dialog box vary according to effect and what you are choosing to animate, but you always have Effect and Timing tabs to allow you to adjust properties and speed or delay for the effect.

CERTIFICATION READY?
How do you create a custom animation?
2.4.3

■ SOFTWARE ORIENTATION

PowerPoint's Slide Master View

Slide Master view, shown in Figure 4-28, provides tools for modifying the master slides on which all of the current presentation's layouts and formats are based.

Figure 4-28

Slide Master view

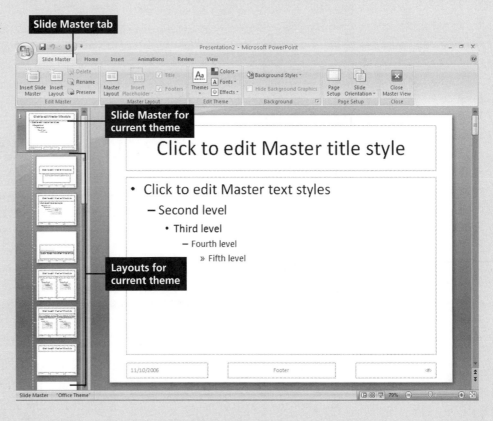

Use the tools on the Slide Master tab and the blank slide in the Slide pane to customize formats that will apply to all slides in a presentation. All layouts used in the current theme appear in the left pane so you can customize each layout as desired. Making a change to the Two Content layout, for example, will change all slides in the presentation that use that layout.

■ Customizing Slide Masters

THE BOTTOM LINE
If you want to make design changes that will apply to many or all slides in a presentation, you can save a great deal of time by modifying the slide master rather than applying changes on each slide. Customizing a slide master makes it easy to apply changes consistently throughout a presentation.

Applying a Theme to a Slide Master

To customize a slide master, you use Slide Master view. Slide Master view has its own tab on the Ribbon to provide tools you can use to change the masters.

⊕ APPLY A THEME TO A SLIDE MASTER

The *Rates* file is available on the companion CD-ROM.

1. Locate and open the *Rates* presentation.
2. With slide 1 active, click the **View** tab.
3. Click the **Slide Master** button in the Presentation Views group. Slide Master view opens with the Title Slide Layout selected in the left pane, as shown in Figure 4-29.

Figure 4-29

Slide Master view with the Title Slide layout selected

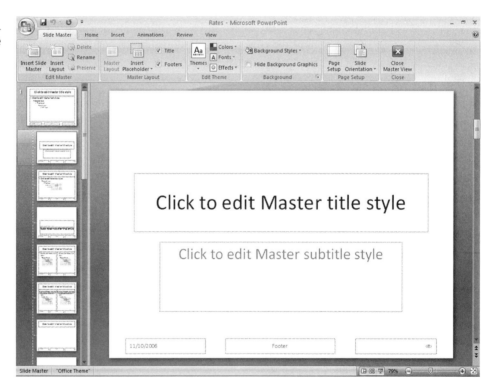

4. Click the first slide in the left pane, the slide master for the current theme.
5. Click the **Themes** button in the Slide Master tab's Edit Theme group.
6. Click the **Solstice** theme. The theme is applied to the slide master as well as all slide layouts in the left pane, as shown in Figure 4-30.

Figure 4-30

A new theme applied to the slide master and layouts

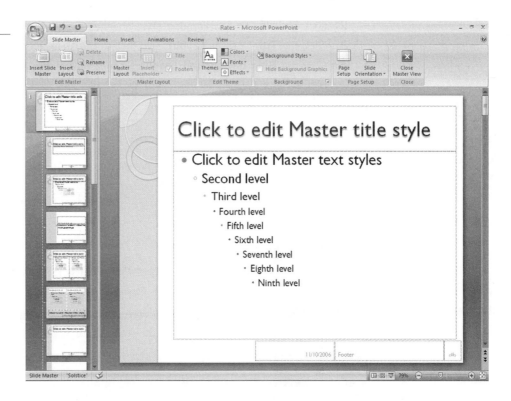

7. **SAVE** the presentation as *Rates Masters*.
   PAUSE. LEAVE the presentation open to use in the next exercise.

TAKE NOTE

Slide Master view shows two layouts—Title and Vertical Text and Vertical Title and Text—that are not available in the default slide layout gallery.

CERTIFICATION READY?
How do you apply a theme to a slide master?
1.2.1

The ***slide master*** for a presentation stores information on the current theme, layout of place-holders, bullet characters, and other formats that affect all slides in a presentation. Slide Master view makes it easy to change formats globally for a presentation by displaying the slide master and all layouts available in the current presentation.

The slide master, displayed at the top of the left pane, looks like a blank Title and Content slide. To make a change to the master, edit it just the way you would edit any slide using tools on any of the Ribbon's tabs. For example, to change the font of the slide title, click the title, display the Home tab, and use the Font list to select a new font. Change bullet characters by clicking in any of the nine levels of bullets and then selecting a new bullet character from the Bullets and Numbering dialog box.

Some changes you make to the slide master display on the masters for other slide layouts. You can also click any of these layouts to display it in the Slide pane so you can make changes to that layout. Any changes you make to these layouts will display on slides that use those layouts. Your changed masters display in the slide layout gallery to be available when you create new slides.

Changing a Slide Master's Background

Change a slide master's background to quickly modify the background for all slides in the presentation. You can apply a different background style or hide background graphics to customize slide backgrounds.

CHANGE A SLIDE MASTER'S BACKGROUND

USE the presentation that is still open from the previous exercise.

1. With the slide master still selected in the left pane, click the **Background Styles** button in the Background group. The Background Styles gallery opens.

2. Click **Style 6.** The background style changes for all layouts.

3. Click the **Title Master Layout,** just below the slide master in the left pane.

4. Click the **Hide Background Graphics** check box in the Background group. The white text panel and the graphic shapes at the left side of the slide are hidden, as shown in Figure 4-31.

Figure 4-31

Hide background graphics to change slide appearance

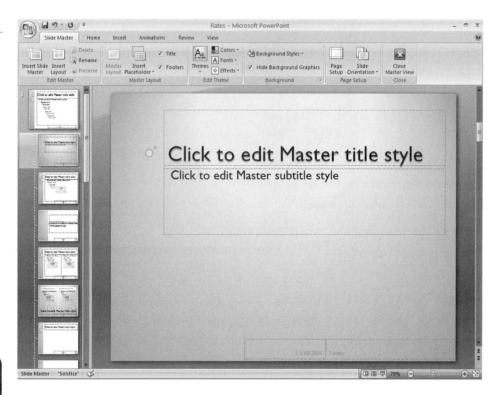

CERTIFICATION READY?
How do you change a slide master's background?
1.2.2

PAUSE. LEAVE the presentation open to use in the next exercise.

Changing the background of a slide master is the same process as changing the background of any slide in Normal view. Keep in mind that any changes you make to a specific slide master will display each time you use that master.

Adding New Elements to a Slide Master

If you add a picture or text to a slide master layout, it will display on all slides that use that layout. To allow the user to insert his or her own content, you can add a placeholder to a layout.

ADD A NEW ELEMENT TO A SLIDE MASTER

USE the presentation that is still open from the previous exercise.

1. Click the **Section Header Layout** in the left pane to display the Section Header master in the Slide pane.

2. Click the **Insert Placeholder** drop-down arrow in the Master Layout group, and then click **Text.** The pointer changes to a crosshair you can use to draw a new text placeholder.

3. Draw a placeholder in the upper-left corner of the slide. As soon as you release the mouse button, a list of bulleted text levels displays in the new text placeholder, as shown in Figure 4-32.

Figure 4-32

A new text placeholder on a slide master

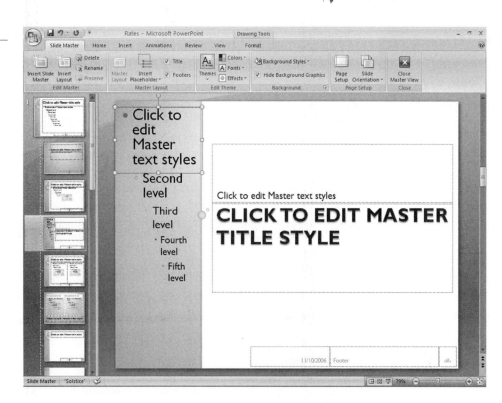

4. Select all text in the new placeholder and press **Delete** to remove the placeholder text.

5. Click the **Home** tab.

6. Turn off bullets for the new placeholder and change the text size of the placeholder to **18 point**.

TAKE NOTE The text in the placeholder still shows the hanging indent needed for a bulleted list. You can remove this indent using the Paragraph dialog box.

7. Click the **Slide Master** tab, and then click the **Close Master View** button to return to Normal view.

8. Go to slide 1, if necessary, click the **Home** tab, and add a slide with the Section Header layout.

9. Key the slide title **Service Rates**.

10. Click in the new placeholder in the upper-left corner of the slide and key **As of [current date]**, replacing *[current date]* with a date such as 11/08/08.

11. **SAVE** and **CLOSE** the presentation.
    CLOSE PowerPoint.

 If you need to create a number of slides with a layout different from any of the default layouts, you can create a new custom layout to your own specifications. Use the Insert Layout button on the Slide Master tab to insert a new layout in the layout list in the left pane of Slide Master view. You can then use tools in the Master Layout group to customize placeholders for your new layout. You can decide whether to display a title or the footer placeholders, and you can use the Insert Placeholder button to select from a number of standard placeholders, such as Text, Picture, Clip Art, or Table.

TAKE NOTE

Custom layouts remain in the presentation in which they are created.

If you have inserted a text placeholder, you should format the placeholder text the way you want text to appear on the slides. Apply formats using options on the Home tab.

CERTIFICATION READY?
How do you add an element
to a slide master?
1.3

When you have completed the custom layout, use the Rename button on the Slide Master tab to give the custom layout a meaningful name. It will then be available in the slide layout gallery any time you want to add a slide in that presentation.

In addition to creating your own custom layout, you can also insert another slide master into any presentation using the Insert Slide Master button on the Slide Master tab. When you insert a new slide master, PowerPoint displays a new default blank slide master and layouts. You can apply a different theme and formatting to the new master and layouts, allowing you considerable freedom when creating slides because you can draw on the layouts of both masters.

SUMMARY SKILL MATRIX

IN THIS LESSON YOU LEARNED	MATRIX SKILL	SKILL NUMBER
To format presentations with themes		
To change slide backgrounds		
To change a slide layout		
To insert a date, footer, and slide numbers		
To insert links and action buttons on slides	Insert hyperlinks	2.3.3
To apply and modify slide transitions	Add, change, and remove transitions between slides	1.4.2
To apply simple, built-in animations	Apply built-in animations	2.4.1
To modify built-in animations	Modify animations	2.4.2
To create custom animations	Create custom animations	2.4.3
To apply a theme to a slide master	Apply themes to slide masters	1.2.1
To change the slide master background	Format slide master backgrounds	1.2.2
To add an element to a slide master	Add elements to slide masters	1.3

■ Knowledge Assessment

Fill in the Blank

Fill in each blank with the term or phrase that best completes the statement.

1. PowerPoint's _____ feature lets you move the mouse pointer over items in a gallery to see instantly how formats look on the current slide.

2. To select a picture for a slide background, use the _____ dialog box.

3. A(n) _____ is text that repeats at the bottom of each slide in a presentation.

4. A(n) _____ is a special effect that occurs as one slide leaves the screen and another enters.

5. The _____ stores information about formats used on all slides in a presentation.

6. The _____ is the page or slide that opens when you click a link.

7. _____ can be used to control how an object enters or leaves the screen during a slide show.

8. You can create a(n) _____ to appear at the top of every page of handouts.

9. To test links, you must be in _____ view.

10. Use a(n) _____ to play a sound file or open a file from another program.

Multiple Choice

Circle the correct answer.

1. A PowerPoint theme includes
   a. a palette of complementary colors
   b. a combination of fonts
   c. placeholder layouts
   d. all of the above

2. A saved color scheme displays in the _____.
   a. Custom area of the Theme Colors gallery
   b. Built-In area of the Themes gallery
   c. My Colors area of the New Presentation dialog box
   d. Saved Colors area of the Theme Colors gallery

3. If you applied a texture that made it hard to read slide text, you could modify the effect by _____.
   a. changing the size of the texture tile
   b. changing the texture gradient
   c. changing the transparency of the texture
   d. changing the underlying slide color

4. PowerPoint's built-in themes offer a choice of _____ layouts.
   a. six
   b. nine
   c. twelve
   d. fifteen

5. If it is important to indicate what day slides were created, you should use a(n) _____ date.
   a. automatically updating
   b. absolute
   c. numeric equivalent
   d. fixed

6. To link to a slide in the current presentation, choose _____ in the Insert Hyperlink dialog box.
   a. Existing File or Web Page
   b. Place in This Document
   c. Create New Document
   d. Show Current Slides

7. By default, transitions display at which speed?
   a. Slow
   b. Medium
   c. Fast
   d. Very Fast

8. To display the items in a placeholder one at a time, you would choose what animation option?

   a. All At Once

   b. One at a Time

   c. By Paragraph

   d. By 1st Level Paragraphs

9. To have the best control over when an animation plays, you would choose the _____ start option.

   a. On Mouse Click

   b. With Previous

   c. After Previous

   d. Either b or c

10. To remove objects from a slide's background, click the _____ check box.

   a. Hide All Slide Objects

   b. Suppress Graphics

   c. Hide Background Graphics

   d. Show Only Background

■ Competency Assessment

Project 4-1: Service with a Smile

You're the sales manager for a large chain of auto dealerships that prides itself on service and warranty packages that give customers a sense of security. The company, Car King, is rolling out a new line of extended warranties to offer its customers. You have created a presentation that details three levels of warranties. Now you need to improve the look of the slides to make customers take notice.

GET READY. Launch PowerPoint if it is not already running.

The *Warranty Plans* file is available on the companion CD-ROM.

1. **OPEN** the *Warranty Plans* presentation.
2. With slide 1 active, click the **New Slide** button to insert a new Title and Content slide.
3. Click the **Layout** button, and then click **Title Slide**.
4. Key the title **Car King** and the subtitle **Extended Warranty Plans**.
5. Drag the slide above slide 1 in the Slides tab so the title slide becomes the first slide.
6. Click the **Design** tab, and then click the **More** button to display the Themes gallery.
7. Click **Foundry** to apply this theme to all slides.
8. Click the **Theme Fonts** button, and then scroll down to locate and click the **Metro** theme fonts combination.
9. Click the **Theme Colors** button, and then click **Create New Theme Colors**.
10. Click the **Accent 1** drop-down arrow, then click the **Tan, Text 2, Darker 25%** color.
11. Click the **Accent 2** drop-down arrow, then click the **Tan, Text 2, Darker 50%** color.
12. Key **CarKing** as the color scheme name, and then click **Save**.
13. Go to slide 1, if necessary.

14. Click the **Background Styles** button, and then click **Style 7**.

15. **SAVE** the presentation as *Warranty Plans Final* and **CLOSE** the file.

LEAVE PowerPoint open for the next project.

Project 4-2: Special Delivery

As a marketing manager for Consolidated Delivery, you have been asked to prepare and present information on the company's services to a prospective corporate client. You need to add some interactive features to a standard presentation to make your delivery especially interesting.

The *Messenger Service* file is available on the companion CD-ROM.

1. **OPEN** the *Messenger Service* presentation.

2. Go to slide 2 and select the text *Contact Consolidated* in the text box at the bottom of the slide.

3. Open the Insert Hyperlink dialog box, click **Place in This Document**, and then click **6. Our Numbers** in the list of slide titles. Click **OK**.

4. Go to slide 4 and click the WordArt graphic to select it.

5. Click the **Animations** tab, and then click the **Custom Animation** button to open the Custom Animation task pane.

6. Click the **Add Effect** button, point to **Emphasis**, and then click **Grow/Shrink**. Leave the default animation options in place and close the task pane.

7. Go to slide 5 and use the Shapes gallery on the Insert tab to select the **Information** action button.

The *Contract Plans* file is available on the companion CD-ROM.

8. Draw a button near the bottom of the slide and set the action to **Hyperlink to: Other File**. Select the file *Contract Plans*.

9. Go to slide 6, select the Web site address, and use the Insert Hyperlink dialog box to create a link to http://www.consolidatedmessenger.com.

10. Insert an automatically updating date, slide numbers, and the footer **Consolidated Messenger** on all slides except the title slide. (You may need to adjust the location of your action button on slide 5 after you add slide numbers and the footer.)

11. Press F5 to run the slide show from slide 1. Advance to slide 2 and test the link at the bottom of the slide. Slide 6 displays.

12. Right-click slide 6, point to **Go to Slide**, and then click **2 Our Services** to return to slide 2.

13. Advance to slide 4 and click the slide to see the emphasis animation take place.

14. Advance to slide 5 and click the action button to open the *Contract Plans* file. Close Microsoft Word to return to the slide show.

15. Advance to slide 6 and click the Web site link. Close the browser and end the slide show.

16. **SAVE** the presentation as *Messenger Services Links* and **CLOSE** the file.

LEAVE PowerPoint open for the next project.

■ Proficiency Assessment

Project 4-3: Animated Speaker

The *Speaker* file is available on the companion CD-ROM.

You are an instructor at the School of Fine Art, and one of your supplementary tasks is to schedule and introduce speakers. You can add animations to a simple introductory slide to jazz up the presentation.

1. **OPEN** the *Speaker* presentation.

2. Select the slide title.

3. Apply the **Fly In** built-in animation.

4. Click in the bulleted list.

5. Apply the Fade **By 1st Level Paragraphs** built-in animation.

6. Open the Custom Animation task pane and modify the built-in animations as follows:

    a. For the title animation, change the start option to **With Previous**, the direction to **From Top**, and the speed to **Fast**.

    b. For the content placeholder animation, change the start option to **After Previous** and the speed to **Fast**.

7. Click the picture to select it and add the **Fade** entrance effect (you may have to go to the More Effects dialog box to locate this effect). Change the start option to **With Previous**.

8. With the picture effect still selected, click the **Re-Order Up** button at the bottom of the task pane to move the picture effect above the content placeholder effect so it will occur just after the title animation.

9. Click the **Slide Show** button to test the animations.

10. **SAVE** the presentation as *Speaker Animated* and **CLOSE** the file.

    LEAVE PowerPoint open for the next project.

Project 4-4: The Wild Blue Yonder, Revisited

As the Sales Manager for Blue Yonder Airlines, you have almost finished a presentation that you want to run at a regional travel exposition. You need to add transitions and set slide timings so the slides will run on their own.

1. **OPEN** the *Blue Yonder Introduction* presentation.

2. Switch to Slide **Sorter** view and click the **Animations** tab.

3. Set a transition speed of **Medium**.

4. Click the **On Mouse Click** check box to deselect it, and then click **Automatically After**.

5. Set an advance timing of 10 seconds, and then apply these settings to all slides.

6. Select slide 1 and apply the **Fade Smoothly** transition.

7. Select slides 2 through 4 and apply the **Wipe Down** transition. Apply the **Wind** sound effect to slide 2 only.

8. Select slides 5 and 6 and apply the **Blinds Vertical** transition.

9. Apply the **Newsflash** transition to slide 7, and the **Fade Smoothly** transition to slide 8.

10. Run the slide show to view the transitions.

11. **SAVE** the presentation as *Blue Yonder Transitions* and **CLOSE** the file.

    LEAVE PowerPoint open for the next project.

The *Blue Yonder Introduction* file is available on the companion CD-ROM.

Mastery Assessment

Project 4-5: The Art of the Biography

You work for the Editorial Director of Lucerne Publishing. She has asked you to fine-tune a presentation on new biographies she plans to deliver to the sales force. You want to make some global changes to the presentation by customizing the presentation's slide masters, and you need to create a new layout that you will use to introduce sections of biographies.

The *Biographies* file is available on the companion CD-ROM.

1. OPEN the *Biographies* presentation.
2. Switch to Slide Master view and apply a new theme of your choice to the slide master.
3. In the left pane, click the **Title and Content** layout and then click the **Insert Layout** button in the Edit Master group to insert a new layout.
4. Deselect **Title** in the Master Layout group to remove the title placeholder from the new layout.
5. Insert a text placeholder in the center of the slide. Delete the sample bulleted text, remove bullet formatting, and change font size to 40 point. Center the text in the placeholder.
6. Apply a new background style to this new layout.
7. Click the **Rename** button in the Edit Master group and key **Introduction** as the new layout name.
8. Close Slide Master view.
9. Insert a new slide after slide 1 using the Introduction layout. Key **American History** in the placeholder.
10. SAVE the presentation as *Biographies Masters* and **CLOSE** the file.

    LEAVE PowerPoint open for the next project.

Project 4-6: Adventure Works

You are a coordinator for Adventure Works, a company that manages outdoor adventures for children and teenagers. To introduce your programs, you have created a presentation to show at local schools and recreation centers. Finalize the presentation with design elements and effects that will catch the eye.

The *Adventures* file is available on the companion CD-ROM.

1. OPEN the *Adventures* presentation.
2. Apply a suitable theme to the presentation. Customize theme colors or fonts if desired.
3. Animate the bulleted text on slides 2, 3, and 4 using effects of your choice.
4. Apply transitions of your choice to all slides.
5. Set an automatic advance time that will allow plenty of time for animations and reading slide content, and apply it to all slides.
6. Run the slide show to make sure your timing is adequate.
7. SAVE the presentation as *Adventures Final* and **CLOSE** the file.

   CLOSE PowerPoint.

INTERNET READY

Have you ever wanted to create your own digital movies? Use an Internet search tool to locate information on digital video cameras. Select two that seem to offer quality for a reasonable price and make a list of their features. Create a new presentation with a theme of your choice, insert a title, and add a Comparison slide. List the two cameras you have researched in the subheading placeholders and key features for each camera in the text placeholders. Save the presentation with an appropriate name.

↻ Circling Back

You are a sales representative for Contoso Food Services. You are preparing a brief presentation to introduce your company to the Food Services Committee at Trey College, in hopes of receiving a contract to provide food services for the campus dining hall.

→ Project 1: **Create a Presentation**

Begin by creating slides from a blank presentation. Then add slides from another presentation, rearrange the slides, and print the presentation.

GET READY. Launch PowerPoint if it is not already running.

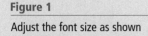

The *Boilerplate* file is available on the companion CD-ROM.

1. Create a new, blank presentation.
2. On the title slide, key **Contoso Food Services** in the title placeholder.
3. Key **Trey College Proposal** in the subtitle placeholder.
4. Reuse slides 2–4 from the *Boilerplate* presentation.
5. Rearrange slides so that slide 2 becomes slide 3.
6. Print the presentation as slides in Grayscale mode.
7. **SAVE** the presentation as *Trey Proposal*.

   PAUSE. LEAVE PowerPoint and your presentation open for the next project.

→ Project 2: **Format Your Presentation**

Now that you have the bare bones of your presentation written, you can concentrate on formatting to improve the presentation's appearance. You will use WordArt, a theme, font styles, and other formatting options to give your slides punch.

USE the presentation that is open from the previous project.

1. Apply the Median theme, and then change theme colors to those for Office.
2. On slide 1, delete the title text and the title placeholder.
3. Create a WordArt graphic using the **Fill - Text 2, Outline - Background 2** style (the first one in the WordArt style gallery). Key the text **CONTOSO FOOD SERVICES**.
4. Make these changes to the WordArt graphic:

   a. Increase the font size so that the title stretches all the way across the slide, as shown in Figure 1. (Hint: Use the Increase Font Size button.)

Figure 1

Adjust the font size as shown

    b. Change the WordArt fill to a gradient, using the **Linear Down** option in the Light Variations section of the Gradient gallery.

    c. Change the WordArt outline color to **Dark Blue, Background 2, Lighter 80%**.

    d. Apply the **Tight Reflection, touching** effect to the WordArt graphic.

5. Apply italics to the slide 1 subtitle.

6. Go to slide 2. Make these changes to the text in the right-hand placeholder:

    a. Select all text in the right-hand placeholder and change the font size to 24 point.

    b. Right-align the last three paragraphs in the quote (the attribution), and adjust line space so there is no extra space above these lines. (Hint: Choose Line Spacing Options at the bottom of the Line Spacing menu.)

    c. Use the Format Painter to copy formats from the quote paragraph and the quote attribution on slide 2 to the quote text and attribution on slide 3.

7. Go to slide 4. Insert a text box below the picture that is as wide as the picture and key the following text:

Contoso Food Services is proud to serve institutions in fifteen states in this country and three Canadian provinces. Our reputation for quality is second to none.

8. Format the text box as follows:

    a. Center the text in the text box.

    b. Apply a Quick Style of your choice to the text box.

9. **SAVE** the presentation.

    PAUSE. LEAVE PowerPoint and your presentation open for the next project.

➔ Project 3: Add Design Touches to Your Presentation

You are ready to do the final formatting and add the finishing touches to the presentation. You will adjust the slide master, add a slide, insert links, and set up transitions and animations.

1. Insert an automatically updating date and slide numbers that appear on all slides except the title slide. Notice that the date is partially obscured on slide 4 by the text box you added.

2. In Slide Master view, right-align the date in the date placeholder on the slide master. Close Slide Master view.

3. Insert a new slide at the end of the presentation using the **Two Content** layout.

4. Key the slide title **Contact Us**.

5. Insert the following contact information in the left-hand text placeholder. Format the information as desired.

Mailing address:

    17507 Atlantic Blvd

    Boca Raton, FL 33456

Phone:

    561 555 3663

    561 555 3664

6. Insert the following information in the right-hand text placeholder:

E-mail:

    sales@contoso.com

Web site:

    www.contoso.com

7. Create a hyperlink from the Web site text to the Web site at http://www.contoso.com.

8. Apply a different background style to slide 5 only to make it stand out.

The *Pricing* file is available on the companion CD-ROM.

9. Go to slide 3. Insert an Information action button above the date in the lower-right corner of the slide that links to the *Pricing* Excel file.

10. Go to slide 2. Animate the text on this slide as follows:

   a. Animate the bullet items in the left-hand text placeholder so that each item flies in from the bottom at a medium speed. Set the start option to **After Previous**.

   b. Animate the text in the right-hand placeholder to fade into view at a medium speed. The effect should start **After Previous**.

11. Apply the same animations to slide 3.

12. Go to slide 1. Apply the **Uncover Down** transition at **Medium** speed to all slides. Apply the **Chime** transition sound effect to slide 4 only.

13. Run the presentation in Slide Show view to test transitions, animations, and links.

14. **SAVE** your changes to the presentation.

15. **SAVE** the presentation as *Trey_2003* in the 97–2003 format, and then **CLOSE** the file.

   CLOSE PowerPoint.

Adding Tables to Slides

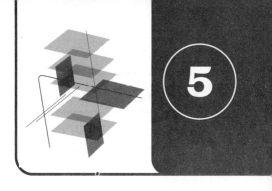

5

LESSON SKILL MATRIX

SKILLS	MATRIX SKILL	SKILL NUMBER
Creating Tables		
Inserting a Table	Insert tables in a slide	3.7.1
Modifying Table Layout		
Formatting Tables		
Changing Table Text Alignment and Orientation	Change alignment and orientation of table text	3.7.3
Applying a Quick Style to a Table	Apply Quick Styles to tables	3.7.2
Adding an Image to a Table	Add images to tables	3.7.4

You are an assistant director of ATM operations at Woodgrove Bank. Your job is to help oversee the placement and use of ATMs in your bank's branches and other locations. You often deliver presentations to bank officers to keep them up to date on ATM activities. The best way to organize information that has several related components is to use a table. Distributing information in rows and columns makes the data easy to read and understand. Use the table features of Microsoft Office PowerPoint 2007 to modify the structure and appearance of a table to improve readability and visual interest.

KEY TERMS
embedded
linked
table
worksheet

■ SOFTWARE ORIENTATION

A PowerPoint Table

Tables are designed to organize data in columns and rows, as shown in Figure 5-1.

Figure 5-1

A PowerPoint table and
table tools on the Ribbon

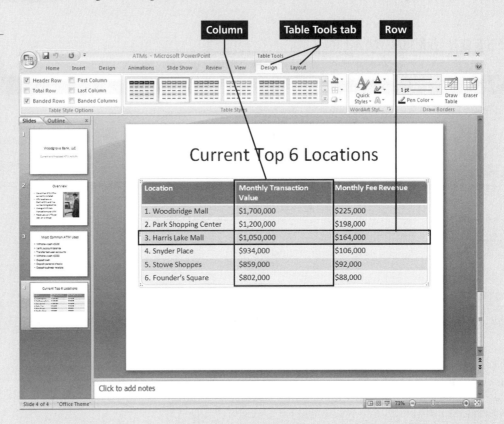

The Table Tools Design tab, shown above, and the Table Tools Layout tab provide tools for
modifying and formatting a table. These tabs become active only when a table is selected.

■ Creating Tables

↓
THE BOTTOM LINE

When you want to organize complex data on a slide, use a table. A table's column-
and-row structure makes data easy to understand. If you need to organize numerical
data that may be used in calculations, you can insert an Excel worksheet right on a slide
and use Excel's tools to work with the data.

Inserting a Table

PowerPoint offers several ways to insert a table. The simplest is to click the Insert Table
icon in any content placeholder.

The *ATMs* file is avail-
able on the companion
CD-ROM.

→ **INSERT A TABLE**

GET READY. Before you begin these steps, make sure that your computer is on. Log on,
if necessary.

1. Start PowerPoint, if the program is not already running.
2. Locate and open the *ATMs* presentation.

3. Go to slide 4. Insert a new slide with the Title and Content layout.

4. Key the slide title **Proposed ATM Locations**.

5. Click the **Insert Table** icon in the group of icons in the center of the content placeholder. The Insert Table dialog box opens, as shown in Figure 5-2.

Figure 5-2

The Insert Table dialog box

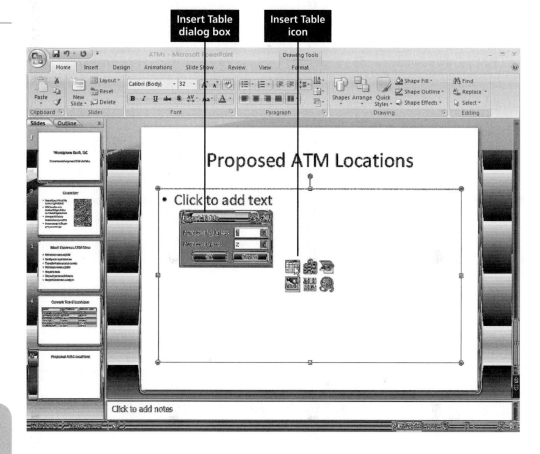

ANOTHER WAY

You can open the Insert Table dialog box by clicking the Table drop-down arrow on the Insert tab and then clicking Insert Table.

6. Key **3** to specify three columns, press Tab, and then key **6** to specify six rows. Click **OK**. PowerPoint creates the table in the content area, as shown in Figure 5-3. Notice that formats specified by the current theme have already been applied to the table.

Figure 5-3

A new table with three columns and six rows

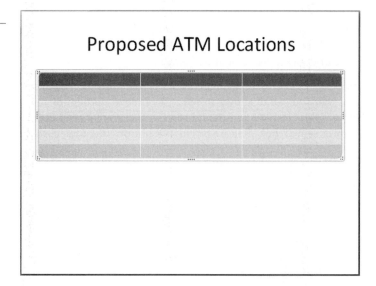

7. Click in the first table cell in the top row and key **Location**. Press `Tab` and key **Site Study Complete**. Press `Tab` and key **Nearest Competing ATM**.

8. Key the following information in the table cells, pressing `Tab` to move from cell to cell. Your table should look like Figure 5-4 when you complete it.

1.	Springdale Cineplex	Yes	More than 2 miles
2.	Glen Avenue BIG Foods	No	Three blocks
3.	Findlay Market Square	Yes	One block
4.	Center City Arena	Yes	One block
5.	Williams State College	No	Half a mile

Figure 5-4

Completed table

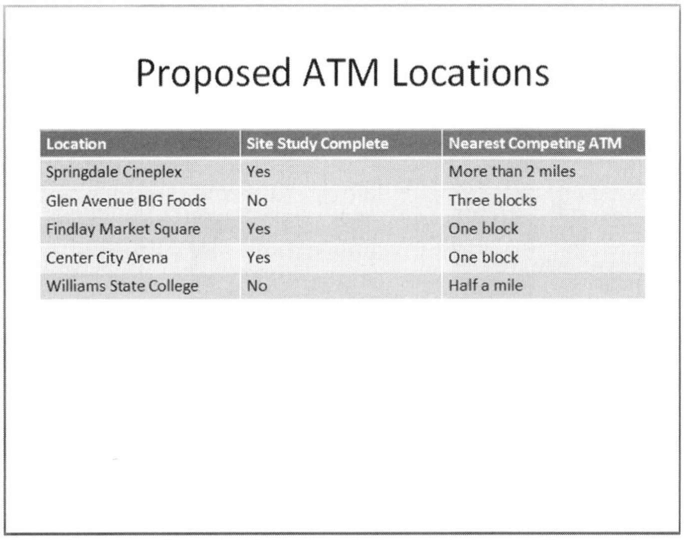

Proposed ATM Locations

Location	Site Study Complete	Nearest Competing ATM
Springdale Cineplex	Yes	More than 2 miles
Glen Avenue BIG Foods	No	Three blocks
Findlay Market Square	Yes	One block
Center City Arena	Yes	One block
Williams State College	No	Half a mile

9. **SAVE** the presentation as *ATMs Final*.

   PAUSE. LEAVE the presentation open to use in the next exercise.

PowerPoint has automated the process of creating a ***table*** so that you can simply specify the number of columns and rows and then key data to achieve a professionally formatted result. By default, PowerPoint sizes a new table to fill the width of the content placeholder. If you have only a few columns, you may find the table a little too "spacious." You will learn later in this lesson how to adjust column widths and row heights to more closely fit the data you have entered.

Once you have become proficient with tables, you may want to use one of the other methods PowerPoint offers to create a new table: dragging over a grid of columns and rows to create a table or drawing the table from scratch.

To create a table by dragging, click the Table button on the Insert tab. PowerPoint displays a grid that you can drag over to select the desired number of columns and rows. As you drag, PowerPoint creates columns and rows in the content placeholder so you can easily see how your table will look. Release the mouse button to complete the table.

To create a table by drawing it from scratch, click the Table button drop-down arrow, then click Draw Table on the menu. The mouse pointer changes to a pencil pointer you can use to draw the table outline and the rows and columns within the table border. This option makes it easy to create a table that does not have a regular arrangement of columns and rows; if, for example, you need to create a table in which one column has three rows while an adjacent column has only one cell.

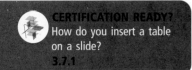

You can adjust a table's size by using the Height and Width options in the Table Size group on the Table Tools Layout tab. If you need to reposition a table on a slide, you can do so by simply dragging it into place using the light-blue table container outline.

Inserting an Excel Worksheet

Microsoft Office 2007 allows for a great deal of integration among its programs. If you need to show numerical data on a slide, for example, you can insert an Excel worksheet directly on the slide and use it to manipulate data just as you would in Excel.

→ INSERT AN EXCEL WORKSHEET

USE the presentation that is still open from the previous exercise.

1. Insert a new slide after the current slide (slide 5) with the Title Only layout.
2. Key the slide title **ATM Cost Analysis**.
3. Click the **Insert** tab, click the **Table** drop-down arrow, then click **Excel Spreadsheet**. PowerPoint creates a small Excel worksheet on the slide, as shown in Figure 5-5. Note that the PowerPoint Ribbon has been replaced by the Excel Ribbon.

Figure 5-5

A new Excel worksheet on a slide

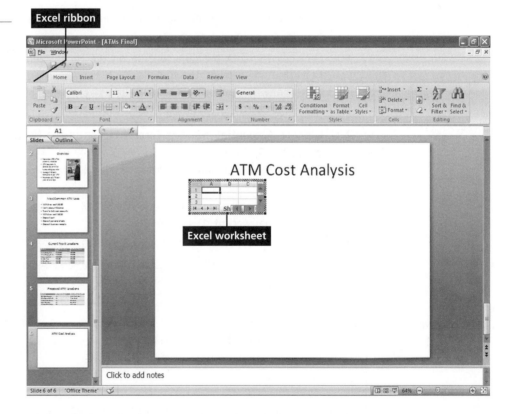

TAKE NOTE When an Excel worksheet is open on the slide, you are actually working in Excel. To return to PowerPoint, click outside the worksheet.

4. Resize the worksheet object by dragging the lower-right corner handle diagonally to the right to display columns A through F and rows 1 through 10.

TROUBLESHOOTING If your worksheet does not show lettered columns, click the Office button, click Excel Options, click Formulas, and remove the check mark from the R1C1 reference style check box.

5. Click the **Select All** area in the upper-left corner of the worksheet object, where the column headers and row headers intersect. The entire worksheet object is selected.

6. Click the **Font Size** drop-down arrow on the Home tab and click **18**.

7. Key data in the worksheet cells as shown in Figure 5-6. To adjust column widths, position the pointer on the border between columns and drag to the right until all data appears.

Figure 5-6

Key the data as shown

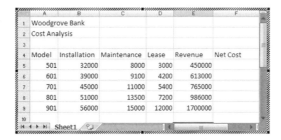

8. Click cell **F5** and key the following formula: **=E5–(B5+C5+D5)**.

9. Press **Enter** to complete the formula.

10. Click cell **F5**, click the **Copy** button on the Home tab, click cell **F6**, and click the **Paste** button to paste the formula.

11. Continue to paste the formula to cells **F7**, **F8**, and **F9**.

12. Drag over the numbers in columns B through F to select them.

13. Click the **Accounting Number Format** button in the Number group on the Home tab to apply a currency format. (Don't worry if some of the cells fill up with # signs.)

14. Click the **Decrease Decimal** button in the Number group twice to remove the decimal points and trailing zeros for the numbers.

15. Click cell **A1** and change the font size to **24**. Click the **Font Color** button and choose **Blue, Accent 1, Darker 25%**.

16. Adjust column widths again if necessary to present data clearly and attractively.

17. Click outside the worksheet object, and then click again to close the worksheet container. Your slide should look similar to Figure 5-7.

Figure 5-7

The completed Excel worksheet

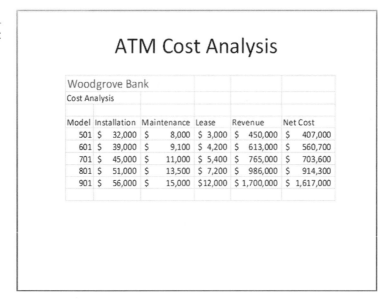

18. SAVE the presentation and **CLOSE** the file.

PAUSE. LEAVE PowerPoint open to use in the next exercise.

Inserting an Excel **worksheet** gives you access to all of Excel's data manipulation and formatting tools. If you want to show Excel data on a slide and have not yet created the worksheet, it makes sense to create the worksheet directly on the PowerPoint slide. A worksheet you insert in this way is **embedded** on the slide—it is stored within the PowerPoint presentation but can be edited using the tools of its source application, Excel.

You can edit the embedded worksheet at any time by double-clicking the worksheet object to open it in Excel. You can remove the object by clicking it once to display the heavy, light-blue container border and then pressing Delete.

> **TAKE NOTE** You know a worksheet is open and ready to edit in Excel when it displays the heavy hatched border.

When you insert a worksheet using the Excel Spreadsheet command, the worksheet consists of only four visible cells. Drag the bottom or side sizing handle (or the lower-right corner handle) to reveal more cells. When you have finished inserting data, use these handles to adjust the border to hide empty cells that would otherwise show on the PowerPoint slide.

You can also resize a worksheet object by clicking it once to display the heavy, light-blue container border, then dragging a bottom, side, or corner of the container. This action enlarges or reduces the object itself; it does not change font size of the embedded data even though the text may look larger.

If you have already created an Excel worksheet and want to use the data on a slide, you have several additional options for getting it from Excel to PowerPoint:

- Select the data in Excel, copy it, and paste it on a PowerPoint slide. This action pastes the Excel data as a PowerPoint table that cannot be edited in Excel but can be modified like any other PowerPoint table.
- Select the data in Excel, copy it, click the Paste button drop-down arrow in PowerPoint, and select Paste Special. In the Paste Special dialog box, choose to paste the data as an Excel worksheet object. The data is then embedded on the slide just as when you used the Excel Spreadsheet command.
- Select the data in Excel, copy it, and open the Paste Special dialog box in PowerPoint. Choose to paste link the data as an Excel worksheet object. The data is then **linked** to the Excel worksheet so that if you make any change to the worksheet in Excel, the data on the slide will show that same change.
- Finally, you can click the Object button on the Insert tab to open the Insert Object dialog box. Here you can choose to create a new worksheet file or navigate to an existing file and paste or paste link it on the slide.

> **TAKE NOTE** The Insert Object dialog box allows you to create a number of objects other than worksheets. You can create formulas, Word documents in various versions, and even sound files.

You can use the same procedures to copy Excel charts to slides. When simply pasted on a slide, an Excel chart can be formatted using the same tools you use to work with a PowerPoint chart.

> **REF** You will work with PowerPoint charts in Lesson 6.

Modifying Table Layout

↓
THE BOTTOM LINE
It is often necessary to modify layout as you work with a table. For example, you may need to add or delete rows or columns, move data in the table, adjust column widths, or merge or split table cells.

Adding and Deleting Rows and Columns

One of the most common reasons to change a table's structure is to add data to or remove data from the table. You can easily insert or delete rows and columns as necessary to keep data accurate and up to date.

→ **ADD A ROW AND A COLUMN**

The *ATM Models* file is available on the companion CD-ROM.

1. **OPEN** the *ATM Models* presentation.
2. Go to slide 2.
3. Click in the **1001** cell.
4. Click the **Table Tools Layout** tab, then click the **Insert Below** button in the Rows & Columns group. A new row appears below the row in which you clicked, highlighted and ready for data entry, as shown in Figure 5-8.

Figure 5-8

New row added below
current row

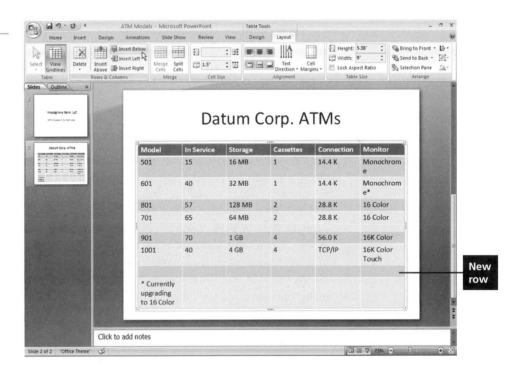

5. Key the following data in the new row:
   2001   10**   8 GB   6   TCP/IP   16K Color Touch
6. Click in the **Cassettes** column heading, then click the **Insert Right** button.
7. In the new column heading cell, key **Encryption**.

ANOTHER WAY You can also right-click in a cell, point to Insert on the shortcut menu, and click an option for inserting cells above, below, left, or right.

8. Key the following entries for the new column. When you finish, your table should look similar to Figure 5-9. (Don't worry about the length of the table; you will adjust column widths later.)

501	No
601	No
701	No
801	Yes
901	Yes
1001	Yes
2001	Yes

Figure 5-9

New column data inserted

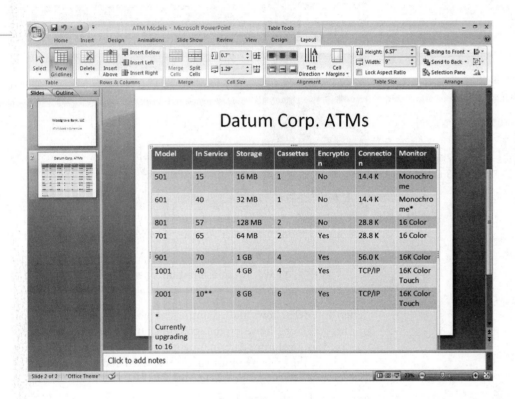

9. SAVE the presentation as *ATM Models Final*.

PAUSE. LEAVE the presentation open to use in the next exercise.

Tools in the Rows & Columns group on the Table Tools Layout tab make it easy to insert new rows and columns exactly where you want them in the table. Simply click in a cell near where you want to add the row or column and then click the appropriate button on the tab.

DELETE A ROW AND A COLUMN

USE the presentation that is still open from the previous exercise.

1. With the table still selected, click in the **501** cell in the second row of the table.
2. Click the **Delete** button in the Rows & Columns group on the Table Tools Layout tab, then click **Delete Rows**. The entire row is removed from the table.

You can right-click in a cell and then click Delete Rows or Delete Columns on the shortcut menu, or you can use the Cut button on the Home tab to remove a selected row or column.

3. Click in the **Cassettes** cell in the column header row.

4. Click the **Delete** button in the Rows & Columns group, then click **Delete Columns**. The entire column is deleted. Your table should look similar to Figure 5-10.

Figure 5-10

A row and column have been deleted

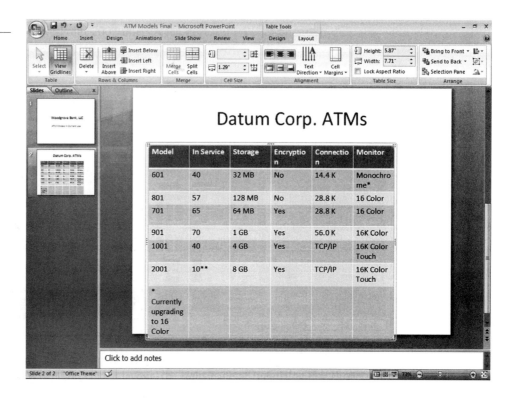

PAUSE. LEAVE the presentation open to use in the next exercise.

When you delete rows and columns, the table automatically resizes to account for the removal of the data. Note, however, that columns do not automatically resize to fill the area previously occupied by a column. After removing columns, you may need to resize the remaining columns in the table to adjust space. You learn about resizing later in this lesson.

Moving Rows and Columns

Move rows and columns when you need to reorder data. You can use drag and drop or the Cut and Paste commands to move row or column data into a new, blank row or column.

⊙ MOVE A ROW AND A COLUMN

USE the presentation that is still open from the previous exercise.

1. Click in the **901** cell, then click the **Insert Above** button in the Rows & Columns group to insert a blank row above the current cell.

2. Drag the pointer over the third row of the table, which contains data for the 801 model, to select all cells.

3. Click cell **801**, hold down the mouse button, and drag the whole row down and drop it in the new, blank row. The ATM models are now in correct numerical order, as shown in Figure 5-11.

Figure 5-11

The table row has been moved

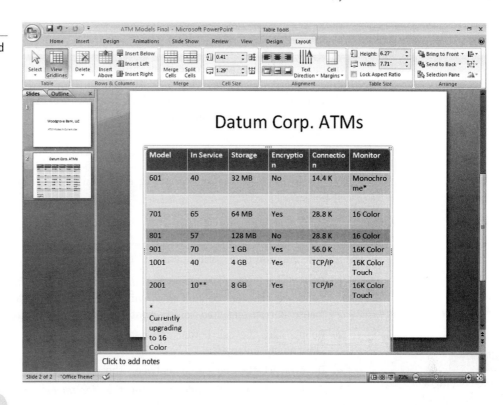

It is sometimes difficult to see the selection highlight on cells formatted with a Quick Style. If you end up moving only a part of row, click Undo and start over.

4. Click in the empty row where the 801 data was previously, click the **Delete** button, and then click **Delete Rows**.

5. Click in the **Monitor** cell, then click the **Insert Right** button. A new, blank column appears to the right of the current cell.

6. Drag the pointer down the *In Service* column to select all cells in the column.

7. Click the **Home** tab, then click the **Cut** button to remove the column from the table.

8. Click in the column header cell in the new, blank column, and then click the **Paste** button. You have moved the column, as shown in Figure 5-12.

Figure 5-12

The table column has been moved

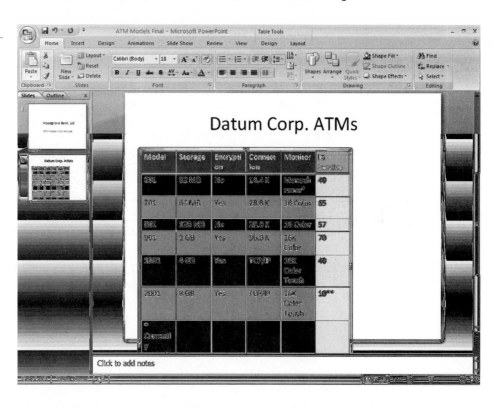

PAUSE. LEAVE the presentation open to use in the next exercise.

Moving rows and columns in PowerPoint 2007 is similar to moving rows and columns in a worksheet program such as Excel: You must make sure you have a blank row or column in which to insert the new data. If you simply drag a row or column to a new location, you will overwrite the existing data at that location.

Resizing Rows and Columns

Row heights and column widths can be easily resized by dragging or double-clicking cell borders.

⊕ RESIZE ROWS AND COLUMNS

USE the presentation that is still open from the previous exercise.

1. Click the cell border between the *Storage* cell and the *Encryption* cell. The pointer takes the shape of parallel lines with outward-pointing arrows. Hold down the mouse button and drag to the right about one-quarter inch to enlarge the column.
2. Double-click the cell border between the *Encryption* cell and the *Connection* cell. The column enlarges.
3. Double-click the cell border between the *Connection* cell and the *Monitor* cell.
4. Double-click the cell border between the *Monitor* cell and the *In Service* cell.
5. Move the pointer near the right edge of the *In Service* cell until it rests on the cell's outer border, as shown in Figure 5-13. (The outer border is obscured by the light-blue table container.)

TAKE NOTE

Double-clicking a column border adjusts column width to fit the column's widest entry.

Figure 5-13

Position the pointer as shown to resize the last column

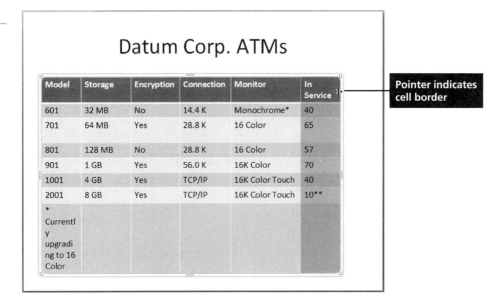

6. Double-click the pointer to resize the last column so the column header fits on a single line.
7. Click the cell border below the *701* cell and drag upward to reduce the row height to match heights of other rows. Your table should look similar to Figure 5-14.

Figure 5-14

Column widths and row height
have been adjusted

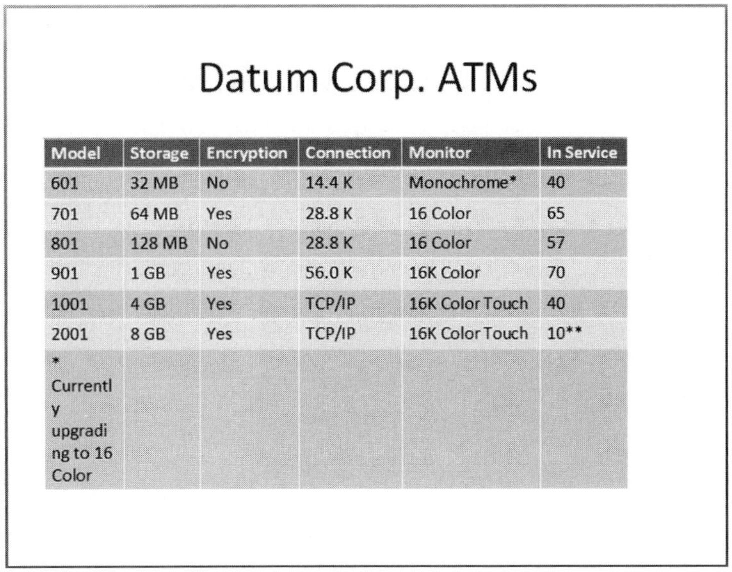

Datum Corp. ATMs

Model	Storage	Encryption	Connection	Monitor	In Service
601	32 MB	No	14.4 K	Monochrome*	40
701	64 MB	Yes	28.8 K	16 Color	65
801	128 MB	No	28.8 K	16 Color	57
901	1 GB	Yes	56.0 K	16K Color	70
1001	4 GB	Yes	TCP/IP	16K Color Touch	40
2001	8 GB	Yes	TCP/IP	16K Color Touch	10**
* Currentl y upgradi ng to 16 Color					

PAUSE. LEAVE the presentation open to use in the next exercise.

Adjust column widths or row heights to eliminate unused space or add space to make table text more readable. Dragging allows you to "eyeball" column widths or row heights so that they look attractive on the slide. Double-clicking allows you to immediately set column width to the width of its widest line. Double-clicking does not adjust row height, however. To resize a row that has been enlarged, drag its bottom border.

You do not have to select an entire column or row to resize all cells in that column. When you click in any cell and resize a row or column, all cells in that row or column are adjusted at the same time.

If you need to be more precise in resizing, you can use the tools in the Cell Size group on the Table Tools Layout tab to specify exact widths and heights for table cells.

You can also adjust column widths or row heights using the Distribute Columns and Distribute Rows buttons on the Table Tools Layout tab. Select the columns or rows you want to resize and click the appropriate button to make all columns the same width or rows the same height.

If space in a table is extremely tight, you may be able to fit more text in columns and rows by adjusting cell margins. The Cell Margins button in the Alignment group on the Table Tools Layout tab allows you to select from four different cell margin options, from None to Wide, or create custom margins.

Merging and Splitting Table Cells

The merge and split features allow you to adjust how content fits in table cells. Merging and splitting can modify the internal structure of a table without increasing or reducing its overall width.

⊕ MERGE AND SPLIT TABLE CELLS

USE the presentation that is still open from the previous exercise.

1. Drag the pointer over the last row in the table to select all cells.
2. Click the **Table Tools Layout** tab, if necessary, and then click the **Merge Cells** button in the Merge group. The entry in the first column can now spread across the bottom row of the table, as shown in Figure 5-15.

Figure 5-15

Cells merged in bottom row
of table

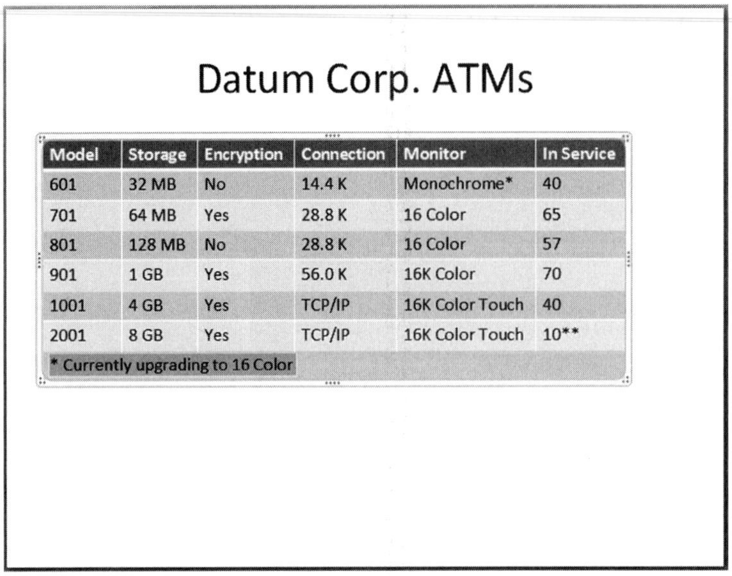

Datum Corp. ATMs

Model	Storage	Encryption	Connection	Monitor	In Service
601	32 MB	No	14.4 K	Monochrome*	40
701	64 MB	Yes	28.8 K	16 Color	65
801	128 MB	No	28.8 K	16 Color	57
901	1 GB	Yes	56.0 K	16K Color	70
1001	4 GB	Yes	TCP/IP	16K Color Touch	40
2001	8 GB	Yes	TCP/IP	16K Color Touch	10**
* Currently upgrading to 16 Color					

ANOTHER WAY   To quickly merge or split, right-click in a cell or selected cells and click Merge or Split on the shortcut menu.

3. Click in the merged row, then click the **Split Cells** button in the Merge group. Accept the default split option of 2 columns and 1 row and click **OK**. The last row of the table now consists of two cells.

4. In the new cell in the bottom row, key ****15 additional on order**.

5. **SAVE** and **CLOSE** the presentation.

   PAUSE. LEAVE PowerPoint open to use in the next exercise.

By merging cells, you can position content so it spans more than one column or row. Merging can give a table visual interest and make it easier to understand.

Use the split feature when you want to divide a single row or column into more parts than surrounding rows or columns. Splitting allows you to accommodate additional entries in a row or column without modifying the remainder of the table.

■ Formatting Tables

THE BOTTOM LINE   PowerPoint provides default formats to all new tables so that they look good right from the start. You may want to modify formatting, however, because you do not like the default colors or you want a different look. Use the tools on the Table Tools Design and Table Tools Layout tabs to apply new formatting options.

Changing Table Text Alignment and Orientation

You have a number of options for aligning text in table cells. You can also change text orientation to create visual interest.

➔ ALIGN AND ORIENT TEXT IN A TABLE

The *Bids* file is available on the companion CD-ROM.

1. **OPEN** the *Bids* presentation.
2. Go to slide 2, and click in the merged cell at the far left of the table.
3. Click the **Table Tools Layout** tab, and then click the **Text Direction** button to display a menu of orientation options.
4. Click **Stacked**. This option will stack text with each letter below the previous one.
5. Key **Vendor**. The text stacks in the merged cell as shown in Figure 5-16.

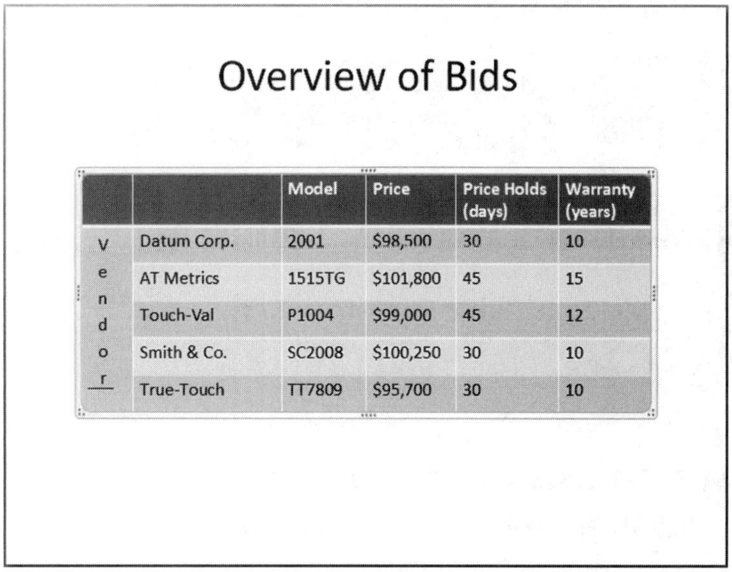

Figure 5-16

Stacked text orientation

Overview of Bids

		Model	Price	Price Holds (days)	Warranty (years)
V e n d o r	Datum Corp.	2001	$98,500	30	10
	AT Metrics	1515TG	$101,800	45	15
	Touch-Val	P1004	$99,000	45	12
	Smith & Co.	SC2008	$100,250	30	10
	True-Touch	TT7809	$95,700	30	10

TAKE NOTE

When you move the I-beam pointer over rotated or stacked text, its orientation changes to match the text orientation.

◆ ANOTHER WAY

Horizontal alignment buttons also appear on the Table Tools Layout tab.

6. Select the text you just keyed. Click the **Home** tab, then click the **Character Spacing** button. Click **Very Tight**.
7. With text still selected, click the **Bold** button.
8. Select the cells with numbers in the *Price* column. Click the **Align Text Right** button in the Paragraph group.
9. Select the cells with numbers in the last two columns. Click the **Center** button.
10. Select the cells in the column header row. Click the **Table Tools Layout** tab.
11. Click the **Align Bottom** button in the Alignment group. All column headings now align at the bottom of the cells, as shown in Figure 5-17.

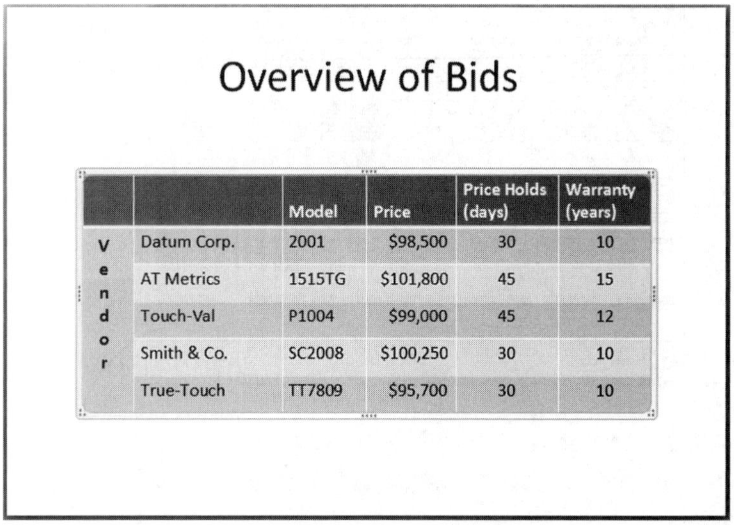

Figure 5-17

Text has been vertically aligned at the bottom

Overview of Bids

		Model	Price	Price Holds (days)	Warranty (years)
V e n d o r	Datum Corp.	2001	$98,500	30	10
	AT Metrics	1515TG	$101,800	45	15
	Touch-Val	P1004	$99,000	45	12
	Smith & Co.	SC2008	$100,250	30	10
	True-Touch	TT7809	$95,700	30	10

12. SAVE the presentation as *Final Bids*.

PAUSE. LEAVE the presentation open to use in the next exercise.

Use the same tools to align content horizontally in a table cell that you use to align text in a text placeholder. Changing alignment in table cells can improve readability as well as make a table more attractive.

Vertical alignment options control how content appears from top to bottom of a cell. The default option is top alignment, but column heads often look better centered vertically in table cells. When column headings have differing numbers of lines, standard procedure is to align all headings at the bottom.

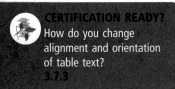

TAKE NOTE You can change vertical alignment in any placeholder as well. Use the Align Text button on the Home tab to choose from Top, Middle, or Bottom vertical alignment.

Use options on the Text Direction menu to change the orientation of text for a special effect. Vertical text or text that reads from bottom to top makes a unique row header, for example.

CERTIFICATION READY?
How do you change alignment and orientation of table text?
3.7.3

Applying a Quick Style to a Table

PowerPoint tables are formatted by default with a Quick Style based on the current theme colors. You can choose another Quick Style to change color and shading formats.

⊙ APPLY A QUICK STYLE TO A TABLE

USE the presentation that is still open from the previous exercise.

1. Click anywhere in the table, then click the **Table Tools Design** tab.
2. Click the **More** button in the Table Styles group to display the Quick Styles gallery, as shown in Figure 5-18. Note that the table styles are organized into several groups—Best Match for Document, Light, Medium, and Dark.

Figure 5-18

Table Quick Styles gallery

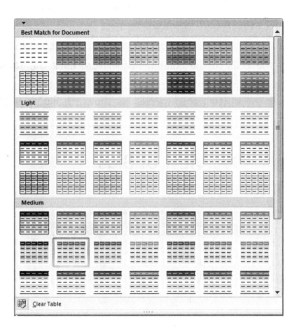

3. Click the **Themed Style 2 – Accent 6** table style. This is a colorful alternative, but not exactly what you want.

4. Click the **More** button again, and then click the **Medium Style 3** style, a black and gray combination in the first column of the gallery. Your table should look similar to Figure 5-19.

Figure 5-19

New Quick Style applied to entire table

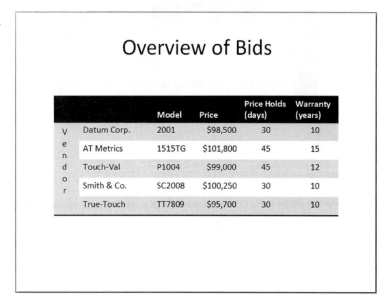

PAUSE. **LEAVE** the presentation open to use in the next exercise.

Colors available for Quick Style formats are controlled by theme. If you apply a Quick Style and then change the theme, the Quick Style colors will adjust to those of the new theme.

You may on occasion want to remove all table formatting to present data in a simple grid without shading or border colors. You can remove formatting by clicking Clear Table at the bottom of the Quick Styles gallery. Once you have cleared formats, you can reapply them by selecting any table style.

CERTIFICATION READY?
How do you apply Quick Styles to tables?
3.7.2

Turning Table Style Options On or Off

Use the table style options to control what parts of a table are emphasized by Quick Style formatting.

⊕ TURN TABLE STYLE OPTIONS ON AND OFF

USE the presentation that is still open from the previous exercise.

1. Click anywhere in the table to select it if necessary.
2. Click the **Table Tools Design** tab if it is not already displayed.
3. Click the **Banded Rows** option in the Table Style Options group to deselect the option.
4. Click the **First Column** option. The first column receives special emphasis.
5. Click the **Banded Columns** option. Color bands are applied to the columns. Your table should look similar to Figure 5-20.

Figure 5-20

New table style options have been applied

Overview of Bids

		Model	Price	Price Holds (days)	Warranty (years)
V e n d o r	Datum Corp.	2001	$98,500	30	10
	AT Metrics	1515TG	$101,800	45	15
	Touch-Val	P1004	$99,000	45	12
	Smith & Co.	SC2008	$100,250	30	10
	True-Touch	TT7809	$95,700	30	10

6. **SAVE** and **CLOSE** the presentation.

PAUSE. LEAVE PowerPoint open to use in the next exercise.

The options in the Table Style Options group on the Table Tools Design tab allow you to adjust what part of a table receives special emphasis. If your table has a row that shows totals of calculations, for example, the Total Row option applies color to that row so it stands out.

You can use any number of these options in a single table, or you can deselect all of them for a plainer effect. Keep in mind that there is sometimes a fine line between emphasis and the visual confusion that can result from too much emphasis.

Adding Shading to Cells

Use the Shading button on the Table Tools Design tab to select your own fill options for table cells.

⊕ ADD SHADING TO CELLS

The *Warranties* file is available on the companion CD-ROM.

1. **OPEN** the *Warranties* presentation.
2. Go to slide 2, and select the cells in the column header row.
3. Click the **Table Tools Design** tab, if necessary, and then click the **Shading** button drop-down arrow in the Table Styles group. The Shading color palette displays.
4. Click the **Gold, Accent 1** color to fill the column header cells with gold.
5. With the column header cells still selected, click the **Shading** drop-down arrow again, point to **Gradient**, and select the **From Corner** gradient style in the Dark Variations section of the gallery. Your table should look similar to Figure 5-21.

Figure 5-21

A gradient shading style applied to table cells

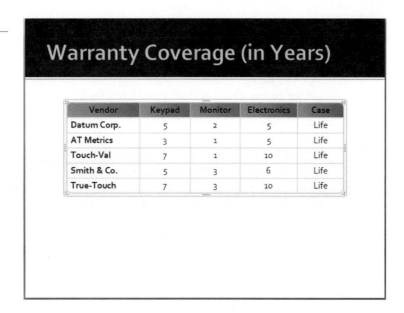

Warranty Coverage (in Years)

Vendor	Keypad	Monitor	Electronics	Case
Datum Corp.	5	2	5	Life
AT Metrics	3	1	5	Life
Touch-Val	7	1	10	Life
Smith & Co.	5	3	6	Life
True-Touch	7	3	10	Life

6. **SAVE** the file as *Warranties Final*.

PAUSE. LEAVE the presentation open to use in the next exercise.

If you do not like the Quick Style options or want more control over formatting, use the Table Tools Design tab's options for creating shading fills, border styles, and effects.

Use the Shading button to display a color palette with the current theme colors. You can also select a color from the Standard color palette or from the Colors dialog box, or choose a picture, gradient, or texture fill.

The Shading menu also offers the Table Background option. You can use this command to insert a color or a picture to fill all cells of a table. You will learn more about inserting pictures as background later in this lesson.

Be careful when applying picture or texture fills to an entire table. Your text must remain readable, so choose a light background, adjust transparency if necessary, or be prepared to boldface text.

Adding Borders to Table Cells

Use the Borders menu to select which borders you want to add to table cells.

⊕ **ADD BORDERS TO TABLE CELLS**

USE the presentation that is still open from the previous exercise.

1. Select all cells *except* those in the first column and the column header cells. (You are selecting the numbers and the *Life* entries.)

2. Click the **Border** drop-down arrow in the Table Styles group. A menu of border options appears, as shown in Figure 5-22.

Figure 5-22

Border options you can apply to cells

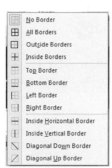

	No Border
	All Borders
	Outside Borders
	Inside Borders
	Top Border
	Bottom Border
	Left Border
	Right Border
	Inside Horizontal Border
	Inside Vertical Border
	Diagonal Down Border
	Diagonal Up Border

3. Click **Inside Horizontal Border.**

4. Click outside the table to deselect the cells, then select only the bottom row of the table.

5. Click the **Border** drop-down arrow, and then click **Bottom Border.** A border is applied to the entire bottom row of the table.

6. Click outside the table to deselect the cells. Your table should look like Figure 5-23.

Figure 5-23

Borders applied to selected cells

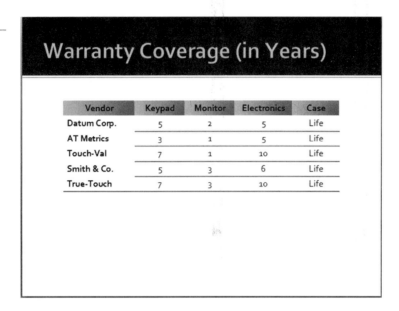

Warranty Coverage (in Years)

Vendor	Keypad	Monitor	Electronics	Case
Datum Corp.	5	2	5	Life
AT Metrics	3	1	5	Life
Touch-Val	7	1	10	Life
Smith & Co.	5	3	6	Life
True-Touch	7	3	10	Life

PAUSE. LEAVE the presentation open to use in the next exercise.

The Border menu allows you to quickly apply borders to all sides of selected cells or to any specific side of a cell, giving you considerable leeway in formatting table cells. You can also remove all borders from a cell or selected cells by selecting No Border.

After you have selected a border option, it displays on the button. You can easily reapply that border option by simply clicking the button.

TAKE NOTE The Shading button also shows the latest shading color you chose, making it easy to apply the same color again.

Note that you can also choose diagonal borders from the Border menu. Use a diagonal border to split a cell so you can insert two values in it, one to the left side of the cell and the other to the right on the other side of the diagonal border.

TAKE NOTE To insert two values in a cell, set left alignment and key the first value, then press Ctrl+Tab or use the spacebar to move to the other half of the cell to key the second value.

Adding Special Effects to a Table

The Table Styles group offers an Effects button to let you apply selected special effects. Some effects apply to individual cells, others to the entire table.

ADD SPECIAL EFFECTS TO A TABLE

USE the presentation that is still open from the previous exercise.

1. Click anywhere in the table to select it.
2. Click the **Effects** button in the Table Styles group, point to **Shadow**, and click **Offset Diagonal Bottom Right**.
3. Click outside the table to see the effect. Your table should look like Figure 5-24.

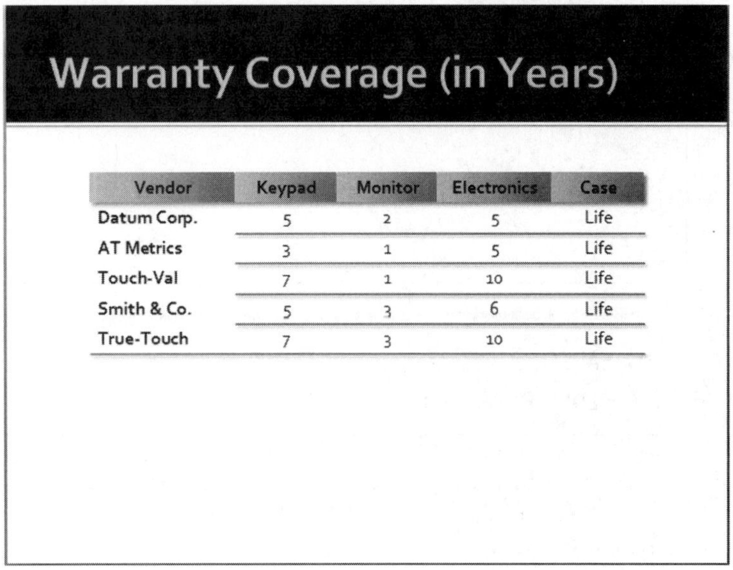

Figure 5-24

Shadow effect applied to table

Warranty Coverage (in Years)

Vendor	Keypad	Monitor	Electronics	Case
Datum Corp.	5	2	5	Life
AT Metrics	3	1	5	Life
Touch-Val	7	1	10	Life
Smith & Co.	5	3	6	Life
True-Touch	7	3	10	Life

PAUSE. LEAVE the presentation open to use in the next exercise.

You have the option to apply bevel, shadow, and reflection effects to a table. Bevels can apply to individual cells or selections of cells, but shadows and reflections are applied to the entire table.

Adding an Image to a Table

You can add an image to create a unique background for an entire table or selected cells.

ADD AN IMAGE TO A TABLE

USE the presentation that is still open from the previous exercise.

1. Select the vendor names in the first column of the table. (Do not select the *Vendor* column heading.)
2. Right-click in one of the selected cells, then click **Format Shape**. The Format Shape dialog box opens.
3. Click **Picture or texture fill**.
4. Click the **File** button and navigate to the location of your data files. Select and open *ATM.jpg*.
5. Click the **Tile picture as texture** check box.
6. Drag the **Transparency** slider until the box to the right of the slider reads 80%.
7. Click **Close**. Click outside the table. Your table should look similar to Figure 5-25.

The *ATM.jpg* file is available on the companion CD-ROM.

Figure 5-25

An image becomes a fill for selected cells

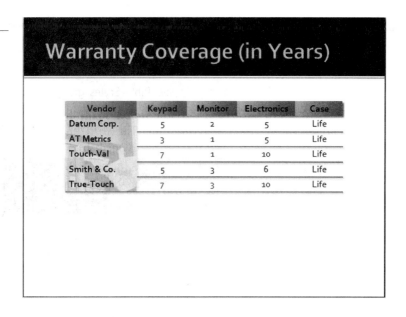

8. **SAVE** the presentation and **CLOSE** it.
   CLOSE PowerPoint.

You learned earlier that you can specify a picture as a background using the Table Background command on the Shading menu. Use this option if the picture you want to use is already formatted in such a way that it will not overwhelm the text in the table.

For the most control over an image to be used as a table background, insert it using the Format Shape dialog box, as you did in this exercise. You can insert a picture in a single cell or selected cells by right-clicking a selected cell and choosing Format Shape. Or you insert the picture in all cells by right-clicking the table's light-blue container and then choosing Format Shape. Tiling options in this dialog box allow you to adjust how the tiles display over the table. If you choose not to tile, the picture will appear in every cell of the table. The Transparency slider lets you wash out the picture to make it appropriate for a background.

Images can be used for more than background effects in tables. You can also insert an image as table content. To do so, click in a cell and use the Picture command on the Shading menu. The picture you select is automatically resized to fit into the selected table cell.

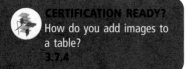
CERTIFICATION READY?
How do you add images to a table?
3.7.4

SUMMARY SKILL MATRIX

In This Lesson You Learned	Matrix Skill	Skill Number
To create a table on a slide	Insert tables in a slide	3.7.1
To modify table layout		
To format tables		
To change alignment and orientation of text in a table	Change alignment and orientation of table text	3.7.3
To apply a Quick Style to a table	Apply Quick Styles to tables	3.7.2
To add an image to a table	Add images to tables	3.7.4

Knowledge Assessment

Matching

Match the term in Column 1 to its description in Column 2.

Column 1	Column 2
1. table	**a.** insert data so that it maintains a connection to a source document
2. Draw Table	**b.** a document used to manipulate numerical data
3. Table Tools Design	**c.** option to click to insert a background color for table cells
4. merge	**d.** insert data so that it can be edited using its original application
5. link	**e.** tab that allows you to insert a new table row
6. Paste Special	**f.** an arrangement of columns and rows used to organize data
7. Shading	**g.** tab that allows you to apply a Quick Style to a table
8. embedded	**h.** option you can use to create a table outline and insert columns and rows where you want them
9. Table Tools Layout	**i.** combine two or more cells to create a larger cell
10. worksheet	**j.** command that allows you to paste or paste link an object to a slide

True / False

Circle T if the statement is true or F if the statement is false.

T | F **1.** The easiest way to create a table is to use the Insert Object button and then select the type of table to create.

T | F **2.** By default, a new table is sized to fit the content placeholder in which it was created.

T | F **3.** To edit a worksheet object, double-click the object to display Excel's tools.

T | F **4.** You can copy and paste any Excel object to a PowerPoint slide.

T | F **5.** You must select an entire row before you can insert a new row above or below it.

T | F **6.** When moving a column, you can simply drag it to a new location in the table and other columns will adjust around it.

T | F **7.** Use Distribute Columns to quickly resize all columns to the same width.

T | F **8.** Use the Blank Table option to quickly remove all formatting from a table.

T | F **9.** Bevel effects automatically apply to an entire table.

T | F **10.** If you do not specify that a picture should be tiled over selected cells, it will display in each table cell.

■ Competency Assessment

Project 5-1: Job Fair

You work for Lucerne Executive Recruiters, a company that specializes in finding employees for a variety of clients. You are planning to give a brief presentation at a local job fair and need to prepare a slide that lists some currently available jobs for which you are recruiting candidates. You can use a table to display this information.

GET READY. Launch PowerPoint if it is not already running.

The *Jobs* file is available on the companion CD-ROM.

1. OPEN the *Jobs* presentation.
2. Go to slide 2, and click the **Insert Table** icon in the content placeholder.
3. Create a table with three columns and seven rows.
4. Key the following information in the table.

Title	Company	Salary Range*
Senior Editor	Litware, Inc.	$30K - $42K
Sales Associate	Contoso Pharmaceuticals	$55K - $70K
District Manager	Tailspin Toys	$65K - $80K
Accountant	Fourth Coffee	$53K - $60K
Production Assistant	Fabrikam, Inc.	$38K - $45K

   *Starting salary based on experience

5. Click in the **Salary Range** column, then click the **Insert Right** button on the Table Tools Layout tab to insert a new column.
6. Key the following information in the new column:

   Posted
   5/01
   5/10
   4/30
   4/27
   5/07

7. Click the **Production Assistant** cell, then click the **Insert Below** button on the Table Tools Layout tab to insert a new row.
8. Key the following information in the new row:

Loan Officer	Woodgrove Bank	$42K - $54K	5/12

9. Select all the cells in the last row of the table, then click the **Merge Cells** button on the Table Tools Layout tab.
10. Adjust column widths by dragging or double-clicking cell borders so that all table entries are on a single line.
11. Format the table as follows:
    a. Select the *Salary Range* and *Posted* columns, then click the **Center** button.
    b. Click in the last row of the table, then click the **Align Text Right** button.
    c. With the insertion point still in the last row, click the **Shading** button on the Table Tools Design tab, then click **No Fill**.
    d. Click the **Border** button, then click **No Border**.
    e. Click the **First Column** table style option to apply emphasis to the first column of the table. Adjust column widths again if necessary to avoid runover lines.
    f. Select all cells in the *Loan Officer* row of the table, click the **Border** button, then click **Bottom Border**.
    g. Apply a bevel effect to the column header cells and the first column cells.

12. **SAVE** the presentation as *Jobs Final* and then **CLOSE** the file.

LEAVE PowerPoint open for the next project.

Project 5-2: Making the Upgrade

You are a production manager at Tailspin Toys. You have been asked to give a presentation to senior management about anticipated costs of upgrading machinery in the assembly area. Because you want to sum the costs, you will use an Excel worksheet to present the information.

The *Upgrades* file is available on the companion CD-ROM.

1. **OPEN** the *Upgrades* presentation.
2. Go to slide 2, click the **Insert** tab, click the **Table** drop-down arrow, and then click **Excel Spreadsheet**.
3. Drag the lower-right corner handle of the worksheet object to reveal columns A through D and rows 1 through 7.
4. Key the following data in the worksheet. (Change the zoom size if desired to make it easier to see the data you are entering.)

Machine	Upgrade	Cost	Time Frame
Conveyor #2	New belt, drive	$28,000	30 days
Conveyor #3	Update software	$5,800	14 days
Drill Press #1	Replace	$32,000	30 days
Vacuum system	New pump, lines	$12,750	30 days
Docks #2 - #5	Doors, motors	$14,500	10 days

5. Click the Excel **Page Layout** tab, click the **Themes** button, and then click **Solstice** to apply the same theme to the worksheet that your presentation uses.
6. Adjust column widths by dragging or double-clicking column borders to display all data.
7. Click in cell **B7**, key **Total Costs**, and then press Tab.
8. Click the **Sum** button in the Editing group on the Home tab, then press Enter to complete the SUM function.
9. Apply Quick Styles to the worksheet as follows:
   a. Select the column headings, then click the **Cell Styles** button in the Styles group on the Home tab.
   b. Click the **Accent5** style.
   c. Click the **Total Costs** cell, click the **Cell Styles** button, and click the **Accent1** style.
   d. Click the cell that contains the sum of costs, click the **Cell Styles** button, and click the **Total** style.
   e. Apply bold formatting to the column heads and the Total Costs cell.
10. Click the **Select All** area at the top left corner of the worksheet, then click the **Font Size** drop-down arrow and click **18**. Adjust column width again if necessary to display all data.
11. Select the entries in the *Time Frame* column, and click the **Center** button.
12. Click outside the worksheet twice to review your changes.
13. **SAVE** the presentation as *Upgrades Final* and then **CLOSE** the file.

LEAVE PowerPoint open for the next project.

■ Proficiency Assessment

Project 5-3: Power Up

You are an operations manager for City Power & Light. You have been asked to give a presentation to department heads about scheduled maintenance of power substations around the city. Use a table to present the maintenance schedule.

The *Power* file is available on the companion CD-ROM.

1. **OPEN** the *Power* presentation.
2. Go to slide 3. On the Insert tab, click **Table** and drag over the grid to create a table with two columns and seven rows.
3. Key the following information in the table:

Substation	Week of
Eastland	July 13
Morehead	October 1
Huntington	June 6
Parkland	May 21
Midtown	July 28
Elmwood	December 11

4. Apply a Quick Style of your choice to the table.
5. Turn on the **First Column** table style, and change any other table style option that improves the look of the table.
6. Click in the last row of the table and then delete the row.
7. Move rows so that the dates in the second column are in chronological order.
8. Click the outside border of the table, hold down the mouse button, and drag straight down to move the table down about half an inch.
9. **SAVE** the presentation as *Power Final* and then **CLOSE** the file.

   LEAVE PowerPoint open for the next project.

Project 5-4: Is It on the Agenda?

You are an assistant director of finance at Humongous Insurance Company. You have been tasked with establishing the agenda for a management meeting. You have created the agenda as a table on a slide, which will appear onscreen throughout the day. You think the table could use some additional formatting to make it easier to read and understand.

The *Agenda* file is available on the companion CD-ROM.

1. **OPEN** the *Agenda* presentation.
2. Center all entries in the second column, and then center the column head only for the third column.
3. Clear all formatting from the table using the **Clear Table** option on the table Quick Styles gallery.
4. Remove all borders using the **No Border** option on the Border menu.
5. Format the table's header row as follows:
   a. Increase the height of the column header row to 0.6 inches, and then center the column header text vertically in the row.
   b. Apply bold, 20-pt formatting to the column header text.
   c. Select the header row cells and use the Format Shape dialog box to apply the **Granite** texture. Change the transparency of the texture to 65%.
   d. Apply the **Circle** cell bevel effect to the header row cells.
6. Select the first *Break* row and apply a shading of **Aqua, Accent 3, Lighter 40%**. Apply the same shading color to the second *Break* row.

7. Select the *Lunch* row and apply a shading of **Lavender, Accent 5, Lighter 40%**.

8. Apply the **Inside Diagonal Bottom Right** shadow effect to the entire table.

9. Add a border around the outside of the table and along the bottom of the header row.

10. **SAVE** the presentation as *Agenda Final* and then **CLOSE** the file.

   LEAVE PowerPoint open for the next project.

■ Mastery Assessment

Project 5-5: Scaling the Summit

You are a district manager for Adventure Works, a travel agency specializing in adventurous destinations. You are preparing a presentation that contains a list of mountain climbing excursions you can use at a travel fair and need to format the table that contains the excursion information.

1. **OPEN** the *Adventures* presentation.

2. Go to slide 3 and select the table.

3. Use the *Mountain.jpg* picture file as a background for the entire table. Tile the picture, and adjust transparency so that the text can be clearly read against the background.

4. Apply shading formatting of your choice to the column heads, and adjust font color and style as desired to improve appearance.

5. Apply borders as desired to the table.

6. Apply an effect of your choice to the table.

7. **SAVE** the presentation as *Adventures Final* and then **CLOSE** the file.

   LEAVE PowerPoint open for the next project.

The *Adventures* file is available on the companion CD-ROM.

The *Mountain.jpg* file is available on the companion CD-ROM.

Project 5-6: Complaint Process

Your employer, Trey Research, has been asked by Center City Hospital to help the hospital conduct an extensive study on patient complaints. You have been asked to tally complaints for the past year and categorize them. You have begun the process of creating a presentation to detail your findings. Your first step is a summary table that lays out the major categories of complaints.

1. **OPEN** the *Complaints* presentation.

2. Go to slide 2 and adjust column widths so that all the summary items are on one line.

3. Move table items to group category items and present the categories in alphabetical order.

4. Split the *Complaints* column into two columns, and move all information from the original *Complaints* column, including the column header, into the right-hand split.

5. Merge the table cells in the left-hand split. (Do not merge the column header row, only the banded cells.)

6. In the merged cell, rotate the text direction 270 degrees and key **Over 375 complaints received from patients in past 12 months**.

7. Apply different shading colors to each category of complaint, with a border at the bottom of each category section.

8. Apply a shading option to the left-hand split column that includes the column header row so the whole column is the same color. Remove the border at the bottom of upper-left column header cell.

The *Complaints* file is available on the companion CD-ROM.

9. Adjust column widths again if necessary and adjust alignment as necessary to improve table appearance.

10. **SAVE** the presentation as *Complaints Final* and then **CLOSE** the file. **CLOSE** PowerPoint.

INTERNET READY

You want to take a vacation over the winter holidays next year, but you have not yet decided whether to go skiing, enjoy the sun on a Caribbean island, or venture down under to Australia. Using Internet search tools, find several interesting ski packages in Canada and Europe, resort packages in the Caribbean, and lodgings in Sydney, Australia. Determine the local price for all these excursions. Create a PowerPoint presentation with a table that lists your possible destinations and dates of travel. Add a new slide and insert a worksheet. Enter the destinations and their costs and the conversion rate to convert local costs to dollars. Create formulas to convert costs so you can compare all package costs in U.S. dollars.

Using Charts in a Presentation

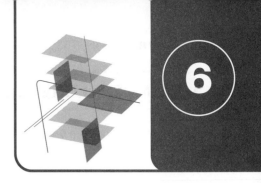

6

You are the general manager of the Alpine Ski House, a small ski resort. One of your responsibilities is to provide information to the group of investors who share ownership of the resort. You use Microsoft Office PowerPoint 2007 presentations to convey that information. PowerPoint's charting capabilities allow you to communicate financial data in a visual way that makes trends and comparisons easy to understand. In this lesson, you learn how to insert different types of charts, as well as how to modify and format a chart so it displays your data in the most attractive and useful way.

KEY TERMS
chart
chart area
data marker
data series
legend
plot area

169

■ SOFTWARE ORIENTATION

A PowerPoint Chart

Charts can help your audience understand relationships among numerical values. Figure 6-1 shows a sample PowerPoint chart with some standard chart features labeled.

Figure 6-1

Components of a
PowerPoint chart

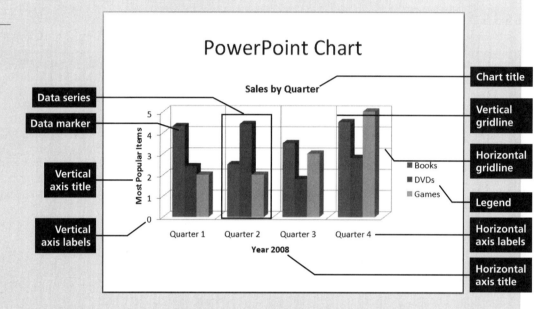

A PowerPoint chart can be as simple as a series of lines or two-dimensional columns, or it can provide a whole range of additional information, such as that shown in the chart above. Legends, titles, and gridlines can help present complex data so it can be easily understood.

■ Building Charts

THE BOTTOM LINE

You can create a chart in any content placeholder. PowerPoint and Excel work in tandem to streamline the operation of inserting and formatting the chart so that all you need to do is key the data for the chart. After you have inserted the chart, you can change the chart type or layout to display the data as you wish.

Inserting a Chart from a Content Placeholder

As with tables and other objects such as diagrams and pictures, the easiest way to insert a chart is to click the Insert Chart icon in any content placeholder. PowerPoint guides you the rest of the way to complete the chart.

⊕ INSERT A CHART

GET READY. Before you begin these steps, make sure that your computer is on. Log on, if necessary.

1. Start PowerPoint, if the program is not already running.
2. Locate and open the *Revenues* presentation.

CD

The *Revenues* file is available on the companion CD-ROM.

3. Go to slide 3. Click the **Insert Chart** icon in the center of the content placeholder. The Insert Chart dialog box opens, as shown in Figure 6-2, showing chart types and subtypes.

Figure 6-2

Select a chart type and subtype

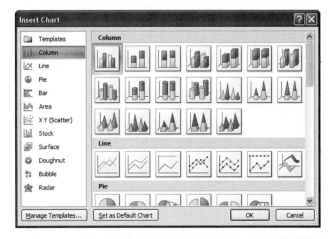

 To insert a chart on a slide that does not have a content placeholder, click the Chart button on the Insert tab.

4. Click the **3-D Clustered Column** chart subtype (the fourth from the left in the top row of the dialog box).
5. Click **OK**. Microsoft Excel opens in a window to the right of the PowerPoint window, as shown in Figure 6-3. The PowerPoint slide displays a sample chart created from the sample data in the Excel window.

Figure 6-3

Creating a new chart requires Excel

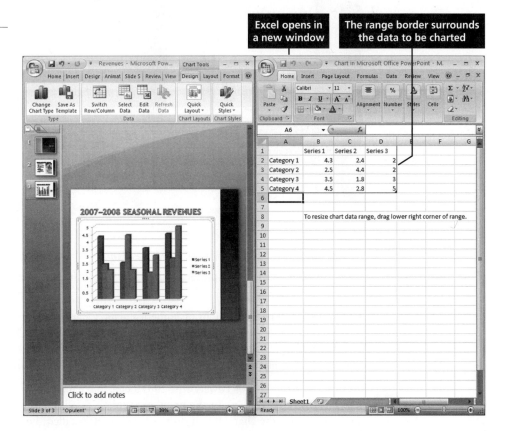

In Excel, notice the bright-blue border that surrounds the data. This *range border* is used to indicate the data being charted. If the data you want to enter has more or fewer columns than the sample data, PowerPoint and Excel may not chart the data accurately unless you adjust this range border.

6. In Excel, click the sizing handle at the lower-right corner of the bright-blue range border. Drag to the left so that the border encloses the range A1:C5.

7. Drag over the cells that contain data in the Excel worksheet and press `Delete`. The chart disappears from the PowerPoint slide because you have removed the data that created it.

8. Click cell **B1** and key 2007, press `Tab`, key 2008, then press `Enter`. Notice that this data appears on the PowerPoint slide in the legend area.

9. Beginning in cell A2, key the following data in Excel to complete the chart. When you have entered the data, your screen should look like Figure 6-4.

Spring	$89,000	$102,000
Summer	$54,000	$62,000
Fall	$102,000	$118,000
Winter	$233,000	$267,000

Figure 6-4

Completed worksheet and chart

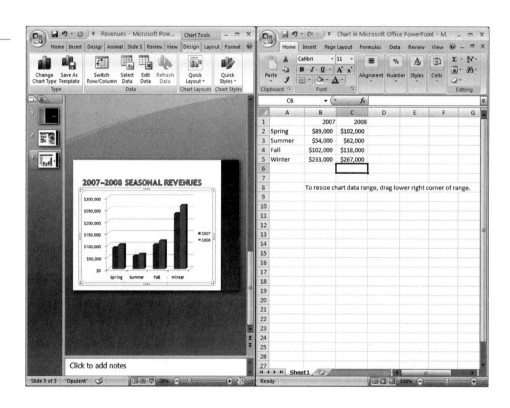

10. **SAVE** the presentation as *Revenues Final*.

   PAUSE. LEAVE the presentation open to use in the next exercise.

Charts are visual representations of numerical data. Chart features such as columns, bars, lines, or pie slices make it easy to understand trends or compare values. Once you have created a chart in PowerPoint, you can easily modify the data on which the chart is based, choose a different type of chart to display the data, change the layout of the chart, or modify its formats.

To take full advantage of PowerPoint 2007's charting capabilities, you must have Microsoft Excel installed. As you saw in the previous exercise, Excel opens to allow you to insert the data that creates the chart. If you do not have Excel installed, PowerPoint instead resorts to Microsoft Graph, the charting application used in previous versions of PowerPoint.

After you key the chart data, you can close Excel to restore the PowerPoint window to its full size. You can, if desired, save the Excel data if you want to work with it later in Excel, but you do not have to save before you close the worksheet. You can redisplay the Excel data any time you want to modify the data by clicking the Edit Data button on the PowerPoint Chart Tools Design tab.

PowerPoint assumes that you will want to key new data for a chart in the Excel worksheet, but you can also use existing Excel data to create a chart in PowerPoint. After Excel opens with the sample data worksheet, use Excel's Open command to open the workbook that contains the data you want to use. In PowerPoint, click the Select Data button to open the Select Data Source dialog box, shown in Figure 6-5.

Figure 6-5

The Select Data Source dialog box

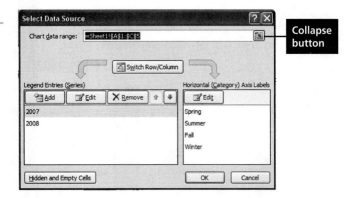

Activate the worksheet you want to use and then click the Collapse button in the Select Data Source dialog box to minimize the dialog box. Drag over the cells that contain the data you need for the chart, then click the Expand button to enlarge the dialog box. The Chart data range box should show the range of cells you want to use. Once you click OK, PowerPoint builds the chart from the specified data.

A somewhat simpler way to use data from an existing worksheet is simply to copy it and paste it in the Excel worksheet that appears when you create a new chart. You may need to adjust the range border to enclose the pasted data. You can do this by dragging the range border in Excel or by using the Select Data Source dialog box to specify the data range for the chart.

You have one other option for putting a chart on a slide: You can copy a chart that has already been created in Excel and paste it on the slide. An Excel chart that is simply pasted on the slide maintains a link to Excel by default so that if you modify the Excel chart, the chart on the slide is also modified. You can format a pasted chart the same way you format any PowerPoint chart.

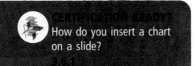

CERTIFICATION READY?
How do you insert a chart on a slide?
3.6.1

Choosing a Different Chart Type

If you decide that the chart type you have chosen does not display the data the way you want, you can choose a different chart type or subtype.

CHOOSE A DIFFERENT CHART TYPE

USE the presentation that is still open from the previous exercise.

1. Click the Excel window's **Close** button to close the data worksheet and restore the PowerPoint window to full size.

2. Click the **Change Chart Type** button in the Type group on the Chart Tools Design tab. The Insert Chart dialog box opens, showing the same options that appeared when you first created the chart.

 **ANOTHER WAY** Right-click almost anywhere in a chart and then click Change Chart Type on the shortcut menu.

3. Click the **Clustered Cylinder** subtype (the first in the second row of column charts), and then click **OK**. The rectangular columns change to three-dimensional cylinders, as shown in Figure 6-6.

Figure 6-6

A new chart type has been applied

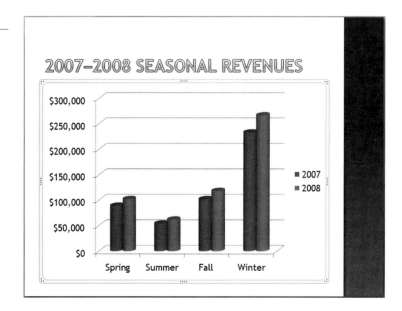

PAUSE. LEAVE the presentation open to use in the next exercise.

In this exercise, you changed one subtype of a column chart to another column subtype. You can also change a chart from one type to another; for example, you can change a column chart to a bar chart without greatly affecting the visual display of information.

Not all chart types are interchangeable. Although you can, for instance, change your column chart to a line chart, the results would not be as informative in line format. And you cannot change a column chart to a pie chart without losing a great deal of information.

When you choose a chart type at the beginning of the charting process, Excel sets up sample data for that type of chart. If you have chosen a pie chart, for example, Excel provides for only one column of data. Thus, if you decide to change chart types completely, you may need to add or remove data in Excel to achieve the desired result.

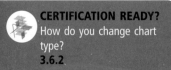 **CERTIFICATION READY?**
How do you change chart type?
3.6.2

If you apply a chart type that does not display your data as you want, use Undo to reverse the change and then try another type.

TROUBLE **SHOOTING** Changing from a two-dimensional chart type to a three-dimensional one can yield unexpected results. For some chart types, PowerPoint may display the new chart type in a rotated, perspective view that you might not like. It is best to decide when you create the original chart whether you want it to use two or three dimensions, and then stick with those dimensions when making any change to the chart type.

Applying a Different Chart Layout

PowerPoint supplies several preformatted chart layouts that you can apply quickly to modify the default layout. These layouts may adjust the position of features such as the legend or add chart components such as titles and data labels.

⊕ APPLY A DIFFERENT CHART LAYOUT

USE the presentation that is still open from the previous exercise.

1. Click the **More** button in the Chart Layouts group on the Chart Tools Design tab. The Chart Layout gallery displays, as shown in Figure 6-7.

Figure 6-7

The Chart Layout gallery

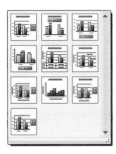

TAKE NOTE*

The thumbnails in the Chart Layout gallery show in miniature the new layout and elements of the chart.

2. Click **Layout 1** in the gallery. The layout is modified to add the Chart Title element at the top of the chart.
3. Click the **Chart Title** placeholder, then drag over the text and press **Delete**.
4. Key **Revenues by Season** in the chart title placeholder. Click outside the placeholder to close it. Your chart should look similar to Figure 6-8.

Figure 6-8

A chart title has been added to the chart

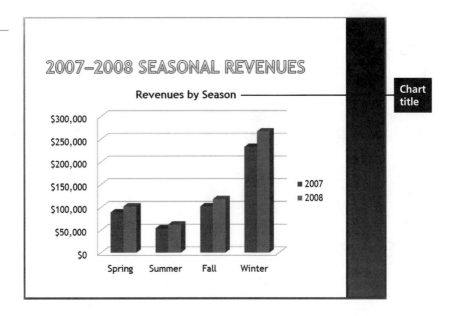

5. SAVE the presentation and then CLOSE the file.

PAUSE. LEAVE PowerPoint open to use in the next exercise.

PowerPoint charts can be customized in a very wide variety of ways by adding and removing chart elements such as titles, labels, and gridlines. If you do not want to take the time to add elements, PowerPoint's chart layouts can provide you with some standard appearance options to choose from. You will learn how to add elements yourself later in this lesson.

Workplace Ready

Choosing the Right Type of Chart

Each PowerPoint chart type is designed to present a specific type of data. When you create a chart, you should select the chart type that will best display your data. Some of the most commonly used chart types are described below.

- **Column charts:** Column charts are generally used for showing data changes over a period of time or for comparing items. Categories (such as Quarter 1 or 2008) display on the horizontal axis (the X axis), and values display on the vertical axis (the Y axis).
- **Bar charts:** Bar charts are used to compare individual items. They are especially useful when values are durations. Categories display on the vertical axis and values display on the horizontal axis.
- **Line charts:** Line charts are best used to display values over time or trends in data. Categories are usually evenly spaced items, such as months or years, and display on the horizontal axis.
- **Pie charts:** Pie charts are used to show the relationship of an individual category to the sum of all categories. Data for a pie chart consists of only a single column or row of data in the worksheet.
- **Area charts:** Area charts are used to show the amount of change over time as well as total value across a trend. Like a pie chart, an area chart can show the relationship of an individual category to the sum of all values.

You can learn more about chart types and subtypes and how they are designed to be used by consulting PowerPoint's Help files.

■ Formatting Charts with Quick Styles

↓
THE BOTTOM LINE

Chart Quick Styles provide instant formatting to change the look of a chart. A Quick Style can change colors and borders of data markers, apply effects to the data markers, and apply color to the chart or plot area.

➔ APPLY A QUICK STYLE TO A CHART

The **Conditions** file is available on the companion CD-ROM.

1. **OPEN** the **Conditions** presentation.
2. Go to slide 2 and click the chart to select it.
3. Click the **Chart Tools Design** tab.
4. Click the **More** button in the Chart Styles group. The Quick Styles gallery appears, as shown in Figure 6-9.

Figure 6-9

Chart Quick Styles gallery

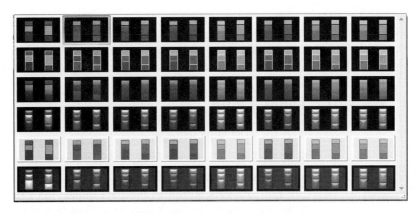

5. Click **Style 7**. The data series' colors change to variations of another theme color. This is not quite dramatic enough for your purpose.

6. Click the **More** button again, and then click **Style 43**. This style applies new theme color, bevel effects, and different chart background colors, as shown in Figure 6-10.

Figure 6-10

The chart is more interesting with the new Quick Style applied

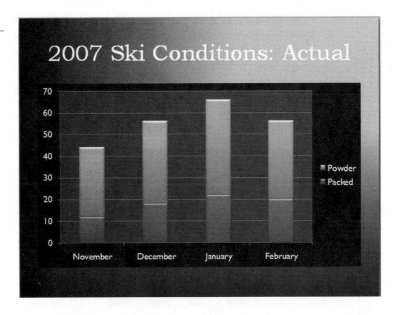

7. **SAVE** the presentation as *Conditions Final* and then **CLOSE** the file.

PAUSE. LEAVE PowerPoint open to use in the next exercise.

Use a Quick Style to format a chart if you do not have time to adjust formatting of chart elements such as *data series* or the individual *data markers* in a series. A data series consists of all the data points for a particular category, such as all the columns for Quarter 1 values. A data marker is one column or point in a series.

Chart Quick Styles give you six appearance options that you can vary by selecting specific theme colors or color combinations. Effects that are applied to the data series, such as bevels, are also applied in the legend.

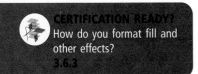

CERTIFICATION READY?
How do you format fill and other effects?
3.6.3

■ Modifying Chart Data and Elements

THE BOTTOM LINE

It is not uncommon to have to modify a chart after it has been created. You can change the data on which the chart is based at any time or change the way in which the data is plotted. You can also add or remove chart elements as desired to customize your chart.

Editing a Chart's Data

Changes you make to the chart data worksheet are immediately reflected on the PowerPoint chart. Use the Edit Data button to reactivate the data worksheet.

⊙ EDIT A CHART'S DATA

1. **OPEN** the *Pricing* presentation.
2. Go to slide 2 and click the chart to select it.
3. Click the **Chart Tools Design** tab.
4. Click the **Edit Data** button in the Data group. The data worksheet appears next to the PowerPoint window. You have noticed that the worksheet uses the wrong year dates.
5. Click cell **B1** and key **2005**. Notice that the new data appears immediately in the PowerPoint chart.
6. Key **2006** in cell C1, **2007** in cell D1, and **2008** in cell E1.
7. Double-click cell **A3** and edit the word *Eqpt.* to read **Equipment**.
8. You think the chart would be more meaningful if the years were plotted on the horizontal axis. In PowerPoint, click the **Switch Row/Column** button in the Data group.
9. **CLOSE** the worksheet. Your chart should look like Figure 6-11.

The *Pricing* file is available on the companion CD-ROM.

Right-click anywhere in the chart and then click Edit Data on the shortcut menu.

Figure 6-11

The chart data has been edited

10. **SAVE** the presentation as *Pricing Final*.

PAUSE. LEAVE the presentation open to use in the next exercise.

Chart data remains "live" as long as the chart remains on the slide. You can reopen the chart worksheet at any time to adjust the data.

The Switch Row/Column feature can be very helpful in adjusting the way data appears in a chart. In essence, the legend entries and the horizontal axis labels switch places. If you find that your chart does not seem to show the data as you wish, try switching rows and columns for a different perspective on the data.

Adding and Deleting Chart Elements

Elements such as axis labels, a chart title, and data labels make your chart more informative. Use the tools on the Table Tools Layout tab to turn chart elements on or off or adjust settings for a particular element.

⊕ ADD AND DELETE CHART ELEMENTS

USE the presentation that is still open from the previous exercise.

1. Click the chart to select it, if necessary, and click the **Chart Tools Layout** tab.
2. Click the **Gridlines** button in the Axes group, point to **Primary Vertical Gridlines**, and click **Major Gridlines**. Vertical gridlines are added to the chart as shown in Figure 6-12.

Figure 6-12

Vertical gridlines added to chart

3. Click one of the Equipment Rental data markers to select the data series.
4. Click the **Data Labels** button, then click **Inside End**. The data point for each data marker appears at the upper end of the marker, as shown in Figure 6-13.

Figure 6-13

Data labels have been added to the data series

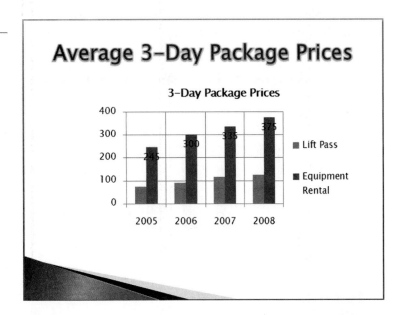

5. Modify the data labels you just inserted as follows:

    a. Click one of the data labels to select all data labels for the series.

    b. Click the **Data Labels** button again, then click **More Data Label Options** at the bottom of the menu. The Format Data Labels dialog box opens, as shown in Figure 6-14.

Figure 6-14

The Format Data Labels dialog box

    c. In the Label Position area of the Label Options pane, click **Outside End** to move the labels outside the data markers.

    d. Click **Number** in the left pane, and then click the **Currency** category.

    e. Select the value in the Decimal places box and key **0** to reduce decimal places to 0.

    f. Click **Close**.

6. Click one of the Lift Passes data markers, and repeat steps 4 and 5 to add and format currency data labels.

7. Click the **Axis Titles** button, point to **Primary Vertical Axis Title**, and then click **Rotated Title**. An axis title placeholder appears to the left of the vertical axis.

8. Drag over the placeholder text and key **In U.S. Dollars**.

9. Click the chart title (*3-Day Package Prices*) and press [Delete].

10. Click outside the chart to deselect it. Your chart should look similar to Figure 6-15.

Figure 6-15

Chart elements have been added and removed

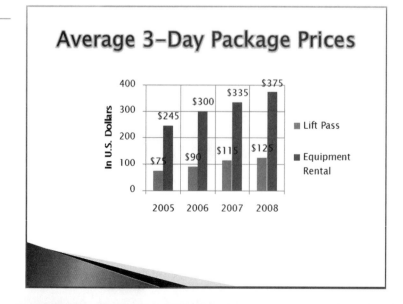

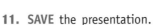

11. SAVE the presentation.

PAUSE. LEAVE the presentation open to use in the next exercise.

The Chart Tools Layout tab has four groups of buttons that control chart elements you can add or remove. When clicked, most of these buttons display a menu of options you can apply by simply clicking. Some include submenus with additional options or a More Options command at the bottom of the menu that takes you to a dialog box where you can find additional formatting options for the element.

You can remove chart elements by turning them off—most of the layout element buttons include a None option—or by simply clicking the item to select it and then pressing Delete.

Applying elements such as a chart title or axis titles generally reduces the size of the plot area and the data markers. You can offset this adjustment by resizing the chart or by reducing the font size of axis labels and titles, as you learn later in this lesson.

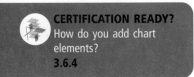

CERTIFICATION READY?
How do you add chart elements?
3.6.4

■ Manually Formatting a Chart

THE BOTTOM LINE

Once you have final data and have added the elements you want to include in the chart, you can make final adjustments to the size and position of the chart and apply final formats to the chart elements. Use the tools on the Chart Tools Format tab to apply formats to any part of a chart, including the entire chart area, the data series markers, the legend, and the chart's labels and titles.

Resizing and Moving a Chart

If you create a chart on a slide that does not have a content placeholder, you may not be entirely happy with its size or location. You can resize and move a chart using its outside container border.

➔ RESIZE AND MOVE A CHART

USE the presentation that is still open from the previous exercise. The chart you have been working with is now a bit small to display the elements you have added. Its right-aligned position is also not very attractive.

1. Click once on the chart to display its blue container border.
2. Position the pointer on the top border so it takes the shape of a four-headed pointer. Press Shift, click the border, hold down the mouse button, and drag to the left until the left container border aligns with the first letter of the slide title. Your slide should look like Figure 6-16.

Figure 6-16

The chart has been moved to the left

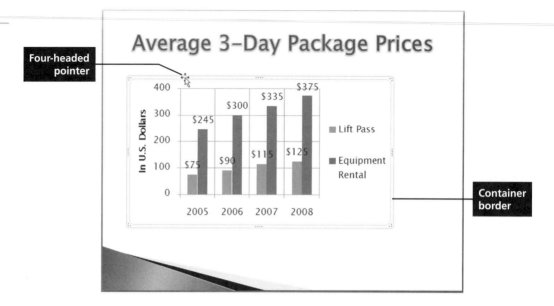

3. Position the pointer on the lower-right corner of the chart container so it takes the shape of a two-headed diagonal pointer. Press **Shift**, click the corner, and drag diagonally until the right border aligns with the last letter of the title. Your slide should look like Figure 6-17.

Figure 6-17

The chart has been resized

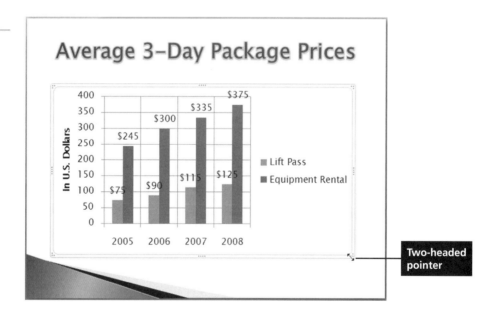

> **TAKE NOTE** *
>
> Pressing Shift when dragging keeps the object on the same horizontal or vertical orientation. Pressing Shift while resizing maintains the current ratio of width to height to avoid distortion.

PAUSE. LEAVE the presentation open to use in the next exercise.

You can resize any object by dragging a side or corner handle of its container. Note that if you drag a side handle, you may "stretch" the container, distorting its contents.

Move any object by dragging it by its container border. When you see the four-headed pointer, just click and drag.

REF

You learn more about aligning and distributing objects on a slide in Lesson 8.

As you reposition objects on a slide, keep in mind that objects on the slide should maintain an obvious relationship; for example, in the previous exercise, you aligned the borders of the table with the beginning and end of the slide title. Aligning objects to the left, right, or center, or distributing them evenly on the slide provides a pleasing appearance that won't distract your audience.

Changing the Fill of the Chart Area

To make a chart really "pop" on a slide, you can change its default fill. When you change the chart area fill, you format the entire area within the outside blue container border.

⊕ CHANGE THE CHART AREA FILL

USE the presentation that is still open from the previous exercise.

1. Click the chart once, if necessary, to select it and display the blue container border.
2. Click the **Chart Tools Format** tab, if necessary. Make sure Chart Area displays in the Chart Elements box at the top of the Current Selection group.
3. Click the **Format Selection** button in the Current Selection group. The Format Chart Area dialog box opens, as shown in Figure 6-18.

Figure 6-18

The Format Chart Area dialog box

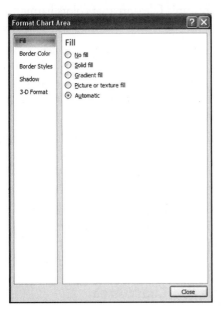

 **ANOTHER WAY**   You can also right-click a blank area of the chart and then click Format Chart Area on the shortcut menu.

4. Click **Picture or texture fill**, and then click the **Texture** button. The texture gallery opens.
5. Click the **Newsprint** texture, and then drag the **Transparency** slider to 25%.
6. Click **Close**. The chart area has been formatted with a light texture background that makes it stand out from the slide, as shown in Figure 6-19.

Figure 6-19

Texture fill applied to the chart area

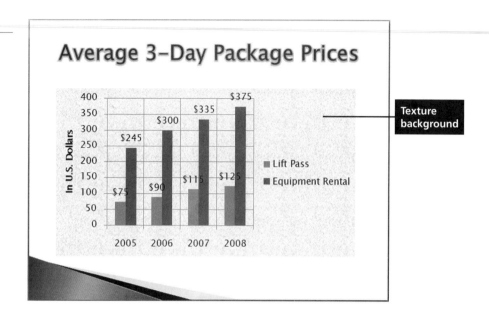

PAUSE. LEAVE the presentation open to use in the next exercise.

When choosing a fill for the *chart area*, you have familiar choices: You can select a theme color, picture, gradient, or texture. Take care that colors harmonize with the current theme and that pictures or textures do not overwhelm the other chart elements.

When formatting parts of a chart, it is sometimes a challenge to make sure you have selected the element you want to change. Use the Chart Elements list in the Current Selection group on either the Chart Tools Layout or Chart Tools Format tab to help you select the element you want. This list clearly identifies all elements of the current chart so that you can easily select the one you want to modify.

You can also select any element on the chart to format by right-clicking it. The shortcut menu displays a Format command at the bottom that corresponds to the element you have clicked. If you right-click one of the columns in the chart, for example, the shortcut menu offers the Format Data Series command.

The dialog box that opens when you select a chart element to format provides options specifically for that element. The Format Axis dialog box, for instance, allows you to change the interval between tick marks on the axis, number style, line color and style, and alignment of axis labels.

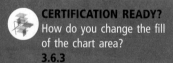

CERTIFICATION READY?
How do you change the fill of the chart area?
3.6.3

Applying a Border to the Chart Area

> By default, the chart area does not display a border. You can create a more finished look for a chart by applying a border that clearly identifies the chart area.

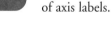 **CHANGE A CHART'S BORDER LINE**

USE the presentation that is still open from the previous exercise.

1. Right-click in the blank area below the legend, then click **Format Chart Area** on the shortcut menu. The Format Chart Area dialog box opens.
2. Click **Border Color**, then click **Solid line**.
3. Click the **Color** button, then click the **Black, Text 1, Lighter 35%** theme color.
4. Click **Border Styles**, then click the **Width** up arrow until the width is 3 pt.
5. Click **Close**, then click outside the chart so you can see the chart area border. Your slide should look similar to Figure 6-20.

Figure 6-20

Chart area border applied

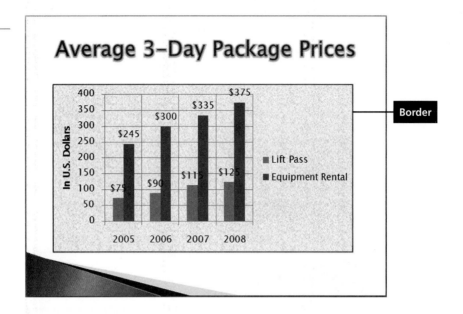

Average 3–Day Package Prices

Border

PAUSE. LEAVE the presentation open to use in the next exercise.

If you have applied a gradient fill to the chart area, you may want to consider using the Gradient line border option. A gradient line border grades from one color to another in the same way a gradient fill does. For a special effect, use the same gradient as for the fill but reverse the direction of the gradient in the border so the light area of the border is adjacent to the dark area of the fill. (Gradient borders are available only for two-dimensional charts.)

The Border Styles options in the Format Chart Area dialog box allow you to select a style other than a plain single border line. You can select compound styles composed of several lines or dashed lines, and you can also choose how to display corners and line ends (caps).

Formatting a Chart's Data Series

As you learned earlier, a chart's data series is the visual display of the actual data points. Data series can be columns, bars, lines, or pie slices. You can give a chart considerably more visual appeal by customizing data series fill and border options and by applying effects.

⊕ FORMAT A CHART'S DATA SERIES

USE the presentation that is still open from the previous exercise.

1. Click the chart to select it, if necessary.
2. Click one of the red data markers. Note that by clicking one of the markers, you have selected the entire data series, so all red markers are selected, as shown in Figure 6-21.

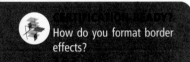

How do you format border effects?

TAKE NOTE

If you want to format a single data marker, click two times on a marker.

Figure 6-21

Click a marker to select the
data series

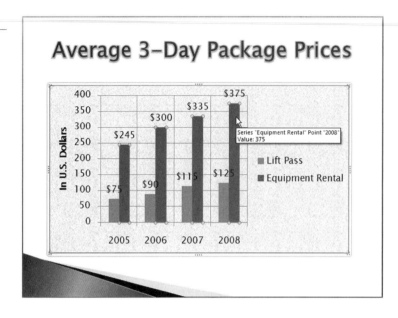

3. Click the **Chart Tools Format** tab, if necessary, and notice that the Chart Elements box in the Current Selection group shows that Series 'Equipment Rental' is currently selected.

4. Click the **Format Selection** button in the Current Selection group. The Format Data Series dialog box opens, as shown in Figure 6-22.

Figure 6-22

The Format Data Series
dialog box

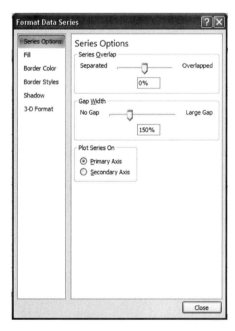

5. In the Series Options pane, drag the Series Overlap slider to the left to −20%. The two data series are now separated on the slide by a small gap so they do not look so crowded.

6. Click **Close** to close the dialog box.

7. With the data series still selected, click the **Shape Fill** button in the Shape Styles group, then click the **Turquoise, Accent 1, Darker 25%** theme color.

8. Click the **Shape Fill** button again, point to **Gradient**, and click the **Linear Down** gradient in the Dark Variations area.

9. With the data series still selected, click the **Shape Outline** button, then click the **Turquoise, Accent 1, Darker 50%** theme color.

10. Click the Shape Outline button again, point to Weight, and click the 1½ pt option.

11. Click the Shape Effects button, point to Shadow, and then click the Offset Diagonal Bottom Right effect. Your chart should look similar to Figure 6-23.

Figure 6-23

Data series formatted with fill, border, and effect

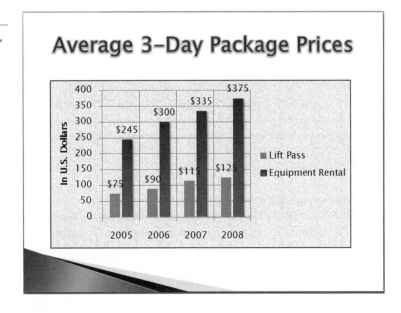

12. Click one of the data markers for the Lift Pass data series to select the entire data series.

13. Click the More button in the Shape Styles group to display the shape Quick Styles.

14. Click the Moderate Effect, Accent 3 style.

15. With the data series still selected, click the Shape Effects button in the Shape Styles group, point to Shadow, and click the Offset Diagonal Bottom Right option. Your chart should look like Figure 6-24.

Figure 6-24

Both data series have been formatted

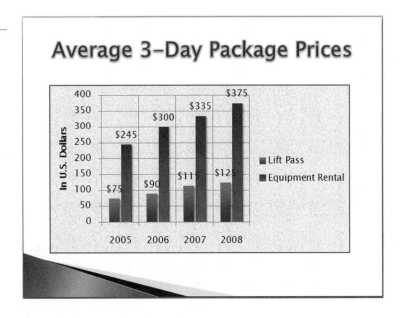

PAUSE. LEAVE the presentation open to use in the next exercise.

You have almost limitless options in formatting the data series for a chart. If you have plenty of time, you can use options in the Format Data Series dialog box and the Shape Fill, Shape Outline, and Shape Effects menus to apply colors, pictures, textures, gradients, shadows, bevels, and many other choices. If your time is limited, you can achieve sophisticated effects by simply applying a Quick Style from the Shape Styles gallery.

In some situations, you may want to apply formats to a specific data marker rather than to the entire data series. To select a single data marker, click it once to select the data series, then click it again to remove selection handles from the other markers. The Chart Elements box will display an item similar to Series 'Equipment Rental' Point '2008' to let you know you have selected only one data point.

You can emphasize a chart's data series by animating the data. Using a custom animation, you can display each data series individually or display data by category. To animate a chart, select the chart, display the Custom Animation task pane, and choose an entrance effect. Right-click the effect in the animation list, click Effect Options, and click the Chart Animation tab. Use the Group Chart settings to control how the chart data displays.

CERTIFICATION READY?
How do you apply fills and other effects to data series?
3.6.3

Modifying a Chart's Legend

You can modify a chart's legend to make it more useful to viewers by repositioning it, applying a fill or border, or changing font options.

 MODIFY A CHART'S LEGEND

USE the presentation that is still open from the previous exercise.

1. Right-click the legend, then click **Format Legend** on the shortcut menu. The Format Legend dialog box opens, as shown in Figure 6-25.

Figure 6-25

The Format Legend dialog box

2. Click **Bottom** in the Legend Options pane. The legend moves to the bottom of the chart below the horizontal axis.
3. Click **Fill** in the left pane, click **Solid fill**, click the **Color** button, and click the **White, Background 1** theme color.
4. Click **Border Color** in the left pane, click **Solid line**, click the **Color** button, and click the **Black, Text 1, Lighter 50%** theme color.
5. Click **Close**. Your chart should look like the one in Figure 6-26.

Figure 6-26

The legend has been moved and formatted

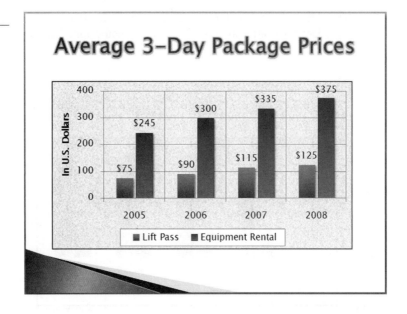

PAUSE. **LEAVE** the presentation open to use in the next exercise.

A chart's *legend* explains what each data series shows. You can modify the legend's formats to make the legend area stand out on the chart.

By default, PowerPoint positions the legend to the right of the *plot area*—the area of the chart where the data series are superimposed on the gridlines. This is a good position for the legend if it lists a number of data series—they will be easier to understand if they are stacked at the right. If you have only a few data series in the legend, you can move the legend to the top or bottom of the chart; this usually frees up a lot of space in the chart area, maximizing the plot area and data marker sizes.

CERTIFICATION READY?
How do you change the fill of the legend?
3.6.3

Modifying Chart Text

Modify other chart elements such as axis labels or titles, using font tools or options in a Format dialog box.

⊙ **MODIFY CHART TEXT**

USE the presentation that is still open from the previous exercise.

1. Click the vertical axis title (*In U.S. Dollars*), click the **Home** tab, click the **Font Size** drop-down arrow, and click **16**. The label is reduced in size.
2. Right-click the vertical axis, and then click **Format Axis**. The Format Axis dialog box opens.
3. Click **Number** in the left pane, click the **Currency** category, and then key **0** in the Decimal places box to remove trailing zeroes. Click **Close**.
4. Click any of the vertical axis data labels to select the entire axis, click the **Font Size** drop-down arrow, and click **16**.
5. Follow step 4 to change the size of the horizontal axis labels to 16 point.
6. Click one of the data labels for the Lift Pass series to select all data labels for the series.
7. Change the font size to **16**, click the **Bold** button, and then click the **Font Color** button and click **Gray-80%, Text 2**.

8. Follow steps 6 and 7 to modify formats for the other set of data labels. Click outside the chart container. Your chart should look like Figure 6-27.

Figure 6-27

The finished chart

9. SAVE the presentation and then CLOSE the file.

CLOSE PowerPoint.

PowerPoint formats the chart text elements with fonts and font sizes controlled by the theme. You may find that the font size looks too large for some chart elements, but you can easily adjust font size using the Home tab's Font group tools. You can also right-click any text label or title to display the Mini toolbar and adjust font formats.

After you change text formats, be sure to check the chart in Slide Show view to make sure the text is still easy to read and attractive. You do not want your audience to have to strain to view numbers, nor do you want text to be so large it overwhelms other chart elements.

SUMMARY SKILL MATRIX

IN THIS LESSON YOU LEARNED	MATRIX SKILL	SKILL NUMBER
To build charts		
To create a chart on a slide from a content placeholder	Insert charts	3.6.1
To choose a different chart type	Change chart types	3.6.2
To apply Quick Styles, fills, borders, and effects to a chart	Format fill and other effects	3.6.3
To add elements to a chart	Add chart elements	3.6.4

Knowledge Assessment

Fill in the Blank

Fill in each blank with the term or phrase that best completes the statement.

1. A single column on a chart that identifies one data point is called a(n) _____.

2. If you want to change a column chart to a line chart, click the _____ button on the Chart Tools Design tab.

3. A(n) _____ is a visual depiction of numerical data.

4. _____ charts display trends in data or values over time.

5. A chart's _____ provides a key to the information plotted on the chart.

6. A(n) _____ displays all the data points for a particular category.

7. Use the _____ key to help you resize a chart without distorting its appearance.

8. The _____ is the entire area within the chart's container border.

9. You can quickly tell what part of a chart you have selected by looking at the _____ box on the Chart Tools Layout or Format tab.

10. The _____ contains the gridlines and elements such as columns or bars.

Multiple Choice

Circle the correct answer.

1. To take full advantage of PowerPoint 2007's charting capabilities, you must also have
   a. Microsoft Word
   b. Microsoft Excel
   c. Microsoft Equation
   d. Microsoft Chart

2. If you want to select a different range of cells for a chart, use the
   a. Select New Data button
   b. Import Data Source command
   c. Select Data Source button
   d. Display New Source button

3. The default PowerPoint chart type is a
   a. Column chart
   b. Bar chart
   c. Line chart
   d. Pie chart

4. If you want to show amount of change over time and total value across a trend, use a(n)
   a. Column chart
   b. Line chart
   c. Area chart
   d. Pie chart

5. You can move a chart on a slide by
   a. Dragging its border
   b. Cutting from one location and pasting elsewhere on the slide
   c. Dragging a sizing handle
   d. Issuing the Move command

6. If you want to move columns on a column chart farther apart, you would adjust the
   a. Column Spacing slider
   b. Plot Area Spacing value
   c. Column Spacing percentage
   d. Series Overlap slider

7. Select a single data marker by
   a. Clicking once on the marker
   b. Double-clicking the marker
   c. Clicking twice on the marker
   d. Triple-clicking the marker

8. To redisplay the chart worksheet at any time, click the _____ button.
   a. Show Datasheet
   b. Edit Data
   c. Show Data
   d. Open Excel

9. The axis that usually shows categories in a column chart is the
   a. Horizontal axis
   b. Vertical axis
   c. Z axis
   d. Y axis

10. Text that identifies information about the values on an axis is called a(n)
   a. Legend
   b. Chart title
   c. Axis title
   d. Axis label

■ Competency Assessment

Project 6-1: Voter Turnout

You are a member of the Center City Board of Elections. You have been asked to create a presentation to deliver to the Board showing how turnout has varied in the city over the past four presidential elections. You can create a line chart to display this data clearly.

GET READY. Launch PowerPoint if it is not already running.

The *Turnout* file is available on the companion CD-ROM.

1. **OPEN** the *Turnout* presentation.
2. Go to slide 2, click the **Insert Chart** icon in the content placeholder, and then click **Line**. Click **OK** to accept the default subtype.

3. Key the following data in the Excel worksheet:

Year	Turnout
1992	0.62
1996	0.74
2000	0.49
2004	0.40

4. Delete the data in the Series 2 and Series 3 columns in the Excel worksheet, and then drag the range border by the lower-right handle until it encloses only the range A1:B5.

5. Close the Excel worksheet.

6. Click **Layout 12** in the Chart Layout gallery.

7. Click **Style 36** in the Quick Style gallery.

8. Click the legend to select it, then press [Delete].

9. Select one of the data points, then click **Data Labels** on the Chart Tools Layout tab. Click **Above**.

10. Right-click one of the data labels, then click **Format Data Labels**. Change the number format to **Percentage** with 0 decimal places.

11. Animate the chart line as follows:

    a. Click the **Animations** tab, then click the **Custom Animations** button to display the Custom Animations task pane.

    b. Click the **Add Effect** button, point to **Entrance**, and then click **Fade**. (If you don't see this effect, click **More Effects** to find it.)

    c. Right-click the effect in the task pane, click **Effect Options**, and click the **Chart Animation** tab.

    d. Click the **Group chart** drop-down arrow, and then click **By Category**.

    e. Click **OK** to close the dialog box.

12. Switch to Slide Show view to see the chart animation. Click the mouse to display the chart background and each segment of the line.

13. **SAVE** the presentation as *Turnout Final* and then **CLOSE** the file.

    LEAVE PowerPoint open for the next project.

Project 6-2: And the Results Are . . .

You are a project manager for Trey Research. You have been asked to create a slide show to present results of a survey you conducted on opinions about violence in the media. You saved your research results as an Excel file that you can use to create a chart in PowerPoint.

1. **OPEN** the *Survey* presentation.

2. Go to slide 2, click the **Insert Chart** icon in the content placeholder, click **3-D Clustered Column**, and click **OK** to create the chart.

3. In Excel, open the *Media* workbook. Select the cell range **A3:C6** and click the **Copy** button on the Excel Home tab.

4. In Excel, display the chart worksheet. Click in cell **A1**, and click the **Paste** button on the Home tab.

5. Delete any unnecessary sample data in the worksheet, and make sure the range border surrounds the range **A1:C4**.

6. Close the Excel worksheet and the *Media* file.

7. Right-click the legend, click **Format Legend**, and change the legend position to **Bottom**.

8. Change the fill colors of both series using the Shape Fill palette.

The *Survey* file is available on the companion CD-ROM.

The *Media* file is available on the companion CD-ROM.

9. Click a vertical axis label to select the axis, click the **Home** tab, click the **Font Size** box, and click **16** to change the font size of all axis labels.

10. Change the horizontal axis labels and the legend labels to 16 points as directed in step 9.

11. **SAVE** the presentation as *Survey Final* and then **CLOSE** the file.

    LEAVE PowerPoint open for the next project.

■ Proficiency Assessment

Project 6-3: **Visitors Welcome**

You work in the Tourist Bureau for the town of Lucerne. As part of your regular duties, you compile a presentation that shows information on visitors. You have created a slide that shows visitors by age. The chart needs some modification and formatting.

The *Tourists* file is available on the companion CD-ROM.

1. **OPEN** the *Tourists* presentation.

2. Go to slide 2 and view the chart. The line chart type does not seem appropriate for the data.

3. With the chart selected, click the **Change Chart Type** button and select the first chart in the Pie category.

4. Apply **Layout 6** and **Quick Style 10**.

5. Click the outside border of the pie to select the entire pie and apply a bevel effect.

6. Reduce the width of the chart by dragging the right container border about 1 inch to the left, and then center the chart horizontally on the slide by dragging it to the right.

7. Delete the chart title *Percent*.

8. Select the legend and apply a light-colored fill. (Change the color of the text if necessary to contrast well with the fill.) Apply a border around the legend.

9. Drag the legend about a quarter of an inch toward the pie, and then apply a bevel effect to the legend.

10. **SAVE** the presentation as *Tourists Final* and then **CLOSE** the file.

    LEAVE PowerPoint open for the next project.

Project 6-4: **Free for All**

You are a marketing consultant hired by Woodgrove Bank. The bank's managers have asked you to determine which freebies customers would find most attractive when opening a new checking account. One of your assistants has created a chart of the survey results. You need to improve the look of the chart by editing the data and applying formats.

The *Freebies* file is available on the companion CD-ROM.

1. **OPEN** the *Freebies* presentation.

2. Go to slide 2 and right-click in a blank area of the chart to select the chart area.

3. Use the Format Chart Area dialog box to apply a gradient fill of your choice to the chart area.

4. Apply a border color and weight of your choice to the chart area.

5. Use the Shape Fill menu to change the color of at least one of the data series. (You may change more than one or all colors if desired.)

6. The data would be more meaningful if the data in columns and rows were reversed. Use the Edit Data command to display the data worksheet and then switch columns and rows in the chart. Close the worksheet.

7. Move the legend to the top of the chart. Then apply a new background fill for the legend and add a border.

8. Format the vertical axis to show numbers as percentages rather than decimal values.

9. Show data labels in percentages, and change alignment of data labels to rotate all text 270 degrees. (Hint: Use the Alignment settings in the Format Data Labels dialog box to rotate the label text.)

10. **SAVE** the presentation as *Freebies Final* and then **CLOSE** the file.

    LEAVE PowerPoint open for the next project.

■ Mastery Assessment

Project 6-5: More Power

You are a financial analyst for City Power & Light. Senior managers have asked you to determine how much power sales increased from 2007 to 2008, based on customer types. You can compare rates of power sales using a bar chart.

1. Start a new, blank presentation and apply a theme of your choice.

2. Change the layout of the first slide to Title and Content, and key the slide title **2007 – 2008 Sales**.

3. Create a Clustered Bar chart, and key the following chart data:

	Industrial	Commercial	Residential
2008	$3,010	$4,273	$5,777
2007	$2,588	$3,876	$4,578

4. Apply Layout 3 to the chart, and change the chart title to **Sales by Customer Type**.

5. Apply a Quick Style of your choice to the chart.

6. Add a horizontal axis title and key the title **In Millions**.

7. Change the size of the horizontal axis labels to 16 point.

8. Insert a border around the legend.

9. **SAVE** the presentation as *Power Sales* and then **CLOSE** the file.

    LEAVE PowerPoint open for the next project.

Project 6-6: Patient Visits

You are a veterinarian hoping to attract investors to your clinic. You have created a chart to be used in a presentation for prospective investors. You want to show investors the reasons for patient visits during a given month, by percentage. You are not satisfied with your chart, however, so you want to improve it before the investor meeting.

The *Patients* file is available on the companion CD-ROM.

1. **OPEN** the *Patients* presentation.

2. In the chart worksheet, edit the values to become percentages (for example, change 38 to 0.38 and apply the Percent style).

3. Change the chart type from bar to a 3-D pie chart.

4. Apply a chart layout to add a legend and data labels. Delete the chart title if your layout added one.

5. Use the 3-D Rotation settings in the Format Chart Area dialog box to adjust the tilt of the pie so you can see the slices more clearly.

6. Apply a Quick Style, or change the fill of some or all of the pie slices.

7. Select the data labels and increase their size by one point size. Apply bold formatting.

8. With data labels still selected, open the Format Data Labels dialog box and specify a light fill for the labels and a border.

9. Add a light-colored fill to the plot area, and apply a shadow effect to the plot area.

10. Apply the same fill and effect to the legend.

11. SAVE the presentation as *Patients Final* and then CLOSE the file.

CLOSE PowerPoint.

INTERNET READY

You have decided you need to improve your fitness levels, but you have not yet settled on whether to take up jogging, biking, or rollerblading. Use the Internet to determine relative costs of these three forms of recreation: What kind of apparel do you need? (You may need different apparel at different times of the year.) What kind of equipment (such as running shoes, stopwatch or other monitor, bike, pads, helmet, rollerblades) is required? How much time per week would you need to spend to achieve a good level of fitness? Tabulate your results and create a column chart in PowerPoint that compares apparel costs, equipment costs, and time expenditures for the three fitness ventures.

Creating SmartArt Graphics

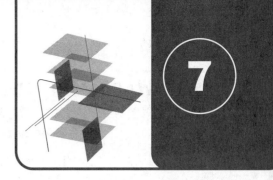

7

You are the director of software development for Litware, Inc., which creates computer games that help children learn to read. One of your responsibilities is orienting new software designers who have just joined the company. You can use SmartArt diagrams to explain your company's organization and standard processes to the newcomers. SmartArt diagrams provide an easy way to share complex information in the form of sophisticated graphics that clearly show relationships and processes.

KEY TERMS
assistant
demote
organization chart
promote
SmartArt diagram
subordinates
Text pane
top-level shape

■ SOFTWARE ORIENTATION

Choosing a SmartArt Graphic

PowerPoint 2007 offers seven different types of SmartArt diagrams, with many layouts for each type. Figure 7-1 shows the dialog box that appears when you choose to insert a SmartArt diagram.

Figure 7-1

Choose a SmartArt Graphic dialog box

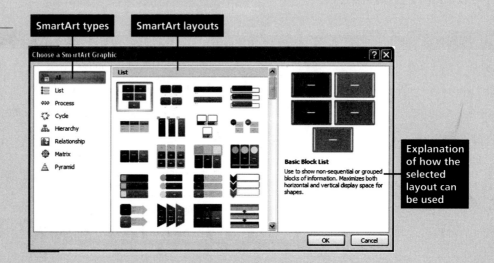

When you click a layout, the right pane of the dialog box shows you a close-up view of the selected layout and provides information on how to use the layout. The layout's description can help you decide whether the layout will be appropriate for your information.

■ Adding SmartArt to a Slide

THE BOTTOM LINE

Use the Insert SmartArt Graphic icon in any content placeholder to start a new diagram. After you have selected a type and a layout, you can add text to the diagram. PowerPoint also lets you use existing bullet items to create a SmartArt diagram.

Creating an Organization Chart

Use an *organization chart* to show the relationships among personnel or departments in an organization. Organization charts are included in the Hierarchy type SmartArt layouts.

⊖ INSERT AN ORGANIZATION CHART

GET READY. Before you begin these steps, make sure that your computer is on. Log on, if necessary.

The *Litware* file is available on the companion CD-ROM.

1. Start PowerPoint, if the program is not already running.
2. Locate and open the *Litware* presentation.
3. Go to slide 3, and click the Insert SmartArt Graphic icon in the center of the content placeholder. The Choose a SmartArt Graphic dialog box opens.

ANOTHER WAY To insert a SmartArt diagram on a slide that does not have a content placeholder, click the SmartArt button on the Insert tab.

4. Click **Hierarchy** in the type list at the left side of the dialog box. The layouts for the Hierarchy type display, as shown in Figure 7-2.

Figure 7-2

The Hierarchy layouts in the Choose a SmartArt Graphic dialog box

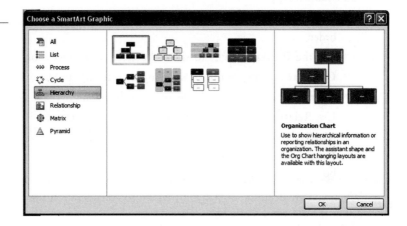

5. Click the first layout in the first row. Read the description of the Organization Chart layout in the right-hand pane of the dialog box.

6. Click **OK** to insert the diagram. The diagram and the fly-out Text pane appear on the slide, as shown in Figure 7-3.

Figure 7-3

A new, blank organization chart diagram

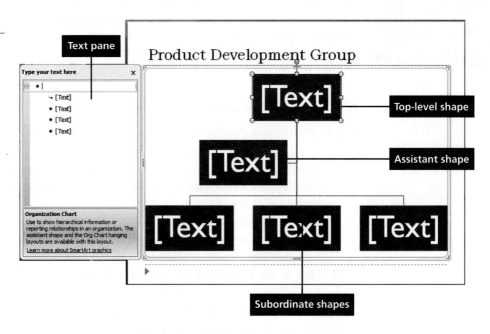

7. **SAVE** the presentation as *Litware Final*.

PAUSE. LEAVE the presentation open to use in the next exercise.

SmartArt diagrams are visual representations of information you want to communicate. SmartArt diagrams show items of related information in a graphical way that makes their relationships easy to understand. You can use SmartArt diagrams to present text information in a more visually interesting way than the usual bulleted or numbered formats.

The Choose a SmartArt Graphic dialog box sorts its many layouts by types such as List, Process, Hierarchy, and so on. The following general descriptions of SmartArt types can help you choose a type:

- Use the **List** layouts to display information that does not have to be in a particular order.
- Use the **Process** layouts to show the steps in a process or timeline.
- **Cycle** layouts are useful for showing a continual process.
- **Hierarchy** layouts show levels of subordination.
- Use **Relationship** layouts to show connections between items.
- **Matrix** layouts show how parts relate to a whole.
- **Pyramid** layouts display relationships in terms of proportion, from largest at the bottom to smallest at the top.

When you are deciding on a layout, take into consideration the amount of text you want to use in the diagram. Some layouts are designed to handle only one or two words in a shape, while other layouts can accommodate longer text entries.

A new SmartArt diagram appears on the slide with empty shapes to which you add text (and in some cases, pictures) to create the final diagram. The appearance and position of these shapes are guided by the layout you chose, and shape color is controlled by the current theme.

An organization chart, such as the one you just created, has some special terminology and layout requirements. In an organization chart, there can be only one *top-level shape*—the person or department at the head of the organization. Persons or departments who report to the top-level entity are *subordinates*. An *assistant* is a person who reports directly to a staff member and usually appears on a separate level.

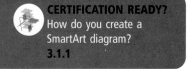

CERTIFICATION READY?
How do you create a SmartArt diagram?
3.1.1

→ ADD TEXT TO A SMARTART DIAGRAM

USE the presentation that is still open from the previous exercise.

1. If necessary, click next to the bullet at the top of the Text pane to place the insertion point there. Key **Ted Hicks** to enter the name in the top-level shape of the diagram. Notice that as you key the text in the Text pane, it appears in the top shape of the diagram.
2. Click in the bullet item below *Ted Hicks* in the Text pane, and then key **Rose Lang**. Rose Lang is an assistant to Ted Hicks and as such has an assistant shape on a level between the top-level shape and the subordinate shapes.
3. Click in the next bullet item in the Text pane and key **Marcus Short**. Marcus Short is a subordinate to Ted Hicks.
4. Click in the next bullet item and key **Ellen Camp**.
5. Click in the last bullet item and key **Pat Cramer**. Your diagram should look like Figure 7-4.

Figure 7-4

Names have been added to the organization chart

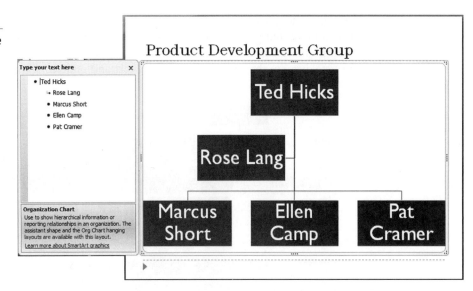

6. Click the **Close** button in the Text pane to hide it. You will complete the text entry by keying directly in the diagram shapes.
7. Click just to the right of the name *Hicks* in the top-level shape, press Enter, and key **Director**. Notice that the text size adjusts in all the shapes to account for the additional entry in the top-level shape.
8. Click after the name *Lang* in the assistant shape, press Enter, and key **Assistant Director**.
9. Key the title **Reading Products** for Marcus Short, **Linguistics Products** for Ellen Camp, and **Writing Products** for Pat Cramer. Your diagram should look similar to Figure 7-5.

Figure 7-5

Titles have been added to the organization chart

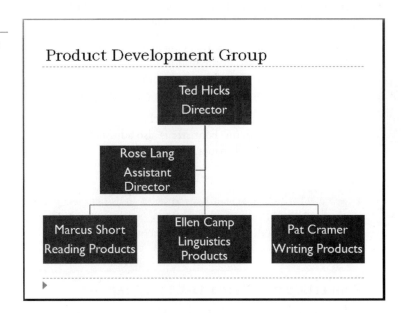

PAUSE. LEAVE the presentation open to use in the next exercise.

Text in a diagram appears either within a shape or as a bulleted list, depending on the diagram type and layout option. In the previous exercise, you inserted text only in shapes, because an organization chart does not offer the option of bulleted text. Figure 7-6 shows a list type diagram that contains both shape text and bulleted text.

Figure 7-6

Shape text and bulleted text in a diagram

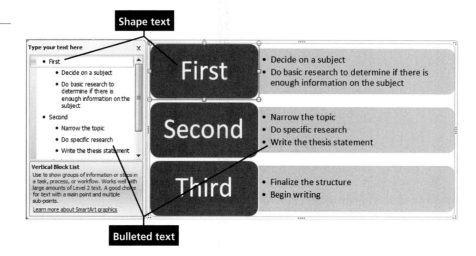

By default, PowerPoint displays the ***Text pane*** to the left of a new diagram. In the Text pane, shape text appears as the first-level bullet item and bulleted text is indented below the shape text, similar to the way several levels of bulleted text appear in a content placeholder.

You can use the Text pane to enter text, or you can enter text directly in each shape. Click next to a bullet in the Text pane or click any [Text] placeholder and begin keying text. If you need more bullet items than are supplied in the default layout, press Enter at the end of the current bullet item to add a new one, or click the Add Bullet button in the Create Graphic group on the SmartArt Tools Design tab.

If you don't want to use the Text pane, you can close it to get it out of the way. To redisplay it, click the tab attached at the middle of the left container border or click the Text Pane button in the Create Graphic group on the SmartArt Tools Design tab. You can also right-click anywhere in the diagram and then click Show Text Pane on the shortcut menu.

As you enter text in the diagram, PowerPoint resizes the shapes to accommodate the longest line of text in the diagram. Font size is also adjusted for the best fit, and PowerPoint keeps the font size the same for all shapes.

CERTIFICATION READY?
How do you add text to a SmartArt diagram?
3.2.1

TAKE NOTE*

If you need to edit text you have entered in a diagram, you can click the text to activate it, then edit the text as necessary. You can also right-click a shape, click Edit Text on the shortcut menu, and then make the necessary changes.

Converting a Bulleted List to a Diagram

PowerPoint provides another way to create a SmartArt diagram: You can create a diagram from any bulleted list on a slide.

⊕ CONVERT A BULLETED LIST TO A DIAGRAM

USE the presentation that is still open from the previous exercise.

1. Go to slide 4 and click in the content placeholder.
2. Click the **Home** tab, if necessary, and then click the **Convert to SmartArt Graphic** button in the Paragraph group. PowerPoint displays the gallery shown in Figure 7-7.

Figure 7-7

The Convert to SmartArt gallery

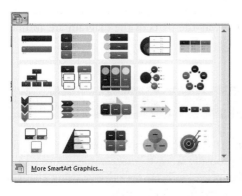

ANOTHER WAY

Right-click in a bulleted list, and then click Convert to SmartArt on the shortcut menu.

3. Click **More SmartArt Graphics** at the bottom of the gallery. The Choose a SmartArt Graphic dialog box opens.
4. Click **Cycle**, then click the **Block Cycle** layout. Read the description of how best to use the Block Cycle layout.
5. Click **OK**. The bulleted list is converted to a cycle diagram, as shown in Figure 7-8.

Figure 7-8

Bulleted list converted to a SmartArt diagram

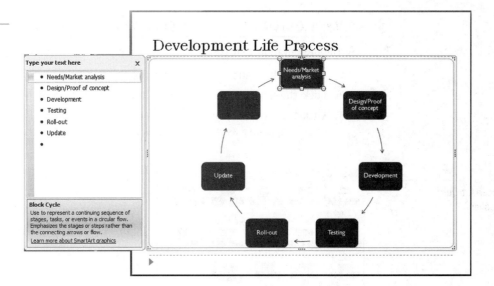

TAKE NOTE
You may notice that the text in the shapes is quite small. You will learn how to modify shape and text size later in the lesson.

6. Notice that the diagram has blocks for six shapes, but because the bulleted list had only five items, one of the blocks is empty. You will learn how to remove this empty shape later in the lesson.
7. **SAVE** the presentation.

   PAUSE. LEAVE the presentation open to use in the next exercise.

As you work with slide text, you may realize that the information would work well as a SmartArt diagram. In this situation, you do not have to re-key the text in the SmartArt diagram shapes. Simply convert the bulleted list to a diagram. You can choose one of the common diagrams in the Convert to SmartArt gallery, or you can access the Choose a SmartArt Diagram dialog box to choose any diagram type or layout.

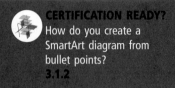

CERTIFICATION READY?
How do you create a SmartArt diagram from bullet points?
3.1.2

You can use animation to make your diagram even more attention-getting. Use the Custom Animation task pane to apply animation effects to a SmartArt diagram. By default, a diagram is animated all at once, but you can use the SmartArt Animation tab in the effect's Options dialog box to change the way the parts of the diagram are animated.

■ Modifying SmartArt Graphics

THE BOTTOM LINE

Although a new SmartArt graphic makes an interesting visual statement on a slide in its default state, you will probably want to make some changes to the graphic to customize it for your use. You can apply a wide variety of formatting changes to modify appearance, and you can also change layout or orientation and add or remove shapes. You can even change the diagram type to another that better fits your data.

Formatting a SmartArt Diagram with a Quick Style

As with other graphic objects, SmartArt diagrams can be quickly and easily formatted by applying a Quick Style. Quick Styles apply fills, borders, and effects to improve the appearance of the diagram's shapes.

⊕ APPLY A QUICK STYLE TO A SMARTART DIAGRAM

USE the presentation that is still open from the previous exercise.

1. Go to slide 3 and click once on the diagram to select it.
2. Click the **SmartArt Tools Design** tab to activate it if necessary.
3. Click the **More** button in the SmartArt Styles group. The SmartArt Quick Style gallery appears, as shown in Figure 7-9.

Figure 7-9

The SmartArt Quick Style gallery

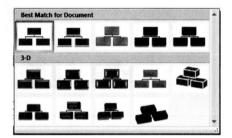

4. Click the **Intense Effect** style. PowerPoint applies the Quick Style.
5. Go to slide 4, click the diagram, and apply the same Quick Style. Your diagram should look similar to Figure 7-10.

Figure 7-10

A Quick Style applied
to a diagram

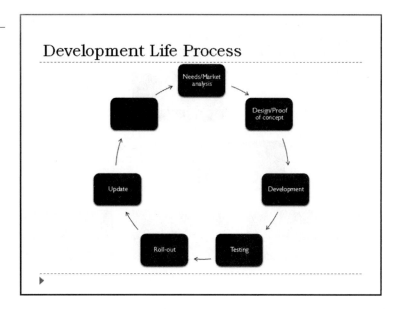

PAUSE. LEAVE the presentation open to use in the next exercise.

Quick Styles can instantly improve a new diagram by applying visual effects to the shapes. Review the results carefully, however, after applying a Quick Style. If your shapes contain several lines of text, some of the three-dimensional styles may obscure the text or cause it to run over on the edges—not a very attractive presentation.

If you do not like the formatting you have applied, you can easily revert to the original appearance of the diagram. Click the Reset Graphic button on the SmartArt Tools Design tab to restore the diagram to its default appearance.

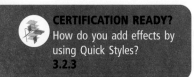

CERTIFICATION READY?
How do you add effects by
using Quick Styles?
3.2.3

Selecting a Theme Color for a SmartArt Diagram

By default, diagrams display using a single theme color. Use the Change Colors gallery to apply a different theme color scheme to the diagram.

⊕ APPLY A THEME COLOR TO A SMARTART DIAGRAM

USE the presentation that is still open from the previous exercise.

1. Go to slide 3 and click the diagram to select it. Click the **SmartArt Tools Design** tab, if necessary.
2. Click the **Change Colors** button in the SmartArt Styles group. The Change Colors gallery opens.
3. Click the first style in the Colorful section. PowerPoint applies theme colors differentiated by level, as shown in Figure 7-11.

Figure 7-11

A new theme color applied to the diagram

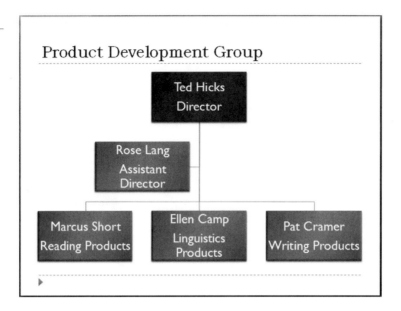

TAKE NOTE Differentiating levels or processes by color gives your audience further visual cues that help them understand the diagram.

4. Go to slide 4 and click the diagram to select it.
5. Click the **Change Colors** button in the SmartArt Styles group, and then click **Colorful Range – Accent Colors 4 to 5**. PowerPoint applies theme colors to create a range of color from light yellow to brown. Your slide should look similar to Figure 7-12.

Figure 7-12

A different color style applied to the cycle diagram

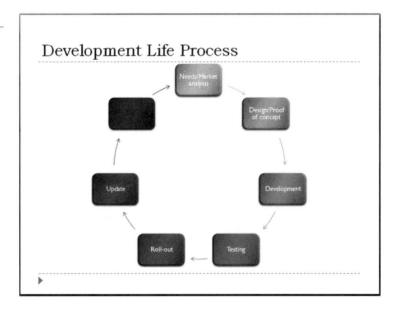

PAUSE. LEAVE the presentation open to use in the next exercise.

The Change Colors gallery provides a quick way to apply variations of theme colors to an entire diagram. If the gallery choices don't strike your fancy, you can manually apply theme colors (or any non-theme color) by using tools on the SmartArt Tools Format tab. Click an individual shape, or use the Shift or Ctrl key to select more than one shape, and then choose

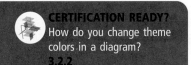

CERTIFICATION READY?
How do you change theme colors in a diagram?
3.2.2

a shape Quick Style from the Shape Styles gallery. Or, use the Shape Fill, Shape Outline, and Shape Effects buttons to choose new colors, outlines, or effects for the selected shapes.

If you do not like the changes you have made to a particular shape, you can reset the shape formats. Right-click the shape, then click Reset Shape on the shortcut menu.

ANOTHER WAY   You can also format a shape by right-clicking the shape, selecting Format Shape, and using the options in the Format Shape dialog box.

Changing a SmartArt Diagram's Layout

If you decide a particular layout does not present your data as you like, you can easily choose a new layout.

⊕ CHANGE THE LAYOUT OF A SMARTART GRAPHIC

USE the presentation that is still open from the previous exercise.

1. Click the diagram on slide 4 to select it, if necessary.
2. Click the **More** button in the Layouts group to display the Layouts gallery, as shown in Figure 7-13.

Figure 7-13

The Cycle Layouts gallery

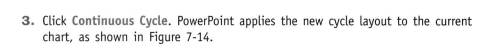

TAKE NOTE

The Layouts gallery displays alternative layouts for the current diagram type.

3. Click **Continuous Cycle**. PowerPoint applies the new cycle layout to the current chart, as shown in Figure 7-14.

Figure 7-14

A new layout has been applied

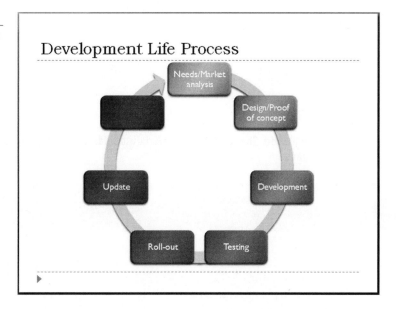

PAUSE. LEAVE the presentation open to use in the next exercise.

When changing a layout, you should generally choose from among the layouts of the current diagram type. In many cases, changing a layout will not result in any additional work for you; PowerPoint simply adjusts the current text into new shapes or configurations, as happened in this exercise.

TAKE NOTE   It is also possible to convert one type of diagram to another type. You will learn more about making this kind of change later in this lesson.

In some cases, however, your information will not convert seamlessly from one layout to another. Some layouts allow only a limited number of shapes, and if your original layout had more than the number allowed in the new layout, you may lose information that cannot be displayed in the new layout.

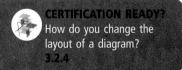

CERTIFICATION READY?
How do you change the layout of a diagram?
3.2.4

You may also need to use the Text pane to modify information so it plots correctly in the diagram. For example, if you had chosen the Basic Radial cycle layout in the previous exercise, you would have had to *demote* some of the shape text items to display them as spokes around the central hub of the diagram. You learn more about demoting and promoting later in the lesson.

Adding a New Shape to a Diagram

As you work with diagrams, you may need to add shapes to accommodate your information. Use the Add Shape button to choose what kind of shape to add and where to insert it in the diagram.

⊕ ADD A SHAPE TO A DIAGRAM

USE the presentation that is still open from the previous exercise.

1. Go to slide 3 and click the diagram to select it.
2. Click the **SmartArt Tools Design** tab.
3. Click the last shape in the last row (*Pat Cramer*) to select it.
4. Click the **Add Shape** drop-down arrow in the Create Graphic group. PowerPoint displays a menu of options for adding a shape relative to the current shape, as shown in Figure 7-15.

Figure 7-15

The Add Shape menu

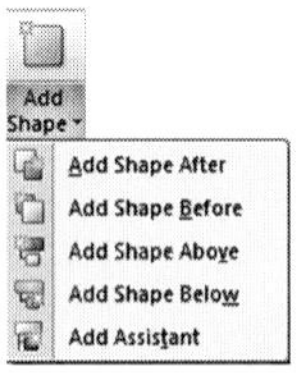

5. Click **Add Shape Below**. PowerPoint adds a subordinate shape to the *Pat Cramer* shape.

TAKE NOTE   Notice that the new shape, which is on a new level, has a different theme color to differentiate it from the level above.

6. Key **Hannah Wong**, press Enter, and key **Product Coordinator**. Your diagram should look similar to Figure 7-16.

Figure 7-16

A new shape has been added to the diagram

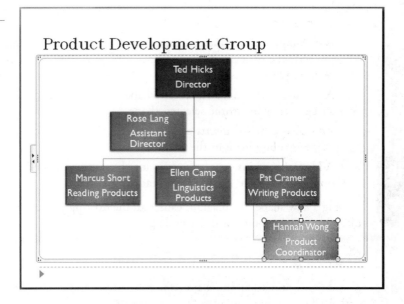

7. With Hannah Wong's shape still selected, click the **Add Shape** drop-down arrow, then click **Add Shape Below**. PowerPoint adds a subordinate shape.

8. Key **Allan Morgan**, press Enter, and then key **Software Design**.

9. With Allan Morgan's shape still selected, click the **Add Shape** drop-down arrow, then click **Add Shape After**. PowerPoint adds a shape on the same level.

10. Key **Kyle Porter**, press Enter, and key **Package Design**. Your diagram should look similar to Figure 7-17.

Figure 7-17

New subordinate shapes have been added

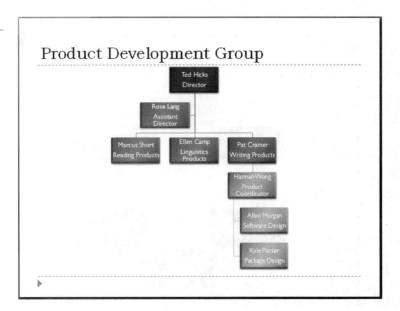

PAUSE. LEAVE the presentation open to use in the next exercise.

The choices available on the Add Shape drop-down menu depend on the type of diagram you are working with. You can choose among some or all of these options:

- **Add Shape After** inserts a new shape to the right of the selected shape on the same level. (If the diagram displays shapes vertically, the new shape may appear below the selected shape.)

- **Add Shape Before** inserts a new shape to the left of the selected shape on the same level. (If the diagram displays shapes vertically, the new shape may appear above the selected shape.)

- **Add Shape Above** inserts a new shape on the level above the selected shape. The new shape is superior to the selected shape.

- **Add Shape Below** inserts a new shape in the level below the selected shape. The new shape is subordinate to the selected shape.

- **Add Assistant** inserts a new assistant shape subordinate to the selected shape. This option is available only in organization charts.

Adding a new shape to a diagram causes all the existing shapes to resize or reposition in the diagram to make room for the new shape.

Removing a Shape from a Diagram

You may not need all the shapes a particular diagram layout provides, or you may find that you can eliminate some of the information in a diagram. You can easily delete shapes you don't need.

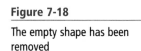 REMOVE A SHAPE FROM A DIAGRAM

USE the presentation that is still open from the previous exercise.

1. Go to slide 4, and click the diagram to select it.
2. Click the empty shape at the upper-left of the diagram.
3. Press [Delete]. PowerPoint removes the shape and reconfigures the diagram, as shown in Figure 7-18.

TAKE NOTE *
You cannot add a shape above the top-level shape in an organization chart.

CERTIFICATION READY?
How do you add a new shape to a diagram?
3.2.6

Figure 7-18

The empty shape has been removed

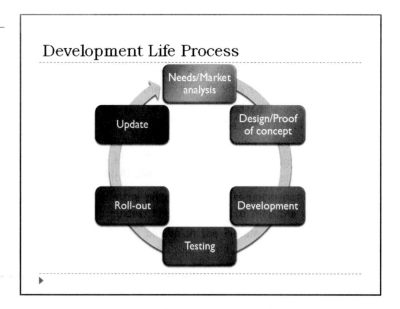

PAUSE. LEAVE the presentation open to use in the next exercise.

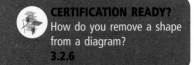

When you remove a shape from a diagram, PowerPoint resizes the other shapes to take advantage of the increased space in the diagram container. Font sizes usually increase accordingly, too. For this reason, you should not do any final formatting on text and shape size until you have finalized the number of shapes in the diagram.

Changing a Diagram's Orientation

Change the look of a diagram by modifying the way shapes are positioned in the diagram. You can use the Right to Left and Layout buttons to adjust diagram orientation.

➔ CHANGE A DIAGRAM'S ORIENTATION

USE the presentation that is still open from the previous exercise.

1. Go to slide 3 and click the diagram to select it.
2. Click the **SmartArt Tools Design** tab.
3. Click the **Right to Left** button in the Create Graphic group. PowerPoint flips the diagram horizontally so that shapes on the left side of the diagram are now on the right side, as shown in Figure 7-19.

Figure 7-19

Use Right to Left to reposition shapes on the slide

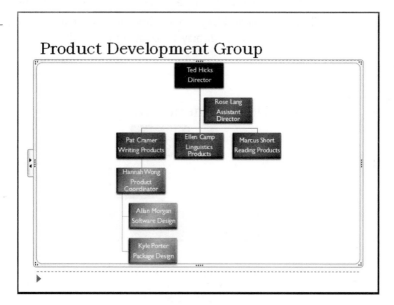

4. Click in the top-level shape (*Ted Hicks*).
5. Click the **Layout** button in the Create Graphic group. PowerPoint displays options for positioning the shapes relative to the top-level shape.
6. Click **Left Hanging**. The subordinate shapes are arranged vertically below the top-level shape, rather than horizontally, as shown in Figure 7-20.

Figure 7-20

Layout has been changed to
Left Hanging

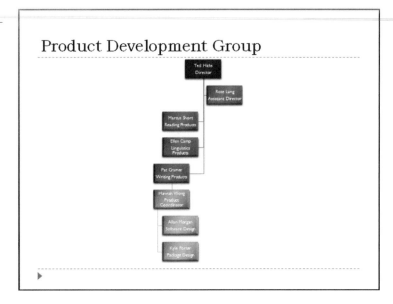

7. Click the **Layout** button, and then click **Standard** to restore the original layout.

8. Click the *Hannah Wong* shape, click the **Layout** button, and then click **Both**. The
subordinate shapes display horizontally rather than vertically, as shown in Figure 7-21.

Figure 7-21

Layout has been changed for
Hannah Wong's subordinates

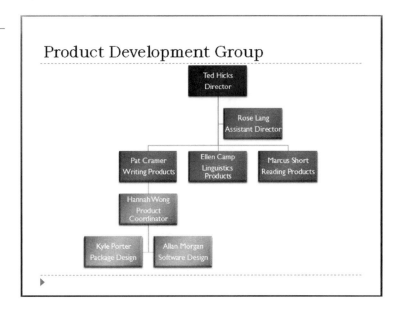

PAUSE. LEAVE the presentation open to use in the next exercise.

You can use the Right to Left button with any diagram that distributes shapes and information horizontally across the slide. Right to Left has no impact on diagrams that center information, such as Pyramid diagrams.

The Layout button is not available for use on all diagram types or layouts. It can be used only
in organization charts with a shape that is superior to subordinate shapes.

You do not have to use the default orientation and positioning of shapes if you would prefer
another arrangement. You can click any shape to select it and drag it to a new location. If the
shape is connected to other shapes, as in an organization chart, the connector lines shift
position or change shape to maintain the connection.

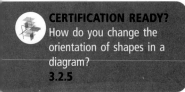

CERTIFICATION READY?
How do you change the
orientation of shapes in a
diagram?
3.2.5

Promoting and Demoting Shapes

You can add, remove, or modify shapes by promoting or demoting diagram text. This procedure is similar to changing the indent level of items in a bulleted list.

⊕ PROMOTE A SHAPE

USE the presentation that is still open from the previous exercise.

1. Click the diagram on slide 3 to select it, if necessary.
2. Click the **Text Pane** button in the Create Graphic group on the SmartArt Tools Design tab. The Text pane reopens.
3. In the Text pane, click the **Hannah Wong** bulleted item. Notice in the Text pane that this item is indented below the *Pat Cramer* bulleted item.
4. Click the **Promote** button in the Create Graphic group. Hannah Wong's shape jumps up one level, and her two subordinates are also promoted, as shown in Figure 7-22.

Figure 7-22

A shape has been promoted

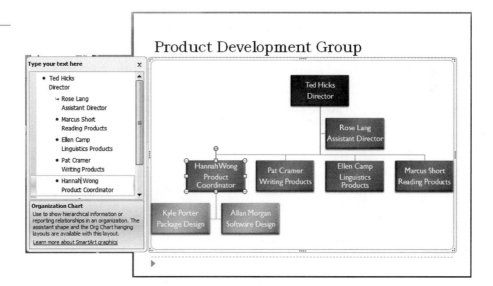

5. Click the **Text Pane** button to hide the text pane again.

PAUSE. LEAVE the presentation open to use in the next exercise.

When you ***promote*** an item, you move it up a level. When you ***demote*** an item, you make it subordinate to the item above it in the hierarchy.

What happens when you promote or demote an item in a diagram depends on whether you are promoting shape text or bulleted text.

- In many diagrams, you cannot promote shape text at all, because shapes are already first-level items by default. An exception is hierarchical charts such as organization charts. You can promote any shape except the top-level shape; when you promote a shape, it jumps up to the level superior to its original position.
- If you promote a bulleted text item, it becomes a shape containing first-level shape text.
- If you demote shape text, it becomes a bullet item.
- If you demote a bulleted text item, it indents further, just as when you make a bullet item subordinate on a slide.

When you promote one bulleted item in a placeholder that contains several bulleted items, the other bulleted items may become subordinate to the new shape text. You may need to move bulleted items back to their original shape in this case. You can use Cut and Paste in the Text pane to move bulleted items from one location to another.

Choosing a Different Type of SmartArt Diagram

Sometimes the hardest part about working with SmartArt is selecting the type and layout that will best display your data. Fortunately, you can easily change the diagram type even after you have created and formatted a diagram.

⊕ **CHOOSE A DIFFERENT SMARTART DIAGRAM**

USE the presentation that is still open from the previous exercise.

1. Go to slide 4 and click the diagram to select it.
2. Click the **More** button in the Layouts group, and then click **More Layouts** at the bottom of the gallery to open the Choose a SmartArt Graphic dialog box.
3. Click the **Process** type in the left pane, and then click the **Upward Arrow** layout in the center pane.
4. Click **OK**. PowerPoint converts the diagram to the process diagram shown in Figure 7-23.

Figure 7-23

The cycle diagram has been changed to a process diagram

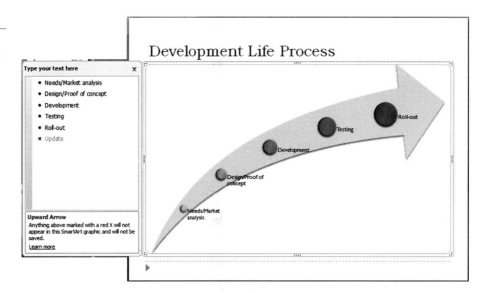

PAUSE. LEAVE the presentation open to use in the next exercise.

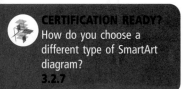

CERTIFICATION READY?
How do you choose a different type of SmartArt diagram?
3.2.7

As when applying a different layout, you are advised to experiment when applying a different diagram type to an existing diagram. Some diagrams will convert very well, while others will not fit the shape layout of the new type at all. You may need to re-key information to display it properly in a different diagram type.

Changing Shape Appearance

Final adjustments to a SmartArt diagram include tweaking the size of shapes and modifying text formats. These appearance changes can improve the look of a diagram and make it easier to read.

⊕ **CHANGING SHAPE SIZE**

Use buttons on the SmartArt Tools Format tab to increase or decrease shape size.

⊕ CHANGE SHAPE SIZE

USE the presentation that is still open from the previous exercise.

> **1.** With the diagram on slide 4 still selected, click the small yellow shape that is nearest the thin end of the arrow graphic to select the shape. When the shape is selected, your diagram will look like Figure 7-24.

Figure 7-24

Selected shape in the diagram

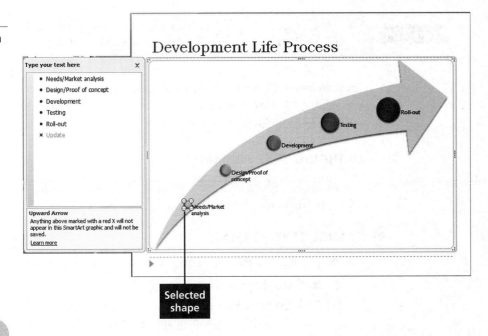

TROUBLESHOOTING

If you select the text box rather than the shape, click outside the text box to deselect it, then try again by clicking the left edge of the yellow shape with the four-headed pointer.

> **2.** Close the Text pane if it opened when you changed the diagram type.
>
> **3.** Click the **SmartArt Tools Format** tab.
>
> **4.** Click the **Larger** button in the Shapes group *twice* to increase the size of the yellow circle shape.
>
> **5.** Click the *Design/Proof of concept* circle shape, then click the **Larger** button once to increase its size.
>
> **6.** Click the *Roll-out* circle shape, then click the **Smaller** button in the Shapes group once to decrease the shape size. Your diagram should look like Figure 7-25.

Figure 7-25

Resized shapes

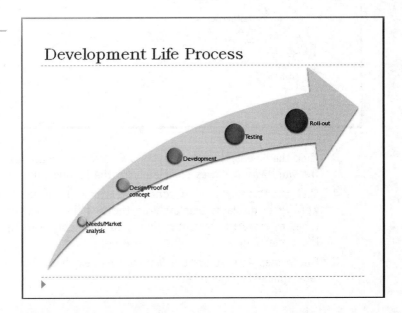

PAUSE. LEAVE the presentation open to use in the next exercise.

PowerPoint formats shapes so that all will fit comfortably in the diagram container. If you have only a few shapes, you might find that this results in a diagram where shapes are much larger than they need to be to hold their text. Conversely, you may want to increase shape size to draw attention to one specific shape.

TAKE NOTE ✳ You can also change shape appearance by selecting a completely new shape: Right-click a shape, click Change Shape, and select the desired shape from the Shapes gallery.

Take care when enlarging or reducing shapes, however. You risk ending up with an inconsistent-looking diagram that is much less attractive than one in which shape sizes are identical or graduated according to an obvious pattern.

CHANGING TEXT FORMATS

If you do not find the size or color of text in a diagram attractive or easy to read, you can use the Home tab's formatting options to adjust text.

⊕ CHANGE TEXT FORMATS

USE the presentation that is still open from the previous exercise.

1. With the diagram on slide 4 still selected, click the **Home** tab.
2. Click the **Font Size** drop-down arrow, and then click **20**. PowerPoint changes the size of all text in the diagram to 20 pt., as shown in Figure 7-26.

Figure 7-26

Text size has been enlarged for easier reading

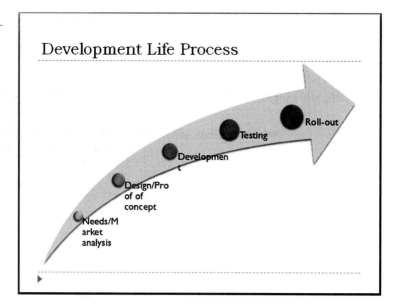

3. Click the **Needs/Market analysis** text box and reduce its width slightly so that the word *Market* moves completely to the second line.
4. Click the **Design/Proof of concept** text box and expand its width so that the word *Proof* displays completely on the first line. Click the ⟶ two or three times to move the text box slightly to the right so its text does not overlap the circle shape.
5. Follow step 4 to adjust the *Development* text box. Your completed diagram should look similar to Figure 7-27.

Figure 7-27

The completed process diagram

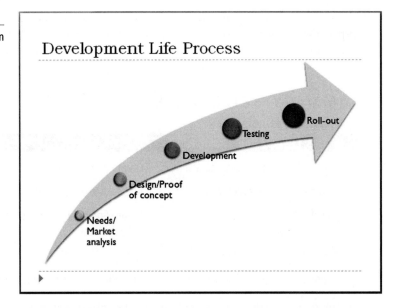

6. Go to slide 3 and click the diagram to select it.
7. Click the outside edge of the *Kyle Porter* shape, hold down Shift, and click the outside edge of the *Allan Morgan* shape.
8. Click the **Font Color** drop-down arrow, and click **Black, Text 1**. The text in these shapes is now easier to read against the light green fill.
9. Click the outside edge of the *Ted Hicks* shape, and then click the **Bold** button on the Home tab. All text in the shape is boldfaced. Your diagram should look like Figure 7-28.

Figure 7-28

The completed organization chart

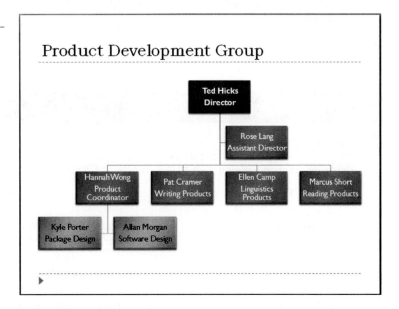

10. **SAVE** the presentation and then **CLOSE** it.
    CLOSE PowerPoint.

PowerPoint automatically adjusts font sizes to fit in or around shapes. In some instances, you may find the sizes too small or too large. Use the text formatting tools with which you are already familiar to adjust font formats such as size, color, or style. You can also adjust alignment in shapes just as you would in any PowerPoint placeholder.

If you modify text formats with the diagram itself selected, all text within the diagram will display the new format. To apply a new text format to a single shape, select that shape first. Text placeholders in a diagram are selected the same way as other slide placeholders are.

SUMMARY SKILL MATRIX

In This Lesson You Learned	Matrix Skill	Skill Number
To add a SmartArt diagram to a slide	Create a SmartArt diagram	3.1.1
To create an organization chart	Add text to SmartArt diagrams	3.2.1
To convert a bulleted list to a SmartArt diagram	Create SmartArt diagrams from bullet points	3.1.2
To modify SmartArt diagrams		
To format a SmartArt diagram with a Quick Style	Add effects by using Quick Styles	3.2.3
To select a theme color for a SmartArt diagram	Change theme colors	3.2.2
To change a SmartArt diagram's layout	Change the layout of diagrams	3.2.4
To add and remove shapes from diagrams	Add or remove shapes within SmartArt	3.2.6
To change a diagram's orientation	Change the orientation of charts	3.2.5
To choose a different type of SmartArt diagram	Change diagram types	3.2.7

■ Knowledge Assessment

Matching

Match the term in Column 1 to its description in Column 2.

Column 1

Column 2

1. promote

a. diagram that shows relationships among departments or personnel

2. assistant

b. diagram type that can show steps in a timeline

3. SmartArt diagram

c. person or department at the head of the organization

4. organization chart

d. a person who reports directly to a staff member

5. Process

e. panel in which you can key diagram text

6. top-level shape

f. change shape text into a bullet item

7. Matrix

g. change a bullet item to shape text

8. Text pane

h. visual representations of information

9. demote

i. departments that report to the head of the organization

10. subordinates

j. diagram type that shows how parts relate to a whole

True / False

Circle T if the statement is true or F if the statement is false.

T | F **1.** List type diagrams show information that has to be in a particular order.

T | F **2.** Text in a SmartArt diagram can appear either in a shape or in a bulleted list.

T | F **3.** Use a Cycle type diagram if you want to show a continual process.

T | F **4.** The Theme Colors gallery allows you to apply variations of theme colors to a diagram.

T | F **5.** If you select a new layout from the same diagram type, you never have to adjust shape text.

T | F **6.** The Add Shape Below option inserts a subordinate shape.

T | F **7.** The Layout button is available for all diagram types.

T | F **8.** To remove a shape, select it and click the Delete Shape button.

T | F **9.** You may have to rekey text if you change from one diagram type to another.

T | F **10.** If a shape is too large, you can use the Smaller button to resize it.

■ Competency Assessment

Project 7-1: Corporate Reorganization

You are a director of operations at Fabrikam, Inc., a company that develops fabric treatments for use in the textile industry. Your company is undergoing reorganization, and you need to prepare a presentation that shows how groups will be aligned in the new structure. You can use a SmartArt diagram to show the new organization.

GET READY. Launch PowerPoint if it is not already running.

The *Reorganization* file is available on the companion CD-ROM.

1. **OPEN** the *Reorganization* presentation.
2. Go to slide 2 and click the **Insert SmartArt Graphic** icon in the content placeholder.
3. Click the **Hierarchy** type, click the **Hierarchy** layout, and then click **OK**.
4. Click in the top-level shape and key **Operations**.
5. Click in the first second-level shape and key **Production**.
6. Click in the second second-level shape and key **R & D**.
7. Click in the first third-level shape and key **Manufacturing**.
8. Delete the other third-level shape under *Production*.
9. Click in the remaining third-level shape (under *R & D*) and key **Quality Assurance**.
10. Click the **Manufacturing** shape to select it, click the **Add Shape** drop-down arrow, and click **Add Shape Below**.
11. Key **Fulfillment** in the new shape.
12. Display the SmartArt Quick Styles gallery and click the **Polished** style.

13. Display the Change Colors gallery and click one of the Colorful gallery choices.

14. Display the Layouts gallery and click the **Horizontal Hierarchy** layout.

15. **SAVE** the presentation as *Reorganization Final* and then **CLOSE** the file.

    LEAVE PowerPoint open for the next project.

Project 7-2: Meeting Agenda

You work for the City Manager of Center City. She has asked you to create an agenda to display at an upcoming meeting of the city's department heads. She has supplied the bulleted text on an existing slide. You can use this text to make a more interesting-looking agenda.

The *Meeting Agenda* file is available on the companion CD-ROM.

1. **OPEN** the *Meeting Agenda* presentation.

2. Click in the content placeholder, click the **Convert to SmartArt Graphic** button, and then click **More SmartArt Graphics**.

3. Click the **Vertical Box List** layout in the first row, then click **OK**.

4. Click the first shape to select it, click the **Add Shape** drop-down arrow, and then click **Add Shape After**.

5. Key **Budget Cuts** in the new shape.

6. Display the Layout gallery and click the **Vertical Bullet List** layout.

7. Display the Change Colors gallery and click the **Transparent Gradient Range – Accent 5** option.

8. **SAVE** the presentation as *Meeting Agenda Final* and then **CLOSE** the file.

    LEAVE PowerPoint open for the next project.

■ Proficiency Assessment

Project 7-3: Wine List

You are the general manager of the Coho Winery, and you are about to present some new wines to your staff. You can make the information more visually exciting using a SmartArt diagram.

The *New Wines* file is available on the companion CD-ROM.

1. **OPEN** the *New Wines* presentation.

2. Convert the bulleted list to the **Vertical Block List** diagram.

3. Click the empty shape at the top of the diagram and remove it.

4. Click at the end of the one Premium bulleted item, press **Enter**, and key **Coho Reserve Chardonnay - $31.99**.

5. Change the orientation of the diagram so that the shape text is at the right and the bulleted text at the left.

6. Reduce the size of the *Whites, Reds, Sparkling,* and *Premium* shapes by selecting each and clicking the **Smaller** button one time.

7. Apply a SmartArt Quick Style of your choice to the diagram.

8. Apply a new theme color scheme of your choice to the diagram.

9. If the words in the shapes to the right are in a white font color that does not contrast well with the shape colors, change the font color to a dark gray.

10. With the diagram still selected, apply an animation effect as follows:

    a. Click the **Animations** tab, then click the **Custom Animations** button to display the Custom Animations task pane.

    b. Click the **Add Effect** button, point to **Entrance**, and then click **Fly In**. (If you don't see this effect, click **More Effects** to find it.)

    c. Change the direction to **From Right** and the speed to **Fast**.

    d. Right-click the effect in the task pane, click **Effect Options**, and click the **SmartArt Animation** tab.

    e. Click the **Group graphic** drop-down arrow, and then click **One by one**.

    f. Click **OK** to close the dialog box.

11. Click the double downward-pointing arrows in the bar below the effect in the animation list to expand the contents so you can see the eight separate Fly In effects.

12. For effects 2, 4, 6, and 8, change the direction to **From Left**.

13. Switch to Slide Show view to see the diagram animation. Click the mouse to display each shape and then the corresponding bulleted text.

14. **SAVE** the presentation as *New Wines Final* and then **CLOSE** the file.

    LEAVE PowerPoint open for the next project.

Project 7-4: On Paper

You are a plant manager for Northwind Paper Company. You are scheduled to give a presentation to a local class of art students to explain how paper is made. You can use a diagram to make the process more visually interesting.

The *Paper* file is available on the companion CD-ROM.

1. **OPEN** the *Paper* presentation.

2. Go to slide 4 and insert a new SmartArt diagram. In the **Relationship** type, choose the **Funnel** layout.

3. Display the Text pane and replace the placeholder text with the following four items:

Pulp

Stock

Press & Dry

Paper

4. Apply the **Subtle Effect** Quick Style to the diagram.

5. Change the diagram to the **Staggered Process** layout in the Process type.

6. The text in the shapes is larger than the slide title. Change the font size of all shapes to **32** pt.

7. **SAVE** the presentation as *Paper Final* and then **CLOSE** the file.

    LEAVE PowerPoint open for the next project.

Mastery Assessment

Project 7-5: Tiger Tales

You are the owner of a karate studio that specializes in teaching youngsters. You are working on a presentation to give at local schools and after-school care centers. You want to add a diagram to your presentation to stress the importance of the proper attitude when learning karate.

1. **OPEN** the *Tigers* presentation.

2. Go to slide 4 and use the bulleted list to create a new SmartArt diagram using the Titled Matrix layout. Note that only the first bulleted item displays in the diagram.

3. Display the Text pane, if necessary, and click the **Respect** item, which is currently grayed out with a red x over the bullet.

The *Tigers* file is available on the companion CD-ROM.

4. Demote this item. It will then display in the upper-left matrix shape.

5. Demote the remaining three bullet items to display them in the diagram.

6. Change the orientation left to right.

7. Apply a Quick Style of your choice.

8. Use the Shape Fill menu to apply a fill color to the *Core Beliefs* shape that is not a theme color but coordinates well with the other shape colors.

9. **SAVE** the presentation as *Tigers Final* and then **CLOSE** the file.

   LEAVE PowerPoint open for the next project.

Project 7-6: Pie Time

You are the franchising manager for Coho Pie Safe, a chain of bakeries specializing in fresh-baked pies and other bakery treats. You are working on a presentation to help potential franchisees understand the company. Use a diagram to display information about revenue sources.

The *Pies* file is available on the companion CD-ROM.

1. **OPEN** the *Pies* presentation.

2. Go to slide 3 and insert a **Basic Pie** diagram from the Relationship type.

3. Use the Text pane to insert the following information in the diagram:

   Birthdays

   Weddings

   Reunions

4. Add two new shapes to the pie with the text **Restaurants** and **Church Socials**.

5. Change the diagram type to a **Vertical Arrow List** layout.

6. Click in the arrow shape to the right of the *Birthdays* shape and key **All ages**.

7. Add bulleted text as follows for the remaining arrows:

Weddings	**Both formal and informal**
Reunions	**Per item or bulk sales**
Restaurants	**Steady income year round**
Church Socials	**Per item or bulk sales**

8. Adjust shape size and bulleted text size as necessary to make the diagram text smaller so it looks more in proportion with the slide title.

9. Apply a Quick Style and a different color scheme of your choice.

10. Click each of the bulleted list arrow shapes and adjust the vertical text alignment to Middle. (Hint: Use the Align Text button in the Paragraph group on the Home tab.)

11. **SAVE** the presentation as *Pies Final* and then **CLOSE** the file.

    CLOSE PowerPoint.

INTERNET READY

The U.S. Department of Agriculture has reworked their Food Pyramid a few times in the past decade. Create a presentation to show how food guidelines have evolved from version to version. Use the Internet to find as many previous versions as you can and create pyramid diagrams in your presentation to display the guidelines. Create a final slide that shows the current guidelines. They are in the form of bands that run from the top of the pyramid to the base, but you can convert these bands to typical pyramid slices.

Adding Graphics and Media Clips to a Presentation

8

LESSON SKILL MATRIX

Skills	Matrix Skill	Skill Number
Adding a Picture to a Slide		
Inserting a Clip Art Picture	Insert clip art	3.3.3
Inserting a Picture from a File	Insert picture from file	3.3.1
Formatting Pictures		
Using the Ruler, Gridlines, and Guides	Use gridlines and guides to arrange illustrations and other content	3.5.4
Rotating an Object	Size, scale, and rotate illustrations and other content	3.5.1
Resizing Objects	Size, scale, and rotate illustrations and other content	3.5.1
Formatting a Picture with a Quick Style	Apply Quick Styles to shapes and pictures	3.4.1
Adding Special Effects to a Picture	Add, change and remove illustration effects	3.4.2
Compressing the Images in a Presentation	Compress images	4.3.5
Adding Shapes to Slides		
Drawing Lines	Insert shapes	3.3.2
Inserting Basic Shapes	Insert shapes	3.3.2
Adding Text to Shapes	Add text to shapes	3.3.4
Organizing Objects on a Slide		
Setting the Order of Objects	Order illustrations and other content	3.5.2
Aligning Objects with Each Other	Group and align illustrations and other content	3.5.3
Grouping Objects Together	Group and align illustrations and other content	3.5.3
Adding Media Clips to a Presentation		
Adding a Sound File to a Slide	Insert media clips	2.3.4
Adding a Movie to a Slide	Insert media clips	2.3.4

You are the director of promotions for the Baldwin Museum of Science. The museum is especially interested in attracting teachers and students to their permanent exhibits, so you have scheduled appearances at a number of high schools in your area, where you plan to present PowerPoint slide shows about the museum and various aspects of science. Power-Point's graphics capabilities allow you to include and customize pictures, shapes, and movies to enliven your presentations. You can also add sounds to provide the finishing touch to a presentation.

KEY TERMS

aspect ratio
clip art
Clip Organizer
constrain
crop
gridlines
guides
keyword
order
rulers
scaling

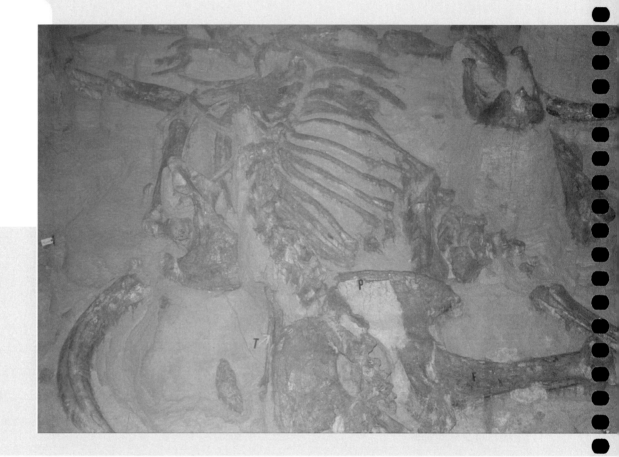

■ SOFTWARE ORIENTATION

Microsoft PowerPoint's Clip Art Task Pane

The Clip Art task pane, shown in Figure 8-1, allows you to search for graphic and multimedia content you can use to embellish and illustrate your slides. The gallery format of the task pane makes it easy to review content and choose a file to insert.

Figure 8-1

The Clip Art task pane

Type a keyword here

Choose a media type

Picture or multimedia files that match the search keyword display here

Click this link to find additional files online

You can use the Clip Art task pane to locate and insert line drawings, photographs, animated graphics, and sound files. If you have a live Internet connection, you have access to thousands of files on the Office Online Web site.

■ Adding a Picture to a Slide

THE BOTTOM LINE

Pictures can be used to illustrate a slide's content or provide visual interest to help hold audience attention. You can insert clip art files that are installed with or accessed through Microsoft Office, or you can insert any picture with a compatible file format.

Inserting a Clip Art Picture

Microsoft Office clip art files include not only drawn graphics but photos and other multimedia objects. Use the Clip Art icon in any content placeholder to open the Clip Art task pane and search for clip art pictures.

 INSERT A CLIP ART PICTURE

The *Exhibits* file is available on the companion CD-ROM.

GET READY. Before you begin these steps, make sure that your computer is on. Log on, if necessary.

1. Start PowerPoint, if the program is not already running.
2. Locate and open the *Exhibits* presentation.

3. Go to slide 4 and click the **Clip Art** icon in the empty content placeholder. The Clip Art task pane opens, as shown in Figure 8-2.

Figure 8-2

The Clip Art task pane

Clip Art task pane

 **ANOTHER WAY**

To insert clip art on a slide that does not have a content placeholder, click the Clip Art button on the Insert tab.

TAKE NOTE

The Clip Art task pane may show the keyword(s) used in the most recent search for clip art.

4. Select any existing text in the Search for box and press **Delete** to remove it.
5. Key **gears** in the Search for box.
6. Click the **Results should be** drop-down arrow, and remove checkmarks from all options *except* Photographs, as shown in Figure 8-3.

Figure 8-3

Choose to search for Photographs only

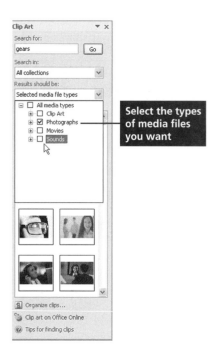

Select the types of media files you want

7. Click the **Go** button near the top of the task pane. PowerPoint searches for clip art photographs that match the keyword and displays them in the task pane.

8. Click the picture of gears shown in Figure 8-4, or one similar to it. The picture is inserted in the content placeholder. (The picture may not take up the entire placeholder.)

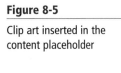

Figure 8-4

Select the photograph of gears

9. Click the **Close** button in the Clip Art task pane to close the pane. Your slide should look similar to Figure 8-5.

Figure 8-5

Clip art inserted in the content placeholder

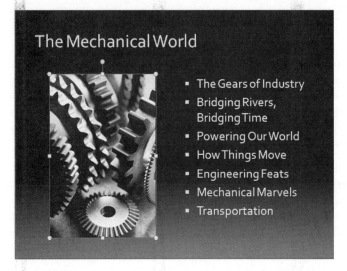

10. SAVE the presentation as *Exhibits Final*.

   PAUSE. LEAVE the presentation open to use in the next exercise.

Clip art is predrawn artwork in a wide variety of styles relating to a wide variety of topics. Microsoft Office supplies access to thousands of clip art graphics that you can insert in documents, worksheets, and databases as well as in PowerPoint presentations. To locate clip art graphics, you use a *keyword* search: In the Clip Art task pane, key a word that relates to the topic you want to illustrate, such as *gears* in the previous exercise.

When you click the Go button, the graphics that appear may be stored on your system in the *Clip Organizer*, a series of folders with keyword names such as Nature and Animals that make it easy for you to locate specific graphic files. You can view files in the Clip Organizer, shown in Figure 8-6, by clicking the *Organize clips* link at the bottom of the Clip Art task pane.

Figure 8-6

The Clip Organizer stores pictures in folders

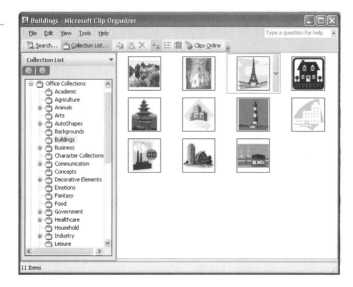

If you have a live Internet connection, PowerPoint will search not only the Clip Organizer on your computer but online graphic files as well and display all of them in the task pane. You can also go directly to the Office Online clip art Web site by clicking the *Clip art on Office Online* link at the bottom of the Clip Art task pane.

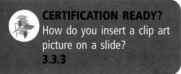

TAKE NOTE

If you find a clip you like on Office Online, you can download it to your computer. Office will store the clip in the Clip Organizer for future use.

Many clip art graphics are humorous in appearance and may not be suitable for corporate communications or presentations on serious topics. You can use the Clip Art task pane to search for photographs as well as clip art graphics. Photographs provide a more sophisticated and professional look for a presentation. The Clip Art task pane also allows you to search for movies and sound files. You will learn how to search for and insert these types of files later in this lesson.

When you insert clip art by using the Clip Art icon in a content placeholder to open the Clip Art task pane, PowerPoint will try to fit the graphic you select into the content placeholder. The graphic may not use up the entire placeholder area, depending on its size and shape. If you insert a graphic on a slide that doesn't have a placeholder, it will generally appear in the center of the slide. You can adjust the graphic's size and position, as you will learn later in this lesson.

CERTIFICATION READY?
How do you insert a clip art picture on a slide?
3.3.3

If you decide you don't like a picture you have inserted, you can easily delete it. Click the picture to select it and then press Delete to remove it from the slide.

Inserting a Picture from a File

You do not have to rely on PowerPoint's clip art files to illustrate your presentation. You can locate many pictures available for free download on the Internet or create your own picture files using a digital camera.

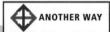 **INSERT A PICTURE FROM A FILE**

USE the presentation that is still open from the previous exercise.

1. Go to slide 3 and click the **Insert** tab to activate it.
2. Click the **Picture** button. The Insert Picture dialog box opens, as shown in Figure 8-7.

Figure 8-7

Locate a picture file in the Insert Picture dialog box

 ANOTHER WAY

Click the Insert Picture from File icon in any content placeholder to open the Insert Picture dialog box.

CD

The *Astronomy.jpg* file is available on the companion CD-ROM.

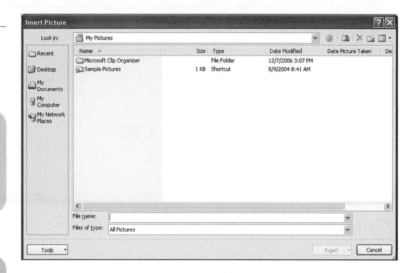

3. Navigate to the location of the data files for this lesson, click *Astronomy.jpg*, and then click **Insert**. The picture appears on the slide, as shown in Figure 8-8.

Figure 8-8

The picture appears on the slide

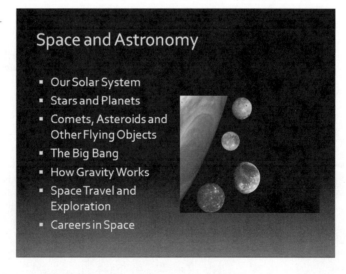

4. **SAVE** the presentation.

PAUSE. LEAVE the presentation open to use in the next exercise.

PowerPoint supports a variety of picture file formats, including GIF, JPEG, PNG, TIFF, BMP, and WMF. Be aware that graphic formats differ in the way they store graphic information, so some formats create larger files than others. GIF files, for example, are generally much smaller than TIFF files because they are limited to only 256 colors, but TIFF files show much greater detail.

If you take your own pictures using a digital camera, you do not have to worry about copyright issues, but you should pay attention to copyright permissions for pictures you locate from other sources. It is extremely easy to save any picture from a Web page to your system. If you are going to use the picture commercially, you need to contact the copyright holder, if there is one, and ask for specific permission to reuse the picture.

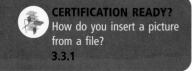 **CERTIFICATION READY?**
How do you insert a picture from a file?
3.3.1

U.S. government sites such as NASA, the source of the picture you inserted in the previous exercise, make images available without requiring copyright permission.

■ Formatting Pictures

 PowerPoint provides many options for improving the appearance of pictures. You can reposition and resize them, rotate them, apply special effects such as Quick Styles, adjust brightness and contrast, and even recolor a picture for a special effect. If you do not like formatting changes you have made, you can reset a picture to its original appearance.

Using the Ruler, Gridlines, and Guides

The ruler, gridlines, and guides can help you position objects such as pictures so that they align with other objects on a slide and appear consistently throughout a presentation. You can move or copy guides to position them where you need them.

⊙ USE THE RULER, GRIDLINES, AND GUIDES

USE the presentation that is still open from the previous exercise.

ANOTHER WAY

Right-click a slide outside of any placeholder, then click Ruler.

1. Go to slide 3 if necessary. Click the **View** tab to activate it, then click **Ruler** in the Show/Hide group if this option is not already selected. The vertical and horizontal rulers appear in the Slide pane.

2. Click **Gridlines** in the Show/Hide group. A grid of regularly spaced dots overlays the slide, as shown in Figure 8-9.

Figure 8-9

Rulers and gridlines

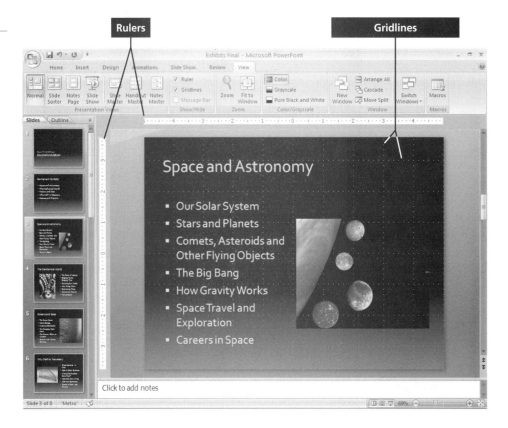

3. Right-click the current slide near the bottom of the slide (outside any placeholder), then click **Grid and Guides**. The Grid and Guides dialog box opens, as shown in Figure 8-10.

Figure 8-10

Grid and Guides dialog box

Press Alt+F9 to show or hide the guides.

4. Click **Display drawing guides on screen**, then click **OK**. The default vertical and horizontal drawing guides display, intersecting at the center of the slide.

5. The guides will be more useful for positioning pictures in this presentation, so you can turn off the gridlines: Click the **View** tab if necessary, and click **Gridlines** to remove the checkmark and hide the gridlines.

6. Click the text placeholder to activate it. You will use the placeholder's selection border to help you position guides.

7. Click the vertical guide above the slide title. You should see a ScreenTip that shows the current position of the guide, 0.0, indicating the guide is at the 0 inch mark on the horizontal ruler.

8. Drag the guide to the left until it aligns on the left border of the text placeholder. The ScreenTip should read 4.50 with a left-pointing arrow. Release the mouse button to drop the guide at that location.

9. Click the horizontal guide to the right of the planet picture and drag upward until the ScreenTip reads 1.67 with an upward-pointing arrow. Drop the guide. It should align with the capital letters in the text placeholder.

10. Click the vertical guide you positioned near the left edge of the slide, hold down **Ctrl**, and drag a copy of the guide to the right until the ScreenTip reads 4.50 with a right-pointing arrow. Drop the guide. Your slide should look like Figure 8-11.

Figure 8-11

Drawing guides positioned on the slide

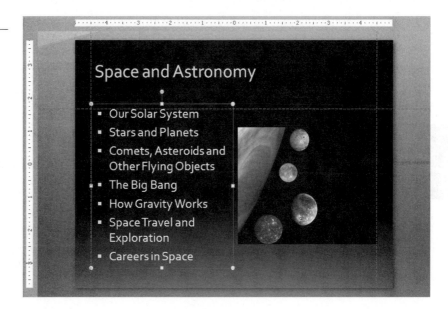

11. Go to slide 4, click the gear picture, and drag it until the upper-left corner of the picture snaps to the intersection of the vertical and horizontal guides. Your slide should look like Figure 8-12.

Figure 8-12

Picture repositioned using the guides

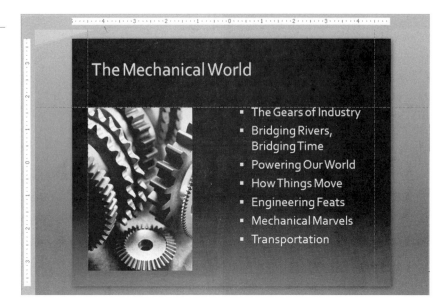

12. Go to slide 5 and drag the picture down and to the left so its upper-right corner snaps to the intersection of the guides.

13. Go to slide 6 and drag the picture up and to the left to snap to the intersection of the two guides.

PAUSE. LEAVE the presentation open to use in the next exercise.

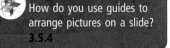

TAKE NOTE

You can adjust the spacing of the dots in the gridlines in the Grid and Guides dialog box.

In Normal view and Notes Page view, you can turn on PowerPoint's horizontal and vertical *rulers*, which help you measure the size of an object on the slide, as well as the amount of space between objects. As you move the pointer on a slide, short dotted lines show the pointer position on both the horizontal and vertical rulers. This allows you to be fairly precise when undertaking tasks such as resizing or cropping.

PowerPoint's drawing *guides* line up with measurements on the ruler to provide nonprinting guidelines you can use when positioning objects on a slide. You can move guides anywhere on the slide and copy them to create additional guides. To remove a guide, drag it off the slide.

PowerPoint also provides *gridlines*, a set of dotted horizontal and vertical lines that overlay the entire slide. Turn on gridlines when you want to arrange a number of objects on the slide or draw shapes to specific sizes.

CERTIFICATION READY?
How do you use guides to arrange pictures on a slide?
3.5.4

By default, objects "snap"—automatically align—to the gridlines even if the gridlines are not currently displayed. This feature can be helpful when you are positioning objects, but you may sometimes find that it hinders precise positioning. You can temporarily override the "snapping" by holding down Alt as you drag an object. Or, you can display the Grid and Guides dialog box and deselect the *Snap objects to grid* check box.

Rotating an Object

Rotate pictures to change their orientation on a slide. You can use the Rotate handle or a Ribbon option to rotate a picture or other object.

 ANOTHER WAY

Click the Arrange button on the Home tab, click Rotate, and choose a rotation option.

ROTATE AN OBJECT

USE the presentation that is still open from the previous exercise.

1. Go to slide 3, and click the picture to select it.
2. Click the **Picture Tools Format** tab, click **Rotate** in the Arrange group, and then click **Flip Horizontal**. The picture reverses its orientation so the planet is on the right and its moons are on the left, as shown in Figure 8-13.

Figure 8-13

The picture has been flipped horizontally

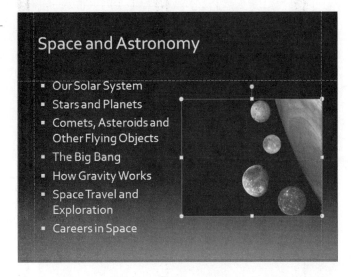

3. Drag the picture up into the upper-right corner of the slide, so that the top and right edges of the picture align with the top and right edges of the slide.

   PAUSE. LEAVE the presentation open to use in the next exercise.

You have rotated objects already in this course, when you changed the orientation of text boxes in Lesson 3. Rotating and flipping can provide additional visual interest for a graphic or fit it more attractively on a slide.

PowerPoint offers some set rotation options, such as rotating right or left 90 degrees. For more control over the rotation, drag the green rotation handle or click More Rotation Options on the Rotate drop-down menu to open the Size and Position dialog box, where you can key a specific rotation amount.

CERTIFICATION READY?
How do you rotate a picture or other object?
3.5.1

Resizing Objects

You have several options for adjusting the size of a picture or other graphic object. You can crop an object to remove part of the object, drag a side or corner, specify exact measurements for an object, or scale it to a percentage of its original size.

CROP AN OBJECT

USE the presentation that is still open from the previous exercise.

1. Go to slide 4 and click the picture to select it.
2. Click the **Picture Tools Format** tab if necessary.
3. Click the **Crop** button in the Size group. The pointer changes to a crop pointer and crop handles appear around the edges of the picture.
4. Position the pointer on the top center crop handle and drag downward until the short dotted line on the vertical ruler is on the 0.5 inch mark, as shown in Figure 8-14.

Figure 8-14

Drag the crop handle down to remove a portion of the picture

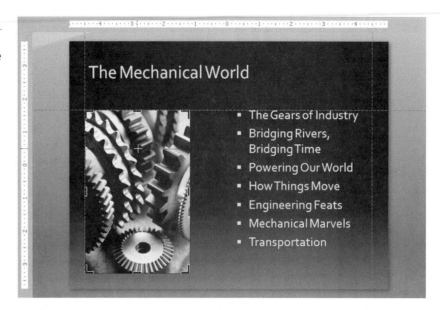

5. Release the mouse button, then click the **Crop** button again to complete the crop.

6. Move the cropped picture back up to the intersection of the two guides. Your slide should look similar to Figure 8-15.

Figure 8-15

The picture has been cropped and repositioned

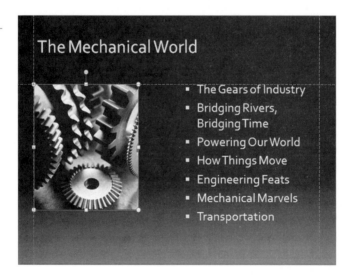

PAUSE. LEAVE the presentation open to use in the next exercise.

When you **crop** a picture, you remove a portion of the graphic that you think is unnecessary. Cropping allows you to focus attention on the most important part of a picture.

The portion of the picture you cropped is not deleted. You can restore the cropped material by using the crop pointer to drag outward to reveal the material that was previously hidden.

⊕ SIZE OR SCALE AN OBJECT

USE the presentation that is still open from the previous exercise.

1. Go to slide 3 and click the picture to select it.

2. Drag the lower-left corner of the picture diagonally until the short dotted line on the horizontal ruler is at 0 inches, as shown in Figure 8-16. (Don't worry that the slide title is partially covered; you'll fix this problem in a later exercise.)

Figure 8-16

Resize a picture by
dragging a corner

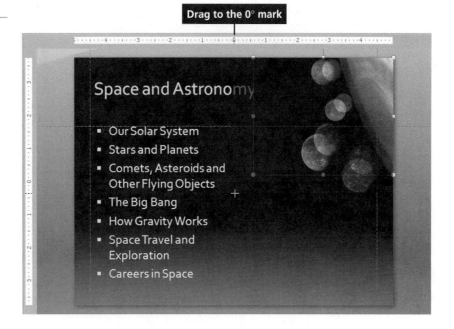

3. Go to slide 4 and click the picture to select it.

4. Right-click the picture, then click **Size and Position**. The Size and Position dialog box opens, as shown in Figure 8-17.

Figure 8-17

The Size and Position
dialog box

 ANOTHER WAY

You can open the Size and Position dialog box by clicking the dialog box launcher in the Size group on the Picture Tools Format tab.

5. Click the **Lock aspect ratio** check box to deselect this option. You can now specify the height and width independently.

6. In the Size and rotate area of the dialog box, click the **Height** up arrow until the height is 4.1 inches. Click the **Width** up arrow until the width is 4.2 inches.

7. Click **Close** to close the dialog box. Your slide should look similar to Figure 8-18.

Figure 8-18

The picture has been resized

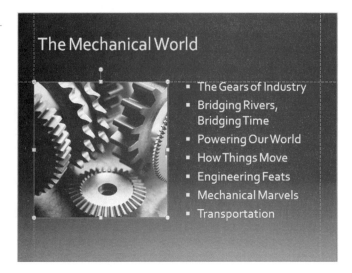

8. Go to slide 5 and click the picture to select it.

9. Click the **Picture Tools Format** tab if necessary, then click the **Width** down arrow in the Size group until the picture's width is 4.2 inches.

10. Drag the picture back over to the intersection of the two guides near the right edge of the slide.

PAUSE. LEAVE the presentation open to use in the next exercise.

In this exercise, you learned three ways to adjust the size of a picture: by simply dragging a corner, by setting measurements in the Size and Position dialog box, and by setting a measurement in the Size group on the Picture Tools Format tab. You can use these options to resize any object on a slide.

Generally, you will want to maintain a picture's *aspect ratio* when you resize it. The aspect ratio is the relationship of width to height. By default, a change to the width of a picture is also applied to the height to maintain aspect ratio. For this reason, you adjusted only the width of the picture on slide 5; PowerPoint took care of adjusting the height to keep the picture in proportion.

Another way to maintain the current aspect ratio is to drag a corner of picture when resizing it. This action adjusts width and height at the same time.

In some instances, you may want to distort a picture on purpose by changing one dimension more than the other. To do so, you must deselect the *Lock aspect ratio* check box in the Size and Position dialog box. You are then free to change width and height independently.

The Size and Position dialog box gives you a number of sizing and positioning options that can help you fine-tune pictures on slides.

- You can specify an exact height and width for the picture, as you did in this exercise, or a percentage of the original height or width. Specifying exact dimensions is generally referred to as *sizing*, and specifying a percentage of the original dimensions is called *scaling*. You can scale a picture larger or smaller than its original size.
- You can crop a picture using a precise measurement for any or all sides.
- You can reset the picture to its original appearance to remove any sizing or format changes you have made to it.

TAKE NOTE

You can also easily distort a picture by dragging a side handle rather than a corner handle.

**ANOTHER WAY**

You can also restore a picture's original appearance by clicking the Reset Picture button in the Adjust group on the Picture Tools Format tab.

CERTIFICATION READY?
How do you size and scale pictures and other objects?
3.5.1

• You can use the Position tab in the Size and Position dialog box to key an exact location on the slide for an object, measuring from either the top left corner or the center of the slide.

Formatting a Picture with a Quick Style

PowerPoint provides a number of Quick Styles you can use to apply borders and other effects to pictures. Use Quick Styles to dress up your pictures or format them consistently throughout a presentation.

⊕ APPLY A QUICK STYLE TO A PICTURE

USE the presentation that is still open from the previous exercise.

1. Go to slide 5 and click the picture to select it.
2. Click the **Picture Tools Format** tab if necessary.
3. Click the **More** button in the Picture Styles group. The Picture Styles gallery appears, as shown in Figure 8-19.

Figure 8-19

The Picture Styles gallery

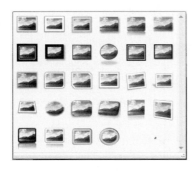

4. Click the **Soft Edge Oval** style. Your picture should look like the one in Figure 8-20.

Figure 8-20

The Quick Style gives the picture a very different look

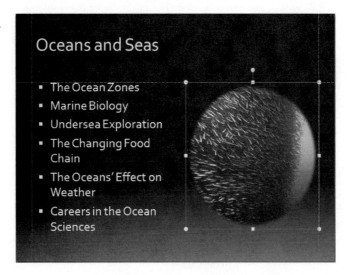

5. Press **Alt** + **F9** to hide the drawing guides.
   PAUSE. LEAVE the presentation open to use in the next exercise.

TAKE NOTE

The Quick Style picture borders are black or white by default, but you can apply any color to the border using the Picture Border button.

The picture Quick Styles give you a number of interesting ways to present pictures on your slides. You can easily apply styles with heavy borders, shadow and reflection effects, and different shapes such as ovals and rounded corners.

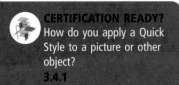

CERTIFICATION READY?
How do you apply a Quick Style to a picture or other object?
3.4.1

If you have a number of pictures in a presentation, be careful not to apply too many different styles to the pictures. Using one or two styles throughout makes a presentation seem more unified and consistent.

Adjusting a Picture's Color, Brightness, and Contrast

> You may need to modify a picture's appearance to make it show up well on a slide. This can be particularly important with pictures you insert from files. Use settings in the Adjust group to improve a picture.

→ ADJUST A PICTURE'S BRIGHTNESS AND CONTRAST

USE the presentation that is still open from the previous exercise.

1. Go to slide 6 and click the picture to select it. This picture is a bit dark.
2. Click the **Picture Tools Format** tab if necessary.
3. Click the **Brightness** button in the Adjust group, then click **+20%**. The picture becomes brighter.
4. Go to slide 5, right-click the picture, and click **Format Picture**. The Format Picture dialog box opens, as shown in Figure 8-21.

Figure 8-21

The Format Picture dialog box

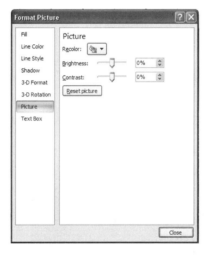

ANOTHER WAY

Open the Format Picture dialog box from the bottom of the Brightness or Contrast menu.

5. Click the **Brightness** up arrow to increase brightness to 15%.
6. Click the **Contrast** up arrow to increase contrast to 25%, and then click **Close**. The picture is now brighter and sharper than previously.

   PAUSE. LEAVE the presentation open to use in the next exercise.

The Brightness and Contrast buttons in the Adjust group allow you to increase or decrease brightness and contrast in set intervals of 10 percent. For more control over brightness and contrast, use the Format Picture dialog box. As you adjust settings in the dialog box, the picture changes to show the modifications, making it easy to control final appearance.

The Adjust group and the Format Picture dialog box also offer the Recolor option. Use the Recolor gallery to apply grayscale, sepia, or one of the current theme colors to a selected picture to create a special effect, as shown in Figure 8-22.

Figure 8-22

The gears picture has been recolored

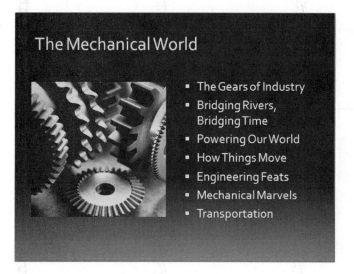

Adding Special Effects to a Picture

Use the Picture Effects options to apply Shadow, Reflection, Glow, and other effects to any picture in a presentation.

⊕ ADD SPECIAL EFFECTS TO A PICTURE

USE the presentation that is still open from the previous exercise.

1. Go to slide 6 and click the picture to select it.
2. Click the **Picture Tools Format** tab if necessary.
3. Click **Picture Effects** in the Picture Styles group, point to **Soft Edges**, and then click **10 Point**. Your slide should look similar to Figure 8-23.

Figure 8-23

Soft edges effect applied to the picture

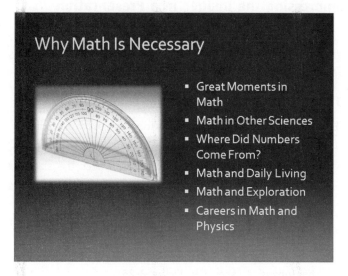

4. This is not quite the effect you want. Click **Picture Effects**, point to **Soft Edges**, and then click **No Soft Edges**.
5. Click **Picture Effects** again, point to **Reflection**, and then click **Tight Reflection, 4 pt offset**. Your picture should look like Figure 8-24.

Figure 8-24

The Reflection effect is a better option for this presentation

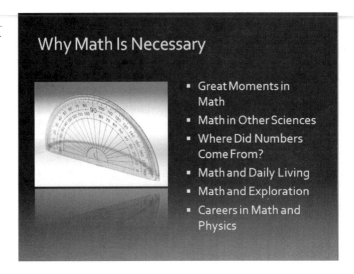

PAUSE. **LEAVE** the presentation open to use in the next exercise.

The effects offered on the Picture Effects gallery should be familiar by now, because you have applied similar effects to other objects such as tables, charts, and diagrams. You add and remove effects using the various submenus from the gallery.

Consider your background when choosing special effects for a picture (or any other object). Shadow effects will not have much impact on a dark background. Glow colors are designed to mix with the background color, so a dark background will make a glow less effective. Reflections, on the other hand, can look especially sharp on a dark background. In the previous exercise, the reflection also added height to the picture, helping it balance out the text placeholder on the right side of the slide.

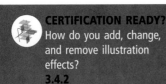

CERTIFICATION READY?
How do you add, change, and remove illustration effects?
3.4.2

Compressing the Images in a Presentation

Compressing images reduces the size of a presentation. This can make the presentation easier to store and speed up display if you have to work on a slow projector or computer system.

➔ COMPRESS THE IMAGES IN A PRESENTATION

USE the presentation that is still open from the previous exercise.

1. Use a file management program such as My Computer to navigate to the current presentation. Use the Details view to check the size of the file.
2. In PowerPoint, click any picture in the presentation to select it, and then click the **Picture Tools Format** tab if necessary.
3. Click **Compress Pictures** in the Adjust group. The Compress Pictures dialog box opens.
4. Click the **Options** button in the dialog box. The Compression Settings dialog box opens, as shown in Figure 8-25.

Figure 8-25

Compression Settings dialog box

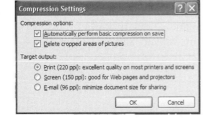

5. Click the **Screen (150 ppi)** option if necessary, then click **OK**.

6. Click **OK** again, and then **SAVE** the presentation. PowerPoint applies the compression settings you selected.

7. In My Computer, note the new file size of the presentation.

PAUSE. LEAVE the presentation open to use in the next exercise.

X REF

You will learn more about sharing a presentation in Lesson 9.

When adding pictures to a presentation, you may need to consider the ultimate size of the presentation. Pictures will add considerably to the presentation's file size. This can make a large presentation difficult to store or work with.

The compression utility allows you to choose several options that can reduce file size. You can choose to delete the hidden portions of cropped pictures, for example. You can also choose a target output setting. If you know your slides will be presented on the Web or projected on a monitor, you can choose the Screen option. Presentations to be presented on a screen do not have to have the same quality as materials that might be printed because the monitor screen itself is limited in the quality it can display. Choose the E-mail option to reduce file size even further to improve transmission time when you are sharing a presentation by e-mail.

CERTIFICATION READY?
How do you compress images in a presentation?
4.3.5

You can select a picture and then click the *Apply to selected pictures only* check box in the Compress Pictures dialog box. This allows you to compress some pictures while maintaining higher quality settings for others in the presentation.

■ Adding Shapes to Slides

↓
THE BOTTOM LINE

PowerPoint offers sophisticated tools that allow you to create both basic and complex drawings. Use line tools and shapes to construct the drawing. You can easily add text to shapes to identify them and format the drawing using familiar fill, outline, and effects options.

Drawing Lines

PowerPoint supplies a number of different line tools so you can draw horizontal, vertical, diagonal, or free-form lines.

→ DRAW LINES

USE the presentation that is still open from the previous exercise.

1. Go to slide 8. You will create a map on this slide to show potential visitors how to get to the museum. As you work, refer to Figure 8-26 for position of objects.

2. Click the **View** tab, and then click **Gridlines** to turn gridlines on.

3. Create the first street for the map as follows:

   a. Click the **Home** tab, then click the **Shapes** button (or the **More** button in the Drawing group) to display the gallery of drawing shapes.

   b. Click **Line** in the Line group. The pointer takes the shape of a crosshair.

   c. Locate the intersection of vertical and horizontal gridlines below the letter *n* in *John*, click at the intersection, and drag downward to create a vertical line three "blocks" long.

TAKE NOTE

You can also access the Shapes gallery on the Drawing Tools Format and insert tabs.

4. Add the street name as follows:

  a. Click **Text Box** on the Insert tab, click anywhere on the slide, and key the text **Matthews Pike**.

  b. Click the outer border of the text box to select all content within the text box, and change the font size to **16**.

  c. Click **Arrange** in the Drawing group, point to **Rotate**, and click **Rotate Left 90°**.

  d. Move the rotated street name just to the left of the vertical line, as shown in Figure 8-26.

5. Click the **Line** tool again, hold down Shift, and draw the diagonal line shown in Figure 8-26.

6. Click the **Line** tool again and draw the horizontal line shown in Figure 8-26.

7. Add the street name for the diagonal street as follows:

  a. Insert a text box anywhere on the slide, and key **Magnolia Parkway**.

  b. Change the font size to **16**.

  c. With the text box still selected, click **Arrange**, point to **Rotate**, and click **More Rotation Options**. The Size and Position dialog box opens.

  d. Key **-45** in the Rotate box, then click **Close**.

  e. Move the rotated text box to the right of the diagonal line, as shown in Figure 8-26.

Figure 8-26

The streets and street names have been added

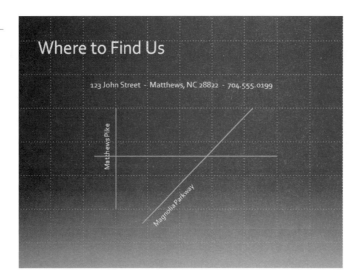

PAUSE. LEAVE the presentation open to use in the next exercise.

The Shapes gallery contains well over a hundred different shapes you can use to create drawings, from a simple rectangle to complex flowchart symbols. If you have worked with previous versions of PowerPoint, you may recognize many of these shapes as AutoShapes.

PowerPoint makes it easy to insert shapes by placing the Shapes gallery on three tabs: Insert, Home, and Drawing Tools Format. When a drawing shape is selected, the Drawing Tools Format tab is active and you can select another drawing tool from the Shapes gallery in the Insert Shapes group. If no shape is currently selected, you can use the Home tab or the Insert tab to select a drawing tool from the Shapes gallery.

To draw a shape with a shape tool, select the tool, click where you want to begin the shape, hold down the mouse button, and drag to make the shape the desired size.

You can use the Shift key to *constrain* some shapes to a specific appearance. For example:

- Hold down Shift while drawing a line to constrain it to a vertical, horizontal, or 45-degree diagonal orientation.
- Hold down Shift while drawing a rectangle to create a perfect square or while drawing an oval to create a perfect circle.
- Hold down Shift while drawing a triangle to create an equilateral triangle.

Selected shapes have sizing handles you can use to adjust the size of the object. Some complex shapes have yellow diamond adjustment handles that allow you to modify the shape. Drag a selected shape anywhere on a slide to reposition it.

Lines and other shapes take their color from the current theme. You can change color, as well as change outline and other effects, at any time while creating a drawing.

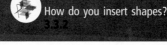

CERTIFICATION READY?
How do you insert shapes?
3.3.2

Inserting Basic Shapes

PowerPoint's many shape tools allow you to create multisided, elliptical, and even freeform shapes.

⊕ INSERT BASIC SHAPES

USE the presentation that is still open from the previous exercise. As you work, refer to Figure 8-27 to help you position and size objects.

1. Click the **Rectangle** tool in the Shapes gallery, hold down the mouse button, and drag to create the tall shape above the horizontal line shown in Figure 8-27.

2. With the shape still selected, click the **Drawing Tools Format** tab if necessary. Note the measurements in the Size group. If necessary, adjust the size so the shape is 1 inch high by 0.9 inches wide.

3. Click the **Rectangle** tool again and use it to create the wider rectangle shown in Figure 8-27. This shape should be 0.7 inch high by 1.2 inches wide.

4. Click the **Oval** tool in the Shapes gallery, hold down (Shift), and draw the circle shown in Figure 8-27. This shape should be 1.2 inches high and wide.

5. Click the **Rectangle** tool and create a rectangle 0.7 inches high by 1 inch wide near the lower end of the diagonal street.

6. Click the shape's green rotate handle and drag to the right to rotate the shape so its right side is parallel to the diagonal road, as shown in Figure 8-27.

7. Click the **Freeform** tool in the Lines group in the Shapes gallery. Near the bottom of the slide (so you can easily see the line you are drawing), draw an irregular oval shape to represent a lake. The shape should be about 1.4 inches high and 1.5 inches wide.

TROUBLESHOOTING

When using the Freeform tool, if you return to the exact point at which you started drawing, PowerPoint will automatically close and fill the shape with color. If your shape does not fill, double-click to end it, click Undo, and start again.

8. Drag the lake shape to the right of the diagonal line, as shown in Figure 8-27.

Figure 8-27

Basic shapes have been added
to the map

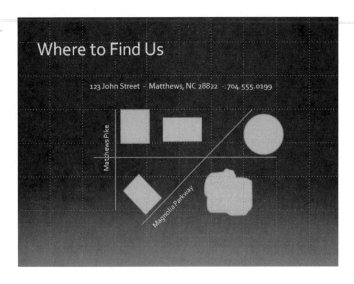

9. **SAVE** the presentation.

PAUSE. LEAVE the presentation open to use in the next exercise.

When creating shapes, you can simply "eyeball" the size, use the rulers or gridlines to help you size, or use the Height and Width settings in the Size group on the Drawing Tools Format tab to scale the objects. Setting precise measurements can help you maintain the same proportions when creating objects of different shapes; for example, when creating circles and triangles that have to be the same height and width.

You can save yourself some time when drawing similar or identical shapes by copying shapes. Copy a selected shape, use Paste to paste a copy on the slide, then move or modify the copy as necessary. Or, select a shape, hold down the Ctrl key, and drag a copy of the shape to a new location.

If you are creating a drawing in which you want to show connections between objects, you can use connectors from the Lines group of the Shapes gallery. Connectors automatically snap to points on shape sides so you can easily draw an arrow, for instance, from one shape to another. As you reposition objects, the connectors remain attached and adjust as necessary to maintain the links between shapes.

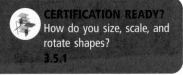

CERTIFICATION READY?
How do you size, scale, and
rotate shapes?
3.5.1

Adding Text to Shapes

You can often improve a drawing by labeling the shapes to clearly state what they represent. In PowerPoint 2007, you can add text by simply clicking and keying.

➔ ADD TEXT TO SHAPES

USE the presentation that is still open from the previous exercise.

1. Click in the tall rectangle above the horizontal street, and then key **West Bank Center**.
2. Click in the wide rectangle shape, and then key **Baldwin Museum**.
3. Click in the circle shape, and then key **Miller Arena**.
4. Click in the rotated rectangle, and then key **Holmes College**. Note that the text is rotated as well.
5. Click in the freeform lake object, and then key **Magnolia Lake**.
6. Drag over the *Baldwin Museum* text to select it, then click the **Bold** button to boldface the text. Your map should look similar to Figure 8-28.

Figure 8-28

Text added to the shapes

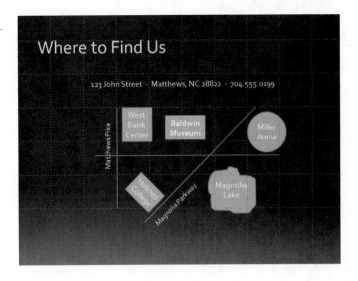

PAUSE. LEAVE the presentation open to use in the next exercise.

When you add text to a shape, the shape takes the function of a text box. PowerPoint automatically wraps text in the shape as in a text box; if the shape is not large enough to display the text, words will break up or the text will extend above and below the shape. You can solve this problem by resizing the shape or changing the text's point size.

TAKE NOTE
To adjust the way text appears in a shape, right-click the shape, click Format Shape, and access the Text Box settings.

You can use any text formatting options you like when adding text to shapes, just as when inserting text into a placeholder or text box. To select text in a shape to edit it, drag over it with the I-beam pointer.

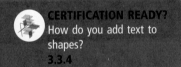

CERTIFICATION READY?
How do you add text to shapes?
3.3.4

Formatting Shapes

You format shapes using the Shape Fill, Shape Outline, and Shape Effects tools on the Drawing Tools Format tab. You can also apply Quick Styles to shapes for immediate impact.

⊕ FORMAT SHAPES

USE the presentation that is still open from the previous exercise.

1. Format the *Matthews Pike* line and label:
   a. Click the vertical line that represents Matthews Pike, click the **Shape Outline** button, and then click the **Gold, Accent 3** theme color.

TAKE NOTE
You can use the Shape Outline button in the Drawing group on the Home tab or in the Shape Styles group on the Drawing Tools Format tab.

   b. Click the **Shape Outline** button again, point to **Weight**, and click **6 pt**.
   c. Click the outside border of the *Matthews Pike* text box to select all content in the text box, click the **Home** tab if necessary, click **Font Color**, and click **Black, Background 1**.
   d. With the text box still selected, click the **Shape Fill** button, and then click **White, Text 1**.

2. Click the horizontal line and repeat steps 1a and 1b to format the line with the **White, Text 1, darker 35%** theme color and **6 pt** weight. (Don't worry about the street crossing over the *Matthews Pike* text box. You will fix this problem in a later exercise.)

3. Click the diagonal *Magnolia Parkway* line, click the **Shape Outline** button, point to **Weight**, and click **6 pt**.

4. Format the *Magnolia Parkway* text box following steps 1c and 1d to change text to black and the fill to white.

5. Format the other shapes as follows:

   a. Click the *West Bank Center* shape above the horizontal street, hold down `Shift`, and click each additional filled shape until all are selected. (Do *not* click any of the lines or the street name text boxes.)

   b. Click **Shape Outline**, and then click **No Outline**. You have removed outlines from the selected shapes.

   c. Click anywhere on the slide to deselect the selected shapes.

   d. Click the *West Bank Center* shape, click **Shape Fill**, and click **Periwinkle, Accent 5, Darker 25%**.

   e. Click the *Miller Arena* shape and fill with **Gold, Accent 3, Darker 25%**.

   f. Click the *Holmes College* shape and fill with **Pink, Accent 2, Darker 25%**.

   g. Click the *Magnolia Lake* shape and fill with **Turquoise, Accent 4, Darker 25%**.

6. You will use a Quick Style for the *Baldwin Museum* shape to make it stand out: Click the *Baldwin Museum* shape, display the Shape Styles gallery, and click **Intense Effect - Dark 1**.

7. Select all the filled shapes *except* the *Baldwin Museum* shape and the street name text boxes, click **Shape Effects**, point to **Bevel**, and click **Circle**. Your map should look similar to Figure 8-29.

Figure 8-29

The map has been formatted

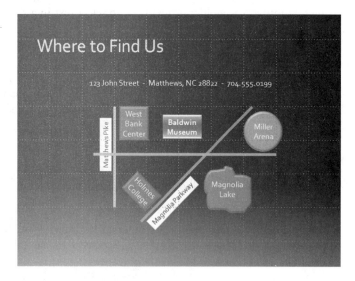

8. **SAVE** the presentation.

   PAUSE. LEAVE the presentation open to use in the next exercise.

You should be familiar by now with applying fills, outlines, and effects. You can format shapes using these options just as you formatted table cells, chart data markers, and SmartArt shapes.

Note that you can access fill, outline, and effect options from either the Home tab or the Drawing Tools Format tab. PowerPoint makes these options available on both tabs to minimize the amount of switching you have to do if you are also formatting text.

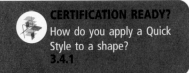
CERTIFICATION READY?
How do you apply a Quick Style to a shape?
3.4.1

Save time when applying the same kinds of formats to a number of objects by selecting all the objects that need the same formatting. You can then apply the format only once to modify all the selected objects. To select several objects, you use the Shift-click method: Click the first object you want to select, hold down the Shift key, and then click additional objects. If you select an object for your group by mistake, click it again to exclude it from the selection group.

■ Organizing Objects on a Slide

 THE BOTTOM LINE

It is not uncommon to have to adjust the layout of objects you have added to slides. You may find that objects need to be reordered so they do not obscure other objects, or need to be aligned on the slide to present a neater appearance. You can also group objects together to make it easy to move or resize them all at once.

Setting the Order of Objects

As you applied formats to the lines in the map, you may have noticed that the lines are stacked on top of each other and the horizontal line appears to cross over a text box. You can adjust the order in which objects stack on the slide by using Arrange commands or the Selection and Visibility pane.

⊙ SET THE ORDER OF OBJECTS

USE the presentation that is still open from the previous exercise.

1. Go to slide 3, and click the picture to select it.

2. Click the **Arrange** button on the Home tab, and then click **Send to Back**. The picture moves behind the slide title placeholder, as shown in Figure 8-30.

Figure 8-30

The picture moves behind the placeholder

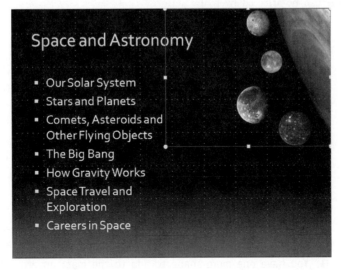

TAKE NOTE*

The Arrange tools are available on both the Home tab and the Picture Tools Format tab.

3. Go to slide 8. Click the **Arrange** button, then click **Selection Pane**. The Selection and Visibility pane opens, as shown in Figure 8-31, showing the current slide content in the order in which it was created, from bottom to top.

Figure 8-31

The Selection and Visibility pane shows the current slide content

 **ANOTHER WAY**   You can also display the Selection and Visibility pane by clicking Select on the Home tab, then clicking Selection Pane.

TROUBLESHOOTING   Don't be concerned if the list in your Selection and Visibility pane doesn't exactly match the one shown in Figure 8-31. The order and numbering of objects in the pane can be affected by many actions.

4. Click the *Matthews Pike* street in the map to see how it is identified in the Selection and Visibility pane—it will have a name such as Straight Connector 4 and should be near the bottom of the list of objects. Then click the horizontal street line to see its name.

5. Click the *Matthew Pike* street line again to select it. Click the **Re-order** up arrow until the selected Straight Connector is above the horizontal Straight Connector in the Selection and Visibility pane. Notice that the gold line is now on top of the light gray line in the map.

6. Click the *Matthews Pike* text box and click the **Re-order** up arrow until the text box is on top of the horizontal gray line in the map.

7. Click the *Magnolia Parkway* street line and click the **Re-order** up arrow until the diagonal street is above the horizontal street in the map.

8. You have one more shape to add to the map: an arrow that labels the horizontal street as John Street and indicates that the street is one way. Click **Shapes** on the Home tab, click **Right Arrow** in the Block Arrows group, and draw a block arrow as shown in Figure 8-32. The arrow should be about 0.7 inches high and 5.2 inches wide.

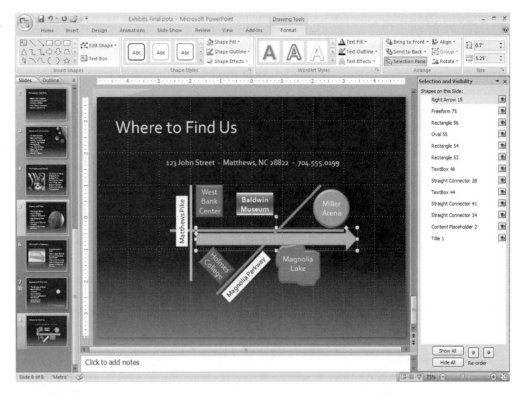

Figure 8-32

Adding the block arrow
to the map

Note that the Right
Arrow object has been
added at the top of the
Selection and Visibility
pane.

9. Remove the shape outline and fill the shape with **White, Text 1**.

10. Key **John Street**, press `Tab` twice, and key **ONE WAY**. You will not be able to see the text because it is white.

11. Click the outside border of the block arrow to select all content in the shape, click the **Home** tab, click **Font Color**, and click **Black, Background 1**.

12. Right-click a blank area of the block arrow (to the left of the words *John Street*, for example), point to **Send to Back**, and click **Send to Back**. The arrow moves behind all lines and shapes, as shown in Figure 8-33. Note the position of the Right Arrow object in the Selection and Visibility pane.

Figure 8-33

The block arrow has been
moved behind all other objects

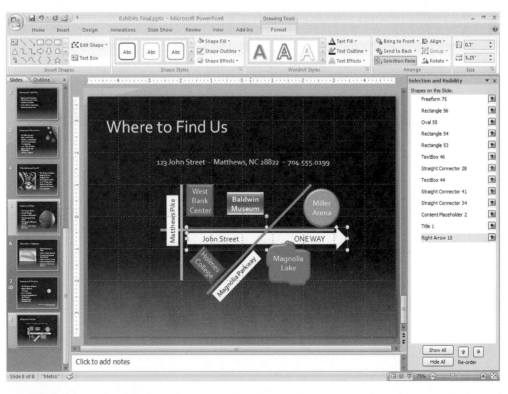

13. Close the Selection and Visibility pane.

14. If any of your shapes obscures the text on the block right arrow, adjust their positions as necessary.

PAUSE. LEAVE the presentation open to use in the next exercise.

Objects stack up on a slide in the order in which you created them, from bottom to top. If you insert a slide title on a slide, it will be the object at the bottom of the stack. The last item you create or add to the slide will be at the top of the stack. You can consider each object to be on an invisible layer in the stack.

As you have seen in the map exercises, some objects can obscure other objects because of the order in which you add them to the slide. You use the ***order*** options to reposition objects in the stack:

- **Bring to Front** moves the selected object to the front or top of the stack, on top of all other objects.
- **Bring Forward** moves an object one layer toward the front or top of the stack. Use this option if you need to position an object above some objects but below others.
- **Send to Back** moves an object all the way to the back or bottom of the stack, below all other objects.
- **Send Backward** moves an object one layer toward the back or bottom of the stack.

You can clearly see the stacking order of objects on a slide using the Selection and Visibility pane, new in PowerPoint 2007. This pane is similar to the Layers palette in a program such as Illustrator or Photoshop. It allows you to easily move objects up or down in the stacking order. You can click the visibility "eye" to hide objects that might be in your way as you work on another object—a handy feature when creating a complex drawing.

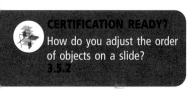

CERTIFICATION READY?
How do you adjust the order of objects on a slide?
3.5.2

If you do not want to use the Selection and Visibility pane, you can use options on the Home tab's Arrange button menu to reorder objects, or you can use buttons in the Drawing Tools Format tab in the Arrange group. You can also access these options readily by right-clicking an object and selecting the appropriate command from the shortcut menu.

TAKE NOTE

Arrange options also display on other Format tabs, such as the Picture Tools Format and SmartArt Tools Format tabs.

Aligning Objects with Each Other

Your drawings will present a more pleasing appearance if similar items are aligned with each other or to the slide. Use PowerPoint's alignment options to position objects neatly.

⊕ ALIGN OBJECTS WITH EACH OTHER

USE the presentation that is still open from the previous exercise.

1. Click the **West Bank Center** shape, hold down (**Shift**), and click the **Baldwin Museum** shape and the **Miller Arena** shape. These landmarks are all different distances from the *John Street* horizontal line but can be aligned for a neater appearance.

2. Click the **Drawing Tools Format** tab if necessary, click **Align**, and click **Align Bottom**. The shapes are now aligned at the bottom so they are the same distance from the horizontal line, as shown in Figure 8-34.

Figure 8-34

Objects have been aligned
by their bottom edges

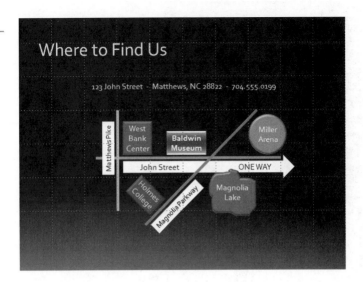

PAUSE. LEAVE the presentation open to use in the next exercise.

PowerPoint's alignment options allow you to line up objects on a slide both horizontally and vertically:

- Use **Align Left**, **Align Center**, or **Align Right** to align objects horizontally so that their left edges, vertical centers, or right edges are lined up with each other.
- Use **Align Top**, **Align Middle**, or **Align Bottom** to align objects vertically so that their top edges, horizontal centers, or bottom edges are lined up with each other.

You can also use distribute options to space objects evenly, either vertically or horizontally. This feature can be a great time-saver when you have a number of objects that you want to spread out evenly across a slide.

PowerPoint allows you to align (or distribute) objects either to each other or to the slide. If you select Align Selected Objects on the Align menu, PowerPoint will adjust only the selected objects. If you select Align to Slide, PowerPoint will rearrange objects using the entire slide area.

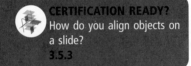

CERTIFICATION READY?
How do you align objects on a slide?
3.5.3

Grouping Objects Together

When a drawing consists of a number of objects, it can be tedious to move each one if you need to reposition the drawing. Grouping objects allows you to work with a number of objects as one unit.

⊕ **GROUP OBJECTS TOGETHER**

USE the presentation that is still open from the previous exercise.

1. Click the **Matthews Pike** text box, hold down Shift, and click each of the other objects in the map until all are selected.
2. Click the **Drawing Tools Format** tab if necessary, click **Group**, and then click **Group**. All objects are surrounded by a single selection border, as shown in Figure 8-35.

Figure 8-35

All elements of the map
are grouped

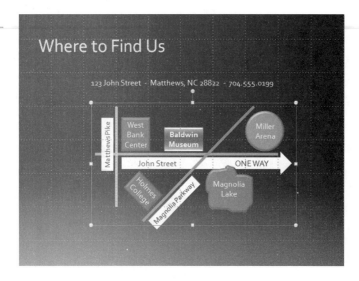

3. Click the **View** tab, then deselect **Gridlines** to hide the grid.

4. Click the **Drawing Tools Format** tab, click the **Align** button, and make sure that **Align to Slide** is selected.

5. Click the **Align** button again, and click **Align Center**. The grouped map is now centered horizontally on the slide, as shown in Figure 8-36.

Figure 8-36

The map is centered
on the slide

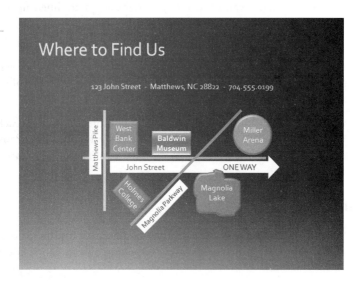

6. **SAVE** the presentation.

   PAUSE. LEAVE the presentation open to use in the next exercise.

If a drawing contains a number of objects, it makes sense to group the objects when you are finished with the drawing. You can more easily reposition a grouped object, and you can also apply formatting changes to all objects in a group much more quickly than by applying formats to each individual object. To select a group, click any object in the group.

If you find that you need to work further with one object in a group, you can simply click it to activate it. It remains part of the group while you modify it. If you need to remove objects or make sweeping changes to a group, you can use the Ungroup option to release the group

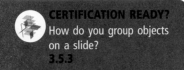

CERTIFICATION READY?
How do you group objects
on a slide?
3.5.3

into its component parts. PowerPoint remembers the objects that are in the group so you can use Regroup if desired to restore the group.

If you are creating a very complex drawing, you can group portions of the drawing, then group those groups. This makes it easy to reuse portions of a drawing—simply ungroup the entire drawing, copy the group you need elsewhere, and regroup the whole.

TAKE NOTE

It is easy to miss an object when selecting parts of a complex drawing to create a group. To check that you have all objects selected, move the group. You will easily see if one or more objects do not move with the group. Undo the move, click the group, click any other objects that need to belong to the group, and issue the Group command again.

Adding Media Clips to a Presentation

THE BOTTOM LINE

Media clips include sounds and movies. You can add media clips to a presentation to present information or to support the mood or ambience of the presentation.

Adding a Sound File to a Slide

You can add sounds from files or from the Clip Organizer. PowerPoint allows you to specify when the sound will play and choose from other sound settings to control playback.

⊕ **ADD A SOUND TO A SLIDE**

USE the presentation that is still open from the previous exercise.

CD

The *Beethoven's Ninth.wma* file is available on the companion CD-ROM.

1. Using a program such as My Computer, copy the *Beethoven's Ninth.wma* file from this lesson's data files and paste the copy in the folder in which you are storing solution files.
2. Go to slide 1 and then click the **Insert** tab.
3. Click **Sound** in the Media Clips group, then click **Sound from File**. The Insert Sound dialog box opens.
4. Navigate to the solution files for this lesson, click *Beethoven's Ninth*, and then click **OK**. A dialog box displays asking how you want to start the sound, as shown in Figure 8-37.

Figure 8-37

Choose how the sound will play

5. Click **Automatically**. A sound icon displays on the slide.
6. Drag the icon down to the lower-right corner of the slide, as shown in Figure 8-38.

Figure 8-38

You can move the sound icon anywhere on the slide

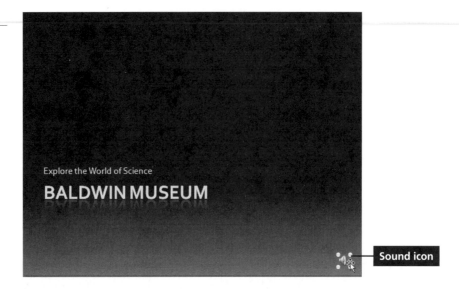

Explore the World of Science

BALDWIN MUSEUM

Sound icon

7. With the sound icon still selected, click the **Sound Tools Options** tab if necessary.

8. Click the **Play Sound** drop-down arrow in the Sound Options group, and then click **Play across slides**. This option allows a sound file to play even after you move to a new slide.

9. Press [F5] to start the slide show from slide 1. The music starts playing. Click the mouse button to progress through the slides. The music will keep playing until you end the show.

   PAUSE. LEAVE the presentation open to use in the next exercise.

You have a number of options for adding sounds to a presentation:

- Use **Sound from File** if you have a sound file in a supported format that you want to insert. PowerPoint can handle AIFF, AU, MIDI, MP3, WAV, and WMA files.

- Use **Sound from Clip Organizer** to open the Clip Art task pane and search for a sound file the same way you searched for clip art. PowerPoint automatically selects Sounds in the *Results should be* list and displays sounds on your system. You can use a keyword search to find specific sounds.

- Use **Play CD Audio Track** to select a track or tracks to play during the presentation. You must have a CD in the computer's CD drive to play music this way during the presentation.

- Use **Record Sound** if you want to record your own sound to play on the slide. You must have a microphone to record the sound.

For best results, your system should have a sound card and speakers. Otherwise, sounds will play with the computer's default speaker, which generally isn't very powerful.

The Sound Tools Options tab provides a number of tools for working with a sound file. You can preview the sound, set its volume for the slide show, hide the sound icon during the slide show (don't use this option if you want to be able to play the sound by clicking on it during the presentation), loop the sound so it repeats until you stop it, adjust whether the sound plays automatically or when you click it, and adjust the maximum sound file size.

Sound files can be either embedded in a presentation or linked to a presentation. Because only WAV files smaller than the default maximum sound file size can be embedded in a presentation, most sound files are actually linked to the presentation. For this reason, you should consider storing a presentation's sound files in the same folder with the presentation itself.

TAKE NOTE

You can also play a sound file while in Normal view by double-clicking the sound icon.

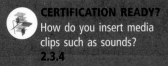

CERTIFICATION READY?
How do you insert media clips such as sounds?
2.3.4

If you run a presentation and discover that objects such as sound files and movies will not play, chances are that PowerPoint cannot find the linked sound or movie file. You can reestablish the link by deleting the object that will not play and reinserting it from a known location.

Adding a Movie to a Slide

You can insert movies from files or movies from the Clip Organizer to add visual interest or information to a presentation.

→ ADD A MOVIE TO A SLIDE

USE the presentation that is still open from the previous exercise.

 CD

The **Sunspot.mpeg** file is available on the companion CD-ROM.

1. Using a program such as My Computer, copy the **Sunspot.mpeg** file from this lesson's data files and paste the copy in the folder in which you are storing solution files.

2. Go to slide 7 and click the **Insert Media Clip** icon in the content placeholder. The Insert Movie dialog box opens.

3. Navigate to the solution files for this lesson, click **Sunspot.mpeg**, then click **OK**.

4. Click **Automatically**. The first frame of the movie appears on the slide and the Movie Tools Options tab becomes active, as shown in Figure 8-39.

Figure 8-39

The movie file has been inserted on the slide

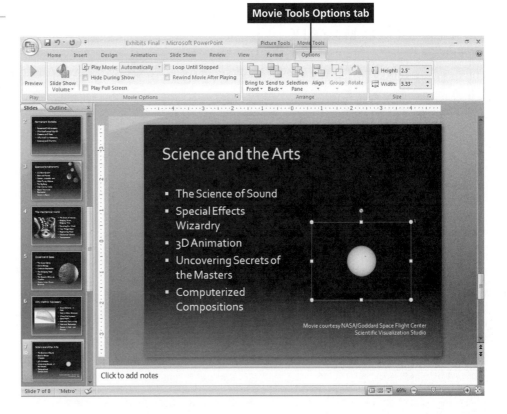

5. Press **Alt** + **F9** to display the drawing guides, and then drag the movie up and to the right so the upper-right corner snaps to the intersection of the two guides. Press **Alt** + **F9** again to hide the guides.

6. Click **Rewind Movie After Playing** in the Movie Options group on the Movie Tools Options tab.

7. Press ⌞F5⌟ to play the presentation from the beginning. When you reach slide 7, watch the movie, which shows an animation of the structure of a sunspot.

8. **SAVE** the presentation and **CLOSE** it.

CLOSE PowerPoint.

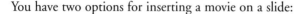

TAKE NOTE

You can play a movie file while in Normal view by double-clicking the movie.

You have two options for inserting a movie on a slide:

- Use **Movie from File** if you have a movie file in a supported format that you want to insert. PowerPoint can handle ASF, AVI, MPEG, or WMV files.
- Use **Movie from Clip Organizer** to open the Clip Art task pane and search for a movie file the same way you searched for clip art. PowerPoint automatically selects Movies in the *Results should be* list and displays movies on your system. You can use a keyword search to find specific movies and search Office Online for more files.

Files identified as movies in the Clip Organizer are actually more like animated clip art graphics. They tend to be relatively small and cannot be significantly enlarged without a corresponding loss of quality. But they can still provide multimedia interest on a slide.

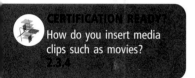

CERTIFICATION READY?

How do you insert media clips such as movies?
2.3.4

The Movie Tools Options tab provides some of the same options you find on the Sound Tools Options tab. In addition, you can choose to play the movie in the full screen during the slide show and rewind it back to the first frame after it finishes playing.

Like most sound files, movie files in formats other than WMF are generally linked to the presentation. For best results, store movie files in the same folder with their presentations.

SUMMARY SKILL MATRIX

IN THIS LESSON YOU LEARNED	MATRIX SKILL	SKILL NUMBER
To add pictures to slides		
To insert clip art pictures	Insert clip art	3.3.3
To add pictures from files	Insert picture from file	3.3.1
To format pictures		
To use gridlines and guides	Use gridlines and guides to arrange illustrations and other content	3.5.4
To resize and rotate objects	Size, scale, and rotate illustrations and other content	3.5.1
To format pictures and shapes with a Quick Style	Apply Quick Styles to shapes and pictures	3.4.1
To add special effects to a picture	Add, change and remove illustration effects	3.4.2
To compress images in a presentation	Compress images	4.3.5
To add shapes to slides		
To draw lines and other basic shapes	Insert shapes	3.3.2
To add text to shapes	Add text to shapes	3.3.4
To adjust the order of objects on a slide	Order illustrations and other content	3.5.2
To align and group objects on a slide	Group and align illustrations and other content	3.5.3
To add media clips to a presentation		
To add a sound file to a slide	Insert media clips	2.3.4
To insert a movie clip on a slide	Insert media clips	2.3.4

■ Knowledge Assessment

Matching

Match the term in Column 1 to its description in Column 2.

Column 1

Column 2

1. order

a. predrawn graphics you can use to illustrate a slide

2. clip art

b. the relationship of width to height for a picture

3. guides

c. a descriptive word or phrase you can use to search for specific types of objects

4. constrain

d. sizing to a percentage of the original size

5. aspect ratio

e. series of folders in which pictures are stored on your computer

6. scaling

f. to force a drawing tool to create a shape such as a perfect square or circle

7. keyword

g. a series of vertical and horizontal dotted lines that help you align objects on a slide

8. crop

h. to move one object behind or in front of another

9. Clip Organizer

i. to remove portions of a picture you don't need

10. gridlines

j. nonprinting lines that you can move or copy to help you position objects on a slide

True / False

Circle T if the statement is true or F if the statement is false.

T | F **1.** When adding clip art to a slide, you are limited to the pictures stored on your computer.

T | F **2.** PowerPoint allows you to insert pictures that are stored in BMP format.

T | F **3.** As you move the pointer, a short dotted line also moves on both rulers.

T | F **4.** The Recolor option lets you select colors in a picture and replace them with other colors.

T | F **5.** One reason to compress pictures is to reduce the number of colors used.

T | F **6.** The color of a new shape is determined by the current theme.

T | F **7.** To add text to a shape, right-click the shape and then click Add Text and begin keying.

T | F **8.** If you want an object to be at the bottom of a stack of objects, you would use Send to Back.

T | F **9.** You can work with a single object in a group without having to ungroup all objects.

T | F **10.** A sound file in MP3 format will be linked to the presentation rather than embedded in it.

Competency Assessment

Project 8-1: Get the Picture

You are a recruiter for Woodgrove Bank, and you have prepared a presentation to be delivered at a local job fair. You need to locate a picture to illustrate one of the presentation's slides. You can use Microsoft Office clip art files to find a suitable picture.

GET READY. Launch PowerPoint if it is not already running.

The *Job Fair* file is available on the companion CD-ROM.

1. **OPEN** the *Job Fair* presentation.
2. Go to slide 5 and click the **Clip Art** icon in the right-hand content placeholder.
3. Key **business** as the keyword, click the **Results should be** drop-down arrow, and select only **Photographs**.
4. Review the results to find a photograph of a professionally dressed business person and then click a picture you like to insert it into the placeholder.
5. Use the Size options on the Picture Tools Format tab to resize the picture to be as wide as the text in the left-hand placeholder if necessary.
6. Click the **View** tab, then click **Gridlines.** Use the gridlines to align the top of the picture with the top of the text in the left-hand placeholder.
7. Click the picture to select it, click **Picture Effects** on the Picture Tools Format tab, point to **Shadow**, and click any shadow effect.
8. Hide the gridlines.
9. **SAVE** the presentation as *Job Fair Final*.

   LEAVE the presentation open for the next project.

Project 8-2: Final Touches

You have decided you need another picture in the Job Fair Final presentation. You have a picture file you think will work.

The *Building.jpg* file is available on the companion CD-ROM.

1. Go to slide 2 of *Job Fair Final* and click the **Insert Picture from File** icon in the right-hand content placeholder.
2. Navigate to the data files for this lesson, locate *Building.jpg*, click the file, and click **Insert**.
3. Right-click the picture and click **Size and Position**. In the Size and Position dialog box, scale the picture to 90% of its current height and width.
4. Press **Alt** + **F9** to display drawing guides. Click the slide title placeholder to display its border, then drag the vertical guide to the right to align with the right border of the slide title placeholder.
5. Drag the horizontal placeholder up to align with the capital letter in the first bulleted item in the left-hand placeholder.
6. Reposition the picture so that its upper-right corner snaps to the intersection of the two guides. Press **Alt** + **F9** to hide the guides.
7. Click the **More** button in the Picture Styles group on the Picture Tools Format tab, and then click the **Drop Shadow Rectangle** Quick Style.
8. Right-click the picture, click **Format Picture**, and change Brightness to 5% and Contrast to 10%.
9. Click **Compress Pictures** in the Adjust group on the Picture Tools Format tab, and then click **Options**.
10. Click **Screen (150 ppi)** if necessary, and then click **OK** twice.
11. **SAVE** the presentation and then **CLOSE** the file.

    LEAVE PowerPoint open for the next project.

■ Proficiency Assessment

Project 8-3: Go with the Flow

You are a professional trainer teaching a class on basic computer skills. For your class today, you need to explain the systems development life cycle (SDLC) to a group of students. You can use PowerPoint's drawing tools to create a flow chart that shows the process.

1. Create a new, blank presentation, and apply the Median theme.
2. Change the title slide to a Title Only slide, and key the slide title **Systems Development Life Cycle (SDLC)**.
3. Draw five rectangles stacked vertically on the slide. You do not have to worry about alignment or distribution at this point.
4. Key **Phase 1: Needs Analysis** in the top rectangle.
5. Add text to the remaining rectangles as follows:

   Phase 2: System Design

   Phase 3: Development

   Phase 4: Implementation

   Phase 5: Maintenance
6. Resize the shapes as necessary so that text fits on a single line.
7. Add connectors between the shapes as follows:

   a. Click the **Shapes** button to display the Shapes gallery, and click the **Elbow Arrow Connector** line in the Lines group.

   b. Move the crosshair pointer over the *Phase 1* shape to see the red connection points on all four sides of the shape.

   c. Click the red connection point at the bottom side of the shape, then drag down toward the next shape. When you see the red connection points on the second shape, click the one at the top center of the shape.

   d. Repeat these steps to create four connection arrows between the five shapes.
8. Click the **Elbow Arrow Connector**, click the right side connector point on the last shape, then drag upward and connect to the right side connector of the top shape.
9. **SAVE** the presentation as *SDLC Final*.

   LEAVE the presentation open for the next project.

Project 8-4: Final Flow

You have the basic flowchart structure on the slide. Now you need to modify and format it to improve its appearance.

1. Select the shape that has the most amount of text and check its size using the Size group of the Drawing Tools Format tab. (If desired, you can adjust the size upward or downward to round numbers.)
2. Use the ⟨Shift⟩-click method to select the remaining four rectangles.
3. Set the width and height in the Size group to the measurements of the rectangle you checked in step 1. All rectangles should now be the same width and height.
4. Select all five rectangles, and use the **Align Left** option to align them with each other.
5. With all five rectangles still selected, use the **Distribute Vertically** option to equalize the space between the rectangles.
6. Apply a different Quick Style color to each rectangle. (Use the same effect for all rectangles, but vary the colors for each.)

7. Select the vertical line connectors between shapes and apply a Quick Style that emphasizes the connectors; for example, **Moderate Line, Dark 1.** If any of the connectors do not quite touch the shape below, adjust the connector by dragging it to the red anchor point.

8. Click the connector that runs from the last shape to the first, change the line weight to **6 pt**, and drag the yellow diamond adjustment handle at the center of the shape to the right about one-quarter of an inch to give more room for the arrowhead at the top of the connector. Change the color of the connector to a darker theme color.

9. Group all drawing objects.

10. Use the **Align Center** option to center the grouped object on the slide.

11. **SAVE** the presentation and then **CLOSE** the file.

   LEAVE PowerPoint open for the next project.

■ Mastery Assessment

Project 8-5: Photo Flair

The *Speaker* file is available on the companion CD-ROM.

You are finalizing a presentation to introduce a speaker and want to do some work on the photo of the speaker you have included on a slide. You can use PowerPoint's picture tools to finalize the photo.

1. **OPEN** the *Speaker* presentation.

2. Go to slide 2 and select the picture.

3. Crop the picture to remove the coffee cup and newspaper at the right side of the picture.

4. Resize the photo so it is 4 inches high and align it with the top of the vertical line at the center of the slide.

5. Increase the contrast in the picture by 10%.

6. Draw a rectangle that exactly covers the picture. Remove the outline from the rectangle.

7. Click the ↓ twice and the → twice to slightly offset the shape from the picture, then send the shape behind the picture to act as a drop shadow.

8. Choose a new theme color for the rectangle shape that contrasts well with the picture but does not overwhelm it.

9. **SAVE** the presentation as *Speaker Final* and then **CLOSE** the file.

   LEAVE PowerPoint open for the next project.

Project 8-6: Media Support

The *Messenger* file is available on the companion CD-ROM.

Your Consolidated Courier presentation needs some additional pizzazz. You can insert media clips to add some life to the slides.

1. **OPEN** the *Messenger* presentation.

2. Copy the sound file *Town.mid* to your solutions folder, and then insert this file on slide 1.

The *Town.mid* file is available on the companion CD-ROM.

3. Choose to play the sound automatically, and then adjust settings so the sound file plays across slides.

4. Go to slide 5. Insert a movie from the Clip Organizer, using a keyword such as *airmail, world,* or *airplane* to convey the idea of global courier service.

5. Position the movie as desired on the slide.

6. Run the presentation in Slide Show view to check the sound file and view the animated graphic.

7. **SAVE** the presentation as *Messenger Final* and then **CLOSE** the file.

   CLOSE PowerPoint.

INTERNET READY

The local library has asked you to prepare a presentation for their book club, which is about to embark on a Famous Novels series of club meetings. The book club will read novels by Austen, Dickens, Melville, and Steinbeck this year. Using the Internet, research some basic facts about the lives of these four authors and locate and save pictures of each. Create a slide show to present the information you have gathered. On the first slide, use drawing tools to draw a stack or row of books with the names of the authors on the spines. Create a slide for each author and insert life details and the pictures you located. Adjust the pictures as necessary to be about the same size and location on each slide and use any picture formatting tools you like to improve the appearance of the pictures.

⟳ Circling Back

You are a managing editor at Lucerne Publishing. You are preparing for an important meeting with the senior managing team, and you are producing a presentation that should serve two purposes: to show how you intend to grow the publishing plan for the coming year and to convince senior management to let you hire several new editors. You can use PowerPoint tools to focus attention on these two goals.

➔ Project 1: Basic Formatting and Tables

In this project, you will open your draft presentation, apply a theme, and add both a table and an Excel worksheet to present data.

GET READY. Launch PowerPoint if it is not already running.

The *Opportunities* file is available on the companion CD-ROM.

1. **OPEN** the *Opportunities* presentation.
2. Apply the Origin theme. Change the theme fonts to those from the Module theme. Change the theme colors to those from the Urban theme.
3. Insert a date that updates automatically, slide numbers, and the footer **Editorial Opportunities**. Apply to all slides except the title slide.
4. Display the slide master and make these changes:
   a. Change the alignment of the date placeholder to right alignment.
   b. Boldface the slide titles.
   c. Change the color of the first-level bullet.
   d. Close Slide Master view.
5. Go to slide 4 and create a table that has three columns and six rows. Key the following data in the table:

Division	Current Year	Next Year
History	23	27
Science Fiction	19	23
Literature	12	16
Nonfiction	26	31
Lifestyle	38	43

6. Format the table with the **Light Style 3 – Accent 1** Quick Style.
7. Turn off banded rows. Select the column heading cells, fill with **Blue-Gray, Accent 6**, and change the font color to **White, Background 1**.
8. Center all entries in the center and right columns. Click the **Table Tools Layout** tab, and in the Table Size group, change the table width to 8 inches.
9. Go to slide 3 and format the existing table to match the one you inserted on slide 4. Be sure to also change column alignment and table size.
10. Go to slide 5 and insert an Excel worksheet. Key the following data in the worksheet:

Division	Current Year	Next Year
History	4.65	4.89
Science Fiction	3.77	4.01
Literature	8.92	9.15
Nonfiction	4.41	4.79
Lifestyle	3.59	3.95

11. In cell A8 of the worksheet, key **Average**. In cell B8, insert the formula =AVERAGE(B2:B6).

12. Copy the formula in cell B8 to cell C8.

13. Format the values in cells B8 and C8 as currency with two decimal places.

14. Format the worksheet as follows:

   a. Apply the Urban theme in Excel (you'll find the themes on the Page Layout tab in Excel).

   b. Select the column headers in row 1, click the **Cell Styles** button in the Styles group on the Excel Home tab, and select **Accent6**.

   c. Boldface the column headings.

   d. Center all entries in the center and right columns.

   e. Change the font of the worksheet cells to Corbel to match the text in the presentation. Change the font size to 18.

   f. Adjust columns to a width of 25.

15. Adjust the size of the worksheet's hatched selection border to hide any empty rows or columns. Click outside the worksheet to deselect it.

16. Go to slide 4. Display the drawing guides and adjust them to align with the table's upper-left corner.

17. Go to slide 5 and drag the worksheet container so its upper-left corner snaps to the intersection of the guides.

18. **SAVE** the presentation as *Opportunities Final*.

   PAUSE. LEAVE PowerPoint and your presentation open for the next project.

⊙→ Project 2: Charting the Data

You are now ready to create a chart that shows the editorial workload for the current year and your projections for the next year. The chart will make it easy for your audience to compare the numbers.

USE the presentation that is open from the previous project.

1. Go to slide 6, and change the layout of the slide to Title and Content.

2. Click the **Insert Chart** icon in the content placeholder to begin a new chart. Select the clustered 3D bar chart.

3. Insert the following data in the chart worksheet:

Division	Current Year	Next Year
History	5.8	6.8
Science Fiction	6.3	7.6
Literature	4	5.3
Nonfiction	4.3	5.2
Lifestyle	5.4	6.1

4. Delete the unneeded sample data in column D and make sure the range border surrounds only the data you need for your chart. Close the worksheet.

5. Change the chart type to a 3-D clustered column chart.

6. Format the chart as follows:

   a. Apply **Layout 4** and the **Style 18** Quick Style.

   b. Change the font size of the vertical and horizontal axis labels to 16 pt.

   c. Display the major gridlines for both the horizontal and vertical axes.

   d. Turn off the data labels for both data series.

7. Click on the four dots at the bottom center of the chart container and drag upward about half an inch to free up some room at the bottom of the slide.

8. Draw a text box below the chart and key the text ***Books per editor, based on current staffing.**

9. Resize the text box so that all text is on one line, and then apply a Quick Style to the text box that coordinates well with the chart.

10. **SAVE** the presentation.

PAUSE. LEAVE PowerPoint and your presentation open for the next project.

Project 3: Add Diagrams

You are ready to add SmartArt diagrams to display additional information about your organization and your department's work processes.

USE the presentation that is open from the previous project.

1. Go to slide 7 and click the **Insert SmartArt Graphic** icon in the content placeholder to start a new diagram.

2. Choose to create an organization chart and add text to the chart as follows:

   a. In the top-level box, key the name **Bill Bowen**, press Enter, and key the title **Managing Editor**.

   b. In the assistant box, key **Eva Corets**, press Enter, and key **Chief Editorial Assistant**.

   c. In the second-level boxes, key the following names, titles, and departments:

Jo Berry	Dan Bacon	Jun Cao
Sr. Editor	Sr. Editor	Sr. Editor
History	Science Fiction	Literature

3. Add a new shape after Jun Cao's shape, key the name **Aaron Con**, the title **Sr. Editor**, and the department **Nonfiction**. Then add a new shape after Aaron Con's shape, key the name **Debra Core**, the title **Sr. Editor**, and the department **Lifestyle**.

4. Apply a Quick Style and a new color scheme to the diagram.

5. Delete Debra Core's shape, and then change the division information for Aaron Con's shape to **Nonfiction & Lifestyle**.

6. Boldface the text in the top-level shape.

7. Go to slide 8, and convert the bulleted list to a Vertical Process diagram.

8. Apply a Quick Style and color scheme that match the ones you used on slide 7.

9. Change the diagram type to the Vertical Box List layout in the List type.

10. Click in the Notes pane and key **We are rolling the production preparation phase into the copyedit phase to save production time and costs.**

11. **SAVE** the presentation.

PAUSE. LEAVE PowerPoint and your presentation open for the next project.

Project 4: Insert and Format a Picture

Now insert additional visual interest in the form of a picture. You will format the picture to improve its appearance.

USE the presentation that is open from the previous project.

1. Go to slide 2, and click the **Clip Art** icon in the content placeholder to open the Clip Art task pane.

2. Use the keyword *award* to search for a photograph of a trophy. You should find several if you have a live connection to the Internet. If do not find a gold trophy on a white background in your results, insert the picture *Award.jpg* in the placeholder.

The *Award.jpg* file is available on the companion CD-ROM.

3. Adjust the picture's brightness to +10% and contrast to +20%.

4. Apply the **Perspective Shadow, White** Quick Style, and then click **Picture Border** and select a different border color, such as **Teal, Accent 2, Darker 25%**.

5. Move the picture down so that it aligns at the bottom with the last line of text in the text placeholder.

6. Compress pictures in the presentation to the Screen setting.

7. **SAVE** the presentation.

   PAUSE. LEAVE PowerPoint and your presentation open for the next project.

Project 5: Add a Drawing and Finalize the Presentation

You have been asked to suggest a new office layout to reorganize departments on the production floor. You can create a simple drawing to show the areas where each department, supporting personnel, and production will be placed.

USE the presentation that is open from the previous project.

1. Go to slide 7 and add a new slide with the Title Only layout. Key the slide title **Revised Office Layout**.

2. Copy the vertical drawing guide and place the copy so that it aligns with the right border of the slide title placeholder. Copy the horizontal guide and drag it down until the ScreenTip reads 0.25 with a downward-pointing arrow. You now have guides to the left and right of the slide and in the center of the content area that can help you position your drawing objects.

Figure 1

Draft reorganization drawing

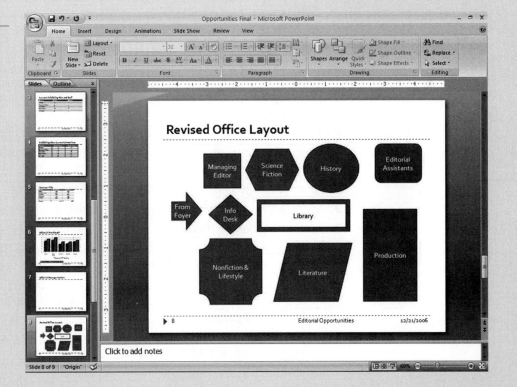

3. Create the drawing objects shown in Figure 1. You can choose your own sizes for objects, but they should be similar in scale to the ones shown.

4. Modify your drawing as follows:

   a. Make all the department objects—the shapes for Nonfiction & Lifestyle, Literature, Science Fiction, and History—the same dimensions, even though they are different shapes; that is, they should all be the same height and width. Make sure all text displays without breaking after resizing.

   b. Position the *From Foyer* block arrow so that its left side square sizing handle is on the center horizontal guide.

   c. Align the *Info Desk* and *Library* shapes to the middle of the block arrow. These three shapes will create a central area for the layout and should all be aligned middle on the guide.

   d. Rotate the *Editorial Assistants* shape to the right so it fits into the corner created by the vertical and horizontal guides.

   e. Align the three shapes above the library by their tops and the *Nonfiction & Lifestyle, Literature,* and *Production* shapes by their bottoms. Make sure the aligned shapes are within the slide content area (below the top guide and above the bottom dashed line).

   f. Align the *Managing Editor, Info Desk,* and *Nonfiction & Lifestyle* shapes to the left, and move them to the right if necessary so the *Info Desk* shape doesn't crowd the block arrow.

   g. Select the three top shapes and distribute them horizontally. Select the two bottom shapes and the *Production* shape and distribute them horizontally.

   h. Make any other adjustments you think necessary to improve the look of the layout.

5. Apply colors and effects or Quick Styles to the layout as desired to improve its appearance.

6. Select all objects in the drawing and group them. Right-click any shape in the group and click **Size and Position**. In the Size and Position dialog box, click **Lock aspect ratio** to select it, and scale the group object to 95% of its original size.

7. If the text in any of the shapes runs over after scaling, click the shape in the group to select it and adjust the shape size or reduce the font size to fit the text.

8. Center the object in the content area below the slide title. Hide the guides.

9. Select a slide transition, choose Medium speed, and apply it to all slides.

10. Apply animations as follows:

    a. On slide 2, apply a built-in fade transition to display the bullet items by first-level paragraphs. Then modify this animation to occur **After Previous**.

    b. Animate the organization chart on slide 7 to fade into view **After Previous**. Use the Effect Options dialog box to specify that the graphic displays **By level one by one**.

    c. Click the group on slide 8 to select it, and then apply the **Diamond** entrance animation starting **After Previous**.

    d. Animate the final SmartArt diagram as desired.

11. Run the presentation in Slide Show view. Make any corrections you think necessary to the animations.

12. **PRINT** the presentation as handouts in grayscale mode.

13. **SAVE** and **CLOSE** the presentation.

    CLOSE PowerPoint.

Securing and Sharing a Presentation

9

LESSON SKILL MATRIX

SKILLS	MATRIX SKILL	SKILL NUMBER
Working with Comments		
Viewing Comments	Show and hide markup	4.1.2
Inserting a Comment	Insert, delete and modify comments	4.1.1
Editing a Comment	Insert, delete and modify comments	4.1.1
Deleting a Comment	Insert, delete and modify comments	4.1.1
Making Sure a Presentation Is Safe to Share		
Using the Compatibility Checker	Identify presentation features not supported by previous versions	4.3.1
Using the Document Inspector	Remove inappropriate information using Document Inspector	4.3.2
Setting Permissions for a Presentation	Restrict permissions to a document using Information Rights Management (IRM)	4.3.3
Using a Digital Signature		
Adding a Digital Signature to a Presentation	Add digital signatures to presentations	4.2.1
Sharing a Presentation Through E-Mail		
Marking a Presentation as Final	Mark presentations as final	4.3.4

You are the Human Resources Director for Contoso, Ltd., a big company that manufactures automotive parts. You must give a 30-minute presentation to senior management and prominent shareholders during the company's annual operations review. You have asked a colleague to give you some feedback, and she has inserted comments that you need to address. You will add some comments of your own before finalizing the presentation to share with the Vice President for Operations, who has promised to look over the slides before you present them. You can use PowerPoint to handle chores such as viewing and working with comments, making sure the presentation is safe to share with others, and adding a digital signature. You can use PowerPoint to e-mail the presentation directly to your contact.

KEY TERMS
comment
Compatibility Checker
digital signature
Document Inspector
encryption
Information Rights Management (IRM)
permissions
properties

■ SOFTWARE ORIENTATION

Microsoft PowerPoint's Review Tab

Tools on the Review tab make it easy for you to add comments to a slide and apply protection to the presentation. Figure 9-1 shows the Review tab.

Figure 9-1

The Review tab

Besides allowing you to add comments, the Review tab lets you check spelling, access references such as encyclopedias, use a thesaurus, translate a word or phrase, or set the current language.

■ Working with Comments

THE BOTTOM LINE

You can insert comments on slides to suggest content changes, add reminders, or solicit feedback. Use comments on your own presentations or on presentations you are reviewing for others. You can also let other people review your presentations and add comments addressed to you. PowerPoint's Review tab makes it easy to view, insert, edit, or delete comments.

Viewing Comments

Use the Show Markup button on the Review tab to show or hide comments. The Next and Previous buttons make it easy to jump from comment to comment in a presentation.

⊕ VIEW COMMENTS

The *HR Review* file is available on the companion CD-ROM.

GET READY. Before you begin these steps, make sure that your computer is on. Log on, if necessary.

1. Start PowerPoint, if the program is not already running.
2. Locate and open the *HR Review* presentation.
3. Note the small comment marker in the upper-left corner of the slide, as shown in Figure 9-2.

Figure 9-2

A comment marker indicates
a comment on the slide

4. Click the **Review** tab, and then click the **Show Markup** button in the Comments group. The comment marker is hidden.

5. Click the **Show Markup** button again to redisplay the comment marker.

6. Rest the mouse pointer on the comment marker to display the comment, as shown in Figure 9-3.

Figure 9-3

Displaying a comment
on the slide

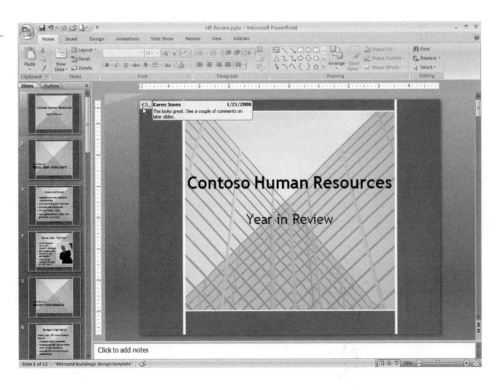

7. Click the **Next** button in the Comments group to go to the second comment by Karen Jones. (You may have to click the button twice to go to the next comment.) Ms. Jones suggests adjusting the diagram.

8. Click the SmartArt diagram, click the **SmartArt Tools Design** tab, click the **Intense Effect**, click **Change Colors**, and click **Gradient Loop-Accent 6**. The diagram now has the "pop" Ms. Jones suggested, as shown in Figure 9-4.

Figure 9-4

Revised diagram and comment marker on slide 9

9. Click the **Review** tab, and then click the **Next** button to go to the next comment by Karen Jones.

10. Click the **Previous** button twice to return to the first comment on slide 1.

11. **SAVE** the presentation as *HR Review Final*.

PAUSE. LEAVE the presentation open to use in the next exercise.

A **comment** is a note you insert on a slide. You can use comments to provide feedback on a presentation you are reviewing or remind yourself of changes you want to make to a slide.

Comments are identified by the initials of the current user. When you display a comment, the full name of the person who inserted the comment displays, along with the date on which the comment was inserted.

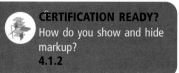

You can change the current user name by clicking the Office button, clicking PowerPoint Options at the bottom of the Office menu, and supplying a new name and initials on the Popular pane in the PowerPoint Options dialog box.

CERTIFICATION READY?
How do you show and hide markup?
4.1.2

When you open a presentation that has comments inserted, the comment markers are visible by default. If you do not want to see the comment markers as you work, you can click the Show Markup button on the Review tab to hide the markers.

Inserting a Comment

To add a comment to a slide, use the New Comment button on the Review tab.

⊙ INSERT A COMMENT

USE the presentation that is still open from the previous exercise. You are now ready to add your own comments to the presentation, which you are going to send to the Vice President for Operations.

1. With slide 1 displayed, click the **New Comment** button on the Review tab. A new comment box opens, as shown in Figure 9-5.

Figure 9-5

A new comment box ready for you to key the comment

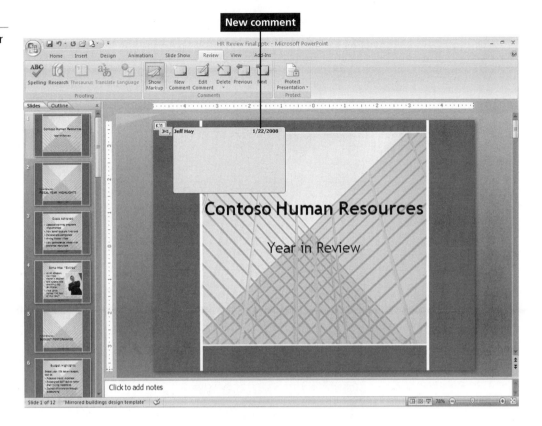

2. Key the following text in the comment box:

Peter, I have already received feedback from Karen Jones. Please suggest any further changes you think necessary to make this a dynamite presentation.

3. Click outside the comment box to close it. Your comment marker should display on the slide slightly overlapping Karen Jones's comment marker.

4. Go to slide 10, then click the **New Comment** button.

5. Key the following text in the comment box:

Peter, please see Karen's comment on this slide. I don't have access to Design Dept. schedules. Can you confirm the lag time is now only 4 to 5 weeks?

6. Click outside the comment box to close it.

PAUSE. LEAVE the presentation open to use in the next exercise.

Comment markers are color-coded, so that if more than one reviewer adds comments, it is easy for you to identify the commenter simply by color. Comments are numbered consecutively as they are inserted, regardless of the order of slides. If you insert your first comment on slide 5, it will be numbered 1. If you insert your second comment on slide 1, it will be numbered 2.

If no object is selected when you insert a comment, the comment marker appears in the upper-left corner of the slide. If an object is selected, the comment marker appears next to the selected object. You can also drag a comment marker anywhere on a slide. Moving a comment marker allows you to associate the comment with a specific area of the slide, such as a picture or a bullet item.

Editing a Comment

Use the Edit Comment button to open a comment box so you can modify the text.

⊕ **EDIT A COMMENT**

USE the presentation that is still open from the previous exercise.

1. Go to slide 1, click your comment marker, then click the **Edit Comment** button on the Review tab. The comment box opens for editing, as shown in Figure 9-6.

Figure 9-6

Open the comment box for editing

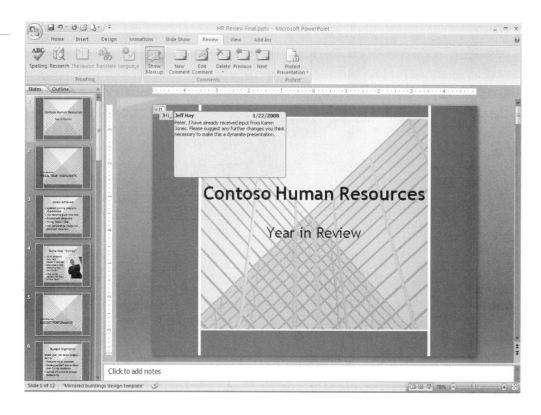

2. Select the text *to make this a dynamite presentation* at the end of the second sentence, and press **Delete**. You have removed text from the comment.
3. Click outside the comment box to close it.

   PAUSE. LEAVE the presentation open to use in the next exercise.

ANOTHER WAY

Right-click the comment you want to edit, then select Edit Comment from the shortcut menu.

If you simply rest the pointer on a comment marker, or click it, you can read the text but cannot edit it. You must use the Edit Comment button or command to open the comment box for editing.

Like any other text in a presentation, comment text should be clear and concise. If you find upon review that your comments do not convey the information they should, you can reword, insert, or delete text in the comment box.

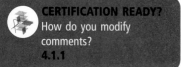

CERTIFICATION READY?
How do you modify comments?
4.1.1

Deleting a Comment

You can easily remove comments from slides when they are no longer needed.

⊕ **DELETE A COMMENT**

USE the presentation that is still open from the previous exercise.

1. With slide 1 displayed, right-click Karen Jones's first comment, then click **Delete Comment** on the shortcut menu. The comment is removed from the slide, leaving only your first comment.
2. Go to slide 9, click the comment, and then click the **Review** tab if necessary.

3. Click the **Delete** button. The comment is removed from the slide.

4. **SAVE** the presentation.

> **PAUSE. LEAVE** the presentation open to use in the next exercise.

If you simply click the Delete button on the Review tab, PowerPoint removes the currently selected comment. Click the Delete button's drop-down arrow for other delete options: You can delete the current comment, delete all comments (markup) on the current slide, or delete all comments throughout the presentation.

■ Making Sure a Presentation Is Safe to Share

 THE BOTTOM LINE

Tools on the Office menu's Prepare submenu can help you check your presentation before you share it with others in your organization. You can make sure a presentation is compatible with other versions of PowerPoint, remove personal information that you don't want others to access, and apply settings that authenticate the presentation and prevent others from making changes to it without permission.

Using the Compatibility Checker

 NEW FEATURE

The Compatibility Checker alerts you to features or objects in your PowerPoint 2007 presentation that may not appear or behave the same way in previous versions of PowerPoint. Use this tool to make sure you do not find yourself unable to edit a slide object if you have to save to a different PowerPoint format.

⊙ USE THE COMPATIBILITY CHECKER

USE the presentation that is still open from the previous exercise.

1. Click the **Office Button**, point to **Prepare**, and then click **Run Compatibility Checker**.

2. PowerPoint runs the check and displays the Microsoft Office PowerPoint Compatibility Checker dialog box shown in Figure 9-7. The dialog box alerts you that you will not be able to edit the SmartArt graphic or its text in earlier versions of PowerPoint.

Figure 9-7

Compatibility Checker
dialog box

3. Click **OK** to accept the message and close the dialog box.

4. Go to slide 12, select the words *lower-rank* in the last bullet item, and key **entry level**.

> **PAUSE. LEAVE** the presentation open to use in the next exercise.

Some of the features that make PowerPoint 2007 slides so attractive, such as reflections, shadows, and SmartArt graphics, are not compatible with previous versions of PowerPoint. Many of these effects are converted to pictures, so the slide may appear more or less the same as in PowerPoint 2007, but you will be unable to change settings or adjust effects for these pictures.

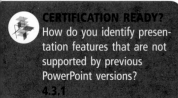

Consult PowerPoint's Help files for a detailed list of how PowerPoint 2007 objects are converted for use in previous PowerPoint versions.

CERTIFICATION READY?
How do you identify presentation features that are not supported by previous PowerPoint versions?
4.3.1

Use the *Compatibility Checker* to identify potential problems with PowerPoint 2007 features before you save a presentation in a previous PowerPoint format. If you find that some of your slide formatting or features are not compatible, consider saving a "master" 2007 version that you can revert to if you need to edit the version you saved to another PowerPoint format.

Using the Document Inspector

Many individuals and organizations are wary of sending or sharing documents that contain information Microsoft Office routinely stores, such as the name of the user who created it. Use the Document Inspector to determine what kinds of information are stored with a document.

⊖ USE THE DOCUMENT INSPECTOR

USE the presentation that is still open from the previous exercise.

1. Before you run the Document Inspector, display the presentation's current properties: Click the **Office Button**, point to **Prepare**, and then click **Properties**. PowerPoint opens the Document Properties pane shown in Figure 9-8.

Figure 9-8

Properties saved with the current presentation appear in the Document Properties pane

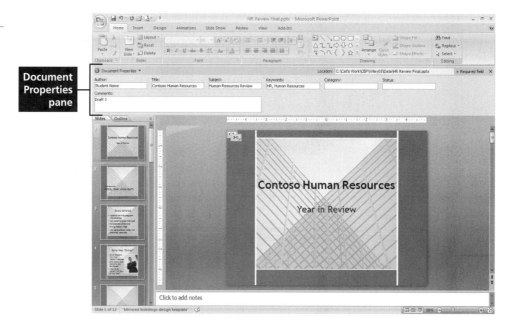

2. Click the **Close** button in the upper-right corner of the Document Properties pane to close it.
3. Click the **Office Button**, point to **Prepare**, and then click **Inspect Document**. PowerPoint displays a message indicating that changes have not been saved and asking if you want to save now.
4. Click **Yes** to save changes. The Document Inspector dialog box opens, as shown in Figure 9-9, to indicate what content will be inspected.

Figure 9-9

Document Inspector dialog box

5. Click **Inspect**. PowerPoint inspects the document and displays a report similar to the one in Figure 9-10 to show the results of the inspection. Note that PowerPoint found comments, document properties, and personal information.

Figure 9-10

The inspection report

6. You do not want to share properties and personal information, so click the **Remove All** button to the right of Document Properties and Personal Information.

7. Click the **Close** button in the Document Inspector dialog box.

8. Click the **Office Button**, point to **Prepare**, and then click **Properties**. Note that the fields in the Document Properties pane are now empty. Close the Document Properties pane.

9. **SAVE** the presentation. Go to slide 1, if necessary, and notice that the user initials on the comment marker have changed to *A*, for *Author*.

   PAUSE. LEAVE the presentation open to use in the next exercise.

TAKE NOTE

Computer forensic examiners can use metadata to determine who might have created files at a particular time.

Properties are details about a document, such as who created it, when it was created or modified, its size, the number of words or slides in the document, and so on. Properties are also known as *metadata*.

Properties can help an author identify a particular document among a number of similar documents or store information about a document, such as its title, category, and keywords that describe it. This information can be keyed in the Document Properties pane, and it will then travel with the document wherever it is stored or sent.

TAKE NOTE To insert more properties, open the Document Properties pane, click the Document Properties drop-down arrow, and click Advanced Properties to open a dialog box with multiple tabs for different types of properties.

Many people prefer not to share the type of properties Microsoft Office applications store automatically. The **Document Inspector** searches a presentation for personal or hidden information that you would not want someone else to have access to. The Document Inspector searches for the following types of information:

- **Comments and ink annotations.** As you have learned, comments show the name of the person who inserted the comment. You may not want to reveal the names of persons who have worked on or reviewed a presentation.

- **Document properties and personal information.** You may not want someone else to know who wrote or edited a document, or when it was created.

- **Custom XML data.** The Document Inspector can locate and remove any custom XML tags you do not want to share.

- **Invisible on-slide content.** It is possible to format objects on a slide to be invisible; the Document Inspector checks such objects to make sure they contain no private information.

- **Off-slide content.** You can drag objects such as text boxes or tables off a slide so that they are not visible during the slide show, but they may still contain information you do not wish to share.

- **Presentation notes.** The Document Inspector will check for text in the Notes pane.

CERTIFICATION READY?
How do you remove information inappropriate for sharing using the Document Inspector?
4.3.2

If the Document Inspector finds information in any of these searches, you have the option of removing all the material. If you are not sure about removing private information, create a copy of the presentation you want to share so you can remove information as desired before sending it out. You can then retain your original presentation intact.

Removing properties also removes the identifying initials and names from comments. Rather than showing the original user name and initials, comments display the generic name *Author*.

■ Setting Permissions for a Presentation

THE BOTTOM LINE The best way to protect a presentation you plan to share with others is to set permissions to restrict who can open or modify the presentation. To set permissions, you use Microsoft's Information Rights Management (IRM) service. With IRM installed on your system, you can specify access and usage *permissions* for a presentation.

⊙ SET PERMISSIONS FOR A PRESENTATION

USE the presentation that is still open from the previous exercise.

TROUBLESHOOTING To use the Protect Presentation button, you need to download and install the Windows Rights Management software. IRM is the use of a server to authenticate the credentials of people who create or receive documents with restricted permission. Some organizations use their own rights management servers. For Microsoft Office users without access to one of these servers, Microsoft provides a free trial IRM service. If you do not already have the software, you will be prompted to download it when you access the Restricted Access command. Downloading and using the software requires a .NET Passport account. (If you have a Hotmail or MSN e-mail account, you already have a .NET Passport.) Check with your instructor about whether you should download the software and install it on the computer you are using. If you choose to download it, a wizard will appear providing step-by-step instructions for installation.

1. Click the **Review** tab, click the **Protect Presentation** button, and then click **Restricted Access**. The Permission dialog box opens.
2. Click the **Restrict permission to this presentation** check box. The options in the dialog box become active, as shown in Figure 9-11.

Figure 9-11

The Permission dialog box become active

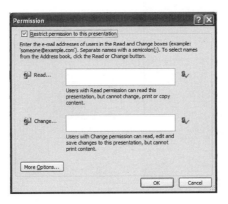

 Click the Office Button, point to Prepare, point to Restrict Permission, and click Restricted Access to open the Permission dialog box.

3. Click in the **Change** box and key **pconnelly@contoso.com**, the name of the Vice President to whom you intend to e-mail the presentation for final review.
4. Click **OK**. A message bar displays below the Ribbon to indicate that permission has been restricted.
5. Click the **Change Permission** button in the message bar. The Permission dialog box opens.
6. Click the **Restrict permission to this presentation** check box to deselect it.
7. Click **OK**. You have removed the permission, so the message bar is also removed.
8. **SAVE** the presentation.

   PAUSE. LEAVE the presentation open to use in the next exercise.

Information Rights Management (IRM) is a feature that allows an administrator to control who can access or use a file. This feature is most useful in the corporate world where file sharing is a daily task and where companies want to safeguard sensitive information. For this reason, IRM is available only in Microsoft Office versions aimed at corporate or enterprise users.

IRM software is generally installed on a corporate server by an IT specialist, but Microsoft has made available a trial version of its Windows Rights Management software for individuals using Microsoft Office 2007 Professional Plus, Enterprise, or Ultimate. If you have one of these versions, you can install the trial version to see how the process of setting permissions works.

If you do not have IRM software on your computer and receive a presentation that has permissions set, you will be prompted to download the rights management client software you need to work with the presentation.

The Permission dialog box allows you to grant permission to specified users to read or to change a presentation (or to do both). Simply key the user's e-mail address in the Read or Change box. Information below each box tells you what that user will be able to do with the presentation. After you set the permission, the information bar at the top of the presentation provides a Change Permission button that lets you modify the permission you have set.

For more control over permissions, click the More Options button in the Permission dialog box to display the options shown in Figure 9-12. You can set the following options:

Figure 9-12

Additional permissions options

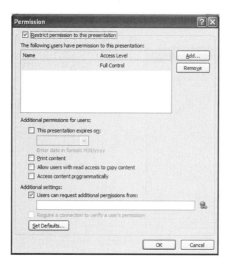

- Add or remove a user from the list of those who have permission to work with the presentation, and set the Access level to Read, Change, or Full Control for any user. Full Control allows a user to both read and change a presentation.
- Specify a date on which the permissions expire.
- Allow a user additional access options, such as to print or copy material.
- Provide an e-mail address a user can employ to ask for additional permissions.

The permissions you set in the Permission dialog box are a rigorous form of protection, because permissions travel with the presentation when you send it to someone else. Your recipient must be on the list of permitted users to work with the presentation.

When an unauthorized recipient opens a presentation that has permissions set, a dialog box will inform the recipient that he or she does not have the credentials to open the presentation and allow him or her to request updated permission to work with the presentation. If you have not supplied an e-mail address for contact in the Permission dialog box, the unauthorized recipient receives an error message when trying to open the presentation.

If your version of Microsoft Office does not support IRM, you can still protect a presentation using the Encrypt Document option on the Prepare submenu. The process of *encryption* translates data into a non-readable form. A key or password is required to restore the encrypted data to readable form. To encrypt a presentation, click the Office Button, point to Prepare, and click Encrypt Document. Then key the password that will be required to open the presentation.

You can also set a password to open as well as a password to modify the presentation contents during the process of saving a presentation using the Save As command. Click Save As on the Office menu, click the Tools button in the Save As dialog box, and then click General Options. Key the password(s) you want to apply in the designated boxes.

TAKE NOTE ✳
Passwords can usually be broken fairly easily using tools that are readily available on the Internet.

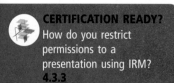

CERTIFICATION READY?
How do you restrict permissions to a presentation using IRM?
4.3.3

■ Using a Digital Signature

↓
THE BOTTOM LINE

Digital signatures are used to authenticate a document. You can create a signature using Office tools or you can purchase a signature from a third-party supplier.

Creating a Simple Digital Signature

Microsoft Office offers a digital signature you can use to sign Office documents. If you already have a digital signature, you may skip to the next exercise.

→ CREATE A SIMPLE DIGITAL SIGNATURE

USE the presentation that is still open from the previous exercise.

1. Click the Windows **Start** button, point to **All Programs**, point to **Microsoft Office**, point to **Microsoft Office Tools**, and click **Digital Signature for VBA Projects**. The Create Digital Certificate dialog box opens, as shown in Figure 9-13.

Figure 9-13

The Create Digital Signature dialog box

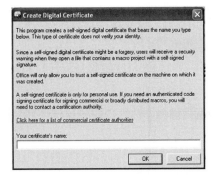

2. Key your name in the *Your certificate's name* text box, then click **OK**.
3. Click **OK** again when the SelfCert Success dialog box tells you that you have successfully created a new certificate. You now have a digital certificate on file that you can use to sign a presentation.

   PAUSE. LEAVE the presentation open to use in the next exercise.

TAKE NOTE

If you do not have the Digital Signature for VBA Projects option, see your instructor for further information.

A ***digital signature*** is used to verify the origin of a presentation by confirming the identity of the signer and ensuring the integrity of the presentation. A digital signature relies on a digital *certificate* that is issued by a trusted authority.

The digital signature you create yourself using Microsoft Office tools is a self-signed signature— you yourself certify that it is valid. Because this type of signature is not backed by any kind of rigorous certification test, it is not worth much as an authenticating device, but it is a quick (and free) way to learn more about using a digital signature.

If you want to acquire a real, robust digital signature that you can use to authenticate your documents, click the *Click here for a list of commercial certificate authorities* link in the Create Digital Certificate dialog box. A Web page appears with a list of companies that provide digital signatures. You can easily compare options offered by these companies and contact them via links provided on the page.

Adding a Digital Signature to a Presentation

PowerPoint allows you to add an invisible signature to a presentation using another of the options on the Office menu's Prepare submenu.

→ ADD A DIGITAL SIGNATURE TO A PRESENTATION

USE the presentation that is still open from the previous exercise.

1. Click the **Office Button**, point to **Prepare**, and click **Add a Digital Signature**. PowerPoint displays a message box to explain some of the legal ramifications of using a digital signature.
2. Click **OK**. The Sign dialog box appears, as shown in Figure 9-14.

Figure 9-14

The Sign dialog box

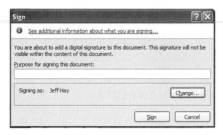

Figure 9-15

Select the certificate for your name

3. Click in the **Purpose for signing this document** box and key **Verify presentation content**.

4. If the name shown next to *Signing as* is not your name, click the **Change** button. The Select Certificate dialog box opens, as shown in Figure 9-15.

5. Select your name, click **OK**, and then click **Sign**. The Signature Confirmation dialog box lets you know your signature has been saved with the presentation.

6. Click **OK**. The Signatures task pane opens to show your signature, and the *This document contains signatures* icon appears in the status bar, as shown in Figure 9-16, to let you know the presentation has been signed.

Figure 9-16

Signature appears in the Signatures task pane

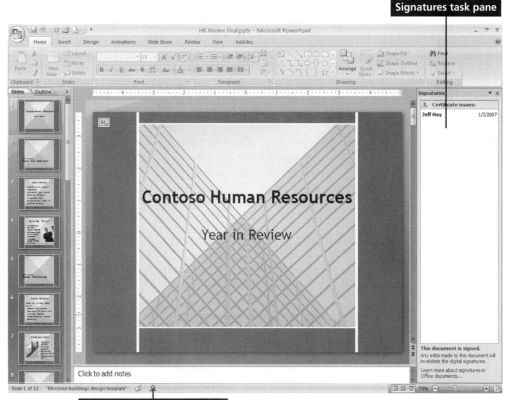

7. Close the Signatures task pane.

8. Click the *This document contains signatures* icon in the status bar to reopen the Signatures task pane.

9. Rest the pointer on your name in the task pane, click the drop-down arrow, and click **Signature Details**. The Signature Details dialog box, shown in Figure 9-17, tells you that the signature is valid and content has not been modified since the presentation was signed.

Figure 9-17

Signature Details dialog box verifies content

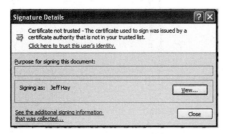

10. Click **Close**, and then close the task pane.

PAUSE. LEAVE the presentation open to use in the next exercise.

A digital signature not only tells a recipient who created a presentation but also indicates that the presentation has not been altered by anyone after the author applied the signature. Editing a document after a digital signature has been applied invalidates the signature. If a signature has become invalid, it displays in red type in the Signatures task pane. You can re-sign to validate the signature again.

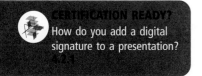

CERTIFICATION READY?
How do you add a digital signature to a presentation?
4.2.1

Applying a digital signature "locks" the presentation so that you cannot edit it and thereby invalidate the signature. You will also find that you cannot use some of the options on the Office menu's Prepare submenu. If you need to edit a presentation you have signed, click the signature's drop-down arrow in the Signatures task pane and select Remove Signature.

■ Sharing a Presentation Through E-Mail

THE BOTTOM LINE

One of the easiest ways to share a presentation is to e-mail a copy of it. Microsoft Office's application integration allows you to e-mail a presentation from PowerPoint using Outlook's mail capability.

⊕ E-MAIL A PRESENTATION

USE the presentation that is still open from the previous exercise.

1. Click the **Office Button**, point to **Send**, and click **E-mail**. A dialog box opens to tell you that using this command will remove all signatures in the presentation.

2. Click **Yes** to continue. A new e-mail message opens, as shown in Figure 9-18, with the presentation already stored as an attachment.

Figure 9-18

New message with presentation attached

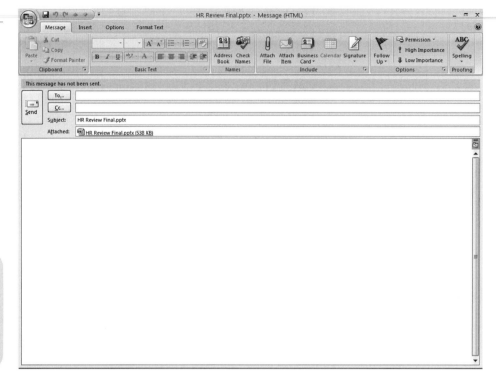

TROUBLESHOOTING

If Microsoft Outlook is not your primary e-mail application, you may not see a message window like the one shown in Figure 9-18.

TAKE NOTE

The message to pconnelly will be returned as undeliverable, but you will receive the copy in your Inbox.

3. Click in the **To** box and key **pconnelly@contoso.com**.

4. Click in the **Cc** box and key your own e-mail address.

5. Click in the message area and key the following message:

   Peter, please review the attached presentation and let me have your comments as soon as possible.

6. Click the **Send** button. The message is sent through Outlook. Open the Signatures task pane if necessary to see the heading *Invalid Signatures* in red, as shown in Figure 9-19. You will re-sign in the next exercise.

Figure 9-19

Invalid signature in the Signatures task pane

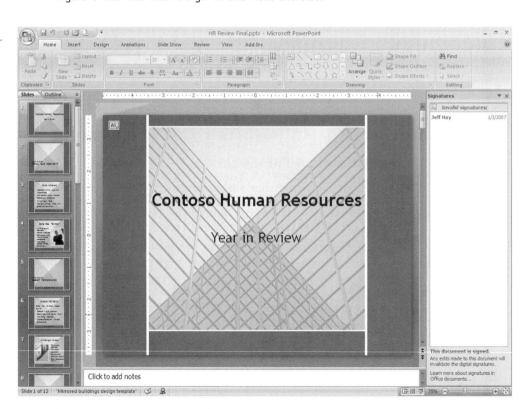

7. Open Outlook and click the **Send/Receive** button in the Standard toolbar. You should receive the message you sent.

8. Click the attachment in the message and then click the **Preview file** button. You should see the first slide of the presentation as a thumbnail. Use the scroll bar to view all slides.

9. Delete the message if desired and exit Outlook.

   PAUSE. LEAVE the presentation open to use in the next exercise.

One advantage to using an integrated application suite such as Microsoft Office is that applications are designed to work seamlessly together. The exercise above is a good example of how integration can make work flow both speedy and efficient. You do not need to go to Outlook, create a new message, and attach the file. Clicking the E-mail command on the Send submenu automatically opens a new message window and attaches the current presentation for you.

The E-mail command may not work this way if your mail program is an application other than Outlook. You can still send the presentation as an attachment, but you must do so in your mail program rather than in PowerPoint.

Another way to send a presentation to a client is to use the Internet Fax option on the Send submenu. This option allows you to fax the presentation without having to leave PowerPoint. You must have access to an Internet fax service to use this option. Microsoft will direct you to a list of fax services if you do not already subscribe to one.

■ Marking a Presentation as Final

 THE BOTTOM LINE   When you have completed all work on a presentation, you can mark it as final to prevent any further editing.

➔ MARK A PRESENTATION AS FINAL

USE the presentation that is still open from the previous exercise.

1. Click the **Office Button**, point to **Prepare**, and click **Mark as Final**. An alert box appears to warn you that this edit will invalidate the signature.

2. Click **Yes** to continue. You may not see any result from this action, but PowerPoint has invalidated the signature.

> **TAKE NOTE**
> The message appears even though the signature is already invalid.

3. Click the **Office Button**, point to **Prepare**, and again click **Mark as Final**. The alert box shown in Figure 9-20 lets you know the presentation will be marked as final and saved.

Figure 9-20

Alert box lets you know the presentation will be marked as final

4. Click **OK**, and then read the information in the dialog box about the impact of marking a presentation as final.

5. Click **OK.** The Marked as Final icon appears in the status bar to the right of the signature icon, as shown in Figure 9-21.

Figure 9-21

Marked as Final icon in the status bar

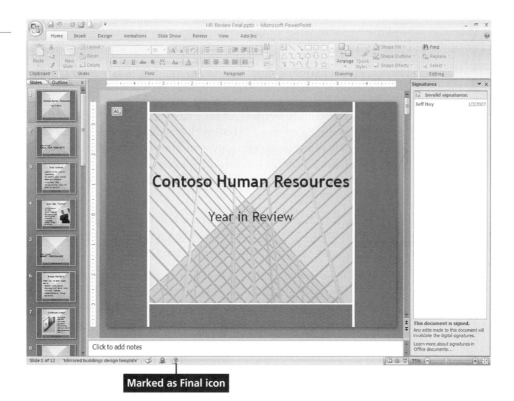

Marked as Final icon

6. If you have closed the Signatures task pane, re-open it by clicking the **Signatures** icon in the status bar. In the task pane, point to your signature in the Signatures task pane, click the drop-down arrow, and click **Sign Again**.

7. Click **OK**, click **Sign**, and then click **OK** again. Your signature has been restored.

8. Close the Signatures task pane.

9. **CLOSE** the presentation.

   CLOSE PowerPoint.

When you mark a presentation as final, you can open the presentation and read it, but you can no longer edit it or add comments. You are also restricted in other chores, such as inspecting or encrypting the document. For this reason, marking a presentation as final should be one of your last tasks when finalizing a presentation.

Marking a presentation as final does not prevent you from ever making additional changes to a presentation. You can reverse the Mark as Final command by simply selecting it again on the Prepare submenu. All features are then available to you again.

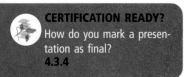

CERTIFICATION READY?
How do you mark a presentation as final?
4.3.4

SUMMARY SKILL MATRIX

IN THIS LESSON YOU LEARNED	MATRIX SKILL	SKILL NUMBER
To work with comments		
To view or hide comments in a presentation	Show and hide markup	4.1.2
To insert, modify, and delete comments on slides	Insert, delete and modify comments	4.1.1
To make a presentation safe to share		
To use the Compatibility Checker	Identify presentation features not supported by previous versions	4.3.1
To use the Document Inspector	Remove inappropriate information using Document Inspector	4.3.2
To set permissions for a presentation	Restrict permissions to a document using Information Rights Management (IRM)	4.3.3
To authenticate a presentation with a digital signature	Add digital signatures to presentations	4.2.1
To share a presentation through e-mail		
To mark a presentation as final	Mark presentations as final	4.3.4

■ Knowledge Assessment

Fill in the Blank

Fill in each blank with the term or phrase that best completes the statement.

1. A(n) _____ is a note you can insert directly on a slide.

2. _____ include the author of a presentation, the size of the file, and when it was created.

3. Use the _____ to make sure there will be no problems with content if you save the presentation to an earlier version of PowerPoint.

4. _____ is a feature that allows an administrator to control who can access a file.

5. You can set a(n) _____ while saving a document to restrict access to the presentation.

6. Use the _____ to make sure your presentation does not contain personal information you don't want to share with others.

7. A(n) _____ authenticates a presentation.

8. When you send a presentation by e-mail from PowerPoint, the current presentation is included in the message as a(n) _____.

9. _____ is the process of transforming data into a non-readable form.

10. You can set _____ to allow a user to read or change a presentation.

Multiple Choice

Circle the correct answer.

1. To hide comments in a presentation, click the _____ button.
   a. Hide Markup
   b. Show Markup
   c. Show/Hide Comments
   d. Change Comment View

2. When you save a PowerPoint 2007 presentation as an earlier version, effects such as reflections are
   a. saved as noneditable pictures
   b. deleted
   c. preserved just as in the 2007 presentation
   d. converted to shapes

3. Properties are also known as
   a. encrypted data
   b. personal data
   c. metadata
   d. permitted data

4. The Document Inspector can find all of the following types of information *except*
   a. custom XML data
   b. off-slide content
   c. comments
   d. HTML data

5. Which of the following is not a permission you can specify in the Permissions dialog box?
   a. A date when the permission expires.
   b. Permission to add a digital signature to the presentation.
   c. Full control of the presentation.
   d. Permission to print the presentation.

6. Comments are identified by
   a. color
   b. author initials
   c. number
   d. any of the above

7. A digital signature relies on a(n)
   a. digital certificate
   b. encrypted key
   c. read permission
   d. personal guarantee

8. How do you know a signature has become invalid?
   a. It is removed from the presentation.
   b. It displays in red in the Signatures task pane.
   c. The presentation cannot be opened.
   d. PowerPoint shuts down.

9. If you have signed a presentation digitally, sending the presentation by e-mail
   a. has no impact on the signature
   b. requires the recipient to know the digital signature before he can open the file
   c. invalidates the signature
   d. transfers the signature to the recipient's computer

10. To edit a presentation that has been marked as final,
    a. click the Mark as Final command again to turn it off
    b. click the Restore command on the Prepare submenu
    c. close the presentation and re-open it to turn off Mark as Final
    d. click the Edit Final command

■ Competency Assessment

Project 9-1: Messenger Messages

You are the new Marketing Manager for Consolidated Messenger. The company owner has given you a presentation to review with his comments already inserted and has asked you to add your own comments responding to his and describing any changes you would make. You will work with comments and check compatibility in case you need to save to a different version of PowerPoint.

The *Sales Pitch* file is available on the companion CD-ROM.

GET READY. Launch PowerPoint if it is not already running.

1. **OPEN** the *Sales Pitch* presentation.
2. Click the **Review** tab, then click the **Next** button to read the comment on slide 1.
3. Click **Next** and read the comment on slide 3, then click **Next** again to read the comment on slide 5.
4. Click the **Previous** button twice to return to the comment on slide 1.
5. Click the **Delete** button to delete the comment on slide 1.
6. Click the **New Comment** button and insert the following comment:

   I think the template is fine as is.
7. Go to slide 3 and insert the following comment:

   I will try to find a picture with color values more in line with the template.
8. Go to slide 5 and delete the comment.
9. Click the **Office Button**, point to **Prepare**, and click **Run Compatibility Checker**. PowerPoint should not detect any compatibility issues.
10. Click **OK** to close the dialog box after the check.
11. Right-click the comment on slide 1, then click **Edit Comment**.
12. Edit the comment to read as follows:

    I think the template is fine as is, but I can apply a different template or theme if you prefer.
13. **SAVE** the presentation as *Sales Pitch Final* and then **CLOSE** the file.

    LEAVE PowerPoint open for the next project.

Project 9-2: Travel Protection

You are a travel agent working for Margie's Travel Agency. Blue Yonder Airlines has asked you to start pitching their services to corporate clients and has sent you a copy of their presentation. Your contact at Blue Yonder has asked you to share the presentation with other agents in your office, but she does not want anyone to change the presentation. You can use PowerPoint features to safeguard the presentation.

1. **OPEN** the *Airline Overview* presentation.
2. **SAVE** the presentation as *Airline Overview Protected*.
3. Click the comment on slide 1 to open it, and then read the comment.
4. Right-click the comment and then click **Delete Comment**.
5. Click the **Office Button**, point to **Prepare**, and then click **Inspect Document**.
6. Click **Yes** to save the presentation, then click **Inspect**.
7. Click **Remove All** twice to remove both document properties and presentation notes, then click **Close**.
8. Click the **Office Button**, point to **Prepare**, and then click **Mark as Final**.
9. Click **OK** twice to save the presentation and mark it as the final version. **CLOSE** the file.

   LEAVE PowerPoint open for the next project.

The *Airline Overview* file is available on the companion CD-ROM.

Project 9-3: Mail-In Feedback

You are the Research Director at Trey Research. You have just completed a confidential presentation for Center City Hospital regarding recent complaints from patients. You need to e-mail the presentation to the hospital's director for patient services, but first you need to make sure the information in the presentation will remain secure.

1. **OPEN** the *Hospital Complaints* presentation.
2. **SAVE** the presentation as *Hospital Complaints Final*.
3. Run the Compatibility Checker from the Office menu's Prepare submenu. Click **OK** after you have read the information about the table.
4. View the properties for the presentation. You do not want the hospital administration to know the author of the presentation.
5. Run the Document Inspector and then remove all document properties. Close the Document Information panel if necessary.
6. Insert the digital signature you created earlier in this lesson.
7. Use the Office menu's **Send** command to open a new e-mail message. (You can click **Yes** to continue even though it will invalidate your digital signature.)
8. Click in the **To** box and key **cc-hospital@hotmail.com**.
9. Key your own e-mail address, or that of your instructor, in the Cc box.
10. In the message area, key the following message:

    As promised, here are the results of the patient complaint survey.
11. Send the message. If desired, go to Outlook, receive the copy of the message, and view the attachment.
12. Re-sign the presentation to validate the digital signature again.
13. **CLOSE** the file.

    LEAVE PowerPoint open for the next project.

The *Hospital Complaints* file is available on the companion CD-ROM.

Project 9-4: Adventure Review

You are the owner of Adventure Works, a company that offers outdoor adventures for groups of young people. The marketing manager has created a presentation to show to some local civic organizations and wants your feedback on it. You can share your ideas using comments.

The *Adventures* file is available on the companion CD-ROM.

1. **OPEN** the *Adventures* presentation.
2. Read the comment on slide 1.
3. Go to slide 2 and add the following comment:
   Don't forget our new Horseback Trekking adventure.
4. Go to slide 4 and add the following comment:
   Can we replace this picture with a more youth-oriented one?
5. Drag the comment marker closer to the picture.
6. Go to slide 5 and add the following comment:
   Good job, Marie. I like the clean, modern look of this theme.
7. Go to slide 1 and delete Marie's comment.
8. Go back to slide 4 and change your comment to read:
   I like this picture, but can we replace it with a more youth-oriented one?
9. Hide all comments.
10. **SAVE** the presentation as *Adventures with Comments* and then **CLOSE** the file.
    LEAVE PowerPoint open for the next project.

■ Mastery Assessment

Project 9-5: Training Day

You are the Training Manager for Northwind Traders. You have just finished a presentation for your trainers to use in training new cashiers. You will send the presentation by e-mail, so you want to protect it from unauthorized access.

The *Training* file is available on the companion CD-ROM.

1. **OPEN** the *Training* presentation.
2. **SAVE** the presentation as *Training Final*.
3. Use the **Encrypt Document** option on the Prepare submenu to set a password for the presentation. Key **North85** as the password.
4. Re-enter the password when prompted.
5. Mark the presentation as final.
6. Close the presentation, and then re-open it.
7. Key the password you set to open the presentation.
8. Send the presentation as an attachment to your instructor. In the message area, indicate that the presentation is encrypted and that you will send the password in a separate e-mail.
9. **SAVE** the presentation with the same name and **CLOSE** the file.
   LEAVE PowerPoint open for the next project.

Project 9-6: Video Marketing

You are the owner of Southridge Video. You are considering hiring a marketing specialist to help you market the company, and the specialist has asked for an example of your current marketing material. You want to send the presentation you use now, but first you need to protect it.

The **Video** file is available on the companion CD-ROM.

1. **OPEN** the *Video* presentation.
2. **SAVE** the presentation as *Video Final*.
3. Run the Compatibility Checker.
4. Run the Document Inspector. Remove all properties.
5. Add your digital signature to the presentation.
6. **CLOSE** the file.

   CLOSE PowerPoint.

INTERNET READY

In this lesson, you learned about digital signatures and created a simple one to use in the exercises. Use the Internet to further investigate digital signatures: Search for information on digital signatures or digital certificates. Choose several suppliers and create a table that compares their services. Be sure to find out if they offer a free trial, and try to determine how much a certificate costs.

Delivering a Presentation

LESSON SKILL MATRIX

SKILLS	MATRIX SKILL	SKILL NUMBER
Adjusting Slide Orientation and Size		
Selecting Slide Orientation	Change presentation orientation	1.4.1
Setting Slide Size	Set slide size	1.4.3
Customizing Audience Handouts	Customize handout masters	4.4.1
Choosing Slides to Display		
Omitting Selected Slides from a Presentation	Show only specific slides in presentations	4.5.1
Creating a Custom Show	Show only specific slides in presentations	4.5.1
Rehearsing Your Delivery	Rehearse and time the delivery of a presentation	4.5.2
Setting Up a Slide Show	Set slide show options	4.5.5
Working with Presentation Tools	Use presentation tools	4.5.3
Packaging a Presentation for Delivery	Package presentations for a CD	4.5.4

You are an engineer for A. Datum Corporation, a contractor specializing in piledriving and heavy concrete construction. Your team has put together a bid on a large bridge construction project for the town of Center City, and you must present the bid package to the client. You will present a slide show for the client before reviewing the bid in detail. Your presentation will introduce your company and provide an overview of the bid itself. PowerPoint provides a number of tools that can help you set up your presentation, rehearse it, and then package it to use in the final presentation.

KEY TERMS
annotate
custom show
orientation

■ Adjusting Slide Orientation and Size

↓ THE BOTTOM LINE

Slides are generally displayed at a standard size and orientation. You can adjust orientation and size for special impact or to meet the requirements of a specific projection device or output option.

Selecting Slide Orientation

By default, slides are displayed so they are wider than they are tall. You can easily change this orientation by using the Page Setup dialog box or a Ribbon command.

⊕ SELECT SLIDE ORIENTATION

GET READY. Before you begin these steps, make sure that your computer is on. Log on, if necessary.

The **Bid** file is available on the companion CD-ROM.

1. Start PowerPoint, if it is not already running.
2. Locate and open the **Bid** presentation.
3. Click the **Design** tab, and then click the **Page Setup** button in the Page Setup group. The Page Setup dialog box opens, as shown in Figure 10-1. Note the current width and height measurements at the left side of the dialog box.

Figure 10-1

Page Setup dialog box

TAKE NOTE

You will see the result of this change to handout orientation later in this lesson.

4. Click **Portrait** in the Slides area of the dialog box. Note that the width and height measurements reverse.
5. Click **Landscape** in the Notes, handouts & outline area.
6. Click **OK**. The slides are now taller than they are wide, as shown in Figure 10-2.

Figure 10-2

The slides display in portrait orientation

7. Click the **Slide Orientation** button in the Page Setup group, then click **Landscape**. The slides return to their default landscape orientation.

8. **SAVE** the presentation as *Bid Final*.

PAUSE. LEAVE the presentation open to use in the next exercise.

Orientation refers to the direction material appears on a page when printed. A page printed in *landscape orientation* is wider than it is tall, like a landscape picture that shows a broad panorama view. A page printed in *portrait orientation* is taller than it is wide, like a portrait picture that focuses on a single upright figure.

Landscape orientation is the default choice for displaying and printing slides. You may want to change the orientation of a presentation for a special case; for instance, if you need to accommodate large graphics that have a portrait orientation or if you want to print slides at the same orientation as other materials.

You cannot mix landscape and portrait orientations in a single presentation, the way you can in a word processing document. All slides in a presentation must have the same orientation. However, if you need to display one or more slides in a different orientation, you can create a secondary presentation with the different orientation and then provide links between the main presentation and the secondary one. You can easily click the link during the slide show to jump to the secondary presentation and then click another link to return to your main presentation.

Presentation materials such as notes pages and handouts print in portrait orientation by default, because this orientation allows the most efficient placement of slide images and text on the page. Adjusting orientation for these materials allows you to fit more information across the longest axis of the page, a plus if you have a great many notes for each slide.

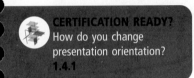

CERTIFICATION READY?
How do you change
presentation orientation?
1.4.1

Setting Slide Size

> Slides have a default size that you can change if you need to accommodate a particular kind of projection system or output. Use the Page Setup dialog box to adjust slide size.

⊙ SET SLIDE SIZES

USE the presentation that is still open from the previous exercise.

1. Click the **Page Setup** button in the Page Setup group on the Design tab. The Page Setup dialog box opens. Note the width and height measurements for the default slide size.

2. Click the **Slides sized for** drop-down arrow, then click **On-screen Show (16:9)**. The width and height measurements change to reflect the new slide size.

3. Click **OK**. The slides are now much wider than they are tall, as shown in Figure 10-3.

Figure 10-3

Slides display at their new size

4. Click the **Page Setup** button again, click the **Slides sized for** drop-down arrow, then click **35mm Slides**.

5. Click **OK**. The slides are now the proper size to create slides that could be used in an old-style slide projector.

6. Click the **Page Setup** button again, click the **Slides sized for** drop-down arrow, then click **On-screen Show (4:3)**.

7. Click **OK**. The slides are now the default size again.

8. SAVE the presentation.

PAUSE. LEAVE the presentation open to use in the next exercise.

Slides are sized by default at a 4:3 aspect ratio that allows them to be shown on a standard monitor without distortion. The *Slides sized for* drop-down list lets you choose from a number of other standard size options, including different screen aspect ratios, standard U.S. and European letter paper sizes, 35mm slides, overheads, and banners. Slide sizes apply to all slides in a presentation, not just the currently selected slide.

If you do not find a suitable size for a specific need, you can create a custom slide size. Adjust the width and height as desired in the Page Setup dialog box to create the custom slide size.

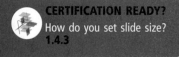

CERTIFICATION READY?
How do you set slide size?
1.4.3

Besides allowing you to set slide size and orientation, the Page Setup dialog box lets you choose the starting number for slides in a presentation. This is useful if you are combining several separate presentations in one comprehensive slide show.

■ Customizing Audience Handouts

THE BOTTOM LINE

You can help your audience follow a presentation by giving them handouts, which show small versions of the slides arranged in various ways on a page. Handout layouts are controlled by a handout master, as slide appearance is controlled by the slide master. You can customize the handout master to create your own handout layout.

⊕ CREATE A CUSTOMIZED HANDOUT MASTER

USE the presentation that is still open from the previous exercise.

1. Click the **Insert** tab, click **Header & Footer**, and click the **Notes and Handouts** tab.
2. Set up headers and footers as follows:
   a. Click in the **Date and time** check box, and make sure the Update automatically option is selected.
   b. Click the **Header** check box, and key the header **A. Datum Corporation**.
   c. Click the **Footer** check box, and key the footer **No Job Is Too Big for A. Datum**.
   d. Click **Apply to All**.
3. Click the **View** tab, and then click the **Handout Master** button in the Presentation Views group. Handout Master view opens as shown in Figure 10-4, with the header and footer you supplied in step 2.

Figure 10-4

Handout Master view

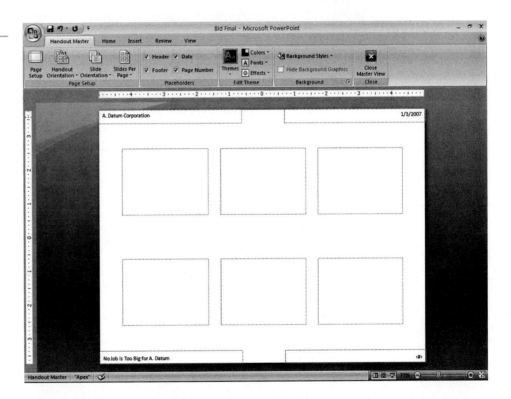

TAKE NOTE✱

The master displays in landscape orientation because you changed the orientation in a previous exercise.

4. Click the **Slides Per Page** button in the Page Setup group, then click **3 Slides**. The handout master displays the layout used to show three slides across the width of the page.

5. Click the Insert tab, click Text Box, and draw a text box above the center slide placeholder, the same width as the placeholder, as shown in Figure 10-5.

Figure 10-5

Add a text box to the handout placeholder

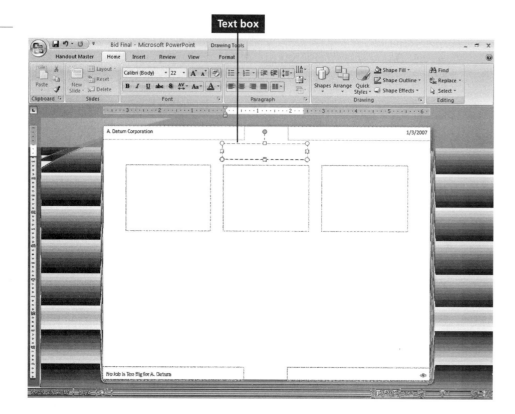

6. Key **Center City Bridge Project** in the text box.

7. Change the font size of the text box text to **18** if necessary, apply bold formatting, change the color to **Dark Blue, Text 2**, and center the text. Adjust the size of the text box as necessary to display the text on one line.

8. Click the outside border of the header placeholder in the upper-left corner of the master, hold down (Shift), and click the date, footer, and page number placeholders.

9. Change the font size to **14**, apply bold formatting, and change the color to **Dark Blue, Text 2**.

10. Click the **Handout Master** tab, and then click the **Close Master View** button to exit Handout Master view.

11. Click the **Office Button**, point to **Print**, and click **Print Preview**. In the Print What list, click **Handouts (3 Slides Per Page)**. Your customized handout master should resemble Figure 10-6.

Figure 10-6

Preview of the customized handout

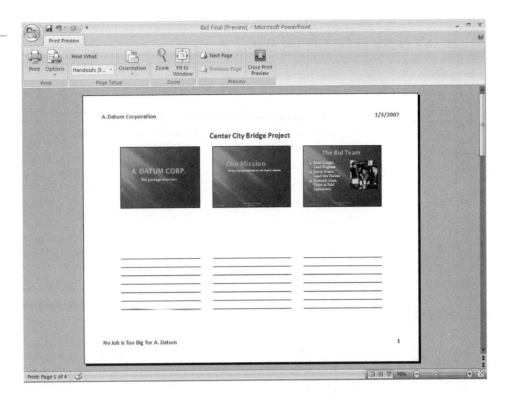

12. Click the **Next Page** button to see that the text box you added displays on each page of the handouts.

13. Click the **Print** button on the Print Preview tab to print the handouts.

14. Click the **Close Print Preview** button to return to Normal view.

15. **SAVE** the presentation.

PAUSE. LEAVE the presentation open to use in the next exercise.

You can create handouts that show one, two, three, four, six, or nine slides on a page. If you make changes to any of these layouts, the changes are reflected on all other layouts. For example, the text box you added to the 3 Slides layout in the previous exercise also appears on the 1 Slide and 9 Slides layouts.

You cannot adjust the position or size of the slide placeholders in the handout master. You can, however, adjust both size and position of the Header, Date, Footer, and Page Number placeholders. You can also choose to hide some or all of these placeholders by deselecting their check boxes in the Placeholders group on the Handout Master tab.

The Handout Master tab allows you to change both slide orientation and handout orientation, using buttons in the Page Setup group. To further modify appearance of handouts, you can change theme colors and fonts (but not the current theme) and apply a different background style. You can format the Header, Date, Footer, and Page Number placeholders like any text box or placeholder using Quick Styles, fills, or outlines.

Note that you can also customize the Notes Page master in many of the same ways that you customize the handout master. Click the Notes Master button on the View tab to display the Notes Master tab. The Notes master allows you to adjust the size and position of the slide image as well as other placeholders on the page.

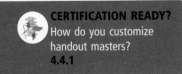

CERTIFICATION READY?
How do you customize handout masters?
4.4.1

✳ Workplace Ready

Ways to Present Slides

You have a number of options for projecting your slides when you are ready to give a presentation. The most popular options include projecting slides on a screen and displaying the slides on a computer monitor. You can also use new technology such as interactive whiteboards.

- **Projection options:** Slide projectors used to be noisy machines that shone bright light through 35mm slides to project the image on a screen. These projectors are still available, as is the technology to create 35mm slides from your PowerPoint files, but the most current projectors are digital devices that accept input from a computer. You can control the slide show from your computer monitor. When you use a digital projector, you project slides onto a screen.

- **Displaying slides on a computer monitor:** You do not need a projection device to present slides. You can display your presentation on a computer monitor, just as you do when using Slide Show view in PowerPoint. The computer monitor should be large enough for your audience to see the slide material clearly. Many computers allow you to connect more than one monitor to the video card, allowing you to use PowerPoint's Presenter view to control the slide show: The audience views the presentation on one monitor, while you use the other monitor to control the show.

- **Self-running or individual presentations:** You can also set up a presentation to run by itself on a monitor (see the *Setting Up the Slide Show* section later in this lesson), allow individuals to view a presentation on their own computers, or broadcast a presentation to viewers over the Internet.

- **Using an interactive whiteboard:** Interactive whiteboards allow you to project or display a presentation (or any other computer application) on a large white surface. The moderator can control slide display by simply touching the screen.

For best results in presenting slide shows from your computer, you should have a high-quality video card, sound card, and speakers. Quality sound and video components will make the most of multimedia files such as sounds and movies and allow transitions and animations to run smoothly.

If you do not have access to current technology, you can fall back on more traditional methods of presenting slides: You can submit PowerPoint files to photographic sources to prepare 35mm slides that can be used in standard slide projectors. You can also print slides onto clear film to create transparencies that can be used with overhead projectors.

■ Choosing Slides to Display

THE BOTTOM LINE
You may want to present only a portion of the slides you have prepared on a specific subject. You can select the slides to display by hiding slides or by creating a custom slide show.

Omitting Selected Slides from a Presentation

You can omit slides from a presentation by hiding them. Use the Hide Slide button or command to hide a slide so it won't appear during the presentation.

OMIT A SLIDE FROM A PRESENTATION

USE the presentation that is still open from the previous exercise.

1. Go to slide 2, then click the **Slide Show** tab.
2. Click the **Hide Slide** button in the Set Up group. The slide is shaded on the Slides tab, as shown in Figure 10-7, and the slide number is surrounded by a box with a diagonal bar across it.

Figure 10-7

A hidden slide is shaded in the Slides tab

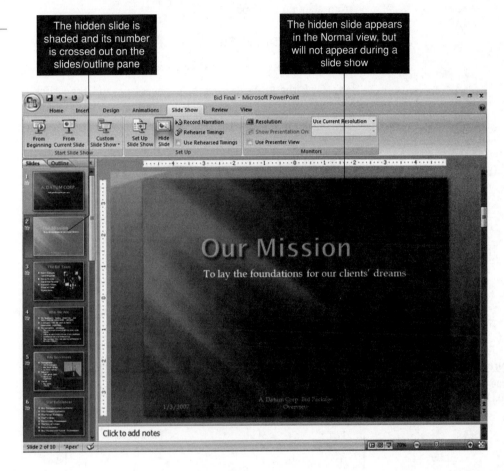

3. Press F5 to start the presentation from slide 1.
4. Click the mouse button and notice that slide 2, *Our Mission*, does not display—you go directly to slide 3, *The Bid Team*.

 Right-click a slide in the Slides tab or in Slide Sorter view, and click Hide Slide on the shortcut menu.

5. Press Esc to stop the slide show.
   PAUSE. LEAVE the presentation open to use in the next exercise.

When you hide a slide, you can still see it in Normal view and Slide Sorter view. It is hidden only in Slide Show view, when you present the slides. You can unhide a slide using the same procedure you used to hide it.

 Another way to omit slides from a presentation is to set a range of slides to show in the Set Up Show dialog box, covered later in this lesson.

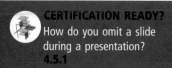

If you find that you want to display a hidden slide during the presentation, you can show it using PowerPoint's presentation tools. You will learn more about controlling a presentation with these tools later in this lesson.

Creating a Custom Show

A comprehensive presentation may contain a number of slides that you can group to show to different audiences. You can create custom shows to organize groups of slides from a single presentation.

 **CREATE A CUSTOM SHOW**

USE the presentation that is still open from the previous exercise.

1. Click the **Slide Show** tab, if necessary, and then click the **Custom Slide Show** button in the Start Slide Show group.
2. Click **Custom Shows**. The Custom Shows dialog box opens, as shown in Figure 10-8.

Figure 10-8

Custom Shows dialog box

3. Click the **New** button. The Define Custom Show dialog box opens, as shown in Figure 10-9.

Figure 10-9

Define Custom Show dialog box

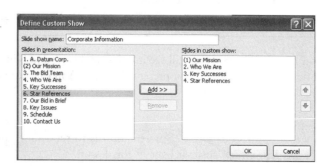

4. In the **Slide show name** box, key **Corporate Information**.
5. Click slide 2 in the *Slides in presentation* list, then click the **Add** button to place this slide in the *Slides in custom show* list.
6. Add slides 4, 5, and 6 to the custom show list. Your dialog box should look like Figure 10-10.

TAKE NOTE*

The parentheses around slide 2's number indicate it is a hidden slide.

Figure 10-10

Four slides have been added to the custom show

 **ANOTHER WAY** You can quickly select more than one slide to add by clicking a slide in the list, holding down Shift, and then clicking additional slides.

7. Click **OK**, then click **Show**. The custom show starts with the second slide you added (the first slide, slide 2, is still hidden).

8. Click the mouse button to proceed through the slides of the custom show until the show ends.

9. **SAVE** the presentation.

PAUSE. LEAVE the presentation open to use in the next exercise.

Create *custom shows* to customize presentations for different groups using slides from a single presentation. A comprehensive year-end corporate review presentation, for example, might include information on the company as a whole as well as on the operations of each department. You could show all of the slides to the board of directors and use custom shows to present to each department the general company statistics and the information specific to that department. Custom shows allow you to focus attention on the material most relevant to a specific audience.

You select the slides for a custom show in the Define Custom Show dialog box. Add slide titles from the main presentation to the custom presentation. You can adjust the order in which the slides display in the custom show: Use the up and down arrows to the right of the *Slides in custom show* list to move a selected title up or down in the list.

TAKE NOTE When you add slides to the *Slides in custom show* list, they are renumbered in the list, but the slide numbers on the slides do not change.

After you create a custom show, its name appears in the Custom Slide Show drop-down list, as well as in the Custom Shows dialog box. You can run the custom show from either list. You can also select the custom show in the Custom Shows dialog box and choose to edit the show, remove it, or copy it.

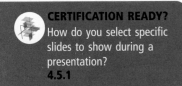 **CERTIFICATION READY?**
How do you select specific slides to show during a presentation?
4.5.1

You can create any number of custom shows in a presentation. When you set up a presentation for showing, you can specify that only the custom show slides will be presented. You can also choose to run the show while you are in Slide Show view.

■ Rehearsing Your Delivery

 THE BOTTOM LINE To make sure that your audience will have enough time to read and absorb the content on your slides, you can rehearse your delivery. After you rehearse, you have the option of saving your timings to use during your presentation.

⊕ REHEARSE THE TIMING OF A PRESENTATION

USE the presentation that is still open from the previous exercise.

1. Click the **Rehearse Timings** button in the Set Up group on the Slide Show tab. The slide show starts from slide 1 and the Rehearsal toolbar appears in the upper-left corner of the screen, as shown in Figure 10-11.

Figure 10-11

The Rehearsal toolbar
appears in Slide Show view

2. Read all the content on each slide, clicking the mouse button to display bullet items and advance slides.

3. When asked if you want to save the slide timings, click **Yes**. The presentation appears in Slide Sorter view, with the timing for each slide displayed below it, as shown in Figure 10-12.

Figure 10-12

Slide timings appear beneath each slide

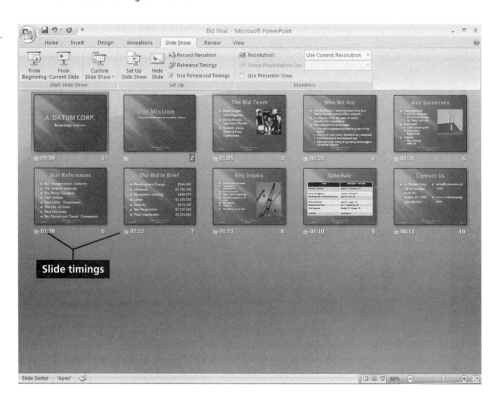

4. Press [F5] to start the slide show again from slide 1. This time, let PowerPoint control the slides according to the rehearsal times you set.

5. After three or four slides have displayed, press $\boxed{\text{Esc}}$ to end the slide show. Switch to Normal view.
6. **SAVE** the presentation.

   PAUSE. LEAVE the presentation open to use in the next exercise.

When you rehearse a presentation, you read it just as if you were a member of the audience viewing the slides for the first time. Look at pictures, charts, and diagrams to read any information they supply.

Slide timings are particularly important if you intend to show the slides as a self-running presentation that viewers cannot control. You should allow plenty of time for viewers to read and understand the content on each slide. (You will learn more about self-running presentations in the next section.)

The Rehearsal toolbar that displays when you rehearse slides shows you how much time you have spent reading the current slide as well as the elapsed time for the entire presentation. You can pause the rehearsal if necessary, then resume it when you are ready to continue. You can also choose to start the time again for a particular slide.

Note that saving your rehearsed times applies timings to the slide that allow PowerPoint to control the slides for you. The presentation can run automatically without your having to click buttons to advance slides. If you have applied animations to slide objects, rehearsing will set the proper timing for those objects to display.

You do not have to save the slide timings after rehearsal if you do not want PowerPoint to control the slides for you. You can tell PowerPoint not to save the timings, or you can deselect Use Rehearsed Timings in the Set Up group on the Slide Show tab to remove slide timings.

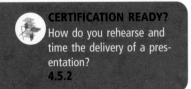

CERTIFICATION READY?
How do you rehearse and time the delivery of a presentation?
4.5.2

SOFTWARE ORIENTATION

The Set Up Show Dialog Box

When you are doing the final setup for a presentation, you have a number of decisions to make. The Set Up Show dialog box, shown in Figure 10-13, allows you to specify settings for any kind of show.

Figure 10-13

Set Up Show dialog box

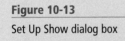

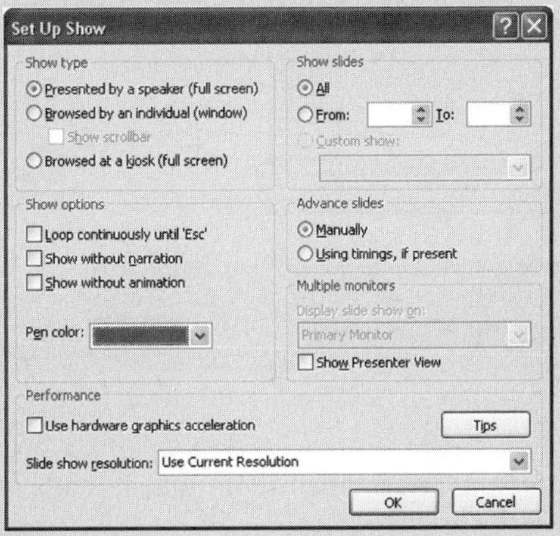

You can specify options such as how the presentation will be shown, what slides or custom show to present, how to advance slides, and whether to use more than one monitor. Choosing options in this dialog box is one of the last chores you'll complete before giving your presentation.

Setting Up a Slide Show

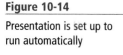 **THE BOTTOM LINE**

You will probably decide how to present your slides early in the process of creating the slide show. Use the Set Up Show dialog box to choose the final settings for the presentation type you have selected.

⊕ SET UP A SLIDE SHOW

USE the presentation that is still open from the previous exercise. Your boss has asked you to save a version of the presentation that can run unattended at a construction industry trade show.

1. **SAVE** the presentation as *Datum Custom*.
2. Adjust the slides for their new use as follows:
   a. Right-click slide 2 in the Slides pane, and then click **Hide Slide**. The slide is no longer hidden in this version of the presentation.
   b. Slide 2 does not have a timing because it was hidden when you rehearsed the other slides. Click the **Animations** tab, and then click the **Automatically After** up arrow four times to set 4 seconds as the timing for the slide.
   c. Click the **Insert** tab, click **Header & Footer**, and change the footer text to **A. Datum Corporation**. Click **Apply to All**.
3. Click the **Slide Show** tab, then click the **Set Up Slide Show** button in the Set Up group. The Set Up Show dialog box opens.
4. Click **Browsed at a kiosk (full screen)** in the Show type area. The *Loop continuously until 'Esc'* option is automatically selected and grayed out.
5. Click **Custom show** in the Show slides area. Your dialog box should look like the one in Figure 10-14.

Figure 10-14

Presentation is set up to run automatically

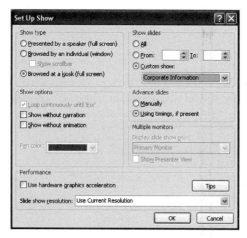

TAKE NOTE The Corporate Information custom show is automatically selected because it is the only custom show in the presentation.

6. Click **OK**.
7. Press **F5** to start the presentation. Note that it starts with the first slide of your custom show, *Our Mission*.
8. Let the presentation run through all slides in the custom show until it displays the second slide (*Who We Are*) for the second time, then press **Esc**.
9. **SAVE** the presentation and then **CLOSE** the file.

PAUSE. LEAVE PowerPoint running to use in the next exercise.

The Set Up Show dialog box allows you to make a number of decisions about how slides display during a presentation. The first and most important decision to make is how the slides will be presented. The Show type area in the dialog box lists three show types that are most commonly used when presenting slides:

- **Presented by a speaker (full screen)** is the option to choose if the slides will be presented by a moderator (you or some other person) to a live audience. The slides will display at full screen size.
- **Browsed by an individual (window)** is the option to choose if you are preparing the presentation for a viewer to review on his or her own computer. The slides display within a window that contains a title bar with size/close controls. You can choose to also display a scrollbar to make it easy for the individual to scroll through the slides.
- **Browsed at a kiosk (full screen)** is the option to choose if you intend to have the presentation run unattended, with no moderator. This option is a standard choice for trade shows or other venues where the slides can loop indefinitely for viewers to watch as long as they desire.

The Show slides area of the dialog box allows you to specify a range of slides to show, or choose a custom show to limit the amount of information presented. You would most likely use these options if you are setting up a show to be browsed by an individual or at a kiosk.

If your slides have timings, you can specify that the show loop continuously until you press the Esc key (as you did in the previous exercise). This option is selected automatically if you choose to have slides browsed at a kiosk. If you have recorded narration for your slides or applied animations, you can choose whether to use those features in your final presentation.

TAKE NOTE If you have a microphone attached to your computer, you can click the Record Narration button on the Slide Show tab and add voice narration to your slides.

If you have rehearsed a presentation to set slide timings, PowerPoint will select the *Using timings, if present* option by default. You can override this setting by selecting *Manually* if you want to control the slides and slide content yourself.

The Multiple monitors area of the dialog box provides support if you can attach more than one monitor to your computer. You can select which of your two monitors will display the slide show, and you can turn on Presenter view to help you control the presentation.

If you intend to make annotations on the slides, you can choose the color of the pen you will use to write with. You learn more about annotating in the next section.

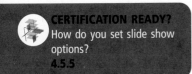

CERTIFICATION READY?
How do you set slide show options?
4.5.5

The Set Up Show dialog box also allows you to control your system's performance. To increase the rate at which your screen displays slides, click *Use hardware graphics acceleration*. To improve graphic appearance, you can choose a higher resolution for the show, but be aware that the higher the resolution, the slower your system is likely to run.

■ Working with Presentation Tools

↓ THE BOTTOM LINE PowerPoint offers a number of tools you can use during a presentation to control the display of slides and mark directly on the slides if desired. You can use keyboard commands, mouse clicks, presentation tools, or menu commands to control the presentation. You can select from several marking options and colors to annotate your slides during the presentation.

⊕ USE PRESENTATION TOOLS

1. **OPEN** the *Bid Final* presentation you worked with earlier in this lesson.
2. Click the **Slide Show** tab, and then click **Use Rehearsed Timings** to turn off slide timings so you can work more easily with presentation tools.
3. Click the **From Beginning** button in the Start Slide Show group on the Slide Show tab to start the presentation from slide 1. Move the pointer on the slide until you can see the presentation tools in the lower-left corner of the screen, as shown in Figure 10-15.

Figure 10-15

The presentation tools appear in the lower-left corner of each slide

4. Click the **Next** button (the right-pointing arrow at the far right of the tools). The next slide displays.
5. Click the **Previous** button (the left-pointing arrow at the far left of the tools).
6. Right-click anywhere on the slide to display the presentation shortcut menu, point to **Go to Slide**, and then click the hidden slide, **(2) Our Mission**, as shown in Figure 10-16. The hidden slide displays.

Figure 10-16

Displaying a hidden slide during a slide show

ANOTHER WAY

To go to the next slide if it is hidden, press H.

7. Press [Page Down] to display the next slide.

8. Click the **Menu** button in the presentation tools (the second button from the right) to display a menu similar to the presentation shortcut menu, and then click **Last Viewed**. The slide you previously viewed (slide 2) displays.

9. Right-click the screen again, then click **End Show** on the presentation shortcut menu to end the presentation.

   PAUSE. LEAVE the presentation open to use in the next exercise.

PowerPoint allows you to use the tools that are most comfortable for you to go forward, backward, or to a specific slide. Table 10-1 summarizes the most popular navigation options in Slide Show view.

Table 10-1

Navigation options in Slide Show view

ACTION	KEYBOARD	MOUSE	SHORTCUT MENU
Show the next slide or animation	N Enter Spacebar Page Down → ↓	left button	Next Advance
Show the previous slide or animation	P Page Up Backspace ← ↑		Previous Reverse
Go to last slide viewed			Last Viewed
Go to specific slide	Type slide number, press Enter		Go to Slide, select slide number
End show	Esc		End Show

TAKE NOTE

Consult PowerPoint's Help files to find many more keyboard shortcuts for controlling a presentation.

If you have chosen the *Browsed by an individual (window)* show type, the presentation tools at the lower-left corner of the screen do not display and you cannot use the mouse button to go to the next slide. You can use the keyboard options to go to the next or previous slide, or you can use the Next Slide and Previous Slide buttons on the scrollbar if you have chosen to display it. You can also right-click the slide and select Advance to move forward or Reverse to move backward through slides.

As you work with PowerPoint, you will find that you develop a feel for the navigation tools that you find easiest. It is often more efficient, for example, to use keyboard options because they can be quicker than right-clicking and then selecting an option from a shortcut menu.

CERTIFICATION READY?

How do you use presentation tools to navigate during a slide show?

4.5.3

ANNOTATE SLIDES WITH THE PEN

USE the presentation that is still open from the previous exercise.

1. Press **F5** to start the presentation from slide 1, key **7**, and press **Enter**. Click the mouse button until all seven bullet items display on the slide.

2. Right-click the slide, point to **Pointer Options**, and click **Felt Tip Pen**. The pointer changes to a small, round, red pen pointer.

3. Right-click the slide, point to **Pointer Options**, and click **Ink Color**. Then click **Orange** in the Standard Colors palette.

4. Use the pen pointer to circle the value for labor, $2,135,000, as shown in Figure 10-17.

Figure 10-17

Making an annotation on a slide

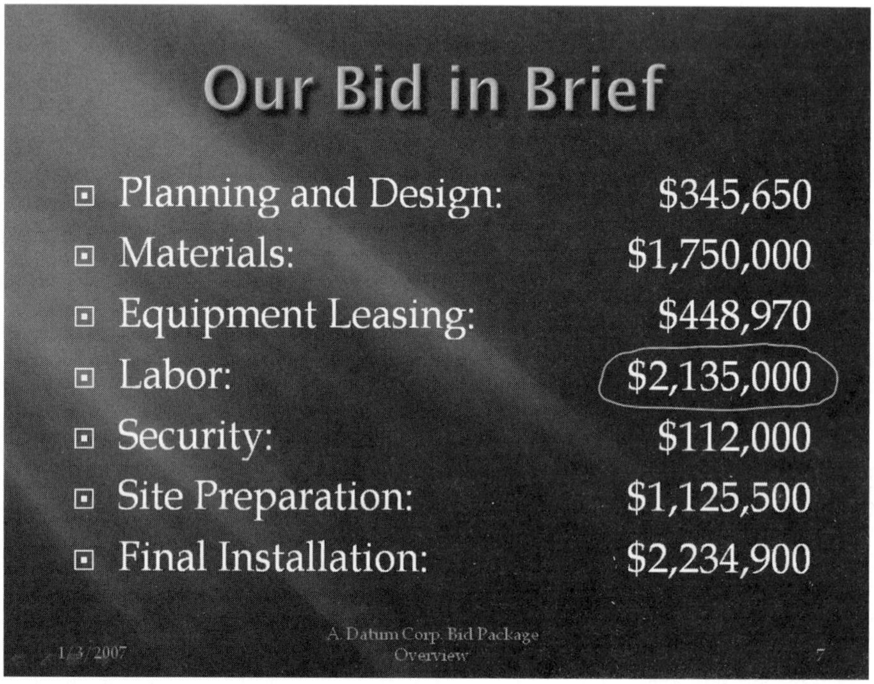

Our Bid in Brief

▫ Planning and Design:	$345,650
▫ Materials:	$1,750,000
▫ Equipment Leasing:	$448,970
▫ Labor:	$2,135,000
▫ Security:	$112,000
▫ Site Preparation:	$1,125,500
▫ Final Installation:	$2,234,900

1/3/2007   A Datum Corp. Bid Package Overview   7

5. Click the **Menu** button in the presentation tools, point to **Screen**, and click **Black Screen**. The screen is blacked out so you can annotate without the distraction of the slide material.

6. Use the pen pointer to draw a large U. S. currency symbol, $, in the middle of the slide.

7. Right-click the slide, point to **Screen**, and click **Unblack Screen**. The slide background is restored and the annotation disappears.

8. Click the **Pointer Options** button in the presentation tools (the second tool from the left) and click **Arrow**. The arrow pointer is restored.

9. Press ⟶ to go to slide 8.

10. Press the spacebar eight times to display all eight bullet items.

11. Click the **Pointer Options** button in the presentation tools, then click **Highlighter**. Drag the highlighter pointer across the *Weather* bullet item to highlight it, as shown in Figure 10-18.

Figure 10-18

Highlighting text on a slide

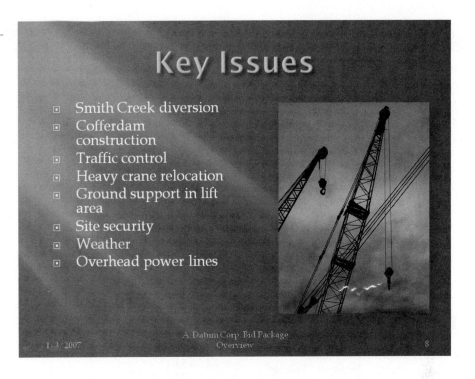

 **ANOTHER WAY**

Press E to remove all annotations on a slide.

12. Click the **Pointer Options** button, then click **Erase All Ink on Slide**. The highlight you added is removed.

13. End the slide show. When asked if you want to keep your annotations, click **Discard**.

14. **SAVE** the presentation.

    PAUSE. LEAVE the presentation open to use in the next exercise.

You can *annotate* slides by drawing or writing with the pointer to draw attention to text or other content on the slide. PowerPoint offers three different annotation pen options: Ball Point Pen, Felt Tip Pen, and Highlighter. These pen options have pointer sizes roughly corresponding to the actual writing instruments. You can change the ink color for any of the pen options.

You can erase any annotation you add to a slide. To remove a single annotation out of several on a slide, click the Eraser option on the Pointer Options submenu and then use the eraser pointer to click the annotation you want to remove. To remove all annotations on a slide, use the Erase All Ink on Slide command.

The Black Screen and White Screen options allow you to replace the current slide with a black or white screen that you can use for annotations or to cover the current material if you want to keep it under wraps while you are discussing some other issue.

If you choose to keep your annotations after ending the slide show, they display as shapes on the slides in Normal view. You can click any annotation in Normal view and press Delete to remove the annotation.

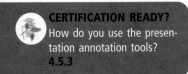 **CERTIFICATION READY?**
How do you use the presentation annotation tools?
4.5.3

■ Packaging a Presentation for Delivery

↓
THE BOTTOM LINE

You may need to transport your presentation materials to another computer to run your slide show. The Package for CD feature streamlines the process of packing up all the materials you need to show the presentation even if PowerPoint is not installed on the other computer.

⊕ PACKAGE A PRESENTATION FOR DELIVERY

USE the presentation that is still open from the previous exercise.

1. Click the **Slide Show** tab, if necessary, and then click **Use Rehearsed Timings** to restore the timings you set in a previous exercise.
2. Click the **Office Button**, point to **Publish**, and click **Package for CD**.
3. Click **OK** when alerted that some files will be updated for use with the PowerPoint Viewer. The Package for CD dialog box opens, as shown in Figure 10-19.

Figure 10-19

Package for CD dialog box

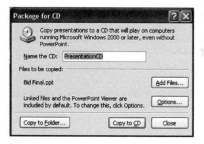

4. Delete the default CD name in the Name the CD text box, then key **Center City Bid**.
5. Click the **Options** button, and then click in the **Embedded TrueType fonts** check box to select the option.
6. Click **OK**.

   If you have the capability to save data on a CD, go to the next step. If you cannot write to a CD, go to step 8.

7. Create the CD package as follows:

   a. Click the **Copy to CD** button.

   b. Click **Yes** when asked if you want to link files. The Copying Files to CD message box shows the progress of the copy. When the copying is complete, the CD drive will open.

   c. When asked if you want to copy the files to another CD, click **No**.

   d. Click **Close**.

8. Copy the package to a folder on your system as follows:

   a. Click the **Copy to Folder** button. The Copy to Folder dialog box opens, as shown in Figure 10-20.

Figure 10-20

Copy to Folder dialog box

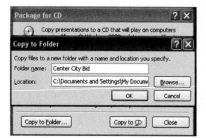

b. Click the **Browse** button. The Choose Location dialog box opens.

c. Navigate to the folder in which you are storing your Lesson 10 solutions, and then click **Select**.

d. Click **OK** and then click **Yes** when asked if you want to link files. The Copying Files to Folder dialog box shows the progress of the copy.

e. Click **Close**.

9. Using a program such as My Computer, navigate to the CD or the folder where you stored your presentation.

10. Start the packaged presentation by clicking on the CD or by opening the Center City Bid folder on your system, double-clicking the **PPTVIEW.EXE** file, selecting **Bid Final**, and clicking **Open**. The presentation starts in Slide Show view.

11. End the show after several slides and close the PowerPoint Viewer.

12. SAVE the presentation and then **CLOSE** the file.

CLOSE PowerPoint.

The Package for CD feature makes short work of packing up all the files you need to show your slides, no matter what kind of system you have to use to run the show. If the system you intend to use does not have PowerPoint, you can use the PowerPoint Viewer to run the presentation.

To make the process of storing files on a CD more efficient, you can choose to copy more than one presentation to the same CD. Click the Add Files button to open additional presentations. This feature can reduce the amount of wasted space that results if you copy a single presentation to a CD.

The Options dialog box that you can access from the Package for CD dialog box gives you additional choices for the packaging process.

- You can choose to create a Viewer Package, in which formats are updated to work with the PowerPoint Viewer, or an Archive Package in which your existing file formats are preserved. If you know the computer on which you intend to show the presentation has PowerPoint, select Archive Package to save file space on your CD.

- Use the *Select how presentations will play in the viewer* drop-down list to choose how to play presentations if you have more than one stored on a single CD. You can play presentations in order, play the first presentation automatically, allow the user to choose which presentation to play, or turn off the option that plays the CD automatically when you click it.

- Linked files, such as large movie and sound files, are included automatically, and you will normally want to retain this setting. You can, however, save the package without linked files if desired by deselecting this option.

- Embedding TrueType fonts is a good idea if you are not sure what fonts you might have access to on the system where you will run the presentation. Embedding fonts will add to file size but ensure the quality of your presentation's font appearance.

- You can specify a password to open or modify the presentation, and you can prompt PowerPoint to inspect the presentation for hidden or personal data you do not want to share.

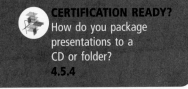

CERTIFICATION READY?
How do you package presentations to a CD or folder?
4.5.4

Besides using Package for CD to create materials to transport for a presentation, you can use this feature to archive presentations onto a CD or into folders for storage. The packaging process pulls together all the files you need for a presentation, so your stored presentation provides an excellent long-term backup for your work.

TAKE NOTE Package for CD works only with CD formats. If you want to store a presentation on a DVD, you can save materials in a folder as in step 8 of the previous exercise and then use your system's DVD burning tools to copy the files to the DVD.

SUMMARY SKILL MATRIX

IN THIS LESSON YOU LEARNED	MATRIX SKILL	SKILL NUMBER
To adjust slide orientation and size		
To set slide orientation	Change presentation orientation	1.4.1
To choose slide size	Set slide size	1.4.3
To create a customized handout master	Customize handout masters	4.4.1
To choose which slides to present	Show only specific slides in presentations	4.5.1
To rehearse the timing of a presentation	Rehearse and time the delivery of a presentation	4.5.2
To set up a slide show	Set slide show options	4.5.5
To work with PowerPoint's presentation tools	Use presentation tools	4.5.3
To package a presentation for delivery on a CD	Package presentations for a CD	4.5.4

■ Knowledge Assessment

Fill in the Blank

Fill in each blank with the term or phrase that best completes the statement.

1. Use the _____ dialog box to adjust slide size.

2. You can set up a presentation to run continuously until you press the _____ key.

3. Use the _____ toolbar to view timings as you rehearse a presentation.

4. _____ refers to the way information displays on a printed page.

5. To display a hidden slide during a presentation, click _____ on the shortcut menu and then click the hidden slide.

6. If the computer on which you will present your slides does not have PowerPoint, you can use the _____ to show the presentation.

7. Customize the _____ to create your own handout layouts.

8. If you want to show your presentation on a screen, you can use a(n) _____ that accepts input from your computer.

9. When you _____ slides, you use the pointer to draw or write.

10. Create a(n) _____ to organize several slides within a presentation into a group that can be shown separately.

Multiple Choice

Circle the correct answer.

1. A slide that is wider than it is tall is displayed in
   a. portrait orientation
   b. 4:3 orientation
   c. picture orientation
   d. landscape orientation

2. Which of the following is not a standard handout layout?

a. 1 Slide

b. 4 Slides

c. 8 Slides

d. 9 Slides

3. If you need to show slides on a wide-screen monitor, you might change their size to

a. On-screen Show (16:9)

b. On-screen Show (3:4)

c. 35mm Slides

d. Ledger Paper (11 × 17 in)

4. To prevent a slide from displaying during a presentation, select it and then choose

a. Delete Slide

b. Hide Slide

c. Show/Hide Slide

d. Conceal Slide

5. If you want to show only a selected series of slides from a presentation, the most efficient option is to

a. hide each slide you do not want to use

b. create an entirely new presentation and copy into it the slides you want to use

c. create a custom show of the slides you want to show

d. copy the presentation and then delete the slides you do not want to use

6. When you rehearse a presentation, you should

a. skim over the content of each slide

b. read the entire content of each slide and look carefully at pictures and diagrams

c. allow yourself a set amount of time to view each slide regardless of its content

d. look only at the slide titles

7. If you set up a slide show to be browsed by an individual, the slides display

a. using the full screen

b. in a virtual kiosk

c. in a window with a title bar

d. within the PowerPoint window

8. Which of the following is *not* a way to advance to the next slide during a presentation?

a. press Home

b. press the spacebar

c. click the left mouse button

d. press Page Down

9. A quick way to restore the arrow pointer after you have used it for drawing is to

a. press End

b. double-click the screen

c. click the arrow pointer tool in the navigation tools

d. press Esc

10. If you are not sure whether the computer you intend to use has PowerPoint, select the _____ option in the Package for CD Options dialog box.

 a. Archive Package

 b. Viewer Package

 c. Add Viewer

 d. Include Viewer

■ Competency Assessment

Project 10-1: Preparing to Fly

You are nearly ready to present the slide show for Blue Yonder Airlines. Use the tools you have learned about in this lesson to finalize the presentation and create handouts.

The *Airline* file is available on the companion CD-ROM.

GET READY. Launch PowerPoint if it is not already running.

 1. **OPEN** the *Airline* presentation.

 2. Click the **Design** tab, click the **Slide Orientation** button, and click **Landscape**.

 3. Click the **Page Setup** button, click the **Slides sized for** drop-down arrow, and click **On-screen Show (4:3)**.

 4. Click the **Slide Show** tab, then click the **Set Up Slide Show** button.

 5. Choose the **Presented by a speaker** show type, deselect the **Loop continuously until 'Esc'** option, and choose to have slides advance **Manually**.

 6. Click the **Insert** tab, click **Header & Footer**, and choose to display the date (update automatically), the header **Blue Yonder Airlines**, and page numbers for notes and handouts.

 7. Click the **View** tab, then click **Handout Master** to open Handout Master view.

 8. Center the header text and date in their placeholders, and right-align the page number in its placeholder. Close Handout Master view.

 9. Hide the last slide in the presentation.

 10. Click the **Office Button**, click **Print**, and set the following print options:

 a. Choose to print handouts with four slides per page, in vertical order.

 b. Deselect the **Frame** option.

 c. Deselect the **Print hidden slides** option.

 11. Print the handouts.

 12. **SAVE** the presentation as *Airline Final* and then **CLOSE** the file.

 LEAVE PowerPoint open for the next project.

Project 10-2: Twin Cities Crawl

You are ready to finalize the presentation you created to publicize the Twin Cities Gallery Crawl. You need to rehearse and set up the show and then package the presentation for delivery.

The *Galleries* file is available on the companion CD-ROM.

 1. **OPEN** the *Galleries* presentation.

 2. Click the **Slide Show** tab, and then click the **Rehearse Timings** button.

 3. Read each slide. When the slide show ends, choose to save the rehearsed timings.

 4. Click the **Set Up Slide Show** button, and set up the show to be browsed at a kiosk using the timings you saved to advance slides.

 5. Click the **Office Button**, point to **Publish**, and click **Package for CD**.

6. Key the package name **Galleries**. If you can copy to a CD, click **Copy to CD** and complete the packaging process. If you cannot copy to a CD, click **Copy to Folder**, select the folder in which you are storing solutions for Lesson 10, and complete the packaging process.

7. Close the Package for CD dialog box.

8. **SAVE** the presentation as *Galleries Final* and then **CLOSE** the file.

   LEAVE PowerPoint open for the next project.

■ Proficiency Assessment

Project 10-3: Final Airline Check

You want to run through the Airline Final presentation before delivering it to make sure you are familiar with content and how to display it during the slide show.

1. **OPEN** the *Airline Final* presentation you created in Project 10-1.

2. Hide slide 7.

3. Press F5 to view the presentation from slide 1.

4. Use the **Next** button in the presentation tools to move to slide 3.

5. Use the **Previous** button in the presentation tools to go backward to slide 1.

6. Right-click to display the shortcut menu, and use **Go to Slide** to jump to slide 4.

7. Right-click the slide, click **Pointer Options**, and select the highlighter.

8. Highlight the bullet items **Caribbean** and **Scuba**.

9. Restore the arrow pointer and press Esc to end the show. Choose not to save your annotations.

10. Rehearse timings for the presentation. When the presentation ends, save the slide timings.

11. Set up the slide show to use the slide timings you saved.

12. **SAVE** the presentation as *Airline Final Check* and then **CLOSE** the file.

    LEAVE PowerPoint open for the next project.

Project 10-4: Year-End Review

You are ready to do the final tweaking of the year-end review for Contoso's Human Resources department. You will create a custom show to send to Contoso's president and CEO, customize handouts for the year-end review meeting, and adjust slide size for printing.

The *Review* file is available on the companion CD-ROM.

1. **OPEN** the *Review* presentation.

2. Create a custom show named **Review Summary**. Include in the custom show slides 1, 3, 4, 6, 7, 9, 10, and 12.

3. Change the slide size to **Letter Paper (8.5x11 in)**.

4. Display a date that updates, the header **Contoso HR Year in Review**, and page numbers for all handouts and notes pages.

5. Display the handout master, and show the **3 Slides** layout.

6. Select the Header and Date placeholders, center the text in these placeholders, and adjust the vertical alignment in these placeholders to Middle. (Hint: Use Align Text on the Home tab to set Middle alignment.)

7. Reduce the width of each placeholder to 2.5 inches wide, and move the placeholders down about half an inch from the top of the page.

8. Center the Header placeholder over the slide image column, and center the Date placeholder over the empty column where the lines will appear to the right of the slide images. (You can check placement by displaying the handouts in Print Preview.)

9. Apply a Quick Style to the Header and Date placeholders. Boldface the text and adjust color if necessary to show up against the Quick Style formatting.

10. Print handouts with three slides per page.

11. **SAVE** the presentation as *Review Custom*.

   LEAVE the presentation open for the next project.

■ Mastery Assessment

Project 10-5: Review Final

You need to complete your preparation of the Review Custom presentation and test it before you send it to the HR executive staff.

1. Set the slides in the *Review Custom* presentation for normal screen 4:3 screen display.

2. Set up the slide show to display only the Review Summary custom show for an individual. Turn on the scrollbar option, and choose to advance slides manually.

3. Start the slide show from slide 1 and view the slides in the custom show, using keyboard options to advance slides.

4. **SAVE** the presentation as *Review Custom Final* and then **CLOSE** the file.

   LEAVE PowerPoint open for the next project.

Project 10-6: Museum Package

The *Museum* file is available on the companion CD-ROM.

You are ready to package the presentation you created for the Baldwin Museum. This presentation contains linked sound and movie files that must be included with the presentation.

1. **OPEN** the *Museum* presentation.

2. **SAVE** the presentation as *Museum Final*.

3. Open the Package for CD dialog box and name the new package **Museum Final**. Choose to embed TrueType fonts and make sure the **Linked files** option is selected.

4. Choose to copy the presentation files to a folder, and select the Lesson 10 solutions folder as the location to store the Museum Final folder. Be sure to click **Yes** when asked if you want to include linked files.

5. Close the Package for CD dialog box.

6. Navigate in My Computer to the Museum Final folder, open the PowerPoint Viewer, and open the *Museum Final* presentation.

7. Proceed through the slides, noting that the linked multimedia files play correctly.

8. **CLOSE** the PowerPoint Viewer, and then **CLOSE** *Museum Final*.

   CLOSE PowerPoint.

INTERNET READY

You have been asked to find out what kind of equipment you would need to project presentations in a medium-sized conference room using a computer to control the show. Using the Internet, research what type of digital projector and pull-down screen you would need to purchase. Read reviews if possible to locate several options for good-quality components that are not the most or least expensive on the market. Create a presentation with your suggestions in a table or diagram. You may also want to research interactive whiteboards as an alternative to the projector-and-screen combination.

Circling Back

You are a project manager at Trey Research. You must give a report to your managers on the status of a major project you are running. Use PowerPoint tools and features you have learned about throughout this course to create, format, and finalize a presentation that you can use to report your project status.

Project 1: Create the Presentation

In this project, you will create your presentation and insert a slide from another presentation. You will also create and format a chart and insert headers and footers for slides and handouts.

GET READY. Launch PowerPoint if it is not already running.

The *Update* file is available on the companion CD-ROM.

1. Create a new, blank presentation.
2. **SAVE** the presentation as *Report*.
3. Key the slide title **Trey Research** and the slide subtitle **Woodgrove Bank Customer Survey**.
4. Insert slide 2 from the *Update* data presentation into the current presentation using the **Reuse Slides** option on the New Slide drop-down list.
5. Apply the **Civic** theme.
6. Go to slide 1 and boldface the slide title. Increase the font size of the subtitle to 18 pt.
7. Add a new slide at the end of the presentation with the Title and Content layout. Key the title **Customer Types**.
8. Insert a 3D pie chart on the slide using the following data:

Main office	23%
Branches	49%
Online	16%
Telephone	12%

9. Remove the chart title and add data labels at the inside end of the pie slices.
10. Apply a Quick Style to the chart.
11. Select the data labels and click the **Increase Font Size** button on the Home tab to make them one size larger.
12. Insert the date (updating automatically), slide numbers, and the footer **Woodgrove Bank Customer Survey** on all slides except the title slide and on notes and handouts. Add the header **Trey Research** for notes and handouts.
13. **SAVE** the presentation.

    PAUSE. LEAVE PowerPoint and your presentation open for the next project.

Project 2: Add Research Data

You are now ready to add a slide to show the data you have collected in your project. Some of the data is still in an Excel worksheet, so you will add an action button link to the worksheet.

USE the presentation that is open from the previous project.

1. Add a new slide at the end of the *Report* presentation with the Title and Content layout, and key the slide title **Overall Responses**.

2. Insert a new table with four columns and eight rows. Key the following data in the table:

Experience	Positive	Negative	No Response
Customer Service: Overall	91%	8%	1%
Customer Service: Tellers	86%	12.5%	1.5%
Customer Service: Managers	75%	23%	2%
Transaction Handling	80%	20%	0%
Wait Times	41%	58%	1%
Convenience of Facilities	89%	9%	2%
Sense of Security	84%	15%	1%

3. Format the table with the Medium Style 1 – Accent 3 Quick Style. Turn off Banded Rows and turn on Banded Columns.

4. Adjust column widths so that all text in the first column appears on a single line and the other three columns are the same width.

5. Add a shadow effect to the table.

6. Insert a text box at the lower-left of the slide (above the green band that contains the footer and date) and insert the following text:

   For detailed results, visit www.treyresearch.net, log in with your password, and click the Woodgrove Survey link.

7. Check the URL to make sure the hyperlink is to http://www.treyresearch.net.

8. Format the text box to be 7.5 inches wide, and apply a Quick Style to the text box that coordinates well with the table.

9. Draw an Information action button to the right of the text box, and link the button to the *Woodgrove Results* Excel file.

10. Adjust the button shape's height to be the same as the text box's height, and align the button and text box at the top.

11. Apply the same Quick Style to the action button that you applied to the text box.

12. SAVE the presentation.

    PAUSE. LEAVE PowerPoint and your presentation open for the next project.

The *Woodgrove Results* file is available on the companion CD-ROM.

→ Project 3: Add Graphic Interest

You need to add some graphic interest to the presentation. You will use a clip art picture to illustrate one of the slides. You also need to insert a diagram to show the process required to change customer interaction behavior.

USE the presentation that is open from the previous project.

1. Add a new slide at the end of the *Report* presentation with the Title and Content layout. Key the title Change Process.

2. Insert the Staggered Process SmartArt diagram in the content placeholder.

3. Display the Text pane if necessary and insert the following text:

   1. Data collection

   2. Present to management

   3. Revise policies and procedures

   4. Management/HR training

   5. Staff training

4. Apply a new style to the diagram such as the Intense Effect, and change colors to one in the Colorful range.

5. Go to slide 1. Click the **Clip Art** button on the Insert tab to open the Clip Art task pane.

6. Search for a photo that has something to do with surveys, business, or communications, such as a person (not a health professional) with a clipboard or a pleasant-looking person talking on a phone or headset.

7. Size and format the picture so it looks attractive in the area below the subtitle. If the picture is taller than it is wide, you may want to crop it so it fits better in the space below the subtitle.

8. Center the picture under the subtitle and apply a picture style. You may want to recolor the picture to integrate it with the theme colors.

9. **SAVE** the presentation.

   PAUSE. LEAVE PowerPoint and your presentation open for the next project.

Project 4: **Prepare for Delivery**

You are ready to apply transitions and animations to add interest during the presentation. You should also check the presentation for compatibility and remove any properties that have accumulated as you've created the show. It is also time to prepare handouts that your audience can use to follow the presentation as you deliver it.

USE the presentation that is open from the previous project.

1. Apply the **Wipe Down** transition at **Medium** speed to all slides.

2. Go to slide 2 and apply the **Fade** animation effect to the text in the content placeholder.

3. Adjust the animation so it begins **After Previous**.

4. Run the Document Inspector and remove any properties in the presentation.

5. Run the Compatibility Checker to make sure you can save the file to an earlier version of PowerPoint if necessary.

6. Open the handout master and make the follow changes:

   a. Display the **3 Slides** layout.

   b. Change the orientation of the handout page to **Landscape**.

   c. Apply the Civic theme colors to the handout master.

   d. Drag the footer placeholder above the first slide placeholder, and then increase the width of the footer placeholder so its right edge aligns with the right edge of the third slide placeholder. (It should form a banner across the top of all three slides.)

   e. Center the text in the footer placeholder and apply a Quick Style to the placeholder.

   f. Adjust font size, color, and style as desired to make it show up well against the Quick Style formatting.

   g. Close Handout Master view.

7. **PRINT** the handouts with three slides per page.

8. **SAVE** the presentation.

   PAUSE. LEAVE PowerPoint and your presentation open for the next project.

➲ Project 5: Final Touches

You are ready to test your presentation. You will review the show, test the annotation options, rehearse timings, and set up the show for its final delivery. Finally, you will package the show so you can transport it easily on the day of the presentation.

USE the presentation that is open from the previous project.

1. Start the slide show from slide 1 and use any combination of keyboard shortcuts, menu commands, or mouse clicks to advance slides until you reach slide 4.

2. On slide 4 (*Overall Responses*), change the pointer to the Felt Tip Pen and circle the URL in the text box.

3. Restore the arrow pointer and test the action button. Close Excel after you have looked at the data and return to the slide show.

4. Continue with the remaining slide and end the show. Do not save your annotation.

5. Run the show again to rehearse timings of slides. Save your slide timings.

6. Open the Set Up Show dialog box and make sure the Advance option is to use slide timings.

7. Package the presentation to a folder named **Trey Report**. Select the **Archive Package** option and choose to embed TrueType fonts.

8. **SAVE** and **CLOSE** the presentation.

   CLOSE PowerPoint.

MATRIX SKILL	SKILL NUMBER	LESSON NUMBER
Create presentations from blank presentations	1.1.1	2
Create presentations from templates	1.1.2	2
Create presentations from existing presentations	1.1.3	2
Create presentations from Microsoft Office Word outlines	1.1.4	2
Apply themes to slide masters	1.2.1	4
Format slide master backgrounds	1.2.2	4
Add elements to slide masters	1.3	4
Change presentation orientation	1.4.1	10
Add, change and remove transitions between slides	1.4.2	4
Set slide size	1.4.3	10
Arrange slides	1.5	2
Insert and remove text boxes	2.1.1	3
Size text boxes	2.1.2	3
Format text boxes	2.1.3	3
Select text orientation and alignment	2.1.4	3
Set margins	2.1.5	3
Create columns in text boxes	2.1.6	3
Cut, copy and paste text	2.2.1	1
Apply Quick Styles from the Style Gallery	2.2.2	3
Format font attributes	2.2.3	3
Use the Format Painter to format text	2.2.4	3
Create and format bulleted and numbered lists	2.2.5	3
Format paragraphs	2.2.6	3
Insert and modify WordArt	2.2.7	3
Reuse slides from an existing presentation	2.3.1	2
Copy elements from one slide to another	2.3.2	1
Insert hyperlinks	2.3.3	4
Insert media clips	2.3.4	8
Apply built-in animations	2.4.1	4
Modify animations	2.4.2	4
Create custom animations	2.4.3	4
Create a SmartArt diagram	3.1.1	7
Create SmartArt diagrams from bullet points	3.1.2	7
Add text to SmartArt diagrams	3.2.1	7
Change theme colors	3.2.2	7
Add effects by using Quick Styles	3.2.3	7
Change the layout of diagrams	3.2.4	7

continued

MATRIX SKILL	SKILL NUMBER	LESSON NUMBER
Change the orientation of charts	3.2.5	7
Add or remove shapes within SmartArt	3.2.6	7
Change diagram types	3.2.7	7
Insert pictures from file	3.3.1	8
Insert shapes	3.3.2	8
Insert clip art	3.3.3	8
Add text to shapes	3.3.4	8
Apply Quick Styles to shapes and pictures	3.4.1	8
Add, change and remove illustration effects	3.4.2	8
Size, scale, and rotate illustrations and other content	3.5.1	8
Order illustrations and other content	3.5.2	8
Group and align illustrations and other content	3.5.3	8
Use gridlines and guides to arrange illustrations and other content	3.5.4	8
Insert charts	3.6.1	6
Change chart types	3.6.2	6
Format fill and other effects	3.6.3	6
Add chart elements	3.6.4	6
Insert tables in a slide	3.7.1	5
Apply Quick Styles to tables	3.7.2	5
Change alignment and orientation of table text	3.7.3	5
Add images to tables	3.7.4	5
Insert, delete and modify comments	4.1.1	9
Show and hide markup	4.1.2	9
Add digital signatures to presentations	4.2.1	9
Identify presentation features not supported by previous versions	4.3.1	9
Remove inappropriate information using Document Inspector	4.3.2	9
Restrict permissions to a document using Information Rights Management (IRM)	4.3.3	9
Mark presentations as final	4.3.4	9
Compress images	4.3.5	8
Save presentations as appropriate file types	4.3.6	1, 2
Customize handout masters	4.4.1	10
Print a presentation in various formats	4.4.2	2
Show only specific slides in presentations	4.5.1	10
Rehearse and time the delivery of a presentation	4.5.2	10
Use presentation tools	4.5.3	10
Package presentations for a CD	4.5.4	10
Set slide show options	4.5.5	10

TO USE MICROSOFT OFFICE PROFESSIONAL 2007, YOU WILL NEED:

COMPONENT	REQUIREMENT
Computer and processor	500 megahertz (MHz) processor or higher[1]
Memory	256 megabyte (MB) RAM or higher[1,2]
Hard disk	2 gigabyte (GB); a portion of this disk space will be freed after installation if the original download package is removed from the hard drive.
Drive	CD-ROM or DVD drive
Display	1024x768 or higher resolution monitor
Operating system	Microsoft Windows XP with Service Pack (SP) 2, Windows Server 2003 with SP1, or later operating system[3]
Other	Certain inking features require running Microsoft Windows XP Tablet PC Edition or later. Speech recognition functionality requires a close-talk microphone and audio output device. Information Rights Management features require access to a Windows 2003 Server with SP1 or later running Windows Rights Management Services.
	Connectivity to Microsoft Exchange Server 2000 or later is required for certain advanced functionality in Outlook 2007. Instant Search requires Microsoft Windows Desktop Search 3.0. Dynamic Calendars require server connectivity.
	Connectivity to Microsoft Windows Server 2003 with SP1 or later running Microsoft Windows SharePoint Services is required for certain advanced collaboration functionality. Microsoft Office SharePoint Server 2007 is required for certain advanced functionality. PowerPoint Slide Library requires Office SharePoint Server 2007. To share data among multiple computers, the host computer must be running Windows Server 2003 with SP1, Windows XP Professional with SP2, or later.
	Internet Explorer 6.0 or later, 32 bit browser only. Internet functionality requires Internet access (fees may apply).
Additional	Actual requirements and product functionality may vary based on your system configuration and operating system.

[1] 1 gigahertz (GHz) processor or higher and 512 MB RAM or higher recommended for **Business Contact Manager**. Business Contact Manager not available in all languages.
[2] 512 MB RAM or higher recommended for **Outlook Instant Search**. Grammar and contextual spelling in **Word** is not turned on unless the machine has 1 GB memory.
[3] Office Clean-up wizard not available on 64 bit OS.

Glossary

A

action A button or text block programmed to perform a specific action, such as jumping to a slide or starting a program.

animation An effect you apply to placeholders or other content to move the content in unique ways on the slide.

annotate To write or draw on a slide during a presentation.

aspect ratio The relationship of width to height in a picture or shape.

assistant In an organization chart, a person who reports directly to a superior.

B

bulleted list Groups of items or phrases that present related ideas.

C

chart A visual representation of numerical data.

chart area The entire area inside the chart container that holds background as well as plotted data.

clip art Predrawn artwork in a wide variety of styles. Office clip art files can include drawn graphics, photographs, sounds, and animated graphics.

Clip Organizer A series of folders in which installed or downloaded clip art files are stored on your system.

comment A note you insert on a slide while reviewing.

Compatibility Checker A PowerPoint 2007 feature that allows you to identify problems that may occur if you save PowerPoint 2007 slides to previous PowerPoint versions.

constrain To force a drawing object into a particular shape or alignment.

crop To remove a portion of a picture or shape that is not needed. The cropped portion is hidden until you compress the picture.

current slide The slide that is currently being edited.

custom show A group of slides in a presentation that can be shown separately from the entire presentation.

D

data marker A single column, pie slice, or point from a data series.

data series All the data points for a particular category of plotted information.

demote To make an item subordinate to another item.

dialog box launcher In some command groups on the Ribbon, a small icon that opens a dialog box related to that group.

digital signature A means of authenticating a document's author and ensuring that the document's content has not been changed since the signature was applied.

Document Inspector A PowerPoint 2007 feature that identifies personal information an author may not want to include when a document is sent for review.

E

embedded Data that has been placed in a destination application so that it can be edited with the tools of its original source applications.

encryption The process of transforming data into a non-readable form for security purposes.

F

fonts Typefaces that are used to display characters, numbers, and symbols in your PowerPoint presentations.

footer Information such as a date, slide number, or text phrase that appears at the bottom of each slide in a presentation.

Format Painter A tool to copy character and paragraph formatting.

formatting The appearance of text or objects on a slide.

G

gridlines A gridwork of horizontal and vertical lines that can be used as guides when positioning objects on a slide.

group A set of related tools on the Ribbon.

guides Nonprinting vertical and horizontal lines that you can move or copy to align objects on a slide.

H

handout A printed copy of a presentation.

header Information such as a date, slide number, or text phrase that appears at the top of each page of a presentation's handouts or notes.

I

indent level The distance of a paragraph of text from the placeholder's left border.

Information Rights Management (IRM) A feature that allows an administrator to control who can access a file.

K

KeyTip A letter or number that appears next to an onscreen tool when the Alt key is pressed; keying that letter or number activates the associated tool.

keyword A word or phrase that describes a subject or category on which you can search.

L

layout A predefined arrangement of placeholders for text or objects (such as charts or pictures).

legend The key to a chart that explains what each data series represents.

line spacing The amount of vertical space between paragraphs.

linked Data that has been placed in a destination application so that it maintains a link with its source file; changes to the source file are also made in the linked object.

M

Mini toolbar A small toolbar that appears when the mouse pointer is placed on a selected text object; provides commands for working with the text.

N

Normal view PowerPoint's default view, suited for editing individual slides; includes the Slide pane, Notes pane, and Slides/Outline pane.

note Additional information associated with a slide.

Notes Page view A view that displays a single slide and its associated notes.

numbered list A group of steps, procedures, or actions that are listed in numeric order.

O

Office Button In the upper-left corner of the PowerPoint window, a button that opens a menu of commands related to creating and managing files; includes commands such as New, Print, and Close.

order The way in which objects stack up on a slide as you create them.

organization chart A diagram that shows the relationships among personnel or departments in an organization.

orientation The direction that material appears on a page when printed.

P

permissions Rights to read or change a document.

placeholder On a slide, a box that holds a specific type of content, such as text.

plot area The area in the chart container that shows the data series compared to the chart's gridlines.

Presenter view A viewing mode that allows the presenter to see notes on one screen while the audience views slides on another screen.

promote To make an item superior to another item.

properties Details about a document such as who created it and when, its file size, when it was last edited, and so on.

Q

Quick Access Toolbar Toolbar at the upper-left corner of the PowerPoint window that provides easy access to tools you use frequently, such as Save and Undo.

Quick Style Built-in formatting for text, graphics, SmartArt diagrams, charts, WordArt, pictures, tables, and shapes.

R

Ribbon A strip of icons that appears across the top of the PowerPoint window; divided into tabs, each of which contains groups of related tools.

rulers Horizontal and vertical measures that help you position objects on a slide.

S

scaling Specifying a percentage of the original dimensions to enlarge or reduce a picture or shape.

slide master A slide that stores information about the formats applied in a presentation, such as theme, fonts, layouts, and colors.

slide show view A view that allows the user to preview a presentation on the screen as it will appear to the audience.

slide sorter view A view that displays all of a presentation's slides in a single window; suited for reorganizing slides.

slide transition A special effect that occurs when one slide is being replaced by another during a slide show.

SmartArt diagram

SmartArt diagram A visual representation of information.

subordinates In an organization chart, persons or departments who are subordinate to another person or department.

T

tab A labeled section of the ribbon; contains a group of related tools.

table An arrangement of columns and rows used to organize information.

target The page, slide, or file that appears when a link is clicked.

template A predesigned presentation.

text box A container that holds text on a slide.

Text pane The fly-out pane that allows you to key information for a SmartArt diagram.

theme A scheme of complementing colors.

thumbnail A small picture of a slide.

top-level shape In an organization chart, the person or department at the head of the organization.

W

WordArt A feature used to turn text into a formatted graphic.

worksheet An Excel document used to organize numerical data that can then be analyzed or otherwise manipulated.